Sue Mosher

SAMS
Teach Yourself

Outlook® 2000 Programming

in 24 Hours

SAMS

201 West 103rd St., Indianapolis, Indiana, 46290 USA

Sams Teach Yourself Outlook® 2000 Programming in 24 Hours
Copyright © 1999 by Sams Publishing

International Standard Book Number: 0-672-31651-X

Library of Congress Catalog Card Number: 99-60557

Printed in the United States of America

First Printing: July 1999

01   00   99   4   3   2   1

Trademarks

Warning and Disclaimer

EXECUTIVE EDITOR
Chris Denny

ACQUISITIONS EDITOR
Chris Denny

DEVELOPMENT EDITOR
Tony Amico

MANAGING EDITOR
Jodi Jensen

PROJECT EDITOR
Dawn Pearson

COPY EDITOR
Kate Talbot

INDEXER
Cheryl Landes

PROOFREADER
Jill Mazurczyk

TECHNICAL EDITORS
Ken Slovak
Diane Roremski

SOFTWARE DEVELOPMENT SPECIALIST
Craig Atkins

TEAM COORDINATOR
Karen Opal

INTERIOR DESIGN
Gary Adair

COVER DESIGN
Aren Howell

COPY WRITER
Eric Bogert

LAYOUT TECHNICIANS
Brian Borders
Susan Geiselman
Mark Walchle

Contents at a Glance

Contents

About the Author

Sue Mosher is the acclaimed author of books and articles on Microsoft Exchange and Microsoft Outlook and founder of the award-winning Slipstick Systems Exchange Center Web site full of tips for users of those email applications. Her company, Slipstick Systems, is dedicated to helping individuals and organizations get the most out of their desktop programs.

She has been working with computers for nearly 20 years, first as a broadcast journalist and technology manager for The Associated Press. She left the AP in 1994 to found Slipstick Systems, whose clients have included the AP, ABC News, American Military University, Turner Broadcasting, and the U.S. Embassy in Moscow.

Much of Sue's work involves researching Outlook and Exchange issues and presenting them in books and articles, on the Slipstick Systems Web site, in her *Exchange Messaging Outlook* newsletter, and in private seminars and projects for clients. She also develops custom workgroup and printing solutions with Outlook and Exchange.

Microsoft recognized the Slipstick Systems Exchange Center Web site at http://www.slipstick.com with one of the 1998 Pathfinder Awards—the Exchange Community Builder Award. The site is often cited as a resource in books and articles on Windows, Exchange, and Outlook. "Sue is amazing," commented Davis Straub, coauthor of *Windows 95 Secrets*. "Her knowledge of Outlook and Exchange surpasses anything we've seen, even at Microsoft."

The desire to share what she learns has led Sue to become a very active participant in Internet newsgroups and mailing lists discussing Exchange and Outlook. In 1994, Microsoft named her as one of the first participants in its MVP—Most Valuable Professional—program recognizing outstanding contributions to the community of Microsoft product users. She continues as an active MVP today.

Sue grew up in Atlanta and attended the College of William and Mary in Williamsburg, Virginia, where she managed the college radio station, helped revive the women's fencing team, graduated with a B.A. degree in sociology, and was elected to Phi Beta Kappa. She later did graduate work in economics at Rutgers University.

She is married to Robert A. Mosher, a career U.S. Foreign Service officer and military historian. They have lived overseas in Kinshasa, Congo, and currently reside in Moscow, Russia. Their daughter, Annie, installs most of the software on the computer she shares with her dad and manages the mailing list for her mom's Exchange Messaging Outlook newsletter. Their perfect Moscow apartment pet is a turtle named Henry. You can reach Sue at sue@slipstick.com.

Dedication

To Lee, John, Dave, and Bill, who helped me to become a programmer despite my best efforts to avoid it.

Acknowledgments

An extraordinarily talented group of people has contributed to this book—knowingly or unwittingly—by showing the way through the oddities of Outlook programming or by providing ideas for some of the projects realized in this book.

Two mentors deserve special mention: Randy Byrne, a fellow Outlook MVP, tolerated my many naive questions and designed the Microsoft Outlook 2000 Object Model map (which I've almost worn out). Siegfried Weber of CDOLive earns my gratitude for his research into the many undocumented aspects of CDO and for sharing his findings with the Outlook/Exchange developer community.

I'd like to thank Outlook MVPs Chris Burnham, Jay Harlow, and Hollis D. Paul for the terrific support they provide in the microsoft.outlook.public.program_forms newsgroup and all the other newsgroup habitués who helped steer me in the right direction. My appreciation also goes to Outlook/Exchange developers Helen Feddema, Tom Howe, Phil Seeman, Rick Spiewak, and Robert Strong for their inspiration and to Office MVPs Cindy Meister and Ken Getz, who helped me get all fired up to finish this book and say something useful about printing and ADO.

I appreciate the project ideas sparked by inquiries from people all over the world: Joyce Clark in Slovakia, Marko Wild in Germany, Christopher Rosevear in the U.K., Tina Buni in Stockholm, John Dale, Dan Yang, Frank Bongers, Dan Shields, Kan Kung, and many anonymous seekers after Outlook enlightenment. Because most of this book was written during Outlook 2000's beta period, it couldn't have happened without the cooperation and assistance of many people at Microsoft, notably Darrique Barton, Todd Dooley, David Hua, Bill Jacob, Tejas Patel, and Joe Turick.

This book would not have seen print without the ideas of Sams Acquisitions Editor Christopher Denny and my dear friend Valda Hilley at Convergent Press. Development Editor Tony Amico, Project Editor Dawn Pearson, and many others at Sams have skillfully and painlessly sped this book toward your hands. I owe a major debt, too, to technical editors Ken Slovak (another Outlook MVP) and Diane Poremsky for their careful reading of the manuscript and excellent suggestions. However, if you find any code that won't run, it's my fault, not theirs.

At home, my husband, Robert, and daughter, Annie, patiently tolerated weeks when I couldn't seem to concentrate on anything but Outlook and often forgot to make dinner. I love you both more than you can imagine and more than I can ever express.

Finally, I thank God for the opportunity to share this knowledge and for the joy that comes from such sharing.

Tell Us What You Think!

As the reader of this book, *you* are our most important critic and commentator. We value your opinion and want to know what we're doing right, what we could do better, what areas you'd like to see us publish in, and any other words of wisdom you're willing to pass our way.

As Executive Editor for Sams Publishing, I welcome your comments. You can fax, email, or write me directly to let me know what you did or didn't like about this book—as well as what we can do to make our books stronger.

Please note that I cannot help you with technical problems related to the topic of this book, and that due to the high volume of mail I receive, I might not be able to reply to every message.

When you write, please be sure to include this book's title and author as well as your name and phone or fax number. I will carefully review your comments and share them with the author and editors who worked on the book.

Fax: 317-581-4770

Email: office_sams@mcp.com

Mail: Chris Denny
           Executive Editor
           Sams Publishing
           201 West 103rd Street
           Indianapolis, IN 46290 USA

Introduction

A friend here in Moscow—a Linux and Netscape die-hard—often asks whether I think Outlook is the best of its breed. Although I haven't done a detailed comparison, I firmly believe that Outlook, especially Outlook 2000, is tops in its capability to be customized to suit either a standalone user or a complete organization. It's not always easy or obvious, but the programming tools now available and the potential interaction with other Microsoft Office applications make Outlook 2000 a real killer.

Who Should Read This Book

I've written this book with two groups in mind: Outlook enthusiasts who want to extend the program's capabilities and experienced developers who need to know how to integrate Outlook into their projects. The early lessons of the book bring the first group up to speed on programming basics, and both groups benefit from a look at Outlook's capabilities and its particular (some might say "peculiar") form design environment.

The heart of the book deals with not one, but two Microsoft programming languages: VBScript in the code behind Outlook forms and Exchange Server folders and Visual Basic for Applications (VBA). Not only is Outlook 2000 the first Outlook version to have VBA, but it also has a vastly expanded object model, giving programmers more ways to harness Outlook as a platform for workgroup and personal information management.

Because this is a book about Outlook, all the VBA work takes place in Outlook's VBA environment. You can, however, use the same techniques to open Outlook items and folders from within Word or Excel or even Visio or the latest version of Corel WordPerfect—any program that uses VBA as its programming language.

Can This Book Really Teach Outlook Programming in 24 Hours?

Yes, it can! What you probably don't realize is that most people doing Outlook programming are themselves self-taught. We all learned by doing and testing and observing and breaking things and then fixing them again.

The early examples are short and simple, but you will soon gain skill with practical techniques for working with Outlook messages, appointments, and other items. You build many procedures and forms that you can use right away to perform tasks that Microsoft left out of the Outlook user interface—things such as replacing one category with another or adding a reminder to all the birthdays in your Calendar folder.

Tables of the most important properties, methods, and other programming components make it easy for you to look up the information you need. However, this is mainly a tutorial, not a reference book, and each hour builds on the techniques you learned in the preceding hour. I think that you will get the most out of it if you work through the lessons in order.

Don't skip the quizzes and exercises at the end of each hour! These are designed to reinforce the lesson's concepts and sometimes provide you with more useful procedures you can reuse.

What You Need

Because this book is about Microsoft Outlook 2000, you obviously need that program installed to work through the examples. Outlook 2000 is part of the Microsoft Office 2000 suite and is also available as a standalone application. I recommend that you install it with the Internet Explorer 5.0 option so that you also have the latest version of VBScript. (Outlook 2000 supports Internet Explorer 4.0, as well as 5.0.)

If you want to generate impressive printed reports with Outlook, you also need Microsoft Word or Microsoft Excel, preferably both, although they don't have to be the Office 2000 versions.

In the advanced discussion of integrating Outlook with databases and Microsoft Exchange Server, it would be helpful to have Microsoft Access installed and have access to Exchange Server public folders.

You should also keep handy my favorite design tools—paper and pencil! Keep a notebook at hand to jot down your ideas for Outlook projects and to draw pictures of forms before you start adding controls. As you work through the projects in this book, write down areas where you'd like to expand them or how you might apply a particular technique to a different kind of form. When you finish this book, you will have a ready roadmap to your next stops along the Outlook programming highway.

Conventions Used in This Book

This book uses different typefaces to differentiate between code and regular English, and also to help you identify important concepts.

Text that you type is presented in **bold monospace** type.

Text that appears onscreen is in monospace font.
```
It will look like this to mimic the way text looks on your screen.
```

Placeholders for variables and expressions appear in *monospace italic* font. You should replace the placeholder with the specific value it represents.

This arrow (➥) at the beginning of a line of code means that a single line of code is too long to fit on the printed page. Continue typing all characters after the ➥ as though they were part of the preceding line.

When you type in the code presented in the listings, do not type the line numbers that appear at the beginning of each line. These are not part of the code.

A Note presents interesting pieces of information related to the surrounding discussion.

A Tip offers advice or teaches an easier way to do something.

A Caution advises you about potential problems and helps you steer clear of disaster.

 New Term icons provide clear definitions of new, essential terms. The term appears in italic.

PART I

Outlook Form Design

Hour

HOUR 1

What You Can Do with Outlook 2000

Welcome to Outlook 2000's world of programming possibilities! This new version of Outlook makes it easier than ever to customize the program. This lesson gets you started by introducing the tools for Outlook programming and suggesting ways to start thinking about projects you want to try.

The highlights of this hour include

- What kinds of projects are possible in Outlook 2000
- What tools you will use the most
- How to decide which tool to use
- Which version of Outlook you have installed
- How to sketch out your plans for Outlook programming projects

Possible Outlook Projects

Whether you have been using Microsoft Outlook for just a few days or more than a year, you've certainly figured out that it does more than e-mail—much, much more. It's not unusual to find people who have organized their entire life with Outlook.

But if you asked each Outlook user how he or she put the program to work, you would receive a different answer every time because people have their own ideas on how to organize the critical information in their lives. Wouldn't it be great if Microsoft could make Outlook so customizable that everyone could use it his or her own way? It might not be 100% possible, but the programming environment included with Outlook 2000 is rich enough to let you make major strides toward bending Outlook to your will— or that of the organization you work for.

This book shows you how to use the programming tools in Outlook to make it your own. It's okay if you have never programmed before—this shows you how! It's much easier than you might think. If you are an experienced programmer, you will see how to put Outlook's special features to work.

To help you get excited about the lessons ahead, take a look at this list of things you can do when you learn how to program with Outlook:

- Distribute a list of company holidays to people in the office so that they can instantly add them to their Outlook calendars.
- Route a message or document through a sequence of people.
- Create your own custom rules to handle incoming e-mail.
- Search and replace data, such as telephone area codes.
- Create custom reports by integrating Outlook data with Word layouts.
- Easily schedule a follow-up call for a meeting.
- Create Outlook forms that duplicate the paper phone message, vacation request, and other business forms you use.

Excited yet? I hope so because I think we're going to have a lot of fun together during the 24 lessons that make up this book.

Outlook Programming Tools

Before digging into the details of Outlook programming, here is a preview of the tools you will be using:

- Outlook forms
- Visual Basic Scripting Edition (VBScript)

- Visual Basic for Applications
- Object models

Customized Forms

The first stop on the road to Outlook programming proficiency is learning how to customize the basic Outlook forms.

Every item that you open in Outlook—whether it's an e-mail message, a contact, or an appointment—uses a particular form to display its data. You can customize these forms to show or hide fields, respond to user input and actions, and control other Outlook tasks. Customized forms can be shared with other users, both within your organization and across the Internet.

In many programming environments, you must start from scratch every time you want to create a new window for the user to interact with. Outlook is different in that it presents you with a group of built-in forms. To build a custom form, you start with one of the built-in forms and then add your own special touches.

For example, Figure 1.1 shows the default Contact form as it normally looks when you add a new item to the Contacts folder. Notice that the E-mail field shows only one address and provides no clue that as many as three addresses can be associated with this contact. In Figure 1.2, you see the same form, this time in Design mode, customized with a NumAddresses box to indicate how many e-mail addresses the contact has. (As you might guess from the title of the form in Figure 1.2, you will build it in Hour 4, "Extend Form Design with a Custom Task Form.")

FIGURE 1.1

This Contact form has not been customized.

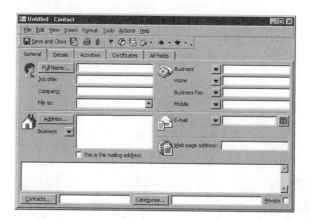

FIGURE 1.2

This Contact form has been customized to show the number of e-mail addresses for this contact.

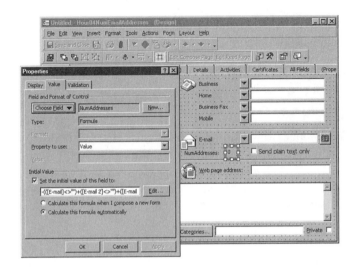

Is programming code necessary to do this? Not really. All it takes is a fairly simple formula, no more complicated than those you might have worked with in Microsoft Excel spreadsheets. You will see how it works in Hour 4.

Is this really programming (no real code is involved)? Sure it is! Designing forms for user interaction is such an important part of programming that whole books have been devoted to that topic alone. Many of the changes you want to make to Outlook might involve nothing more than adding new fields and pages to existing forms to hold the data. Without writing any code at all, you can perform simple validation to make sure that the data meets your criteria for correctness and develop simple formulas such as the one for counting e-mail addresses.

Visual Basic Scripting Edition

A time will come, however, when you want your forms to do more. Maybe you will want to generate a task for a follow-up telephone call from an appointment and have Outlook automatically fill in the contact name for you, or perhaps you would like to be reminded to add a category to each outgoing message you send.

When you are ready to go beyond entering data and manipulating it in simple ways, you move up to *VBScript*, the shorthand name for Visual Basic Scripting Edition, the programming language behind Outlook forms.

You might have heard of VBScript in the context of Web pages. VBScript is one of several languages that can control what you see when you interact with a Web page. It also works with the Windows Scripting Host included with Windows 98 (or downloadable from Microsoft's Web site) to allow you to write programs that are stored as simple text files.

Scripts don't run as fast as other kinds of programs, but they enjoy the advantages of small size and portability. Having a script associated with an Outlook form hardly increases the size of the item at all. If you're using a form to interact with other people via the Internet, this means that your message won't balloon into megabytes just because you want it to support more actions than replying or forwarding.

VBScript is a little scary, though. It's like working without a net, because the built-in editor for building VBScript programs is, well, a text editor. Figure 1.3 shows a sample script for a form to create a bulk reply to a group of e-mail messages in any Outlook folder. Notice the lack of any toolbars or color coding.

FIGURE 1.3
The Outlook form Script Editor is just a text editor.

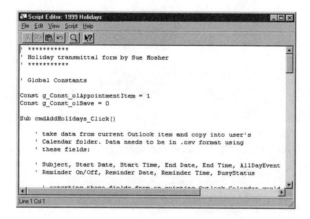

Visual Basic for Applications

Fortunately for those of us who find writing programs in a text editor a bit challenging, Outlook has another development environment, one of the richest available. It's called Visual Basic for Applications (or VBA for short). Outlook shares it with not only the other Office programs, but also programs such as Visio and AutoCAD that have licensed VBA as their programming environment, too.

The VBA programming environment, shown in Figure 1.4, includes all the tools a professional developer might want:

- Visual forms designer
- Intelligent editor with color coding and drop-down lists to avoid code errors

- Detailed help on the things you can do with Outlook
- Debugging windows and other tools

FIGURE 1.4

VBA includes a richer form and code environment (compare with Figure 1.3).

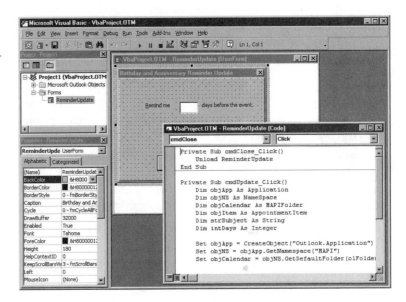

One sneaky technique you will learn in this book is to write and test your Outlook form code in the superior VBA environment, make a few minor adjustments to adapt it to VBScript, and then copy and paste it into the script window of an Outlook form. This method cuts down on the programming time immensely.

However, that great code editor is not the only reason to explore VBA. You need to learn about VBA to control Outlook at the application level, not just at the form level. Outlook 2000 gives you the ability to react to many events that take place when you work with your Outlook information—such as creating new items, switching from one folder to another, or synchronizing with an Exchange Server.

VBA also gives you the ability to design two other kinds of forms: dialog boxes that pop up to get information from the user and windows that stay on the screen to provide information to the user, as well as gather input. One example is a form displaying how many vacation days you have used so far this year.

Office Integration, Object Models, and Beyond

Outlook can create Word or Excel documents, and Microsoft Office programs such as Excel and Word can create messages, appointments, and other Outlook items. You can even integrate Outlook with a Microsoft Access database. This integration occurs thanks to something called the Outlook Object Model. All the Office programs and many other Windows components have object models that reveal what these programs can do, the types of items they can work with, and the characteristics of those items.

Besides the Outlook Object Model, you also work with the Collaboration Data Objects (CDO) model, sometimes called the MAPI object model. MAPI is short for Messaging Application Programming Interface. CDO can reach some corners of e-mail that Outlook by itself can't, such as the fields in the Global Address List on Microsoft Exchange Server. You will see several examples of how CDO delivers details that Outlook can't access.

As you read what other people have done with Outlook programming—in this book and others, on the Web, or in newsgroups—you might hear about other object models relevant to designing with Outlook, such as those listed in Table 1.1.

TABLE 1.1   Object Models Commonly Used When Programming with Outlook

Object Model	Description
ActiveX Data Objects (ADO)	Exchange information with Access and other databases.
Active Directory Services Interface (ADSI)	Interact with the Exchange and Windows 2000 directory.
Collaboration Data Objects (CDO)	Access MAPI properties of Outlook items, as well as many Exchange Server properties.
Outlook Object Model	Create and manipulate Outlook items, as well as react to application-level events.
Other Office application object models	Work with Excel, Word, PowerPoint, and Access objects from within Outlook.

In particular, you will be using the Excel and Word object models to write reports from Outlook objects because Outlook has fairly limited print layout functions. Integrating Outlook with Access is a bit beyond the scope of an introductory book such as this one, but you will find many references in more advanced Outlook programming books and on the Internet.

Furthermore, you can use VBA to create macros that you can add to the Outlook toolbar to launch your telephone message form, search and replace text in all the items in a folder, and expand Outlook's capabilities in many other ways. A macro is a program, too, and not always a small one. You might have created macros in Word or Excel by turning on a macro recorder that watches your actions and then builds the appropriate code. Outlook does not include a comparable macro recorder, but the examples in this book show you how to use VBA to perform all the basic actions of creating messages and other items, addressing them, and sending them.

How to Start

At this point, you might feel the hardest task in Outlook programming is knowing where to start. Do you start with VBScript or VBA? Do you work with the form first and then write the program code, or vice versa?

Start by choosing one or more compelling projects—ideas that will save you time in the long run, make repetitive tasks less burdensome, or perhaps just display information that is hard to get to in the basic Outlook interface. Try to be as specific as possible. Don't decide to build a project to "make Outlook work just like Goldmine" (a popular sales contact management program). Instead, pick a particular Goldmine feature you want Outlook to duplicate.

When you choose a project, don't start writing code or moving fields around on a form right away! Instead, take some time to outline what you want the project to accomplish, using what programmers call *pseudocode*.

But wait! You say you don't know how to write programming code. (That's why you bought this book, you protest.) No, we're not asking you to write a program (not yet), only to lay the groundwork. When you write pseudocode, you're walking through the logic of what you want to happen, without worrying about the exact language required to make it work.

For example, say you want to enhance Outlook's appointment form with a button that would create a new task for a follow-up telephone call to the person you met with. The pseudocode might look something like this:

```
User clicks button
    Show task form
    Copy details of meeting to task body
    Copy contact from meeting to the task's Contact field
    Set task due date for one week from the meeting date
    If task due date falls on a weekend, holiday, or vacation day
        Adjust the due date to the next business day
    EndIf
    ...and so forth
```

1

Nothing in this list looks like programming (except the `If...EndIf` syntax), but it describes in detail what you want Outlook to do when the user clicks the follow-up call buttons. It won't take much to move from this pseudocode to the program code to implement these steps.

Which tool is appropriate for a particular project? Table 1.2 provides some recommendations of the tools you are most likely to use in particular situations.

TABLE 1.2   Choosing Outlook Tools

If You Want To...	You Will Probably Use This Approach
Show additional information on an Outlook form.	Modify an Outlook form.
Make something happen in response to something the user does with an Outlook item.	Modify an Outlook form with VBScript code.
Write a macro that can be run from the Outlook toolbar.	Write a routine in VBA.
Make something happen when the user starts Outlook, switches to a different folder, or performs other actions that don't involve a particular Outlook item.	Write a routine in VBA.
Display status information as the user performs various Outlook tasks.	Create a form in VBA with a routine to show the status information.

However, in many cases, you can approach a project in several ways. As you work through the examples in the lessons that follow, you will develop a better feel for which Outlook tool works best where.

A Word on Outlook Modes

Among Microsoft Office programs, Outlook 2000 has the peculiar distinction of being two applications in one. Depending on how you install Outlook, you may be working in Internet Mail Only mode or in Corporate or Workgroup mode. Each mode includes features not available to the other. For example, the Send Plain Text Only check box on a Contact form (shown in Figure 1.2) works only in Internet Mail Only mode.

To check your version, choose Help, About.

Most developers probably use Corporate or Workgroup mode because it includes a Manage Forms function omitted from Internet Mail Only. However, depending on whether you design Outlook applications for yourself or for others, you might have to test your projects in both modes.

Another factor that makes a difference in how Outlook operates is whether you connect to Microsoft Exchange Server, Microsoft's enterprise e-mail and collaboration server. In Hour 23, "Exchange Server Collaboration," you will look at some particular issues related to creating applications for Exchange Server users.

Summary

At first, Microsoft Outlook programming can seem complex because there is more than one tool and no clear picture of where to start. However, by modifying Outlook forms and creating custom programs in VBA, you can build powerful applications that use electronic messaging as a vehicle for all kinds of other interactions.

The next hour introduces the various Outlook forms and shows you how to enter and exit the forms design mode and how to get help with Outlook forms design.

Q&A

Q Can I use VBA to put programming behind Outlook forms and distribute them to others?

A No, the programming language behind Outlook messages and other forms is VBScript, which is much more compact than VBA. However, you can use Outlook's VBA environment to write and test the code you want to use in scripts. Converting VBA code to VBScript code is not difficult.

Q Are all the capabilities of Outlook available to a programmer?

A No, some functions (such as the nifty calendar pull-down control) are private to Outlook and cannot be accessed by a programmer. In many cases, though, you can write your own functions to duplicate those hidden inside Outlook.

Workshop

Work through the quiz questions and exercises so that you can understand Outlook programming better. See Appendix A for answers.

Quiz

1. Why does Outlook support both VBA and VBScript as programming languages?

2. Why are object models important to programming in Outlook?

3. What are the two versions of Outlook?

Exercise

Write the pseudocode for a routine that forces the File As field on an Outlook Contact item to display the name in first name/last name order with the company name in parentheses. Do you want Outlook to update the File As field whenever any of the related name fields change or only when you save the contact? (Hint: It's your decision!)

HOUR **2**

Six Forms in Search of a Designer

This hour gets you started with Outlook forms. You will take a guided tour of the six main built-in forms. This will give you an idea of which form would be the best fit for a particular project.

The highlights of this hour include

- How to start and end an Outlook forms design session
- Where to find forms you can use as models
- What information each form can store
- How to get help with forms design
- Where to save finished forms

Starting the Forms Designer

Every Outlook form starts from another Outlook form, rather than from a blank page. To start designing an Outlook form, choose Tools, Forms,

Design a Form from the main Outlook menu. The Design Form dialog box shown in Figure 2.1 appears, listing the forms in the Standard Forms Library. This library holds the six basic forms that appear when you click the New button in any Outlook folder, as well as two hidden forms Outlook uses for meeting invitations and task assignments.

FIGURE 2.1

Select a form to modify for your project.

Select the form you want to use as the basis for your new form (for example, the Appointment form), and then click Open.

The Look In list can show you other places where Outlook forms may be stored. The forms you find there have already been modified in some fashion. You can use them to create new forms, too. Later in this lesson, you will learn more about where forms are stored.

The Basic Outlook Forms

For many Outlook applications, you only have to make a few changes to an existing form. The next few sections introduce all six basic forms to help you understand which form would be best suited for a particular task.

The Appointment Form

You will start with the Appointment form, opening it with the Tools, Forms, Design a Form command. Figure 2.2 shows the Appointment form open to the Appointment page. Each tab on the form, starting with Appointment and ending with (Actions), represents a page you can either show the user or hide. The pages whose names appear in parentheses are hidden. When users create new appointments in their Calendar folders, they normally see only the Appointment page and the Attendee Availability page, shown in Figure 2.3.

FIGURE 2.2

The Appointment form holds information about meetings and events.

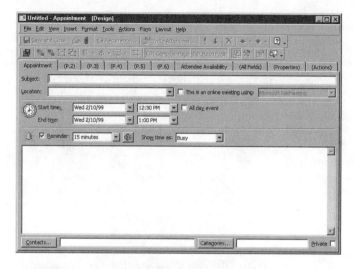

FIGURE 2.3

The Attendee Availability page of the Appointment form shows the times when people are free for meetings.

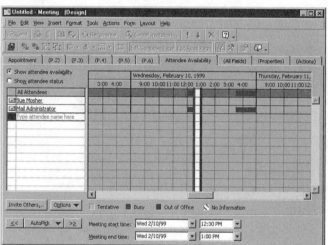

After you use the Attendee Availability page to invite someone, the title of the item changes from *Appointment* to *Meeting*.

You cannot customize the Appointment or Attendee Availability page of the Appointment form. Any customization takes place on the five pages labeled (P.2)–(P.6). Figure 2.4 shows the (P.2) page.

In general, you cannot customize the built-in pages of the various forms, except for the Message and Post forms and the first page of the Contact form. However, you can hide the built-in pages and use the same fields on your own custom pages. You can make the custom pages look, if not exactly the same as, very much like the built-in pages.

FIGURE 2.4

Each form contains five blank pages you can customize.

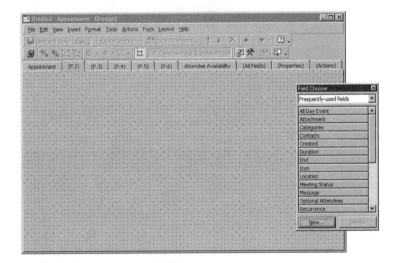

The (All Fields), (Properties), and (Actions) pages are common to all Outlook forms. You will look at them a little later in the chapter.

The Contact Form

Next, take a look at the Contact form. Figures 2.5–2.8 show its built-in pages. Unlike the Appointment form, you can customize the first page of the Contact form, although you still cannot make changes on the other built-in pages.

If you customize the first page of the Contact form, you cannot use the customized form with Outlook 97. Only Outlook 98 and Outlook 2000 support making changes to the first page of the Contact form.

FIGURE 2.5

The grid of dots indicates that you can customize the General page of the Contact form.

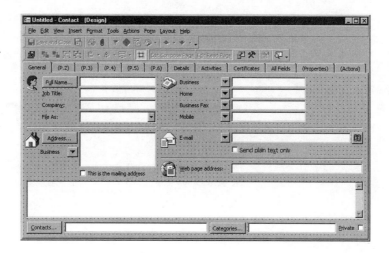

As you work with the various forms, you will discover that some features appear or disappear, depending on the type of Outlook installation you have. Outlook has two main modes: Corporate or Workgroup and Internet Mail Only. (There is also a No E-mail mode, but it is rarely used.) Some features work only in one mode or the other. For example, on the General page of the Contact form (see Figure 2.5), users see the Send Plain Text Only check box only in Internet Mail Only mode, although it appears in the form design when you work in Corporate or Workgroup mode.

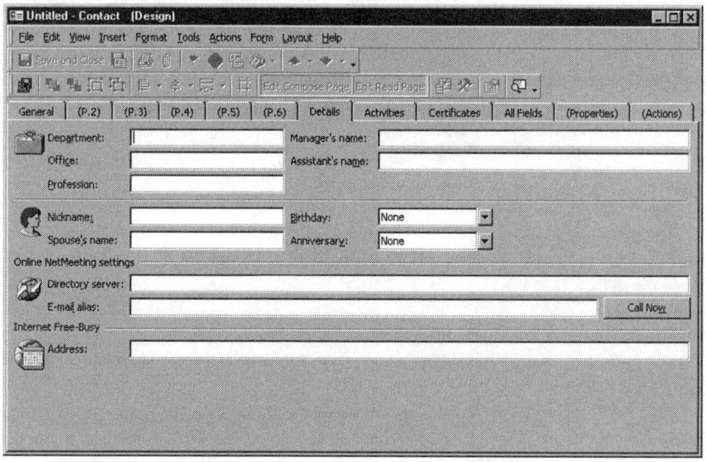

FIGURE 2.6

The Details page holds additional information about each contact.

The Activities page (see Figure 2.7) searches other Outlook folders to find items related to the current contact. The Show field always defaults to All Items; you cannot customize that selection. If you change it to, say, Upcoming Tasks/Appointments, and then save the form, the new form still defaults to All Items.

FIGURE 2.7

The Activities page of the Contact form tracks related items in other Outlook folders.

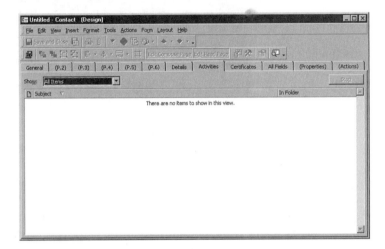

You also cannot customize the Certificates page, shown in Figure 2.8.

FIGURE 2.8

The Certificates page stores digital security certificate information.

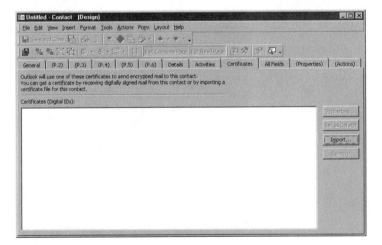

The Journal Entry Form

The Journal Entry form, shown in Figure 2.9, has just one built-in page, the General page. The unique feature of the Journal Entry form is that it includes buttons to start and stop a timer that keeps track of how much time you spend on a particular activity.

FIGURE 2.9

The Journal Entry form tracks the time you spend on tasks.

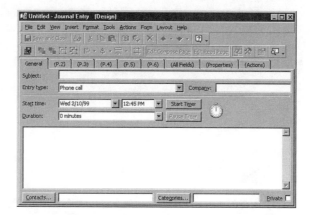

The Message Form

The Message form, shown in Figure 2.10, is probably the most familiar of all the Outlook forms because it appears every time you create a new e-mail message. Because the built-in Message page of this form can be customized, it is used as the basis for many kinds of Outlook projects, especially those that involve routing information from one person to another.

FIGURE 2.10

Use the Message form to create forms that exchange information with other Outlook users.

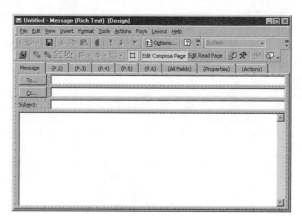

Click the Edit Read Page button to see a different layout for the Message form, such as that in Figure 2.11. Click the Edit Compose Page button to return to the original layout. These two layouts help to explain why a message you compose looks different from a message you receive.

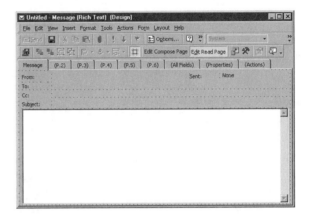

All forms support individual compose and read pages, as you will see in Hour 4, "Extend Form Design with a Custom Task Form." However, only the Message and Post forms show separate compose and read pages by default.

The Post Form

The Post form, shown in Figure 2.12, is even simpler than the Message form. It is always used for posting information directly to a particular folder and, therefore, does not require the To or Cc buttons and boxes associated with the Message form.

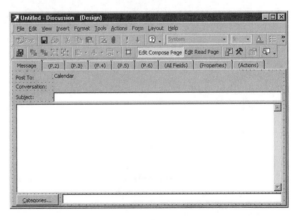

The Task Form

The last built-in form is the Task form. Its two pages, Task and Details, are shown in
Figures 2.13 and 2.14. Users typically create task items to build a to-do list for themselves or for the group of people they work with.

FIGURE 2.13

*The first page of the
Task form holds the
most important infor-
mation about each
task.*

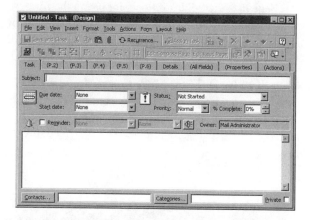

FIGURE 2.14

*The Details page of the
Task form holds track-
ing and other details.*

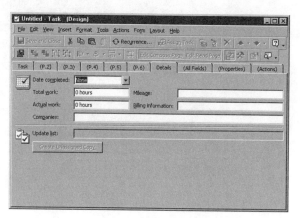

Hidden Forms

In addition to the six basic forms, the Design Form dialog box (refer to Figure 2.1) also
lists Meeting Request <Hidden> and Task Request <Hidden>. These are actually variations on the Appointment and Task forms and add a To button and box for addressing the
form to meeting attendees or a task recipient.

Common Form Pages

Here are the other pages every form includes: (All Fields), (Properties), and (Actions). The names appear in parentheses because these pages are normally hidden, except on the Contact form, which shows the All Fields page by default.

The All Fields page lists the fields available for use in the form. A *field* is a single fact related to an item. Each type of Outlook form uses a distinct set of fields. For example, a Contact form has three fields for holding fax numbers, but these do not appear on a Task form.

From the Select From list at the top of the Contact form, you can choose which set of fields you want to work with and can see the names of the fields, along with their current values. For example, to see all the fields available in a Contact form, choose All Contact Fields. You then see the list shown in Figure 2.15. You can also choose Frequently-Used Fields or Name Fields, and so on, to see a smaller subset of the many fields available in a Contact item.

FIGURE 2.15

The All Fields page shows every field available in a Contact form.

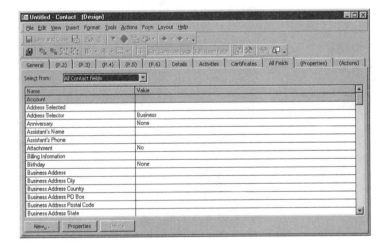

You might also notice the choices for User-Defined Fields in This Item and User-Defined Fields in This Folder, as well as a New button at the bottom of the page. You can create your own fields in Outlook (which you will do in Hour 4).

On the (Properties) page, shown in Figure 2.16, you control various settings for the form, including

- The icon it displays
- The version number

- An optional category and subcategory to help you track forms if you have many of them

- A contact for the form

- A description

FIGURE 2.16

The (Properties) page allows you to control information that identifies the form.

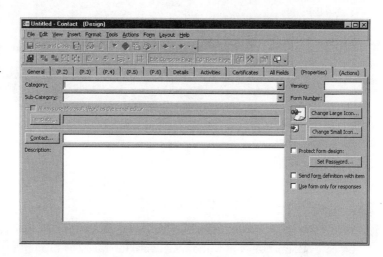

Many of these properties are especially important if you are creating forms that other people will be using.

The last page is the (Actions) page, shown in Figure 2.17. It controls what happens when the user performs standard actions, such as Reply, Reply to All, Forward, and Reply to Folder. You can also add custom actions (as you will learn in Hour 14, "Working with Forms") that add new commands to the Actions menu and toolbar.

Although every form lists the form actions shown in Figure 2.17, not every action is relevant to the current form. For example, the Reply action means something to a Message item, but not to a Contact. On the other hand, the Forward action works on any form because you can forward any type of Outlook item to someone else.

When to Use Which Form

How do you know which form to use? One approach is to make a pencil-and-paper sketch of the form you have in mind for your project and then find the closest match among the six Outlook forms.

You can also look at the (All Fields) page for a sense of which forms include which fields. You should use the built-in fields as much as possible.

FIGURE 2.17

The (Actions) page controls commands that appear on the Actions menu.

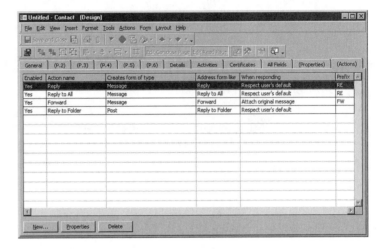

If your project involves sending messages back and forth between people to gather and process information, you will probably use the Message form. If the information is gathered in one specific folder, rather than through an exchange of messages, the Post form is often appropriate.

However, don't feel that you have to use a particular form only for its original purpose. For example, if you want to keep track of how much time is spent on a project, you can use any of the three forms that include fields measuring time: the Appointment, Journal Entry, and Task forms.

As you saw at the beginning of this chapter, the Design Form dialog box (refer to Figure 2.1) has a Look In list where you can select from various locations where forms are stored. Any form you previously modified can be located in one list or another. You can select that modified form and base a new form on it. For example, if you create a new Contact form that includes more fields and want to use those same fields in a new project, start with your modified form, rather than go back to the original Contact form.

You can also open any Outlook item, make changes to it, and choose Form, Design This Form to use that particular item as the starting point for a custom form. This is a good approach when the form you want to customize is not in the Standard Forms list, such as the form for creating distribution lists in a Contacts folder. Another good example is a form with voting buttons. Although you can set the voting options in VBScript code, it's more often convenient to set the voting options in the normal message form, by clicking the Options button. You can then publish the form, as described later in this lesson, to make it easy to reuse. Figure 2.18 shows a custom document transmittal form with three response buttons, as the recipient would see it.

FIGURE 2.18
Voting buttons provide an easy method of creating a custom transmittal form.

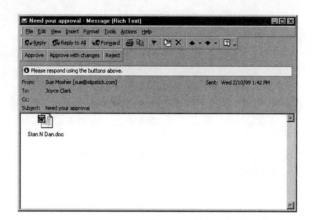

Working in the Forms Designer

To complete this tour of the Outlook forms design environment, here are two of the tools you will be using: Field Chooser and Control Toolbox. Figure 2.19 shows the toolbar buttons for these and two other tools, Properties and View Code, which are covered in upcoming lessons.

FIGURE 2.19
The Field Chooser, Control Toolbox, Properties, and View Code buttons (left to right) display the form design tools.

The Field Chooser

When you view any customizable page, the Field Chooser appears. As shown in Figure 2.20, it lists the fields you can add to the page. It defaults to Frequently-Used Fields, but like the All Fields page, you can click the drop-down arrow at the top of the Field Chooser to see either all available fields or a particular subset.

FIGURE 2.20

The Field Chooser provides a list of all fields available for the current form.

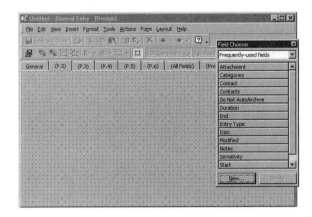

To turn off the Field Chooser, click the close (×) button in its upper-right corner, or choose Form, Field Chooser from the menu. You can also click the Field Chooser button on the toolbar to turn it on and off.

The Control Toolbox

The buttons, check boxes, drop-down lists, and boxes for entering text on the form are all examples of controls that make up the form's user interface. To see the types of controls you can use, click the Control Toolbox button on the form's toolbar, or choose Form, Control Toolbox from the menu to display the Toolbox, shown in Figure 2.21. The easiest way to learn the names of the controls is to place your mouse pointer over a button without clicking. After a moment, the name of the control appears in a ToolTip.

FIGURE 2.21

Pause the mouse pointer over any control in the Toolbox to see the name of the control.

You can add ToolTip pop-up text to controls on your own customized form pages to make it easier for users to understand what each control does.

Getting Help in Outlook Forms Design

Like all Microsoft Office programs, Outlook includes a detailed system of help topics designed to assist you in various tasks, including designing forms. Getting to the help on

Outlook forms is a bit tricky, though. First, if you want to use the Office Assistant, make sure that it is displayed; choose Help, Show the Office Assistant. Then, press Alt+F11 to start a VBA session. If you see a prompt for Disable Macros or Enable Macros, it doesn't matter which you choose because you will not be doing any macro editing in this lesson.

After the Microsoft Visual Basic window opens, press F1, type your question in the Office Assistant box, and then press Enter or click Search. Figure 2.22 shows the Office Assistant suggesting topics related to Customize Outlook Forms. Click on any topic to view it in the separate Microsoft Visual Basic Help window, shown in Figure 2.23.

FIGURE 2.22

The Office Assistant provides answers to your programming questions.

FIGURE 2.23

A general help topic introduces Outlook design concepts.

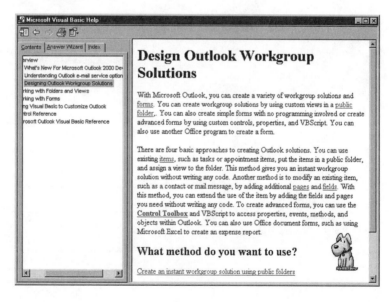

If you do not see the Contents, Answer Wizard, and Index tabs shown on the left in
Figure 2.23, click the Show button on the left of the Help window toolbar. These three
tabs provide ways of getting to the information in the help system, depending on whether
you want to browse through topics in a logical sequence, ask a question, or search a
detailed index.

> If you prefer not to use the Office Assistant, you could type customize
> Outlook forms in the box on the Answer Wizard tab of the Help window
> and find the same topics as in Figure 2.22.

Many help topics cover particular procedures. You usually see a series for numbered
steps, such as that in Figure 2.24. Text shown in blue and underlined, as on a Web page,
represents a linked topic. Click on the link to see the topic.

FIGURE 2.24

*Don't overlook the
notes and links to
additional information
at the bottom of many
Help topics.*

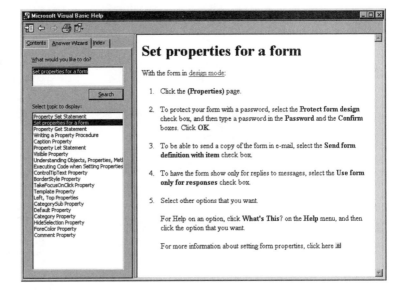

> Whenever you read a procedural topic, be sure to check the bottom of the
> topic for tips and links to additional information.

To close the Help window, click the close (×) button in the upper-right corner. While you are working on forms design, you might want to leave Help open so that you can return to it if you have more questions.

Saving Forms and Ending a Design Session

When you have done enough work on a form for the day, you will want to save the form and end the forms design session. You can save the form in three ways:

- As an item in an Outlook folder
- As an Outlook template file anywhere on your computer
- As a published Outlook form, either in a forms library or in a particular folder

If you close the form with the close (×) button in the upper-right corner, Outlook asks whether you want to save changes. If you respond Yes, Outlook saves the item to the default folder for that type of item. For a Message form, this is the Drafts folder. For a Post form, it's the Inbox. Other forms go into the corresponding folder, an Appointment form to the Calendar folder, and so on.

I don't recommend storing custom forms as items in Outlook folders because it's too easy to delete them accidentally and not that easy to reuse them. You are better off saving them as template files or publishing them.

To save a form as a template file, choose File, Save As; under Save as Type, choose Outlook Template (*.oft). You also have to provide a filename and choose a location. If you installed Outlook on the C: drive, the best location is C:\Program Files\Microsoft Office\Templates. This corresponds to the User Templates in File System location, from which you can open forms with the Choose Form dialog (refer to Figure 2.1).

When you are designing a new form, you might want to save interim versions as .oft template files so that you can revert to a version without the most recent changes.

Publishing a form means saving it to a form library. Table 2.1 lists the three types of form libraries. If you don't use Microsoft Exchange Server, you won't see Organization Forms.

TABLE 2.1 Outlook Forms Libraries

Library	Description
Personal Forms	A library of forms stored in your Personal Folders or Exchange Server mailbox.
Organization Forms	A library of forms stored on the Exchange Server for group use. You need permission from the Exchange Server administrator to publish to this library.
Folder Forms	A library of forms associated with a particular folder, either in your mailbox or Personal Folders or in a public folder on the Exchange Server. You must have folder owner permission to publish to a public folder.

If a form has any code behind it and is saved as an Outlook item or template, when you open it, you will see a dialog box with the choices Enable Macros and Disable Macros. To avoid that dialog box (which you will certainly want to do if you design forms for others to use), you must publish the form.

To publish a newly customized form based on one of the built-in forms, choose Tools, Forms, Publish Form. If you used a previously customized form as the basis for your new form, choose Tools, Forms, Publish Form As so that you can give it a new name. In the Publish Form As dialog box (see Figure 2.25), use the Look In drop-down list or the Browse button to select a location. Then, give the form a display name and form name, and click Publish.

In Hour 24, "Deploying Forms and Applications," you learn how to remove old forms, make a form the default for new items in a folder, and convert old items to use the new form.

After you save a form as an .oft template file or publish it, you can end the design session by clicking the close (×) button and responding No to the Save Changes prompt.

FIGURE 2.25

Publishing a custom Contact form to the Contacts folder.

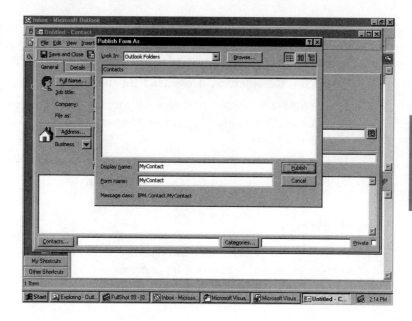

Summary

This hour introduces you to the six basic Outlook forms you can customize and the techniques required to start and end a design session, save your design work, and display the Field Chooser and Control Toolbox. You also learned several methods and locations for saving forms.

In the next hour, you will create your first customized form by modifying the Contact form in several ways.

Q&A

Q Can I build a form from scratch, without using one of the existing forms?

A No, you must always begin with one of the built-in forms or an existing Outlook item. However, if you want to build something that looks nothing like a built-in form, you can hide the default pages and display only custom pages that you yourself create.

Q How do I reuse a form after I've published it?

A Choose Tools, Forms, Choose Form, and select a form from one of the forms libraries, your Outlook folders, or the file system.

Q What is the difference between a field and a control?

A The field contains the actual data in the item, whereas the control displays it in a particular form. Controls can also display information unrelated to the Outlook item being shown.

Q Can I customize the Note form (the one used to make yellow sticky notes)?

A No, this is one Outlook form you cannot modify.

Workshop

Work through the quiz questions and exercises so that you can understand Outlook programming better. See Appendix A for answers.

Quiz

1. How many pages can you customize on a Message form? on a Task form?
2. What fields do the Appointment, Journal Entry, and Task forms use to measure time?
3. What field(s) do all six basic forms show on their main page?
4. What is different about the button in the upper-left corner of the Control Toolbox?

Exercises

1. Search help until you find information on publishing forms.
2. In a Contact form, examine the list of frequently used fields. Which of these do not appear on the General or Details page of the built-in Contacts form?
3. Use voting buttons to create a document transmittal form that looks like Figure 2.17, and publish it to your Personal Folders with an appropriate display name and form name. (Hint: Click the Options button, and enter the names of the buttons in the Use Voting Buttons field, separated by semicolons.)

HOUR 3

Create Your First Custom Contact Form

In the preceding hour, you became acquainted with the Outlook forms design environment. Now, it's time to go to work and create your first custom Contact form. After a review of the overall process, you will get down to the business of adding and modifying form pages and controls.

The highlights of this hour include

- How to add controls to a form
- What constitutes a good control name
- Where to change control properties
- How to rename a page
- What form properties you should always set

The Process in a Nutshell

Creating a custom form involves a series of steps that occur in the same order every time:

1. Pick a form to start with, as discussed in Hour 2, "Six Forms in Search of a Designer."
2. Add and modify controls on either built-in or customized pages.
3. Test the form.
4. Repeat steps 2 and 3 as necessary to complete the form.
5. Set the basic properties for the form.
6. Save the form.

Add and Modify Controls and Pages

Controls are the building blocks of your form's user interface. They determine how users will enter data, retrieve information, and otherwise interact with the form. You can add up to five custom pages, and on the Message, Post, and Contact forms, you can also modify the first page. You will build a new page on a custom Contact form to learn some of the frequently used fields that don't appear on either the General or the Details page. (If you skipped exercise 2 from Hour 2, go back and do it now because I'm about to reveal the answer!)

> If you modify the first page (the General page) of a Contact form, the form cannot be used with Outlook 97. If you must keep the form compatible with Outlook 97, leave the General page alone, and do all your modifications on the available custom pages.

Add Fields

Open the Contact form in design mode, and click on the (P.2) page to start. The Field Chooser should appear with the list of frequently used fields displayed. If it doesn't, click the Field Chooser button, or choose Form, Field Chooser.

To place a field on the form, drag it from the Field Chooser to the form page. Start with the Business Home Page field. Outlook automatically places the field at the top left of the blank page. Next, drag the Personal Home Page field to the form. See how Outlook places it directly beneath the first field. Check your form against Figure 3.1.

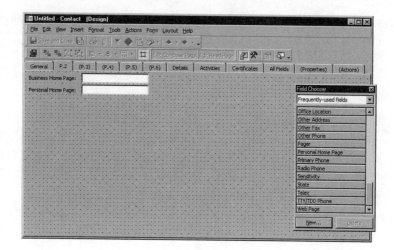

FIGURE 3.1

*This custom page
contains two fields
dragged from the
Field Chooser.*

3

Also, notice that the name of the page, P.2, is no longer in parentheses. Outlook assumes that if you add fields to a custom page, you want users to see them, so it shows the page.

Both these fields display their data in a control called a Text Box (because the user can normally type text into it). Text Boxes are probably the most commonly used form control.

The text that tells you the name of the field, such as Business Home Page for the first field, is called a *label*. Label controls are a key element in making forms that are easy to understand. Not only do they describe different controls, but you can also use them to provide detailed instructions on the form page.

> Outlook saves you time by adding a Label control for most fields that you drag from the Field Chooser. Some controls, such as Check Box controls, do not require Label controls nearby because they include captions.

Now, drag two more fields from the Field Chooser: Flag Status and Follow Up Flag. Finally, in the Field Chooser, switch from the Frequently-Used Fields list to All Mail Fields (That's right, All Mail Fields), and drag the Due By field to your form. Your form should look like Figure 3.2.

FIGURE 3.2

Now you have dragged
three additional fields
to the custom page.

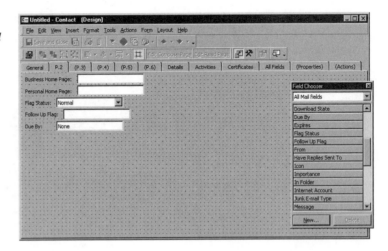

The Flag Status field uses a Combo Box control. This type of control combines elements of a Text Box control (users can type in it) with a List Box control, where users pick an item from a list. Combo Box controls usually work so that when users type the first letter or two of the item they want to select, the Combo Box control automatically selects that item without a mouse click.

Some Outlook fields do not appear in the fields list for the type of item you're working with. It is worth experimenting to see what fields you can use from other types of items. For example, the Due By field is used for both Mail and Contact item message flags, but appears only on the list of Mail fields. In Hour 13, "Working with the Object Models," you will learn how to use the Outlook Object Model and its help system to explore the various Outlook fields.

If you're eager to learn more about the different types of controls, you might want to peek ahead to Hour 6, "A VBA Birthday/Anniversary Reminder Tool," and Hour 7, "An Area Code Search and Replace Tool."

Rearrange Controls

When you drag fields from the Field Chooser, Outlook lines up any accompanying Label controls on the left side of the form. This leaves the right side looking sloppy. Your next task, therefore, is to make the text and combo box fields align neatly by their right edges.

You could move each control individually. For example, click the box with the word *Normal* in it (in other words, the control for the Flag Status field) to select it. The box now appears with a gray line around it and eight white boxes called *drag handles* at the corners and sides; these are used for resizing the control. If you move the mouse pointer over one of the sides (but not over a drag handle), it turns into a four-sided arrow. When you see the four-sided arrow (see Figure 3.3), hold down the left mouse button, and drag the field to a new location on the form.

FIGURE 3.3

To move a single control, select it, move the mouse pointer until it turns into a four-headed arrow, and then drag.

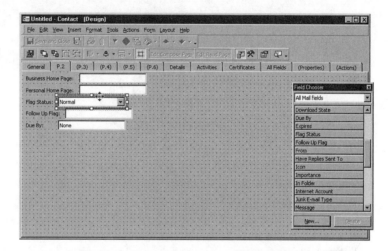

There's an easier way to line up those controls, though. You can select a group of controls and then use a layout command to right-align them.

First, you have to know how to select multiple controls. Earlier, you clicked on one control to select it. To add another control to the selection, hold down the Ctrl key as you click it. Continue using Ctrl+click to include the four text boxes and the one combo box in your selection.

If you select one of the labels by mistake, use Ctrl+click to deselect it. You can also click anywhere on the background of the form to clear all selections and start over completely.

Did you notice that the drag handles for the last control you clicked are white, whereas those for the others are black? The control with white drag handles acts as the model for alignment and resizing operations. In this case, you want to line up everything along the right edge of the Business Home Page and Personal Home Page fields, so make sure that one of those fields has the white drag handles. If one of the other fields was the last selected, use Ctrl+click twice on the Business Home Page field to make it the last selected. Figure 3.4 shows how the selected controls should look.

FIGURE 3.4

FIGURE 3.4

When multiple controls are selected, the one with the white drag handles controls any group sizing and alignment operations.

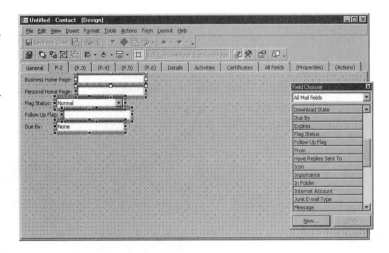

Here is a really quick method for selecting a group of adjacent controls: Drag a rectangular shape (with the mouse pointer) that covers a bit of each control you want to select and doesn't touch any other controls. For this form, position the mouse pointer slightly to the right of the Business Home Page field, the one you want to use as your alignment model. Then, hold down the left mouse button, and drag the mouse diagonally toward the lower left until you see a rectangle touching all the Text Box and Combo Box controls, as shown in Figure 3.5. When you release the left mouse button, the controls will be selected, just as they are in Figure 3.4.

FIGURE 3.5

Quickly select adjacent controls by dragging across them.

With the controls selected, click the small arrow next to the Align Left button on the toolbar (see Figure 3.6), and then click the Right button. You can also choose Layout, Align, Right from the menu. After aligning the controls, they should look like Figure 3.7.

Several buttons on the Form Design toolbar include small arrows that display a list of additional commands.

FIGURE 3.6

The Align commands on the Form Design toolbar.

3

FIGURE 3.7

Controls aligned along their right edge are easier on the user's eye.

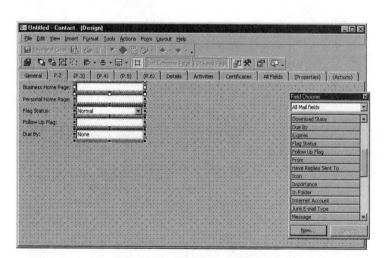

If you change the layout of your form and don't like the way it looks, press Ctrl+Z or choose Edit, Undo to reverse the last change you made.

The Layout menu and Form Design toolbar contain many other helpful commands for rearranging and resizing controls and setting the tab order. (The tab order controls what field is next when a user presses the Tab key to move out of a control (or what field is previous, if the user presses Shift+Tab).) To resize a control, you select it, and then you drag it by one of the white drag handles.

Show, Hide, and Rename Pages

Now that your five controls are looking neat, you can give that custom page a more descriptive name. To rename a page, choose Form, Rename Page, and type in the new name: **Home Pages & Flag** would be appropriate for this page.

To hide or show a page, choose Form, Display This Page. A check next to the Display This Page command indicates whether the user will see the current page. You can also look at the page name; Hidden pages have their names in parentheses.

Set Control Properties

To finish working with controls in this lesson, you have to learn about their properties. Think of *properties* as the adjectives that describe the characteristics of each control. Forms have properties, too, as you will shortly see.

Outlook divides control properties into two groups: the basic ones you are most likely to want to use and advanced properties less commonly changed. To work with the basic properties, select a control, and then click the Properties button on the Form Design toolbar. You can also right-click a control and then choose Properties from the pop-up menu. Figure 3.8 shows the basic display properties.

FIGURE 3.8

The basic control display properties include name, position, font, and color.

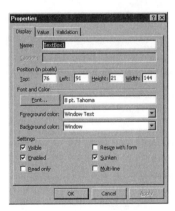

You will learn about the properties on the Value and Validation pages in the next hour.

Every control needs a name to distinguish it from other controls in the tab order and in any programming code you write. Outlook assigns a name automatically. You should change the name, at least for Text Box controls and other controls where the user enters data. Changing the name of Label controls is a less urgent task. Names should be descriptive, not cryptic, and use the prefix from Table 3.1 appropriate for the control; no spaces are allowed in control names.

For example, on your form, Outlook gave the names ComboBox1 to the Combo Box control for the Flag Status field and TextBox1 to the Text Box control for the Follow Up Flag field. Good, clear names for these would be cboFlagStatus and txtFollowUpFlag. The prefix (cbo or txt) makes it easy, when you're writing code, to know whether you are working with a Combo Box or Text Box control. Because the two have different properties, it's important to keep track of what kind of control you're working with.

TABLE 3.1   Outlook Form Control Name Prefixes

Control	Prefix
Label	lbl
Text Box	txt
Combo Box	cbo
List Box	lst
Check Box	chk
Option Button	opt
Toggle Button	tgl
Frame	fra
Command Button	cmd
Tab Strip	tab
Multipage	mlt
Scroll Bar	hsb (horizontal) or vsb (vertical)
Spin Button	spn
Image	img

3

Table 3.2 lists Name, along with the other display properties you can set in the basic Properties dialog box for a form.

TABLE 3.2   Outlook Form Control Display Properties

Property	Description
Name	Unique descriptive name
Caption	Text on label, check box, option button, toggle button, frame or command button
Position	Top, left, height, and width, measured in pixels
Font	Font size, style, and color
Foreground color	Text color, using the Windows color scheme
Background color	Background color, using the Windows color scheme
Visible	Can the user see the control? (Yes/No)
Enabled	Can the user click or enter information in the control? (Yes/No)
Read only	Can the user change the control's data? (Yes/No)
Resize with form	Shrink and enlarge the control when the overall form changes size? (Yes/No)
Sunken	Add a 3-D look? (Yes/No)
Multi-line	Wrap text in a text box, and create a new line when the user presses Enter? (Yes/No)

Additional properties are listed on a different Properties dialog box that appears when you right-click any control and then choose Advanced Properties from the pop-up menu. You can leave this Properties box open as you select controls, even multiple controls.

The two Properties dialog boxes work differently with respect to multiple controls. If you select multiple controls and click Properties, the dialog box controls the properties only for the last control you selected. To set properties for a group of controls, select them. Then, right-click any selected control, and choose Advanced Properties from the pop-up menu.

Text Box controls have a total of 42 properties; Combo and List Box controls, even more; and other controls, more or less as needed. These properties include the display properties from the basic Properties dialog, as well as many others. To change any property, select it in the Properties list, and then look at the top of the advanced Properties dialog box for either a drop-down list of choices or a text box where you can type in a value. Click the Apply button after you make your choice or type in a new property value.

For example, Figure 3.9 shows the Properties for the Follow Up Flag text box. Outlook provides this field so that you can specify how you want to follow up on a contact (or a mail message), with a phone call, visit, reply, or some other activity. In case the user is not familiar with this feature, you can change the `ControlTipText` property to add text that pops up when the user pauses the mouse over the Text Box control. When you click the Apply button, Outlook adds the text `Follow up activity, such as phone call` to the properties for the text box as the new control tip. Figure 3.10 shows how a user will see the control tip works on the finished form.

FIGURE 3.9

Set advanced properties for an Outlook form text box with this window.

Control tips are a great way to document your custom form as you build it.

Complete the Form

After you finish placing controls on the form and setting their properties, you need to test the form, set its properties, and then save it.

Test the Form

At any time, you can see how your form will look to a user by choosing Form, Run This Form. A new instance of the form appears, as in Figure 3.10, with all the changes you have made to the form so far. You can close it with the close (×) button at the upper-right corner of the form and return to your working copy of the form, which remains open in design mode.

Figure 3.10

The user sees the control tip by pointing the mouse at the control.

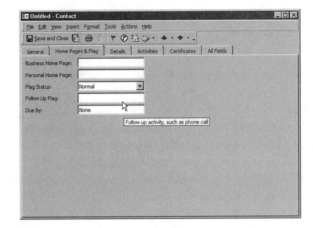

Set Form Properties

Forms have properties, too, just as controls do. Right-click on any blank area of the form background, and then choose Advanced Properties to display the Properties window, where you can set the background color and other properties.

When you are satisfied with the form and have tested it, it's time to set the operational properties for the form, before you save it. Click on the (Properties) tab to switch to that page, which is normally hidden from users.

> If the form is too wide for your display and you can't see the (Properties) tab or other tabs on the right side of the form, press Ctrl+PageDown to move through the different form pages one by one. You can use Ctrl+PageUp to cycle through the pages in the opposite order.

On the (Properties) page, you will almost always want to set the version, icons, contact, and description. Other settings may be optional, depending on the purpose of the form and the environment in which it will be used.

The version should be a number, increased every time you update the form with new enhancements. You can use a numbering sequence for the various versions, such as 1.0, 1.1, 1.2, and so on, or 1, 2, 3, 4, 5, and so on. Because of the way Outlook caches forms the user recently opened, incrementing the number ensures that everyone who uses the form will have the latest version.

To change either the large or small icon, click the appropriate button. Then, choose an icon from the *.ico files on your system in the C:\Program Files\Microsoft Office\ Office\Forms\1033\ folder. (Yours might be in a different location, depending on where you installed Outlook.) Figure 3.11 shows the Contactl.ico icon for the large icon. You will want to use the matching Contacts.ico for the small icon. The 1 and s at the end of the name stand for the large and small versions of the same icon.

Use the Windows Start, Find, Files or Folders command to search for *.ico files located elsewhere on your system.

FIGURE 3.11
Set the form's operational properties on the (Properties) page.

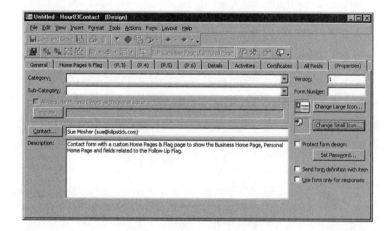

The Contact and Description fields should contain information about how the form should be used and whom to contact in case of questions or problems. This information appears when the user uses the Tools, Form, Choose Form command to run a published form. You also see it on the Help, About This Form dialog on a published form (see Figure 3.12).

Now, take a quick look at the less frequently used form properties. Set a Category and optional Sub-Category if you use a hierarchy of categories to organize forms either in your own folders or in the Organization Forms library. You can add a Form Number, in addition to the Version number, to identify your form as part of your organization's classification scheme.

FIGURE 3.12

*For published forms,
when users choose
Help, About This
Form, they see the
details you set on the
(Properties) page.*

FIGURE 3.12

*For published forms,
when users choose
Help, About This
Form, they see the
details you set on the
(Properties) page.*

Custom forms based on the Message form can require the user to use Word as the e-mail editor, with a particular .dot Word template. These options are available only if the default message format is set to Microsoft Outlook Rich Text. You can change the message format by choosing Tools | Options, and then switching to the Mail Format tab. Set these Word as editor options with the Always Use Microsoft Word as the E-Mail Editor check box and the Template button.

If you don't want anyone to change your form design or see the code for your form, check Protect Form Design and click Set Password to give the form a password.

If you plan to send the form to people outside your organization, check Send Form Definition with Item. Otherwise, leave this box clear.

> You can send custom messages and other Outlook forms to other Outlook users via the Internet if you use Rich Text Format for the message and set the user's address for Rich Text Formatting.

If you to want to keep the form from appearing in the form libraries that the user sees with the Choose Form command, check Use Form Only for Responses. That way, the form works only in conjunction with another custom form that includes the current form among its custom actions. You learn about custom form actions in Hour 14, "Working with Forms."

Save the Form

You have finished your first customized Contact form! Now, save it by following the Hour 2 instructions for saving or publishing a form. Try both saving it as an Outlook template .oft file to a system folder and publishing it to your Personal Forms library.

Remember that when you publish it, you must give it both a display name that will appear on the title bar of new instances of the form and a unique form name. Often, these are the same. In Figure 3.12, you can see that I used the name Hour03Contact for the form created during this hour.

Summary

Creating a custom form is a simple matter of adding controls, adjusting their properties and those of the form itself, and saving the form so that you can easily reuse it.

Q&A

Q Why do many Outlook fields use a Text Box control when I drag them from the Field Chooser?

A You can actually use a Text Box control to display any type of data. That's why it is one of the most commonly used controls.

Q Does every data entry control need a matching Label control?

A With the exception of controls that include their own captions (such as the Check Box control), it's good practice to include a Label control for every data entry control. When you drag a field from the Field Chooser, Outlook includes a Label control automatically.

Workshop

Work through the quiz questions and exercises so that you can understand Outlook programming better. See Appendix A for answers.

Quiz

1. What would be a good name for a Text Box control displaying the Due By field?
2. What is the difference between the Combo Box and List Box controls?
3. The default icon for custom forms is the same as the icon for which basic built-in form?

3

Exercises

1. Change the name and add text in the `ControlTipText` property for each control on the custom Home Pages & Flag page of the customized Contact form.

2. Add a Frame control to the page, give it the caption `Follow Up`, and move the three fields related to flags so that they appear inside the frame.

3. After you save or publish the form, open it using the Tools, Forms, Choose Form command. Does it appear as you expected it to?

HOUR 4

Extend Form Design with a Custom Task Form

You're doing great! Now that you know how to create and save simple customized forms, you can add more controls and create some custom fields. You will also learn how to make Outlook forms display different information, depending on whether you are composing a new item or reading an existing item.

The highlights of this hour include

- How controls are linked to fields
- How to create custom fields and add them to forms
- Why it's a good idea to use Outlook's built-in fields whenever possible
- How to use formulas to combine information from various fields and prevent users from making data entry mistakes
- What gives read messages a different layout from newly composed messages

Bound and Unbound Controls

In the previous lesson, you added several built-in fields to an Outlook form to make it easier for the user to store and retrieve the information in those fields. This is the key idea behind a field: It stores information permanently, as part of an Outlook item.

You will also find uses for unbound controls. These controls don't correspond to a particular field. Unbound controls store information, but only temporarily. The data they hold disappears when the user closes the current item, unless the programmer adds code to the form to save it first.

The fields you added to the form in the last lesson are all fields built in to Outlook. Even the Due Date field is a built-in field, although the Field Picker shows it as a Mail field instead of a Contact field.

You will probably want to use built-in fields as much as possible. For one thing, you cannot import from another data source into user-defined Outlook fields. The only way to import into user-defined fields is with programming code. Therefore, using built-in fields can save you time if you plan to import data.

You also cannot import directly into a custom form. However, as you will learn in Hour 15, "Working with Folders," changing the form for all items in a folder is a simple task.

The Contact form includes four extra generic fields, listed in the Field Picker as User Field 1, User Field 2, User Field 3, and User Field 4, for storing any kind of text information.

Adding User-Defined Fields

First, you will work with the Task form. You will create a new field and then add a control to display it on a custom page. Use the Tools, Forms, Design a Form command to open the built-in Task form to get into design mode.

To add a new field, switch to one of the customizable pages, and then click the New button on the Field Picker. In the New Field dialog box, give the field a name, choose the type, and specify the format. You will start with a field named Project, using the Text type and Text format, as shown in Figure 4.1.

FIGURE **4.1**

Specify the name, type, and format for a user-defined field.

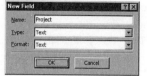

It's time to talk about types. Table 4.1 lists those available on the New Field dialog box. Experienced programmers might be perplexed because the user-defined field types available in Outlook are a little different from data types in other programming environments.

TABLE 4.1 Types for Outlook User-Defined Fields

Field Type	Can Contain
Text	Any string; up to 255 characters long
Number	Any number
Percent	Any number; displayed as a percentage
Currency	Any number involving money; displayed in the currency format for your country
Yes/No	Yes (-1) or No (0), True/False, or On/Off
Date/Time	Date and time data
Duration	The number of minutes
Keywords	Multiple strings, separated by commas
Combination	A combination of values from other fields, showing either all values or the first non-empty value
Formula	A calculation based on other fields and built-in functions
Integer	Any nondecimal number

For example, Outlook lists a Text type, instead of a String data type. To programmers, string data contains zero or more characters, and those characters can be numbers, letters, punctuation—any characters at all. Two Outlook field types can contain string data: the Text type and the Keywords type, which consists of several strings separated by commas.

The concept of a zero-length string might be a philosophical challenge, but it's an extremely useful programming concept. Think of it as what a blank box on the form contains before you fill it in. Zen, anyone?

Notice the several types for holding numeric data: Number, Percent, Currency, and Integer. The Yes/No type is actually a special number type that can hold either of just two values, -1 and 0, which stand for Yes, True, or On and No, False, or Off, respectively.

> Outlook does not allow you to change the name or data type for a user-defined field after you create it.

Fields using the Date/Time and Duration types allow you to enter data using "natural language," in other words, with ordinary words. For example, if you type **today** into a Date/Time field, Outlook converts that to the current date. You can type **next Tues**, and it will calculate the date automatically. Try **typing 2 wks from Fri**, and you will get an idea of just how smart and useful this feature can be. (If you really want a thrill, type in **New Year's Eve**.)

Duration fields store time measured in minutes, but allow you to enter it in days or hours as well. Use the letters d for day and h for hours. Try typing **2d** into any Duration field, and watch it turn into 2 days.

> To learn the type used by a built-in Outlook field, select the field on the (All Fields) page, and then click the Properties button. For example, the Categories field uses the Keywords type. For some fields, you will see Internal Data Type listed as the type. The values and behavior of these fields are controlled by Outlook itself, not by the user directly.

Combination Fields

Combination fields let you combine the values in one or more fields with optional text. For example, you can use a Combination field to show the first non-empty phone number or to put the text This task is due: in front of the due date.

You can add a Combination field to show either the date a task was completed or the date it is due. As you did for the Project field, click the New button on the Field Chooser. Type **Completed or Due** for the Name, and choose Combination for the Type. Then, click the Edit button to display the Combination Formula Field dialog box in Figure 4.2. At the top, select Showing Only the First Non-Empty Field, Ignoring Subsequent Ones.

FIGURE 4.2

To create the formula for a Combination field, use several fields or combine fields and text.

Before going further, take a moment to think through the logic of which field should come first. If the user has already finished the task, you don't have to see the due date, right? Therefore, the completed date should come first. When you decide on the field order, click the Field button, pick a field, and repeat until you see the fields you want in the Formula box. Click OK to save the combination formula. The New Field dialog box should look like Figure 4.3, using the formula [Date Completed] [Due Date]. Click OK to save the new field.

FIGURE 4.3

Combination and Formula fields have a Formula setting instead of a Format setting.

Formula Fields

Now, you will create one more new field so that you can see how Formula fields work. In particular, you are going to create a field to tell you whether this is a newly created, unsaved task or an existing task. Create the field by clicking the New button on the Field Chooser. Name the field **IsNew**, choose Formula for the Type, and then click Edit. In the Formula Field dialog box (see Figure 4.4), you will see not only a Field button, but also a Function button.

Functions are programming routines that return a value based on input values you supply. (Some functions don't require you to provide any input values.) Although you will be writing your own functions in upcoming lessons, you can use only intrinsic functions when creating Formula fields on Outlook forms. Intrinsic functions are those built into a programming environment. The Outlook forms design environment includes conversion, date/time, financial, general, math, and text functions.

FIGURE **4.4**

Use text, fields, and
functions to create a
Formula field.

To create a formula for a field, you combine fields, functions, and operators. Operators
are symbols that perform various mathematical and data operations, such as addition,
division, joining strings, or comparing two numbers to find out whether one is greater
than the other. Table 4.2 lists those you are most likely to use in Outlook formulas. Many
of them should be familiar from your earliest arithmetic books.

For the complete list of operators, ask the Office Assistant for the help topic
Operator Summary.

TABLE 4.2   Commonly Used Operators

Operator	Description
+	Addition
-	Subtraction
*	Multiplication
/	Division
&	String concatenation
=	Equal to
>	Greater than
>=	Greater than or equal to
<	Less than
<=	Less than or equal to
<>	Not equal to
And	True if both expressions are true; otherwise, false
Or	True if either expression is true; otherwise, false
Not	True if the expression is false; false if the expression is true

For your IsNew field, you can use the item's built-in Size field to determine whether an item is new. If the size equals 0, it's a new and unsaved item. If it's greater than 0, the item is not new. You want the IsNew field to have the value True if the item's size is equal to 0.

> Peek ahead to Hour 8, "Code Basics," to see how to use the size of a form to set a variable you can use in other routines. This is an alternative to putting it in a user-defined field.

To create the formula in the Formula Field dialog box, click the Fields button, and choose Size from the All Tasks Fields list. Then, type = 0. The formula should look like Figure 4.4. Click OK to save it as part of the definition of the IsNew field (see Figure 4.5).

FIGURE 4.5

This Formula field returns either True *or* False.

In Hour 1, "What You Can Do with Outlook 2000," do you remember the customized Contact form that showed the number of e-mail addresses for a contact? This is another example of a Formula field. Here is its formula, slightly more complex than the IsNew field's formula:

```
-( ( [E-mail] <> "") + ( [E-mail 2] <> "" ) + ( [E-mail 3] <> ""))
```

Each of the three expressions involving an e-mail field compares it to an empty string (""). For example, if there is no address in the [E-mail] field, the term ([E-mail] <> "") returns True, which is actually the number -1. Each of the three expressions returns -1 if there is an address and 0 if the field is blank. The minus sign (-) at the left of the formula changes the result from a negative to positive number. Therefore, the formula yields 0 if no e-mail address is present and a number between 1 and 3 if any of the fields is filled in.

> If you know the functions and fields you want to use, you can type formulas directly, rather than use the Field and Function buttons. Also, feel free to put spaces around operators and fields to make the formula easier to read.

4

Parentheses control the order in which expressions in a complex formula are evaluated, and they also enhance readability.

If you make a mistake in a Formula or Combination field and want to change it later, after already adding it to a form, make your change through the control that uses the field. Right-click the control, choose Properties, and then switch to the Value tab. Edit the formula under "Set the initial value of this field to." Your change will not be reflected in design mode. However, when you run the form, the new formula should be in effect.

You can also make changes to the formula by double-clicking it in the Field Chooser. However, a change made through the Field Chooser does not affect the form that you're currently working with in design mode   unless you first remove any controls that use the field and delete the field from the "User-defined fields in this item" list on the All Fields tab. Otherwise, a change to the formula made through the Field Chooser will become effective only when you open another form in design mode—one where you haven't used this field before—and then add the field to the form.

Outlook does not allow sorting and grouping on Combination or Formula fields in a view. One way around this limitation is to use a normal field of the appropriate type and then put code behind the form to perform the calculation.

Working with Controls

Now that you've created some user-defined fields, you can add them to the task form's (P.2) page. Drag the Project and IsNew fields from the Field Chooser to the custom page so that it looks like Figure 4.6

Where did the IsNew field's value of –1 come from? The formula for IsNew can return only True or False, that is, –1 or 0. Normally, you use a Check Box control to display the value in a Yes/No field because few users know that True equals –1. However, because IsNew is a Formula field, not a Yes/No field, Outlook does not automatically create a Check Box control when you drag IsNew to the form.

FIGURE 4.6

Drag user-defined fields from the Field Chooser to the form.

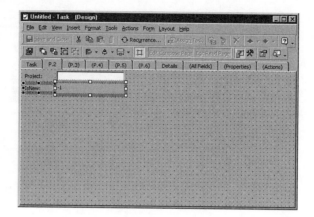

You must use a different technique: Create the Check Box control first, and then bind it to a field. First, select the IsNew field and its label, and delete them. Display the Toolbox, if you don't see it already, and then follow these steps:

1. Drag a Check Box control to the form, positioning it where the IsNew field originally appeared.

2. Open the basic Properties dialog box for the control.

3. On the Value tab, click the Choose Field button, and select the IsNew field from the User-Defined Fields in Folder list. Outlook fills in the details for the field automatically, as shown in Figure 4.7.

4. Switch to the Display tab, and enter **chkIsNew** for the Name of the control. You can leave the Caption as IsNew, which Outlook filled in for you, or change it to something more descriptive, such as Is a New Task.

4. Click OK to save the changes to the control's properties.

> When you drag a control from the Toolbox, you can place it precisely on the form.

The Value page in Figure 4.7 deserves a bit more explanation. All the controls on the Value page and the Validation page are disabled until you click the Choose Field button and bind a control to a field. You probably noticed the New button. Like the New button on the Field Chooser, this creates a new user-defined field.

FIGURE 4.7

*When you use the
Toolbox to create a
control on the form,
bind a field to the con-
trol in the control's
Properties dialog.*

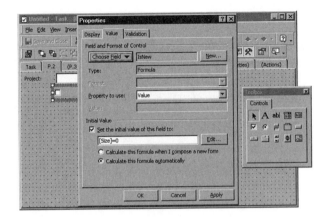

For field types other than Formula and Combination, you can change the Format of the
data. Each data type has its own format choices. For example, there are 16 formats for
Date/Time fields.

Under Initial Value, you can set the initial value of any field (not just formula fields) to a
formula. If you want the initial value to appear when you create a new item but allow
later changes, select Calculate This Formula When I Compose a New Form. If you
always want to use a calculated value, select Calculate This Formula Automatically.

Validation

For fields other than Combination and Formula fields, you sometimes want to specify
that a field must not be left blank or that it can accept only certain values. This technique, called *validation*, is an important method for preventing users (including yourself!) from making mistakes. Validation is the third page of the basic Properties dialog
for each Outlook form control. Figure 4.8 shows a possible validation rule for the Project
field created earlier.

If you just want to require a value, check the top box, labeled A Value Is Required for
This Field. If the user leaves the field blank, a message pops up that a value is required
for a field. Outlook doesn't tell you which field is missing a value, but when you click
the OK button on the pop-up message, it does take you directly to the field that needs
attention.

It's nicer for the user, though, to know right away which field is blank. Click the box for
Validate This Field Before Closing the Form if you want to give the user a specific message. Also, use this setting if you want to check the actual value of the field before the
item is saved. Either type a validation formula in the Validation Formula box, or click the

Edit button to see a Validation Formula dialog box, similar to that for Formula fields. Look in Table 4.3 for examples of validation formulas.

FIGURE 4.8

Validation rules help users enter data correctly.

TABLE 4.3 Sample Validation Formulas and Failure Messages

Formula	Result	Suggested Validation Failure Message
[Project] <> ""	Requires that the [Project] field is not left blank	You cannot leave the Project field blank.
[Due Date] > Date()	Requires that the [Due Date] field is in the future, using the special Date() function for the current date	Enter a Due Date later than today's date.
Len([Project Code]) = 10	Requires that the [Project Code] field has exactly 10 characters	The Project Code must be exactly 10 characters.

As you can see, validation formulas can use fields, functions, and operators. The one thing these examples have in common is that the formula includes the field you want to validate. It wouldn't make any sense, would it, to have a validation formula that ignored the very value you wanted to test?

4

Before you delete a control from a form, check its Validation properties. If validation is active and you remove the field from the form, Outlook still tries to validate it. The user will almost always get an error message, but will not be able to correct the error because the control is no longer present on the form.

If you use a validation formula, you should always add an expression in the box labeled Display This Message If the Validation Rule Fails. Otherwise, the user gets a cryptic, generic message that the field didn't pass the validation rule. In your validation failure message, don't just tell the user that something is wrong; explain how to fix it. Table 4.3 includes examples of validation failure messages that match the validation rule.

Control Limitations

Outlook users can become spoiled by some elements of the application's user interface, particularly the drop-down calendar for picking dates, the automatic phone number formatting, and the automatic breaking of the Full Name and Address fields into their constituent parts.

The bad news is that you can't duplicate the drop-down calendar on your custom form pages (not without adding a component called an ActiveX control, as you will see in Hour 20, "ActiveX and Other Controls." Nor can you create new phone number fields and have Outlook include them in the list of phone numbers and format them into international style automatically.

Another limitation is that Text fields can hold only 255 characters. If you want to store larger quantities of text data, you can use the large Text Box control that appears at the bottom of each form. On Appointment, Message, and Post forms, this appears as the Message field in the Field Chooser. For Contacts, Journal Entry, and Task forms, Outlook calls it the Notes field. However, you can use this field only once on a form.

When you work with the Message or Notes field in code, it has yet another name, the Body property. At least in that context, the property name is the same for every type of Outlook item.

The good news is that some fields, such as the Full Name field and the various address fields, do work the same on custom pages as on built-in pages. For example, if you type **Alex Smith** into a Full Name field on a custom page, Outlook stores Alex in the First

Name field and Smith in the Last Name field. Also, as noted earlier, any user-defined Date/Time or Duration fields support Outlook's shortcuts for entering dates and duration.

Compose and Read Pages

Have you ever sent an e-mail message to yourself? Did you think about why the message you receive looks different from the one you create? Outlook allows you to design two versions of every page, one used when you compose the item, the other when a user reads it.

Open the standard Message form in design mode to see how this works. Figure 4.9 shows the Compose page for a new message, with the To, Cc, and Subject fields enabled for the user to fill in. Click the Edit Read page to see the Read page (shown in Figure 4.10) for the same form. This time, you see the From and Sent fields, and all the fields in the header are displayed in gray, so the user won't change them.

If you are using an automatic signature, you may want to turn it off before opening a Message form in Design mode. Otherwise, the signature will be included in the message body. To turn off the signature, choose Tools | Options, then on the Mail Format tab, select <None> under "Use this Signature by default."

While you're on the Mail Format tab, you may also want to change the default message format so you can control the format used by the form. When you open a Message form in Design mode, it uses the default mail format. It retains that format when you save the form as a template or publish it. When you later run the form, the new message uses the form's format, not the user's default mail format.

4

FIGURE 4.9

The default Message form has separate Read and Compose pages. (Compare with Figure 4.10.)

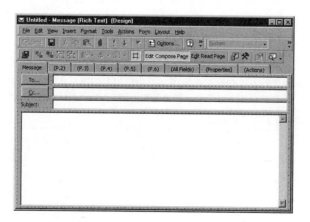

FIGURE 4.10

Use the Edit Compose Page and Edit Read Page buttons to switch between layouts. (Compare with Figure 4.9.)

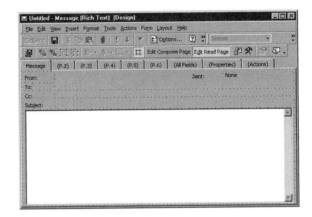

Surprise! On a normal Message form, the user can actually edit the header fields, even though they are shown in gray, which normally means the fields are disabled.

To set up a page for separate Compose and Read versions, choose Form, Separate Read Layout. Outlook copies all the fields from the original page (making it the Compose page) to the new Read page. Switch between two layouts with the Edit Compose Page and Edit Read Page buttons. The page will have the same name in both layouts.

You can save yourself a lot of time if you refrain from separating the Compose and Read layouts until you have placed and configured all the controls that you want to appear on both versions. After you separate them, if you want the same control on both pages, you must add it to each page separately.

Be extremely careful if you decide to use the Form, Separate Read Layout command to revert to a single page instead of two layouts. Outlook discards the page that is not currently visible.

Summary

In this hour, you learned how to create your own custom fields and add them to Outlook forms. You also worked with validation rules and fields based on formulas. For additional flexibility, Outlook allows you to maintain separate Compose and Read layouts for each customized form page.

In the next hour, you will switch gears, leaving the Outlook forms environment behind as you start working with Visual Basic for Applications (VBA).

Q&A

Q **Is it better to store a telephone number or employee ID number as a Number or Text field?**

A You can use a Text field to store any kind of data, even numbers and dates. However, if you plan to perform any mathematical operations, a Number field is the best approach. Because you don't normally perform addition and subtraction on number-like data such as phone numbers, postal codes, and employee ID numbers, store these in Text fields, not Number fields.

Q **Is there a limit to the number of user-defined fields I can create on a form?**

A Not really. If there is a limit, you will probably run out of room on your form long before you reach that limit.

Q **Why might I need to use separate Read and Compose pages?**

A One reason might be to hide certain information from readers of the form. Another would be to prevent the reader from making changes to some of the data in the form.

Workshop

Work through the quiz questions and exercises so that you can understand Outlook programming better. See Appendix A for answers.

Quiz

1. What is the difference between a bound and an unbound control?
2. What is the difference between a Duration field and a Date/Time field?

3. Why is a Check Box control better for displaying a Yes/No field than a Text Box control? Can you use a Check Box control to display fields other than Yes/No fields?

4. What section of the Field Chooser lists fields you yourself create?

5. Can you create separate Compose and Read layouts for any form or just the Message form?

Exercises

1. On the Task form you modified in this lesson, drag the Completed or Due field to the form. Choose Form, Run This Form to create four Task items with the custom form: one with no Due Date, one with both a Due Date and a Status of Completed, one with a Due Date, and a Status of Not Started, and one with no Due Date and a Status of Completed. For each of these items, check the value of the Completed or Due field. What is odd about some of the values? Can you think of a way to fix the problem by using a Formula field instead of a Combination field?

2. On the custom Task form, create a field named Next Status Check as a Date/Time field, and add it to the form's P.2 page. Use the basic Properties dialog for the control to change the format, trying out each of the 16 formats for Date/Time fields. Which do you think works best for this field?

3. Modify the built-in Contact form to use separate Read and Compose layouts for the General page. On the Read layout of the General page, add a Formula field to indicate the number of e-mail addresses for the contact, using the formula you saw in this lesson. Publish the form. Now run the form to try it out: Enter one, two, or three e-mail addresses, and then save the item. Open the item you just saved. Do you see the number of addresses?

4. Open the modified Contact form from exercise 3 again in design mode. Switch to the Compose page, and choose Form, Separate Read Layout to use just one layout for both composing and reading. Publish this form using a different name from that in exercise 3. Then run it, enter e-mail addresses, and save it. Open the saved item. Do you still see the number of addresses?

Part II

Design with VBA

Hour

HOUR 5

The VBA Design Environment

It's time to shift gears for a few lessons and leave Outlook forms behind while you look at Visual Basic for Applications, the other major programming environment in Outlook 2000. VBA, as I'll call it from now on, is the place where you will write and test your program code and design forms for users to interact with. (These are different from forms used to gather and display Outlook data.) VBA is new to Outlook 2000, although other Office applications have had it for some time.

The highlights of this hour include

- How to start and end a VBA session
- What the basic windows in VBA are used for
- Where to enter program code
- How to add a new form
- How to avoid a security message when you start VBA
- Where Outlook saves your VBA project

Starting VBA

To start a VBA session, first start Outlook, and then press Alt+F11. You can also choose Tools, Macro, Visual Basic Editor. A new window opens, as shown in Figure 5.1. It's a little scary if you haven't previously worked with Visual Basic or with VBA in other programs. Don't worry. In this lesson, you will learn about those two windows on the left and fill out the blank space with a form and a module, your first VBA programming components.

FIGURE 5.1

The VBA environment contains no program code and forms when you first start it.

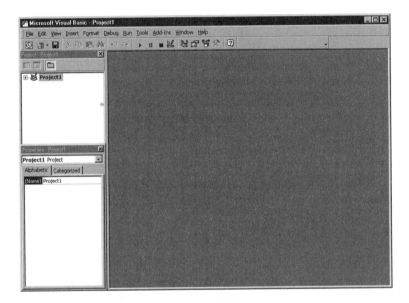

Working in VBA does not mean you can't get your e-mail messages. Outlook remains open. Just click the View Microsoft Outlook button on the VBA toolbar, or click the Outlook icon in the Windows taskbar.

After you add your first form or module, you will start receiving the message shown in Figure 5.2 every time you start VBA. You can either live with it (and choose Enable Macros to enter VBA each time) or change the VBA security settings.

To change the security level, from the main Outlook menu, choose Tools, Macro, Security. On the Security Level tab of the Security dialog box (see Figure 5.3), choose Low if you always want to open Outlook macros, regardless of the source.

FIGURE 5.2

This message appears when you start VBA after creating any modules or forms.

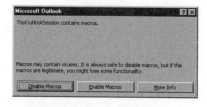

FIGURE 5.3

Medium is the default security-level setting for Outlook macros.

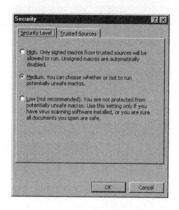

If you choose Disable Macros in the dialog shown in Figure 5.2, you can still work on your VBA project, but you will not be able to run any program code until you exit and restart Outlook.

You use the Security dialog's Trusted Sources tab to view and remove trusted sources for your Outlook project or add-ins. The developer must sign the project or add-in with a digital ID. You learn more about digital IDs in Hour 23, "Exchange Server and Database Collaboration."

5

Saving Your Work and Ending a VBA Session

You should save your work periodically, perhaps after you finish positioning controls on a form or after you finish coding a module. You do this by clicking the Save button, pressing Ctrl+S, or choosing File, Save.

To end a VBA session, click the close (×) button in the upper-right corner of the VBA window, or choose File, Close and Return to Microsoft Outlook. If any modules or forms are unsaved when you leave VBA, Outlook prompts you to save the VBA project VbaProject.OTM when you exit Outlook. This saves all modules and forms in the project.

VBA Windows

When you use VBA, the first two windows that appear are called the Project Explorer and Properties windows. You can close either of them with the close (×) button in the upper-right corner of the window. Probably, you will want to keep them open unless you have limited space on your screen.

 If you close the Properties or Project Explorer window, you can restore either window with the appropriate command on the View menu or the corresponding toolbar button.

Besides these two, you will also look at module and form windows (the windows you use to create Outlook applications) and the Object Browser, which helps you discover what you can do with Outlook.

Project Explorer

The Project Explorer window lists the currently loaded VBA elements that make up your programming application. For example, compare Figure 5.4 with Figure 5.1. Figure 5.4 shows the Project Explorer after I added a form and a module (more on those shortly). You will always see ThisOutlookSession, but you can ignore it because you never work with it directly.

The three buttons at the top of the Project Explorer are (left to right) View Code, View Object, and Toggle Folders. When working with a form, use the View buttons to switch between its code and layout. The Toggle Folders button flattens the list of elements in the project, hiding the folders and listing everything in alphabetical order.

Properties Window

The Properties window, which appears below the Project Explorer window, is similar to the Advanced Properties you saw when working with Outlook forms. It lists all the attributes of any project elements.

FIGURE 5.4

Use the Project Explorer as a map or index to the components you are currently working on.

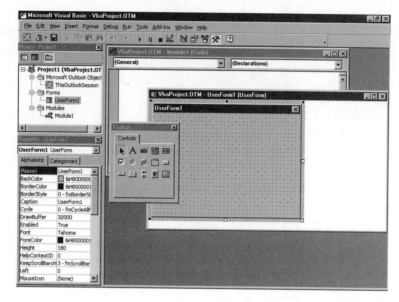

In Figure 5.5, you see the properties for your single project. The only property is its Name, Project1 by default. To change the Name property, click next to (Name) and replace Project1 with a different name.

FIGURE 5.5

Every programming component in VBA has properties.

5

Notice that VBA's Properties window works differently than the Properties dialog box in Outlook forms design, where you had to type the new value at the top of the dialog, rather than in the property list.

As you will see when you start designing VBA forms, there are many, many more properties. Some you change by typing in a new value. Others you pick from a list. Most can also be changed with program code. An example would be turning the text in a control red when the value of the control meets certain criteria.

If you drag the Properties window by its title, you can float it over another part of the VBA environment. Both the Properties window and the Project Explorer (and most other VBA windows) are *dockable*; you can either park them against one side of the main window or float them anywhere inside the VBA window.

Forms

Now, add your first form to the VBA environment by choosing Insert, UserForm. Does the resulting form look familiar? Compare the form shown in Figure 5.6 with the (P.2) page of an Outlook form in design mode—same gray background, same grid of dots to help you place controls, and same Toolbox showing the controls you can add to the form.

FIGURE 5.6

The design tools for VBA forms are very similar to those for Outlook forms.

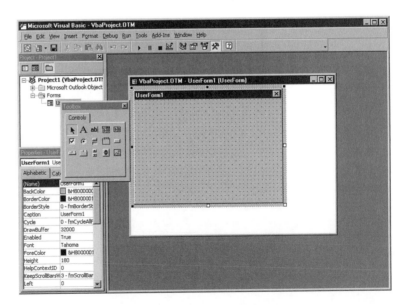

Like Outlook forms, VBA forms use controls to display information to the user and gather data. No data resides in the form itself, except for the short time that the form is visible. VBA forms can be linked to Outlook items or to databases (which is beyond the scope of this book), or they can collect information independently.

Most of the VBA forms you will build in Outlook are called *dialog boxes* because they force the user to carry on a conversation with the program. The user can't return to the Outlook application until the conversation ends with the user clicking OK, Cancel, or some other button that closes the dialog box.

Modules

Now, add a module. A *module* is a collection of programming procedures. Choose Insert, Module, and you should see something like Figure 5.7.

FIGURE 5.7

Modules contain programming procedures.

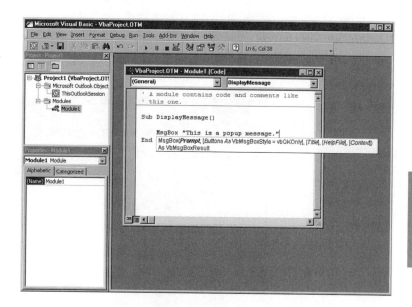

The module window is a rather smart text editor. It checks your code against the VBA programming language, reminds you of the parameters of every function, and colors your text to distinguish different code elements.

You can also insert another kind of module, called a *class module*. I touch on class modules only briefly in this book, in Hour 17, "Responding to Outlook Events in VBA."

5

For example, the text shown at the top of Figure 5.7 appears in VBA in green because it is a *comment*, text in a program module that is not executed as code. To create a comment, start your text with an apostrophe (').

Choose Tools, Options if you want to experiment with the settings for the code editor.

In Figure 5.7, notice the pop-up about the MsgBox function that tells you what parameters it can use and what order to put them in. This information disappears automatically after you finish typing the current function.

Did you know that you already have another place to write programming code for your project? Select UserForm1 in the Project Explorer, and then click the View Code button or choose View, Code. A code window such as the one in Figure 5.8 appears, ready for you to type in the first procedure that applies directly to the form. (Don't be concerned just yet about what to type; that's coming in the next few lessons.)

FIGURE 5.8

Forms also include programming code, shown in a separate window.

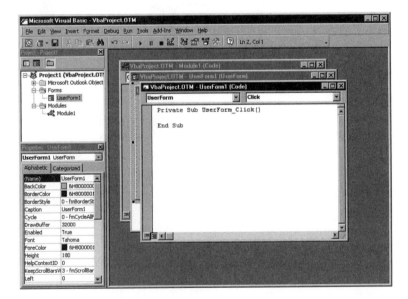

You can switch among the forms and modules either with the Project Explorer or by using the Window menu.

> From now on, any figures illustrating work in VBA will show only the particular form or code window, not the entire VBA environment.

Object Browser

You need to take a look at one more window, the Object Browser. Choose View, Object Browser, or click the Object Browser toolbar button. You will probably want to maximize it so that it fills whatever space is not occupied by the Project Explorer and Properties windows, as shown in Figure 5.9. In the drop-down list at the top of the Object Browser, switch from <All Libraries> to Outlook.

FIGURE 5.9

The Object Browser describes the various objects you can program with and their properties, methods, and actions.

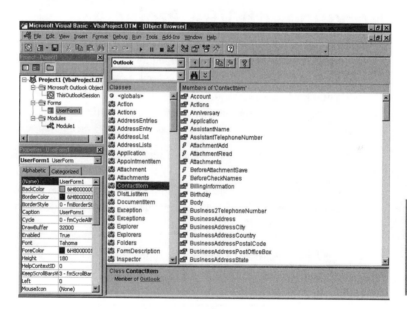

5

The Object Browser is your cookbook, your roadmap, and your index to the world of Outlook items, folders, and other components. Under Classes, you see each Outlook object. Click on ContactItem, for example, and under Members of 'ContactItem' on the right, you see the characteristics of Contact items: what they can do, what you can do to them, and their properties. After you select a class or member, click the question mark button to read the help topic about the item. For many topics, you will find a link to examples that contain sample code you can copy and paste into your application.

Similarly, you can use the Object Browser to explore the characteristics of VBA forms or of other Office applications. You will look at the Object Browser in more detail in Hour 13, "Working with the Object Models." However, you should go ahead and start browsing it to learn more about what you can do in Outlook.

> The fields you see in the (All Fields) page on an Outlook form match the object properties for different items, but the names do not always match. For example, the Company field on a Contact form is actually the CompanyName property of a Contact item.

Working with VBA Projects

Take a look at the project in more detail. Both the Project Explorer and the title bar for the Microsoft Visual Basic window include the name VbaProject.OTM. This is the actual name of the file that contains your Outlook VBA project. Outlook stores it in the C:\Winnt\Profiles\<*profile name*>\Application Data\Microsoft\Outlook\ folder or, if you use Windows 98 without user profiles, in C:\Windows\Application Data\Microsoft\Outlook\.

You can't change the default name of this file or store it in a different location. You can, however, exit Outlook, rename the VbaProject.OTM file, restart Outlook, and start VBA to create a new, empty project. To return to the original one, exit Outlook, rename the current VbaProject.OTM, and then rename the original project back to VbaProject.OTM.

> Unlike other Office applications (such as Excel or Word) that include a VBA project for each document, Outlook allows you to work only on one project at a time.

Setting Project Properties

As you saw in Figure 5.5, the project has only one obvious property, Name, and you can give it a new name in the Properties window.

To change other project properties, choose Tools, Project1 Properties, and you will see the Project Properties dialog in Figure 5.10. Aside from Name and Description, most of the settings on the General tab are used by advanced developers building applications for distribution to other people.

FIGURE 5.10

FIGURE 5.10

Because Outlook allows you to work with only one project at a time, you will probably change the project properties only rarely.

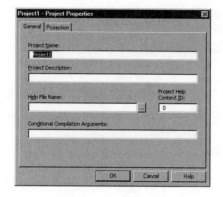

On the Protection tab, you can assign a password to your project to prevent other people from seeing your work.

Backing Up Your Work

Because the VbaProject.OTM file contains all your Outlook VBA work, including it in your regular system backup is a good idea. You can also make copies of individual modules and forms, either as backups or for reuse on a different computer. In the Project Explorer, select any form or module, and then choose File, Export File. Outlook exports modules as Basic .bas files and forms as Form .frm files.

On the File menu, you find an Import command to bring in a module or form that was previously saved, as well as a Remove command. When you remove a module or form from the project, Outlook asks whether you want to export it first. It's a good idea to go ahead and export, just in case you want to recover the routines in that module or form later.

Getting Help in VBA

I have already talked about getting help for Outlook forms (in Hour 2, "Six Forms in Search of a Designer") and about using the Object Browser as an index to Help. Even more extensive help is available for VBA functions and general Outlook programming topics.

To obtain help with a function, select the function in your module code, and press F1 to get details about it. For example, in the routine in Figure 5.7, select MsgBox, and then press F1 to see the MsgBox help topic, shown in Figure 5.11. Topics on functions always give the basic syntax, and most also include hints on how to use it, notes on situations where the function might be appropriate, and one or more code examples.

5

FIGURE 5.11

Detailed help topics on VBA functions help you learn programming fast.

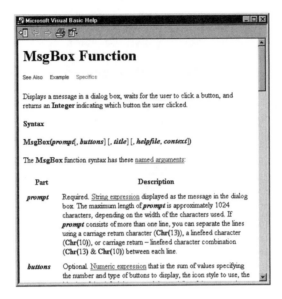

When you first run Microsoft Visual Basic Help, its window docks at the right side of the Windows screen and causes the VBA window to resize. Drag the Help window toward the middle of your screen, and it will change size. You can then resize Help so that you can read the detailed topics better and so that it won't resize your VBA environment every time you view a help topic.

If you are not interested in a particular function, click the Office Assistant, or if the Office Assistant is not visible, click the Help button on the toolbar. Then, type the text you want to search for, and click OK to see a list of related topics.

Summary

The Visual Basic for Applications environment is very different from the Outlook forms designer. It supports the creation of dialog boxes and other user input and display forms, as well as program code modules.

In the next hour, you will learn how to create forms with VBA. Many of these new techniques can be transferred back to the Outlook forms design environment.

Q&A

Q Why does the VBA environment look so complicated?

A Because the *V* in VBA stands for *visual*, you have a variety of tools, each of which performs a different design task with simple typing or a few mouse clicks or drags. Before visual programming environments, elements such as forms had to be hand-coded, with the size and position of each element precisely calculated. If you find the VBA environment too complex, try closing all the windows except the form or module you're working with.

Q What's the difference between a code module and the code in a form's code window?

A Code behind a form runs only when something happens to that form—the form opens or closes, or the user clicks or enters data. Modules contain more generic code—subroutines and functions that can be used outside any particular form.

Workshop

Work through the quiz questions and exercises so that you can better understand Outlook programming. See Appendix A for answers.

Quiz

1. How do you start and end an Outlook VBA session?
2. Name six VBA windows that you studied in this lesson.
3. Describe two ways you can back up your Outlook VBA project.
4. If you switch from a VBA session back to Outlook, how can you return to the VBA session?

Exercises

1. Examine the properties of a VBA project, form, and module. What property do they all have in common?
2. Locate the Outlook VBA project file on your computer.
3. Type **InputBox** into a module window, and then press F1 to view the help topic on the InputBox function.
4. Using the Office Assistant, type **Outlook fields and equivalent properties**, and retrieve and read the help topic by that name. (This is one topic you will come back to again and again.)

HOUR 6

A VBA Birthday/Anniversary Reminder Form

Now that you know your way around the VBA design environment, you are going to start working on a form to accomplish something that Outlook can't do by itself: Update specific information in Outlook items. In the process, you will learn the basics of designing VBA forms.

The highlights of this hour include

- How to add controls using the VBA Toolbox
- Which controls can be useful for data entry tasks
- When to use modal and nonmodal forms
- How to start adding code to a form
- What makes a good dialog box or other form

Search and Replace in Outlook

One of Outlook's major missing features is a global search and replace tool. You can't even replace text inside a message. Therefore, in this and later lessons, you will build several VBA tools to handle particular search and replace tasks, culminating in a general search and replace form.

This first search and replace form is designed to set a reminder for all birthdays and anniversaries in your Calendar folder. Whenever you add a birthday or anniversary on the Details page of the built-in Contact form, Outlook automatically creates a corresponding recurring event in your Calendar folder and adds a shortcut to that event in the Contact item.

However, the events in the Calendar folder don't have reminders. Unless you check the Calendar well in advance, those birthdays are going to sneak up on you. Therefore, you need a tool to globally update all the birthdays and anniversaries to make sure that they have reminders. You can use it periodically to ensure that any newly added anniversaries or birthdays also have reminders.

> For a user-defined Date/Time field added to the Contact form, entering a date does not automatically create a matching Calendar entry. If you want this kind of functionality, you must add it in VBScript code. In Hour 16, "Working with Items," you learn how to create new items with code, using information from an existing item.

Step 1: What Controls Do You Need?

Key first steps in designing any form are to decide what the form will do and what information it needs to complete its task.

The purpose of your form is already decided: Add a reminder to all birthdays and anniversaries. To accomplish this, the form requires information from the user on when to set the reminder, as a specific number of days, weeks, or months in advance of the event.

> Another key decision you will make in designing forms is what kind of feedback to provide the user as the form goes about its work. I discuss this in Hour 12, "Handling User Input and Feedback."

How many ways are there to enter the reminder interval? Here are a few:

- A Text Box control where the user enters the number of days
- A Text Box control where the user types **3 days**, **2 wks**, or **1m**, and so on
- A Spin Button control that the user clicks until the desired number of days is shown
- A Spin Button control to show the number, as well as Option Button controls to select days, weeks, or months
- Option Button controls to select from the most frequently used reminder intervals (as you want to define them)

Which approach would be best? The first and third approaches are somewhat limited because they count only days, not weeks or months. The second approach takes some work because you would have to write code to convert what the user types into the corresponding number of days. (Controls bound to duration-type data fields on Outlook items perform this conversion automatically, but VBA controls do not include that feature.) The fourth approach might be a little too complicated. The last approach is too limited if you later decide to share the form with other people.

> If you are designing a form for your personal use, don't feel that you have to cover every possible option or exception. You would, of course, in a program for wider distribution, but for a personal application, it might be easier to create a form that doesn't offer unlimited options for setting reminders.

In other words, it's hard to know which would be best without creating the form and using it for a while (or being a mind reader). On the other hand, in the long run, it often doesn't matter; every project can have many good approaches to data entry.

Step 2: Create the Form

The next step is to create the form and set its particular properties. You will have to start VBA, as you learned in the previous lesson.

To add a form, choose Insert, UserForm. A blank form appears, along with the Toolbox. The Properties window shows the properties for the form. Figure 6.1 shows the form, Toolbox, and Properties window. Table 6.1 lists key properties you should set right away.

6

To Do

FIGURE 6.1

*A newly created VBA
form uses the name
UserForm1, which you
should change as soon
as possible.*

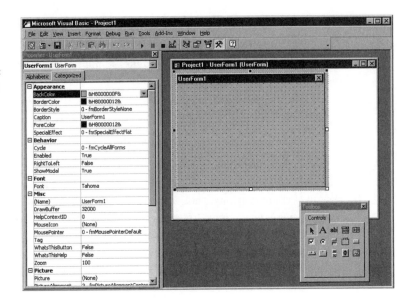

TABLE 6.1 VBA Form Properties to Set Immediately

Property	Description	Suggested Value
(Name)	The form name as shown in the Project Explorer and as used in program code	ReminderUpdate
Caption	The name shown in the title bar of the form	Birthday and Anniversary Reminder Update

If you plan to work with the same form for a while, you don't have to keep the Project Explorer on the screen. Choose View, Project Explorer to hide it, or click its close (×) button. The Properties window will grow taller, making it easier to use. To see the values for the properties more easily, make the Properties window wider by dragging its right border toward the right.

> Make sure that you set the (Name) property before you start writing program code. If you change the (Name) after you write code for the form, you must use search and replace in your code to update the form name wherever it appears.

Exploring Form Properties

Click on the Categorized tab of the Properties window to see the properties organized into different groups: Appearance, Behavior, Font, Misc, Picture, Position, and Scrolling. Because the properties in a group are often related, viewing the categories helps to remind you to change those allied properties. For example, if you change the BackColor property, you might also want to change the BorderColor.

> Did you notice how many more form properties you can customize with VBA than you could in Outlook forms?

> If you are not familiar with a particular property, select it, and then click F1 to bring up a help topic that explains it.

As you explore form properties, notice that different properties use different methods to enter new values. For some properties, such as BackColor or Enabled, you click on a drop-down list and select a value. For others, you type in the value; Caption is a good example. In other cases, such as Font and Picture, you click a button with an ellipsis (...) to get a dialog where you can select the new value.

What about those cryptic values for some of the Appearance properties? What does &H8000000F&, the value for BackColor mean? The value for each color property is a long integer, a number whose value can range from –2,147,483,648 to 2,147,483,647, shown in the Properties window in hexadecimal format.

Don't worry, you don't have to know the values for all the colors, nor do you need the ability to convert a decimal number to hexadecimal. VBA makes it easy to select colors

6

▼ with a couple mouse clicks. For example, click on the `BackColor` property to select it, and then click the arrow button at the right side of the property's value box. A list of colors appears, shown in Figure 6.2.

FIGURE 6.2

Select colors for the form and its controls from among the System colors or by using the Palette.

Now, look at the `SpecialEffect` property, shown in Figure 6.3. First, notice that it supports only a few values: `0`, `1`, `2`, `3`, and `6`. Also, see how each numeric value has a word associated with it. For example, the value `1` also has the word `fmSpecialEffectRaised`. This is an example of an *intrinsic constant*, a value built in to VBA that doesn't change and has a special keyword associated with it.

FIGURE 6.3

Many properties allow only certain values, which have equivalent intrinsic constants.

▼

▼ You use intrinsic constants in VBA code to work with the values of forms and other objects. Hundreds of intrinsic constants are associated with VBA itself and with various Outlook components. As you might imagine, they make it much easier to read and write program code. For example, for a form named ReminderUpdate, this line of code changes the form from flat to raised:

```
ReminderUpdate.SpecialEffect = 1
```

This line does the same thing, but is much easier to understand because it contains an intrinsic constant instead of a number.

```
ReminderUpdate.SpecialEffect = fmSpecialEffectRaised
```

Many form and control properties can be changed with program code while the form is running. The help topic on each property tells you for sure. You will see some examples in Hour 8, "Code Basics."

You cannot use intrinsic constants in VBScript code, only in VBA.

Should You Use a Modal or NonModal Form?

Another important form property is ShowModal, which can have the values True or False. While a modal form is on the screen, you cannot return to the main application window. This is the typical behavior of a dialog box: It opens, the user makes a change, and then the user closes the dialog to return to the application. From a programming standpoint, modal forms are important to controlling program flow. No other code executes until the modal form is either hidden or unloaded.

If a form is modeless, the user can work both with the main application windows and with the form. An example would be a form that provides information to the user, either on demand or according to a schedule. (How about a form that counts down the number of minutes until your own birthday?)

The capability to create modeless forms is new to VBA in Office 2000. Previous VBA versions are limited to modal forms.

▼

6

Because the ReminderUpdate form is designed to perform a quick, occasional update, no need exists to make it a modeless form. Because the default for ShowModal is True, you don't have to make a property change for this form.

Step 3: Add User Input Controls

Ready for the next step? Now that you have a blank form and understand its properties, you can add some controls to it. You will use the simplest of the approaches described earlier: a text box where the user types the number of days. There are two ways to add a text box to the form:

- To get a standard size text box, drag a TextBox control from the Toolbox to the form.

- To set a custom size, select the TextBox control in the Toolbox. Position the mouse pointer over the form where you want one corner of the text box to go. Hold down the left mouse button, and drag the mouse to trace a rectangle the size of the text box you want, just as in Figure 6.4.

Don't forget to leave room for Label controls that indicate how to use the Text Box.

FIGURE 6.4

Select the TextBox control in the Toolbox, and then drag with the mouse to create a text box of the desired size.

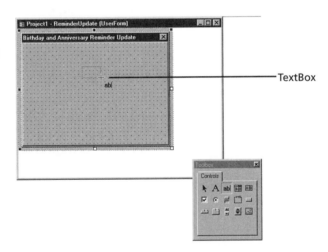

As you learned with Outlook form controls, it is important to give a name to each control that holds data. For the Text Box that will display the number of days, use the name txtDays. You might also want to add ControlTipText, as you did with Outlook form controls, to pop up information when the user pauses the mouse over the control.

▼ Now, use the Label control (to the left of the TextBox control in the Toolbox) to add two Text Label controls, one to the left and one to the right of the TextBox. The form should look like Figure 6.5.

FIGURE 6.5

Whenever you add a Label control, you must replace the default Label1, Label2, and so on, text.

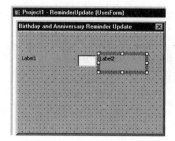

To add your own text to the Label1 control, click the Select Objects button in the Toolbox to switch the mouse pointer back to an arrow. Click the Label control once to select it; then click a second time. When you see the blinking vertical insertion point inside the control, you can delete the Label1 text and replace it with your own, as shown in Figure 6.6.

> That's click once to select the Label control, pause briefly, and then click again to edit its caption. The timing is important. If the clicks are too close together, VBA interprets them as a double-click and opens a program code window to the Click event for the control.

You can also enter text for a Label control by typing in the text as the value for the Caption property.

To make the form look better, you might want to resize or move the labels. You could also change the TextAlign property of the label on the left so that its caption appears closer to the text box. VBA controls use essentially the same sizing and positioning tech-
▲ niques as controls on Outlook forms. Look on the Format menu for essential commands.

Step 4: Add Command Buttons

The form in Figure 6.6 now has a Text Box and two Label controls to give the user an idea of what kind of information to enter. What's missing? There's no way to actually start the process of updating the Calendar events to add a reminder. You need at least one

6

▼   Command Button control to run the code you will be adding to the form. Command but-
     tons are those ubiquitous form controls that make things happen. The code associated
     with a button runs when you click it.

FIGURE 6.6

Change the text for a
Label control by typ-
ing it into the control
or updating the
`Caption` *property.*

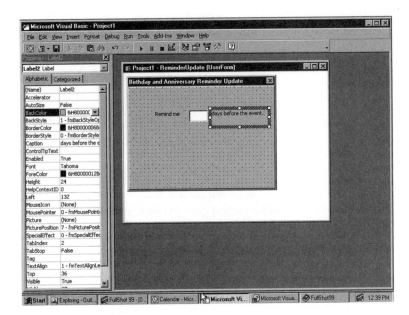

You can add two Command Button controls, one to run the update and the other to close
the form. Drag two CommandButton controls from the Toolbox to your form, and set the
properties shown in Table 6.2.

TABLE 6.2   Properties for ReminderUpdate Command Buttons

Property	CommandButton1	CommandButton2
(Name)	cmdUpdate	cmdClose
Accelerator	U	
Cancel	False	True
Caption	Update	Close
▼ Default	True	False

The form has a close (x) button in the upper-right corner, but putting a command button on the form as well makes it just a little more obvious to the user that the form should be closed when the update has completed.

The most important of these properties are (Name) and Caption, which you should already be familiar with from working with Outlook forms. To see the effect of the other properties in Table 6.2, you must see what the ReminderUpdate form will look like to a user. Click on the background of the form to select the entire form. Then, click the Run button on the toolbar, or choose Run, Run Sub/UserForm. Your form should like the one in Figure 6.7.

FIGURE 6.7

The ReminderUpdate form is starting to look like a real user form, buttons and all.

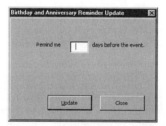

Until now, you have been working in design mode. Figure 6.7 shows the form in run mode. In other words, the form is active. If the buttons had program code associated with them, it would run when you click them. However, if you click the buttons, nothing happens because you have added no code to the form yet.

You can select the form or any control on it by picking it from the drop-down list at the top of the Properties window.

6

Basic Command Button Properties

Take a closer look at the cmdUpdate and cmdClose buttons in Figure 6.7. The property settings from Table 6.2 are responsible for giving them a look similar to that on dialog box command buttons in most Windows programs.

▼ First, setting the `Accelerator` property for the cmdUpdate button to U causes the letter *U* to be underlined. This means the user can press Alt+U as an alternative to clicking the button. Keyboard accelerators such as this make forms more usable and friendlier to those people who prefer the keyboard to the mouse.

See how the cmdUpdate button has a dark border, whereas the cmdClose button doesn't. This is a visual clue that you set the cmdUpdate button as the default button by setting its `Default` property to `True`. Pressing the Enter key is the same thing as clicking on the default button.

Similarly, pressing the Esc key is equivalent to clicking on the cmdClose button because you set its `Cancel` property to `True`. This made cmdClose the cancel button.

A form can have only one default button and one cancel button. Neither is required. Setting a command button's `Default` or `Cancel` property for a button to `True` makes it the new default or cancel button.

In this example, you made cmdUpdate the default button so that you could see what a default button looks like. In reality, though, the default button should never be a button that runs code that can make irreversible changes to many items.

Because the cmdClose button does not do anything yet when you click it, click the close (×) button in the upper-right corner of the ReminderUpdate form to close the running version and return to the design environment. Alternatively, switch back to the design environment, and click the Design Mode button.

Adding Code

Making the command buttons do something is a matter of adding code. You can start with an easy routine to close the form when the user clicks the cmdClose button.

To add code to any command button, double-click the button on the form. A code window, such as that in Figure 6.8, appears. VBA automatically creates the first and last lines of the subroutine that runs when you click the cmdClose button. The name of the routine is `cmdClose_Click`. The keyword `Private` means that this routine runs only in

▼ the context of the current form; no other components in your VBA project can use it.

▼

FIGURE 6.8

A form's code window gives you quick access to all the controls and the events they support.

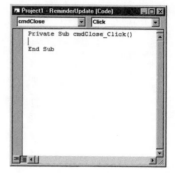

Notice the two drop-down lists at the top of the code window. The one on the left includes the name of every control on the form, as well as UserForm to represent the form itself and a (General) section where you declare variables and constants (more on that in Hour 9, "Code Grammer 101").

The list on the right includes Click, as well as all the other events that can take place on the form or relative to a control. You learn more about events in Hour 8, "Code Basics." For now, you will work just with the Click event for your two command buttons.

In the space between Private Sub cmdClose_Click() and End Sub, type

Unload ReminderUpdate

This is the command to remove the form named ReminderUpdate from memory and from the computer display.

To add code for the other command button, you do not have to switch back to the form. Instead, choose cmdUpdate from the drop-down list of controls at the top of the code window. For the cmdUpdate_Click() procedure, type

MsgBox "This is the update button."

This is the code to pop up a simple message to the user. The code window should now look like Figure 6.9.

6

The indenting in Figure 6.9 helps make the code more readable, but doesn't affect how it runs.

▼

FIGURE 6.9

The two command buttons now have code that will run when the user clicks each button.

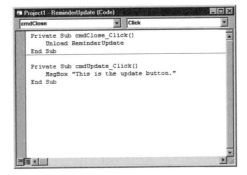

Congratulations! You have now written your first program code! Click the Run button on the toolbar, or choose Run, Run Sub/UserForm to see the form in action. First, click the Update button. You should see a message box such as the one shown in Figure 6.10.

Message boxes are useful, not only for displaying information to the user, but also for forcing the user to make a choice. You will look at message boxes in more detail in Hour 12, "Handling User Input and Feedback."

FIGURE 6.10

It's easy to pop up a simple message box.

After you click OK to dismiss the message box, click the Close button, or press Esc. The `cmdClose_Click()` procedure runs, unloading the form.

Anatomy of a Procedure

No doubt, you're eager to design applications that do more than just open message boxes. To give you some additional practice adding code to a command button, replace the `cmdUpdate_Click()` procedure with the procedure shown in Listing 6.1.

LISTING 6.1   Code for the `cmdUpdate_Click()` Procedure

```
1: Private Sub cmdUpdate_Click()
2:
3:    Dim objApp As Application
```

```
▼    4:        Dim objNS As NameSpace
     5:        Dim objCalendar As MAPIFolder
     6:        Dim objItem As AppointmentItem
     7:        Dim strSubject As String
     8:        Dim intDays as Integer
     9:
    10:        Set objApp = CreateObject("Outlook.Application")
    11:        Set objNS = objApp.GetNamespace("MAPI")
    12:        Set objCalendar = objNS.GetDefaultFolder(olFolderCalendar)
    13:
    13:        intDays = 24 * 60 * txtDays.Value
    14:        For Each objItem In objCalendar.Items
    15:            strSubject = objItem.Subject
    16:            If InStr(strSubject, "Birthday") > 0 Or _
    17:              InStr(strSubject, "Anniversary") > 0 Then
    18:                objItem.ReminderSet = True
    19:                objItem.ReminderMinutesBeforeStart = _
    20:                  intDays
    21:                objItem.Save
    22:            End If
    23:        Next
    24:
    25: End Sub
```

This procedure is divided into three sections. The first section, where each line begins with Dim (lines 3–8), defines the variables used. The next section, where each line begins with Set (lines 10–12), is a series of assignment statements setting up the Outlook object variables. You will learn how to set up variables and work with objects in Hour 8.

The real work is done by the intDays = ... line and the For Each...Next loop. The line

```
intDays = 24 * 60 * txtDays.Value
```

calculates 24 hours/day times 60 minutes/hour times the number of days specified on the form and places the result in a variable named intDays. This, of course, determines the number of minutes before the event and the only place where the procedure has to use a value from the form.

The For Each...Next loop examines each item in the Calendar folder and tests whether the words *Birthday* or *Anniversary* are part of the item's Subject, using the very useful Instr() function. For those that are birthdays or anniversaries, it adds a reminder based
▼   on the value in the txtDays control on the form.

6

For Each...Next loops get a real workout in Outlook. You use them extensively to cycle through every subfolder in a parent folder, every item in a folder, every recipient in a message, and so on.

Did you notice that olFolderCalendar is another intrinsic constant?

The underscore (_) character at the end of the line that begins with objItem.ReminderMinutesBeforeStart = (line 19) is a continuation character. It means that the following line of code is connected to the current line. Rather than use very long lines, use continuation characters to make your code more readable.

Try running the form again, as you did earlier, but with the new code for the cmdUpdate button. (Be sure to back up your Calendar folder, as noted in the next Caution.) Does it operate as you expected?

Although Outlook has an Undo command for single actions, you cannot undo bulk changes made by procedures such as the preceding one. Before you run any procedure that alters all the items in a folder, you should back up the contents of that folder. You can use Outlook's File, Import and Export command to export the folder to a Personal Folders file, or you can copy the items to another folder.

Step 5: Plan the Next Development Stage

 To Do

In one sense, no development project is ever finished because you can always think of ways to improve it. Here are some possible ways to enhance the ReminderUpdate form:

- Allow the user to update just birthdays, just anniversaries, or both. (Hint: This requires two check boxes and a little more code.)
- Before running the update routine, validate the entry in the txtDays control to make sure that a number greater than zero is present.

▼
- Don't update any Calendar item that already has a reminder.
- Speed execution of the update routine by examining only all-day events, instead of every item in the Calendar folder.
- Add feedback to tell the user how many items were updated.
- Ask the user to confirm each change to a birthday or anniversary.

▲ In upcoming lessons, you will return to this form and work through some of these enhancements, which are typical of the operations found in Outlook applications.

Summary

You should be proud of your accomplishment in this lesson—building your first working Outlook application in VBA, one that performs a very useful function that is not built in to Outlook. In the process, you learned how to add Text Box, Label, and Command Button controls to a VBA form; how to work with VBA form and control properties; and how to add code to a Command Button control.

In the next hour, you continue working with this form to add more controls, and you begin working on another search and replace form, one to handle changes in telephone area codes.

Q&A

Q Can form and control names contain spaces?

A No, they can't. The value for the (Name) property must follow the naming convention for form objects, which allows internal capitalization, but no spaces. You can (and should) include spaces in the Caption property.

Q What makes a good dialog box?

A A dialog box should be logical, unambiguous, and consistent. The user should have no doubt about what kind of data to enter in each control. Validation code behind the form should protect the user from "wrong" entries. Controls should be grouped in a clear sequence. They might follow a cycle that mimics the boxes on a paper form, or they might just be grouped in an orderly fashion, either left to right or top to bottom. Lining up controls and using similar size controls makes it visually easy for the user to follow the sequence. If your application uses several dialog boxes, they should have the same color scheme, unless you vary the colors for a particular reason.

6

Q Can I add keyboard accelerators to other controls besides command buttons?

A By all means, add accelerators everywhere. For many users, keyboard accelerators speed up data entry. For Check Box, Command Button, Option Button, and Toggle Button controls, use the `Accelerator` property for the control. For other Text Box, List Box, Combo Box, and Spin Button controls, add a Label control next to the data entry control, and use the Label control's `Accelerator` property. Then, adjust the tab order (which is covered in the next hour) so that the Label control appears immediately before the data entry control. Remember that in a modal dialog box, the user cannot access the main menu for the application. Therefore, you can use any letter of the alphabet for an accelerator, without any conflict with the main application.

Workshop

Work through the quiz questions and exercises so that you can better understand Outlook programming. See Appendix A for answers.

Quiz

1. What is the difference between a Label control and a Text Box control?

2. How do you run a VBA form to test it? How do you close it when you finish testing?

3. What command removes a form from the display and from memory?

4. If you added a Command Button control to a form and named it cmdDoThis, what would be the name of the code procedure that runs when you click that button?

5. Why does pressing Esc close the ReminderUpdate form after you add code to the cmdClose control, but not before?

Exercises

1. Write pseudocode to validate the entry in the txtDays control to make sure that a number greater than zero is present. What should happen if the control does not contain a valid number?

2. Replace the txtDays control on the form with a Spin Button control. Give it an appropriate name, and update the `cmdUpdate_Click()` procedure to use your new control.

3. Can you think of other ways to enhance the ReminderUpdate form?

HOUR 7

More on Controls

The ReminderUpdate form you created during Hour 6, "A VBA Birthday/Anniversary Reminder Tool," is certainly functional, but it would be hard to find a more unsightly form. In this hour, you're going to jazz it up by adding more controls.

The highlights of this hour include

- When to use Option Button and Check Box controls
- What property of a control contains data from the user
- How to set the default value for a control
- Why defaults make a form more usable
- How to work with List Box and Combo Box controls
- How to manage the way users move around in a form

Check Boxes and Option Buttons

In the previous lesson, the last ideas discussed about the ReminderUpdate form are some possible enhancements. You are going to tackle the first idea: allowing the user to choose whether to update just birthdays, anniversaries, or code. As the hint for that idea indicates, it takes just a couple of Check Box controls.

When you add a Check Box control, you don't have to drag a box on the form to trace out the size of the control. Just select the CheckBox tool in the Toolbox, and then click on the form where you want the check box to appear. Check boxes do not need separate Label controls to identify them because they include their own Caption property.

Figure 7.1 shows the ReminderUpdate form with two check boxes added, one for Birthdays and one for Anniversaries.

FIGURE 7.1

Check Box controls give users more choices.

The properties of the first check box should be

(Name)	chkBirthdays
Accelerator	B
Caption	Birthdays
Value	True

For the second check box, use these properties:

(Name)	chkAnniversaries
Accelerator	A
Caption	Anniversaries
Value	True

The `Accelerator` property is case-sensitive. If you enter **a**, instead of **A**, for the accelerator letter for the chkAnniversaries box, the second *a* in the word will be underlined, instead of the initial capital *A*.

Why set the `Value` for the check boxes to `True`? This is where you must know your users—or your own needs, if you are designing in VBA for yourself. Most people probably want to update both birthdays and anniversaries. Setting the `Value` for the check boxes to `True` means that most people won't have to interact at all with the check boxes. They can go straight to the text box and type in the reminder period.

An initial value such as this is called the *default* for the control. Setting the right defaults so that users have to enter as little new information as possible is a key technique for making highly usable forms.

You're probably wondering how to change the code from Hour 6 to use the information in these check boxes. Most check boxes can contain only one of two values, either `True` or `False`. If the chkBirthdays box is checked and the user's Calendar includes a birthday event, you want to add a reminder. The same goes for anniversaries.

The Check Box control includes a property, named `TripleState`, that changes a check box to allow the user to set the value to `Null`. In this situation, `Null` means neither `True` nor `False`. In other words, the check box has no value at all.

This is one case in which writing out what you want to happen provides a clue to how to code it—the word *If*. `If...Then` statements are commonly used to program exactly this type of situation: when you know the values in question are either `True` or `False`. You have already seen an `If...Then` statement in the Hour 6 code for the ReminderUpdate form, where you tested whether an item is a birthday or anniversary. You must update the `For Each...Next` loop to integrate the new check boxes into the procedure. Add the code in Listing 7.1 to the `Click` event for the cmdUpdate button.

7

LISTING 7.1   Use If...Then Statements to Test Conditions

```
 1: Sub cmdUpdate_Click()
 2:     Set objApp = CreateObject("Outlook.Application")
 3:     Set objNS = objApp.GetNamespace("MAPI")
 4:     Set objCalendar = objNS.GetDefaultFolder(olFolderCalendar)
 5:     For Each objItem In objCalendar.Items
 6:         strSubject = objItem.Subject
 7:         If InStr(strSubject, "Birthday") > 0 And _
 8:           chkBirthdays.Value = True Then
 9:             objItem.ReminderSet = True
10:             objItem.ReminderMinutesBeforeStart = _
11:              24 * 60 * txtDays.Value
12:             objItem.Save
13:         End If
14:         If InStr(strSubject, "Anniversary") > 0 And _
15:           chkAnniversaries.Value = True Then
16:             objItem.ReminderSet = True
17:             objItem.ReminderMinutesBeforeStart = _
18:              24 * 60 * txtDays.Value
19:             objItem.Save
20:         End If
21:     Next
22: End Sub
```

If you get a `Variable not defined` error message when you try to run the code in Listing 7.1, this means that you must either declare variables such as `strSubject` before using them or remove the `Option Explicit` statement from the beginning of the form's code module. The next lesson covers both these issues.

You probably noticed that the steps inside the two `If...End If` code sequences are exactly the same. Normally, you wouldn't have such repetition in a routine. In Hour 11, "Controlling Program Flow," you will look at ways to streamline such code.

As you saw in Hour 6, you use the `Value` property of a control to get the data the user has entered. For a Check Box control, the `Value` indicates whether the user has checked the box (`chkBox.Value = True`) or not (`chkBox.Value = False`).

Check Box controls are ideal for obtaining information from the user when the desired answer is Yes or No, True or False, or On or Off. If more than two answers are possible, Option Button controls might work better.

Option Button controls are sometimes called *radio buttons*, in reference to older car radios, which had buttons you pushed to change stations. The last button pressed remained pushed in, until you pressed another button for another station. Only one button at a time could be pushed in.

Option buttons on forms work the same way: No more than one can be selected. In other words, whether it's a choice of five radio stations or four flavors of ice cream at a picnic, you can choose only one. (Well, actually, you could have two scoops if you like.)

Option buttons are also sometimes used when only two choices exist, but they don't reduce so easily to a True/False selection. For example, Outlook users in Corporate or Workgroup mode can choose Tools, Options and find a pair of option buttons on the Mail Services tab of the Options dialog, offering a choice between Prompt for a Profile to Be Used and Always Use This Profile.

To see how option buttons work, you can use them instead of check boxes on the ReminderUpdate form. Here are three choices:

- Update birthdays only.
- Update anniversaries only.
- Update both birthdays and anniversaries.

> Option buttons are a good way to force the user to make a choice. If one button is already selected when the form opens, the user has to either select another button or be content with the default.

To replace the check boxes with option buttons, select and delete the check boxes. Next, before you put the buttons on the form, you're going to add a Frame control to hold them. Select the Frame tool in the Toolbox, and then drag a rectangular shape in the blank area at the top of the form. Set these properties for the frame:

```
(Name)               fraOptions
Caption              Add reminders to:
```

7

If you look at the properties for the frame, you will see that it has no Value property. The frame itself doesn't hold data. Instead, it lassos the controls you put inside it and either organizes them visually or, in the case of option buttons, coordinates their operation.

> If you have only one set of option buttons on a form, putting a frame around them is optional. If you have two sets of buttons, however, at least one set requires a frame to indicate which buttons work together. Using frames for both sets makes your form more consistent.

Add option buttons to the frame by selecting the OptionButton control in the Toolbox and then clicking inside the frame. You might have to rearrange controls to make more room or enlarge the frame by dragging the white size handle boxes on each side and at each corner of the frame. Give your option buttons these properties:

Option button 1:

(Name)	optBirthdays
Caption	Birthdays
Value	False

Option button 2:

(Name)	optAnniversaries
Caption	Anniversaries
Value	False

Option button 3:

(Name)	optBoth
Caption	Both
Value	True

> From now on, the suggested property settings shown for new controls won't include the Accelerator property. You already know how to set it and know that it makes forms easier for keyboard users to navigate.

Setting the `Value` property for the optBoth button to `True` makes it the default choice for the form. Run your form. It should look like Figure 7.2. Try clicking on each of the three option buttons. Can you select more than one at a time?

FIGURE 7.2

Option buttons make it easy to select among three or more choices.

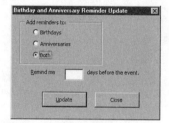

List Box and Combo Box Controls

Check boxes and option buttons make it easy for users to choose among several preferences. However, these can take up a lot of space on a form. Sometimes, you have so many choices that no room would be left for other controls if you used an option button to show each choice.

This is where List Box and Combo Box controls come in. These controls, which have much in common, let users select from a potentially large number of choices. List boxes restrict users to the range of choices you provide. Combo boxes allow users to either pick from a list or type in a new value. The familiar drop-down list boxes that you see in many Windows programs (such as the Priority field on any Outlook item) are a special type of combo box. Figure 7.3 shows various styles of list and combo boxes on an Outlook Post form. The style and behavior of list and combo boxes are controlled by the properties listed in Table 7.1.

FIGURE 7.3

List and combo boxes come in many varieties to suit many purposes.

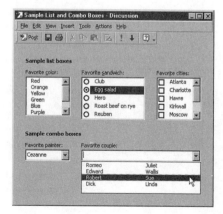

7

TABLE 7.1   Key List and Combo Box Properties

Property	List Box	Combo Box	Description
BoundColumn	X	X	In a multicolumn list or combo box, which column is bound to a data field (default = 1).
ColumnCount	X	X	Number of columns (default = 1).
DropButtonStyle		X	Sets the symbol on a combo box's button (default = 1 - Arrow).
ListRows		X	Number of rows to display in a combo box's drop-down list.
ListStyle	X	X	Shows the list with or without a check box or option button for each item. Use 0 - Plain for no check boxes and 1 - Option for option buttons on single-selection list and combo boxes and check boxes on multiselect controls.
MatchEntry	X	X	Controls how the list or combo box tries to match what the user types. Use 0 - FirstLetter to display the next entry on the list matching the last character the user typed, 1 - Complete to search for an entry matching all user-typed characters, and 2 - None to not try to match what the user types.
MatchRequired		X	Determines whether the user's text must match an item on the list (default = False)
MultiSelect	X		Determines whether the user can select more than one item from a list box. Use 0 - Single to restrict the user to one selection, 1 - Multi to allow multiple selections with additional mouse clicks, and 2 - Extended to allow the user to click and then Shift+click to select a range from within the list.
ShowDropButtonWhen		X	Determines when the user sees a combo box's button. Use 0 - Never to always hide the button, 1 - Focus to show it only when the user is in the control, and 2 - Always to always show it.

Property	List Box	Combo Box	Description
Style		X	Determines whether a user both types in a value and picks from the list. Use `0 - DropDownCombo` to allow both and `2 - DropDownList` to allow the user only to pick from the list.
TextColumn	X	X	In a multicolumn list or combo box, which column to use for the `Value` property of the control.

If you set the `MultiSelect` property to anything other than `0 - Single`, you cannot use the `Value` property of the control to find out what the user has chosen. Instead, you must check the `Selected` property to find out whether each row is marked. `lstbox.Select(index)` returns `True` if the index number row is selected. Hour 11, "Controlling Program Flow," includes an example of how to check the `Selected` property with a `For...Next` loop.

For properties that support only specific values, like many of those in Table 7.1, try double-clicking in the VBA Properties window or Outlook form advanced Properties dialog to cycle through all the possible values.

Until now, the controls you've encountered behave essentially the same on Outlook forms and on VBA forms, although Outlook form controls sometimes have fewer properties. You will, however, find one major difference between list and combo boxes on Outlook forms and on VBA forms: On Outlook forms, if a list or combo box is bound to a user-defined field, you can set the possible values for the list in the Properties dialog for the form, as shown in Figure 7.4. On VBA forms, you can only use code to set the possible values; there is no manual method.

On an Outlook form, you can also use the `PossibleValues` property of a list box in program code. Hour 10, "Working with Expressions," includes an example.

7

FIGURE 7.4

For list and combo boxes bound to user-defined fields on an Outlook form, you can set the list values on the Properties dialog box for the control.

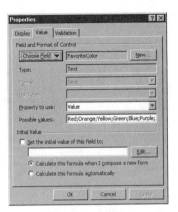

In VBA forms, you can use the AddItem method to fill a list box, one row at a time. This works in Outlook forms, too. Here is what the code would look like to fill a list box named lstColors on a custom Outlook form page named Favorites.

```
Set objPage = Item.GetInspector.ModifiedFormPages("Favorites")
Set lstColors = objPage.Controls("lstColors")
lstColors.AddItem "Red"
lstColors.AddItem "Orange"
lstColors.AddItem "Yellow"
lstColors.AddItem "Green"
lstColors.AddItem "Blue"
lstColors.AddItem "Purple"
lstColors.AddItem "Black"
lstColors.AddItem "Brown"
```

On a VBA form, you would use exactly the same code, minus the two Set statements at the top. Those are required only for VBScript code behind an Outlook form. For both types of forms, code to initialize a list box like this usually runs when the form opens—in the Form_Open event of an Outlook form or in the UserForm_Activate event of a VBA form. Sometimes, you also see a list box's contents change in response to a change in the value of another control.

For multiple column list and combo boxes, such as the Favorite Couple list in Figure 7.3, you would use a different method to fill the list box: the List method, which fills it from a two-dimensional array. See Hour 10, "Working with Expressions," for an example.

Accelerators and Tab Order

Hour 6 introduces the Accelerator property of VBA form controls as one means of helping keyboard-preferring users to get around your form easily. Another key technique for controlling navigation is to set the tab order in a logical fashion. You've probably noticed that as you press Tab in a dialog box or other form, you can enter information in each control in turn. The current control is said to be the one with the *focus*. The tab order determines which control gets the focus as the user presses Tab to move through the controls. You will now look at the method for setting the tab order in both VBA and Outlook forms.

You can direct the user's attention to a particular control programmatically, using the SetFocus method.

First, return to the ReminderUpdate VBA form. Right-click on any empty area of the form, and then choose Tab Order to display the Tab Order dialog (see Figure 7.5). (You can also choose View, Tab Order.) Now you see why it's so important to give distinctive names to your controls! If we had left the command buttons as CommandButton1 and CommandButton2 instead of renaming them to cmdUpdate and cmdClose, it would have been much harder to figure out how to adjust the tab order.

FIGURE 7.5

Compare the order of controls listed here with the form in Figure 7.2.

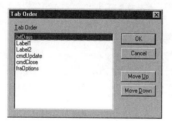

Did you notice that the Tab Order dialog consists of a List Box control and four Command Button controls?

7

Use the Move Up and Move Down buttons to rearrange the Tab Order list to match the order in which controls appear on the form itself. The final order should be

fraOptions

txtDays

cmdUpdate

cmdClose

> To exclude a control from the tab order, set its TabStop property to False. The control will still appear in the Tab Order window but will be bypassed when the user presses Tab or Enter to move through the form's controls.

After you adjust the tab order, run the form, and press Tab to move through the controls. Does the order seem logical to you?

> Most forms use a left-to-right tab order, moving through the controls at the top of the form and then going to the next row of controls. However, some forms use a clockwise order. Others go from top to bottom for the set of controls on the left and then start at the top again for the next column of controls. The important thing is to be consistent, both within a form and within a group of forms in an application.

The process of setting the tab order is similar in an Outlook form. Open the form in design mode, and then choose Layout, Tab Order to access the Tab Order dialog.

Although you can often ignore Label controls in setting the tab order for VBA forms, they play an important role in controlling navigation on Outlook forms because not all Outlook form controls have an Accelerator property. Critically, the commonly used Text Box, List Box, and Combo Box controls do not include an Accelerator property. Setting an accelerator for these controls on an Outlook form involves three steps:

1. Add a separate Label control related to the text box, list box, or combo box.

2. In the advanced Properties dialog, set the label's Accelerator property. (Alternatively, in the Properties dialog, you can add an ampersand (&) to the Caption text to set the accelerator to the following letter.)

3. Adjust the tab order so that the label appears immediately above the related text box, list box, or combo box.

For example, in the tab order for the form in Figure 7.3, the lblColor label control (Favorite color:) appears just above the lstColors list box. Therefore, when the user presses Alt+C, the focus goes to the lstColors box.

 When you use the Tab Order dialog, you are actually changing the TabIndex property of each control.

Summary

You should now have a solid collection of controls to work with, having studied option buttons, check boxes, frames, list boxes, and combo boxes in this hour. When you have more than a few controls on a form, it becomes important to make navigating them easy with accelerators and a logical tab order. Programmers usually write code to initialize list and combo boxes when a form first appears.

The next lesson introduces the basics of writing programming code in Outlook, so you can begin to really put your forms to work!

Q&A

Q Why don't the option buttons inside a frame appear in the tab order?

A Framed option buttons have a tab order of their own, inside the context of the frame. To set their order, right-click the frame, and then choose Tab Order.

Q Where does the focus rest when a form or Outlook item first opens?

A The focus on a newly ordered form is on the first control in the tab order.

Workshop

Work through the quiz questions and exercises so that you can understand Outlook programming better. See Appendix A for answers.

7

Quiz

1. When a user clicks on a check box or makes a selection in a combo box, what property of the control changes?

2. What methods can you use to fill a list box on an Outlook form? Do they all work on a VBA form list box?

3. If you have to present two choices to a user, which is better: check boxes, option buttons, a list box, or a combo box? What if you have three choices to present? Four?

Exercises

1. What do you think should happen if, in the form in Figure 7.1, both check boxes are unchecked when the user clicks the Update button?

2. You omitted keyboard accelerators for the option buttons in Figure 7.2. What would be good choices for the Accelerator property?

3. In the option button example in Figure 7.2, do you agree that the optBoth button should be the default (optBoth.Value = True)? Why or why not?

4. Using the code in Listing 7.1 for the check box form as a model, write a series of If...Then statements to handle the three option buttons. Don't worry about the exact syntax. Just see if you can get the logic and sequence right.

PART III
Adding Code

Hour

Hour **8**

Code Basics

Get ready to dig into coding. In this lesson and the four that follow, you will learn the basics of writing programming code in Microsoft Outlook, both in VBA and in VBScript behind Outlook forms. First, you need to understand when code runs. Then, you will look at the mechanics of writing code in VBA and transferring it to VBScript so that you spend as little time as possible in the Notepad-like VBScript editor.

The highlights of this hour include

- What triggers program routines to execute
- When to use a function versus a subroutine
- How to run an Outlook subroutine from a toolbar button
- How to write code in VBA so that you can transfer it to VBScript with as little effort as possible

Understanding When Code Runs

Think about the Windows applications you use every day. If you have a money management program, take that as an example. When you start the program, it probably pops up reminders that you have bills to pay or investments to check on. You click a button or maybe a menu command to enter a new transaction. Perhaps you can type **May 15**, and the program converts it to May 15, 1999 or May 15, 2000 (or whatever the current year might be). Although virtually all the program runs out of sight, it depends on you, the user, for the key interactions that tell it what to do.

Each time you interact with the program—choosing a menu item, clicking a button, saving an item, and even pressing Tab to move from one control to another—you cause one or more events to fire. Each event can have a programming routine associated with it.

Each type of object (VBA forms, Outlook items, command buttons, text boxes, and so on) has its own set of possible events. Not every event will have code related to it. As you build Outlook programs, you must decide which events are important to your program and which you can ignore.

Outlook as an application has events, too. You use these events, for example, to perform certain tasks every time you start Outlook or every time you end the program.

In addition to routines that run when events are triggered, you can have other procedures that launch directly from the macros list or a toolbar button. Finally, you will write many nonevent procedures that support macros and event procedures by performing calculations and automating routine tasks.

VBA Form Events

Let's take a closer look at events that take place on VBA forms. An easy way to see what events a form supports is to use View, Code to display the code window for the form (see Figure 8.1). From the left drop-down list at the top of the form, choose UserForm. (This will place the Sub...End Sub shell for a subroutine named UserForm_Click in the code window; you can delete or ignore it.) Use the right drop-down list to see all the events for the UserForm object, in other words, for the current form.

If you display the Office Assistant in the main Outlook window, it's also available in the VBA code window, so you can ask about such things as Initialize Event. The Object Browser is another tool for learning about events. You will learn about it in Hour 13, "Working with the Object Models."

It's important to distinguish between form-level events and control events. For example, the Click event for a form fires only when you click outside the area of any controls. If you click on a control, the Click event for that control fires, not the Click event for the form. Initially, you will probably find the form events listed in Table 8.1 the most useful.

FIGURE 8.1

The drop-down lists at the top of the code window help you understand what events are supported by your form and its controls.

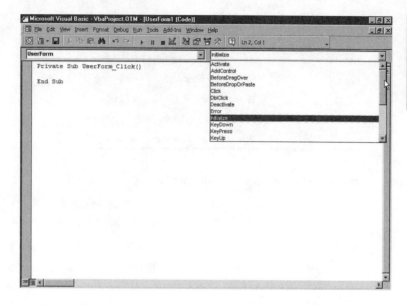

TABLE 8.1 Key VBA Form Events

Event	Occurs
Activate	When a form becomes the active, visible window in Outlook
Deactivate	When the focus moves away from the form to another Outlook window
Initialize	After the form is loaded, but before it becomes visible
Terminate	After the form has been unloaded, but before it is removed completely from memory

Notice that loading a form and showing it are two different things, each with its own set of events. (`Initialize`/`Terminate` and `Activate`/`Deactivate`). These events can fire either because of something the user does or because you load or show a form through code.

With most of the forms you create in Outlook VBA, you will be more interested in control events than form events.

Controls on forms have their own events, too. In Hour 6, "A Birthday/Anniversary Reminder Tool," you saw an example of code attached to the `Click` event for a command button. Table 8.2 lists that and other important events for VBA controls.

TABLE 8.2   Key VBA Control Events

Event	Occurs
AfterUpdate	After the user's change to a control takes effect
BeforeUpdate	Before the user's change to a control takes effect
Click	When a user clicks on a control
Enter	Just before the focus enters a control
Exit	When the focus leaves a control

Here are some notes on control events:

- Because it can be cancelled to roll back the control to its previous value, the BeforeUpdate event is often used to validate the data entered in a control.
- Of the events in Table 8.2, command buttons support only the Click event.
- Text boxes do not support the Click event.
- For check boxes, the Click event occurs not only when the user clicks in the box, but also when the user changes the value by pressing the spacebar or the accelerator key for the control.
- The Exit event can be cancelled if you want the user to remain in the control.
- Visual Basic programmers will recognize that the Enter and Exit events in VBA are analogous to the GotFocus and LostFocus events in VB.

A good way to become acquainted with the order in which these events fire is to create a simple form with one check box, one text box, and one command button. Don't worry about changing the default names of the controls; this is just a test form. To enter code for each event for each control and for the form itself, in the code window, follow these steps:

1. Select the control or form from the left drop-down list.
2. Select the event from the right drop-down list.
3. Between the Private Sub and End Sub statements, enter one line for each event to pop up a message box with the name of the event. You can use the code in Listing 8.1 as a model.

LISTING 8.1   A Series of Message Boxes Shows the Sequence in Which Control and Form Events Fire

```
1: Private Sub CheckBox1_AfterUpdate()
2:     MsgBox "CheckBox After Update"
3: End Sub
```

```
 4:
 5: Private Sub CheckBox1_BeforeUpdate(ByVal Cancel)
 6:     MsgBox "CheckBox Before Update"
 7: End Sub
 8:
 9: Private Sub CheckBox1_Click()
10:     MsgBox "CheckBox Click"
11: End Sub
12:
13: Private Sub CheckBox1_Enter()
14:     MsgBox "Checkbox Enter"
15: End Sub
16:
17: Private Sub CheckBox1_Exit(ByVal Cancel)
18:     MsgBox "Checkbox Exit"
19: End Sub
20:
21: Private Sub CommandButton1_Click()
22:     MsgBox "Command Button Click"
23: End Sub
24:
25: Private Sub TextBox1_AfterUpdate()
26:     MsgBox "Text Box After Update"
27: End Sub
28:
29: Private Sub TextBox1_BeforeUpdate(ByVal Cancel)
30:     MsgBox "Text Box Before Update"
31: End Sub
32:
33: Private Sub TextBox1_Enter()
34:     MsgBox "Text Box Enter"
35: End Sub
36:
37: Private Sub TextBox1_Exit(ByVal Cancel)
38:     MsgBox "Text Box Exit"
39: End Sub
40:
41: Private Sub UserForm_Activate()
42:     MsgBox "Form Activate"
43: End Sub
44:
45: Private Sub UserForm_Deactivate()
46:     MsgBox "Form Deactivate"
47: End Sub
48:
49: Private Sub UserForm_Initialize()
50:     MsgBox "Form Initialize"
51: End Sub
52:
53: Private Sub UserForm_Terminate()
54:     MsgBox "Form Terminate"
55: End Sub
```

After you enter the code, run the form, and use the mouse and keyboard to move through the various controls, enter data, delete data, and so forth. Each event will pop up a message box to tell you which event is occurring.

What Is a Sub Anyway?

After entering the code in the preceding section, you're probably wondering about the `Private Sub` and `End Sub` statements. These mark the beginning and end, respectively, of a code procedure called a *subroutine*. The `Private` keyword means that each of these routines runs only in the context of the particular form. That's normal for forms, but as you will see, in other code modules, you may choose to make a subroutine public so that it can be used elsewhere.

To start a new subroutine, just type **Sub** on a new line in the code editor, followed by the name you want to use for the procedure. Procedure names can't contain spaces. When you press Enter at the end of the `Sub` line, VBA adds an `End Sub` statement automatically.

Did you notice that each subroutine name is followed by a pair of parentheses? These contain the arguments for the subroutine—any inputs to the routine.

In most cases, form events have no arguments. `BeforeUpdate` and `Exit` are exceptions. They both have `Cancel` as an argument. If you set `Cancel` to `True`, you cancel the event. In the case of `BeforeUpdate`, the control returns to the value it had before the user updated it. With `Exit`, setting `Cancel` to `True` makes the focus stay in the control, rather than move on to the next control.

Here is some code you can use with the `txtDays` control on the ReminderUpdate form from Hour 7, "An Area Code Search and Replace Tool." It uses the `BeforeUpdate` event to make sure that the user enters a valid number:

```
Private Sub txtDays_BeforeUpdate(ByVal Cancel _
  As MSForms.ReturnBoolean)
    If IsNumeric(txtDays.Value) = False Then
        Cancel = True
    MsgBox "Please enter a number."
    End If
End Sub
```

IsNumeric() is a built-in function that is True if its argument is a number and False if not.

Also, note that this validation procedure runs only if the user actually enters data in the txtDays control. You also need validation in the Click event for the cmdUpdate button to handle the case of the user leaving txtDays blank and then clicking the Update button.

8

Performing validation with cancelable events can make a form friendlier to the user because you can use message boxes and other clues to tell the user precisely what to do.

Outlook Form Events

Outlook forms have their own set of events, but they're quite different from the VBA form events. Table 8.3 lists the Outlook form events and tells you which can be cancelled.

TABLE 8.3 Outlook Form Events (* = new in Outlook 2000)

Event	Occurs
AttachmentAdd*	When an attachment is added to an item.
AttachmentRead*	When the user opens an attachment.
BeforeAttachmentSave*	Just before an attachment is saved (cancelable).
BeforeCheckNames*	Before Outlook starts to resolve names in the To, Cc, and Bcc fields against the Address Book (cancelable).
Close	When a displayed Outlook item is closed (cancelable).
CustomAction	When a custom action associated with an item occurs (cancelable). See Hour 14, "Working with Forms," for details on custom actions.
CustomPropertyChange	When the value of a user-defined property changes.
Forward	When the user forwards the item (cancelable).
Open	Just before Outlook displays an item in its own window (cancelable).
PropertyChange	When the value of a built-in property changes.
Read	When the user opens an item for editing, either in its own window or using in-cell editing in a folder view.
Reply	When the user replies to the item (cancelable).
ReplyAll	When the user replies to the item using Reply to All (cancelable).
Send	When the user sends the item (cancelable).
Write	When an item is saved (cancelable).

The syntax for canceling an event in VBScript code is different from that in VBA. You will see an example in the upcoming section "Adding VBScript Code to an Outlook Form."

Outlook controls have just one event, Click, which fires only on unbound controls, not on those linked to a particular field. To detect changes in the data stored in controls (so that you can perform validation and other tasks), you must use the

`CustomPropertyChange` and `PropertyChange` events because Outlook forms don't support a `BeforeUpdate` event.

Application-Level Events

One of the big changes in Outlook 2000, compared with previous versions, is the introduction of application-level events. These events allow you to create procedures to initialize Outlook with particular settings; automatically process new items; and respond to synchronization, switching views, switching folders, and many other interesting events. For example, you can use the `FolderSwitch` event to display a custom toolbar when the user switches to a particular folder.

Programming responses to application-level events is more complicated than programming VBA and Outlook forms. Therefore, a discussion is deferred until Hour 17, "Application-Level Events."

Macros to Run Programs on Demand

A frequently asked question in Outlook 97 and Outlook 98 is "Can I create a toolbar button to..." perform a particular task (such as launching a custom form or switching to a particular view)? The Outlook 2000 answer is yes, with macros.

Macros are simply subroutines that are stored in VBA modules, not forms, and have no arguments. If a macro requires some input information, it must either display a VBA form to get the information from the user or use one of the other methods discussed in Hour 12, "Handling User Input and Feedback."

Any argumentless subroutine in a VBA module that does not use the `Private` keyword is automatically listed among the macros that you see when you choose Tools, Macro, Macros (see Figure 8.2). You don't have to do anything special to get your subroutines on the list.

Press Alt+F8 to open the Macros dialog quickly.

Don't look for a macro recorder, such as the ones in Microsoft Word and Excel. You must write all Outlook macros from scratch.

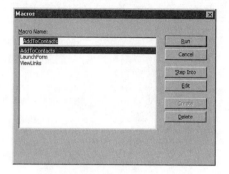

FIGURE 8.2

Run any Outlook macro from the Macros dialog.

To add any macro to an Outlook toolbar, follow these steps:

1. Close the VBA window, if it's open.

2. In the main Outlook window, choose View, Toolbars, Customize. (If you want to run the macro from the toolbar of an Outlook item, open an item first, and then choose View, Toolbars, Customize.)

3. From the Commands tab in the Customize dialog box (see Figure 8.3), drag the macro from the Commands list to the toolbar where you want it to appear. This will create a button for that macro on the toolbar.

FIGURE 8.3

Add any macro to your Outlook toolbars.

4. With the Customize dialog still open, right-click the new button to pop up a menu of commands for customizing it (see Figure 8.4). You will certainly want to change the name to remove the `Project1.` prefix. You might also want to choose Change Button Image to pick an icon.

5. When you finish customizing the button and toolbar, close the Customize dialog box.

FIGURE 8.4

*Customize the macro
toolbar button by
changing its name
and icon.*

 When you're customizing toolbar buttons, the Default Style command (see
Figure 8.4) really means *image only — show this button only as an icon.*

Modules

You first encountered modules in Hour 5, "The VBA Design Environment," while
exploring the VBA programming environment. Any code that is not associated with a
particular form is stored in a module. You can keep everything in just one module or,
more likely, organize your procedures into several modules.

Writing VBA Code

Now, to write some VBA code! If you don't already have a module in the Project
Explorer, choose Insert, Module to add one.

Your first project is to write a macro to launch a customized Contact form. This will let
you display that form from a toolbar button, rather than go through the Tools, Forms
menu.

To start, type **Sub LaunchContactForm** into the code window, and then press Enter. `Sub`
indicates that this is a subroutine, not a function (you will get to functions shortly).
`LaunchContactForm` is the name of the procedure. Procedure names can't contain spaces
and must be unique within a module. When you press Enter, VBA automatically adds
parentheses after the procedure name and then adds the `End Sub` statement marking the
end of the procedure.

Public procedures, those that don't start with `Private Sub`, instead of just `Sub`, need names that are unique not only within the current module, but also within your project. Don't worry too much about this. VBA will warn you if you create a public procedure with a duplicate name.

Because this is a macro, you don't want to put any arguments inside the parentheses. Next, add this line, which supplies the name of your form to a variable named `strMessageClass` that you will use later. If used a different name for the custom Contact form created in Hour 3, "Create Your First Custom Contact Form," use it instead of `IPM.Contact.Hour03Contact`.

```
strMessageClass = "IPM.Contact.Hour03Contact"
```

This is an assignment statement. It assigns the value `IPM.Contact.Hour03Contact` to the variable `strMessageClass`. This means that everywhere you see `strMessageClass` in the code, it's the same as `IPM.Contact.Hour03Contact`. Variables have names and hold the data used in your procedures. Many statements in programming code manipulate variables and then return new values based on those operations. In the next lesson, you will look in more detail at variables.

The next step is to initialize two object variables that Outlook VBA uses every time you have to work with folders or items in folders. Add these two lines:

```
Set objApp = CreateObject("Outlook.Application")
Set objNS = objApp.GetNamespace("MAPI")
```

Compare these object assignment statements with the preceding statement. They require a `Set` keyword because that's the way the VBA programming language works. It has a very specific syntax or grammar, just like English, Russian, or any spoken language. To make yourself understood, you must follow the VBA syntax. The VBA editor makes it easy, as you will see, because it often suggests the right words and warns you when you make common mistakes.

Using `obj` as a prefix for all object variables helps you remember to initialize them with a `Set` statement.

These two lines are *boilerplate*. You use them so many times in Outlook VBA applications that you might want to create a separate module containing sample procedures with these statements and other standard object variable assignment statements used to get the current Outlook folder, the current Outlook item, and so forth.

Next, add these three lines:

```
Set objFolder = objNS.GetDefaultFolder(olFolderContacts)
Set objItems = objFolder.Items
Set objItem = objItems.Add(strMessageClass)
```

Do you recognize these as three more object assignment statements? The last statement is the key; it actually creates a new Outlook item using the message class of your form. You can't just start with the `Set objItem = objItems.Add(strMessageClass)` statement. You must lay the groundwork with the two preceding `Set` statements. It might seem long-winded, but this is the way Outlook works.

Now that you have created a new item using your custom Contact form, you will want Outlook to show it. The last statement above assigns the new item to the `objItem` variable. To make the new item appear takes just one line:

```
objItem.Display
```

The `Display` keyword is called a *method*. By applying a method to an object, you make something happen—display a form, save an item, and so forth. Each object supports its own set of methods. You just used several methods:

GetDefaultFolder	In the Set objFolder statement
Items	In the Set objItems statement
Add	In the Set objItem statement

For example, the `Add` method creates a new item within the `objItems` object, which represents the set of items in the Contacts folder.

How do you know it's the Contacts folder? The key is the `olFolderContacts` keyword in the `Set objFolder` statement. `olFolderContacts` is an intrinsic constant. Constants are similar to variables in that they hold a particular data value. However, they differ in that when you set a constant's value, the value doesn't change later in the program. Intrinsic constants are built into Outlook; you don't have to set their values. They are great coding shortcuts because they usually have very descriptive names. For example, it's not difficult to remember that `olFolderContacts` is a constant that represents the Contacts folder, when used with the `GetDefaultFolder` method.

VBScript on Outlook forms does not support the intrinsic Outlook constants. You must explicitly declare these constants or use their literal values. As you will see in Chapter 13, "Working with the Object Models," you can use the Object Browser to see all the intrinsic constants and get their values.

8

You've not only written a very useful macro, you've also seen how assignment statements, methods, variables, and intrinsic constants comprise key code building blocks. Reward yourself by running the procedure and watching your custom form appear!

Subroutines Versus Functions

Not every procedure you write is a subroutine. You also write *functions*. These are procedures that return data to the program, usually by performing some operation on data you provide to the function. Here's an example:

```
Public Function Quote(varInput)
    Quote = Chr(34) & varInput & Chr(34)
End Function
```

This Quote() function can take anything as its argument (varInput) and returns that data surrounded by quotation marks. Chr() is a built-in function that returns a string consisting of the single ASCII character corresponding to a given number. (In this case, an ASCII 34 is a quotation mark.) You will remember the ampersand (&) concatenation operator from Hour 4, "Extend Form Design with a Custom Task Form," which discusses operators.

> Think of a function as a magic box with an opening at the top, an opening at the bottom, and a crank on the side. Pour something into the top, turn the crank, and something completely different comes out the bottom. Your job as a programmer is to supply the "magic" that makes the box perform its trick.

A function always includes one or more statements that assign the value of the function to some expression. Here, that Quote = statement is the only statement in the whole function. Table 8.4 shows the results the Quote() function delivers for various sample arguments.

TABLE 8.4 Sample Results for the Quote() Function

Argument	Result
Quote("Microsoft Outlook")	"Microsoft Outlook"
Quote(2)	"2"
Quote(Null)	""

A function can have more than one assignment statement, and assignment statements can occur anywhere in a function. However, for beginners, it's easiest to always make the assignment statement the last line in a function's code. That way, you will be able to easily spot a function with a missing assignment statement.

If you add the Quote() function to the module you're building in VBA, you can reuse it in other procedures. You will definitely use it later in message boxes and in searching and filtering for particular Outlook items.

Referring to VBA Forms and Controls

You have one more VBA issue to address before moving on to VBScript: how to refer to VBA forms and controls in your code. It's really simple. You use the name you give the form or control.

You already saw an example of this in Hour 6 in the cmdUpdate_Click procedure on the ReminderUpdate form. In the statement

```
objItem.ReminderMinutesBeforeStart = _24 * 60 * txtDays.Value
```

txtDays.Value represents the Value property of the txtDays text box on the form. You don't have to use the name of the form anywhere because the code is running inside the form, attached to the Click event for one of the form's command buttons.

If the code is in a separate module or behind a different form, refer to the form by its name and to a control on the form with the syntax *formname.controlname*. For example, these three lines load the ReminderUpdate form, display it to the user with the Show method, and then disable the cmdUpdate button by setting its Enabled property to False:

```
Load ReminderUpdate
ReminderUpdate.Show
ReminderUpdate.cmdUpdate.Enabled = False
```

Why disable the cmdUpdate button? Maybe you don't want it to be active until the user puts a valid entry in the txtDays text box.

Adding VBScript Code to an Outlook Form

To complete your introduction to writing code, you must explore VBScript, as well as VBA. You must understand the critical differences in the syntax of these two languages and grasp the special syntax for referring to Outlook form controls and fields.

To add code to an Outlook form, open the form in design mode; then, click the View Code button, or choose Form, View Code. All code on Outlook forms is event driven. A routine runs either from a form event (see Table 8.3) or from the Click event on a control. You can add other subroutines and functions, but they must be called from one of the event procedures.

To add code for a form event, choose Script, Event Handler, and select from the list of events in the Insert Event Handler dialog box (see Figure 8.5). A Function...End Function wrapper is added to the code window.

FIGURE 8.5
Add Outlook form-level event handlers through this dialog.

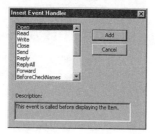

You must type in your own wrapper for a Click event. For example, this would be the wrapper for a Click event on a command button named cmdShowSpouse:

```
Sub cmdShowSpouse_Click
    your code goes here
End Sub
```

VBScript Versus VBA

Here are some of the key differences between VBScript and VBA code:

- VBScript does not support the Outlook intrinsic constants. You must either include declarations for these constants in your module and procedures or use the actual literal values that correspond to the constants.

- In VBScript, you don't have to use a

  ```
  Set objApp = CreateObject("Outlook.Application")
  ```

  statement because the Application object is intrinsic to VBScript behind an Outlook form.

- The Item object representing the current item is also intrinsic to Outlook form code. In VBA, you must use an object variable to represent any Outlook item.

- VBScript supports only the Variant data type, which can represent any type of data. (You will find a discussion of data types in the next lesson).

- Outlook forms don't include a form object and use a complex syntax for referring to form controls that you'll see in the next section.

What does this mean for your code? You will see the implications as you go along. Some differences, such as the intrinsic Application and Item objects, make VBScript coding easier. Others, such as the lack of support for intrinsic constants, make you work a little harder.

Some language differences also exist between VBA and VBScript: functions or statements that work in one but not the other. As you encounter a few in this book, they'll be clearly noted.

Referring to Outlook Form Controls and Fields

Flip back to Hour 3, "Create Your First Custom Contact Form," and Hour 4, and look at the various Outlook forms. Remember how each form has multiple pages, and you can customize only certain pages, depending on the form? This is an important concept to remember, because to access the properties of a control, you must refer to both the page and the control. This next example should help you see how to do that.

Go back to the custom task form created in Hour 4, and add a command button named cmdChangeProjectColor. Then, add this procedure to the code on the form:

```
Sub cmdChangeProjectColor_Click()
    Set objPage = Item.GetInspector.ModifiedFormPages("P.2")
    Set objControl = objPage.Controls("txtProject")
    If objControl.ForeColor = RGB(204, 0, 153) Then
        objControl.ForeColor = RGB(0, 128, 128)
    Else
        objControl.ForeColor = RGB(204, 0, 153)
    End If
End Sub
```

Clicking the command button toggles the color of the text in the Project box between fuchsia and teal, because of the If...Else...End If block of statements. Here are a few additional notes on this procedure:

- Use Item.GetInspector.ModifiedFormPages("pagename") whenever you need to refer to a page on a form. If you renamed the custom page on the task form, use your name instead of *P.2*.

- Controls is a property of a page that gives you access to a particular control, either by name or an index number.

- ForeColor is a property of the Text Box control.

- RGB(red,blue,green) is a built-in function that uses as its arguments the three color components you can get from many graphics programs' color picker.

To get at the data in the control, you can either use the control's Value property or, if the control is bound to an Outlook field, the data field itself. In Hour 4, you created an IsNew field as a Formula type field. This time, create an IsNew2 field as a Yes/No field, and place a check box on the custom page so that you can see its value. Add this code to the form to calculate the value of IsNew2 every time you open an item using this function:

```
Function Item_Open()
    Item.UserProperties.Find("IsNew2") = (Item.Size = 0)
End Function
```

Notice the difference in syntax between intrinsic properties and user-defined properties. Use Item.*property* as the syntax for intrinsic properties (as in Item.Size in the preceding snippet). However, for user-defined Outlook properties, you must use the Item.UserProperties.Find(*myproperty*) syntax. For the *myproperty* argument, use the exact name of the custom property, and enclose it in quotation marks or use a String expression that evaluates to the property name.

> The expression (Item.Size = 0) might look odd, but it's quite logical. If the Size equals 0, it evaluates to True; otherwise, it's False. Using a comparison expression such as this produces much more compact code than an equivalent If...End If block.

Summary

This has been a busy hour, in which you have learned how program code consists of subroutines and functions. You have written code to react to events and used object methods to make something happen. Other new concepts include variables to store the data that your program will manipulate and constants to store data that doesn't change. Finally, you have briefly explored the differences between VBA and VBScript code.

In the next hour, you will continue learning code basics by refining your knowledge of modules, variables, and constants.

Q&A

Q Can you run a VBA macro or form from an Outlook form?

A No, because an Outlook form cannot call a VBA subroutine. It is possible for an Outlook form to activate an existing toolbar button that runs a VBA macro. However, this is a moot point because the form's code cannot pass any data directly to the macro. (Remember that macros have no arguments.)

Q Why don't VBA and VBScript use the same syntax to refer to controls?

A It's not so much a limitation of the programming language, but a function of the different object models. VBA forms and Outlook forms are really different types of objects, even though they both present windows containing information to the user. Outlook forms have to be self-contained so that the design they contain can be transported, even across the Internet. When you work with Outlook forms in VBA, you must still use the `Item.GetInspector.ModifiedFormPages("pagename")` and `objPage.Controls("txtProject")` syntax.

Workshop

Work through the quiz questions and exercises so that you can understand Outlook programming better. See Appendix A for Answers.

Quiz

1. What's the difference between a variable and a constant? Between a method and an event?

2. What steps must occur to create a new Outlook item using a custom form? (Hint: In your own words, summarize the macro you created.)

Exercises

1. Open any Outlook form, add one or more custom fields, and write VBScript code to pop up a message box whenever any form event fires. Use the same `MsgBox` syntax as in Listing 8.1. Run the form, and experiment with changing data, saving, closing without saving, and so on.

2. For the custom Contact form you created in Hour 3, create a macro to launch the form, and customize the Standard toolbar with a button to run the macro.

HOUR 9

Code Grammar 101

So far, your excursion into Outlook programming code has been a lot like beginning language lessons. Most of the initial work in learning a language is oral: You work with a teacher or tape, memorizing phrases and repeating them. Sooner or later, though, you have to learn more about the structure of a language; you have to study grammar. Welcome to VBA and VBScript Grammar 101, the hour in which you study the basic syntax of these programming languages.

Highlights of this hour include

- How to make a procedure available to any VBA routine
- Where and when to add global constants
- What data types VBA and VBScript support
- How to name your variables
- Which features of the VBA editor make it easier to write accurate code quickly

Option Explicit

I'm going to let you in on a little secret: To create the macro in Hour 8, "Code Basics," you did more typing than you had to. Outlook can do more of the work for you and at the same time avoid common errors. The key is to set up VBA so that it forces you to declare all your variables.

First, it helps to see what happens when you have a mistake in your code. Go back to the LaunchContactForm macro in Hour 8, and change the objItem.Display line to

```
objMyItem.Display
```

Then, run the routine. You should receive an Object Required error message, shown in Figure 9.1. Click the Debug button, and VBA takes you directly to the statement with a problem, the one you changed. It's wrong because objMyItem isn't the right name for the object variable for new item; it should be objItem instead.

FIGURE 9.1

A wrong variable name causes an error.

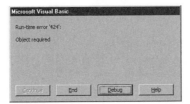

I want you to notice this error because it's a common one—you might change a variable name midprocedure or just make a typo—and because you're going to make a couple changes to the macro code to help prevent such errors.

Reset your procedure to get out of debug mode and back to design mode: Click the Reset button, or choose Run, Reset.

Press Ctrl+Home to move to the top of the module containing the LaunchContactForm procedure. The drop-down lists at the top of the code window should show (General) and (Declarations). You are now in the declarations section of the module, before the first procedure. This is where you place statements that affect the entire module and declare variables and constants that you want to use in more than one procedure.

Make this statement the first line in the declarations section:

```
Option Explicit
```

The Option Explicit statement tells VBA that, within this particular module, all variables must be declared before you use them. This means that you can't just throw in a new variable any time you need it. You must declare it first, either in the declarations section if it's a global-level or module-level variable, or at the beginning of a procedure.

Otherwise, when you try to run the procedure, you receive a compile error. VBA compiles code before it runs any procedure and detects errors, such as undeclared variables. You can also use the Debug, Compile command at any time to compile the project and check for compile errors. Detecting an error early, at the compile stage, is better than finding the error only when you run the procedure.

To add Option Explicit automatically to the declarations for any new module, choose Tools, Options. In the Options dialog box, shown in Figure 9.2, check Require Variable Declaration. This change affects only new forms and modules. If you want to use Option Explicit in existing modules, you must add it to the declarations section of the code module.

FIGURE 9.2

Options for the VBA code editor include requiring all variables to be explicitly declared.

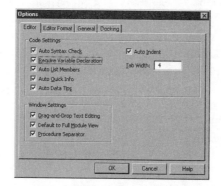

To use Option Explicit in VBScript, you must type it at the beginning of the script, before any event handlers or other procedures.

Declaring Variables

If you try to run the LaunchContactForm macro at this point, you will receive a compile error because you didn't declare any variables. Use the Dim statement to declare any variable at the beginning of the procedure, right after the Sub or Function statement that marks the beginning of the procedure. To declare all the variables used in the LaunchContactForm macro, add these statements to your code:

```
Dim objApp As Application
Dim objNS As NameSpace
Dim objFolder As Folder
Dim objItems As Items
Dim objItem As ContactItem
Dim strMessageClass As String
Dim blnUseDefault As Boolean
```

Did you notice that, when you type the space after As, VBA pops up a list of possible ways to complete the Dim statement? This feature, Auto List Members, will save you hours of typing and avoid many errors. Select an item from the list, and then press Tab to add that text to the current statement. It helps you complete a statement or expression by offering a set of appropriate choices.

For example, after you type Dim strMessageClass As Str, you see String selected in the list of data and object types. Press Tab to select String, completing the Dim statement.

Variable Data Types

In Hour 4, "Extend Form Design with a Custom Contact Form," you created custom Outlook form fields and, in the process, selected a data type for each field. When you declare a variable in VBA, you specify a data type. If you don't, the variable uses the Variant data type. Because Variant-type variables can support all kinds of operations, VBA cannot optimize the code when it compiles it, as it can if you use explicit data types. Therefore, using explicit data types can make your VBA code run more efficiently. Table 9.1 lists the data types that VBA supports.

 VBScript supports only the Variant data type. The Variant data type is often used in VBA for variables that hold data from a form control, because users can type numbers and letters or leave the control blank.

TABLE 9.1 VBA Data Types

Data Type	Prefix	Can Contain
Boolean	bln	True (-1) or False (0)
Byte	byt	Any nondecimal number between 0 and 255
Integer	int	Any nondecimal number between $-32{,}768$ and $32{,}767$
Long	lng	Any nondecimal number between $-2{,}147{,}483{,}648$ and $2{,}147{,}483{,}647$
Single	sng	Numbers from $-3.402823E{+}38$ to $-1.401298E{-}45$ for negative values and from $1.401298E{-}45$ to $3.402823E{+}38$ for positive values (single-precision floating point)
Double	dbl	Numbers from $-1.79769313486231E{+}308$ to $-4.94065645841247E{-}324$ for negative values and from $4.94065645841247E{-}324$ to $1.79769313486232E{+}308$ for positive values (double-precision floating point)
Currency	cur	Numbers between $-922{,}337{,}203{,}685{,}477.5808$ and $922{,}337{,}203{,}685{,}477.5807$ (limit of four decimal places)

Data Type	Prefix	Can Contain
Decimal	dec	Any integer up to +/–79,228,162,514,264,337,593,543,950,335; any decimal number up to +/–7.9228162514264337593543950335 with 28 places to the right of the decimal; smallest nonzero number is +/–0.0000000000000000000000000001
Date	dte	Date and time values from January 1, 100, to December 31, 9999; time values are resolved to the second
Object	obj	Reference to any object
String	str	For variable-length strings, from 0 to approximately 2 billion alphanumeric characters; for fixed-length strings, from 1 to 65,400 characters
Variant	var	Any kind of data, including numbers, strings, and objects

In Table 9.1, *E+38* means *10 to the power of 38*, and *E–45* means *10 to the power of –45*. This scientific notation, as it's called, is used to simplify the writing of very large and very small numbers.

Date/Time fields in Outlook items do not support the full range of dates that a VBA Date variable can hold. Dates on Outlook forms must fall between April 1, 1601, and August 31, 4500, inclusive. Dates that appear in Outlook form fields and folder views as "None" are really January 1, 4501.

Even though VBA includes an Object data type, most of the time you should declare an object variable as a specific type of object, as you saw in the Dim statements earlier in this section. Use the Object data type when you don't know what type of object you might be dealing with. For example, when accessing items in an Outlook Contacts folder, you don't know in advance whether any given item is a ContactItem or a DistListItem (distribution list) object.

Variable Naming Conventions

Variable names must follow certain rules. They must begin with a letter, not a number, and cannot contain a period. Most programmers use a naming convention—a specific pattern for variable names—for a variety of reasons:

- To distinguish variables from constants and intrinsic objects
- To provide a reminder of the type of data a variable contains

- To make the code easier to read, especially if someone else might be maintaining it in the future

Don't invent your own naming convention. Use one of the accepted methods. The simplest is to begin a descriptive name of a variable with a prefix, such as those in Table 9.1, that gives the data type.

> Being consistent with a naming convention is like sticking to your weekly exercise routine. If you keep it simple and manageable, you're more likely to succeed.

For example, the `strMessageClass` variable is used to hold the `MessageClass` property of a form, and it's a `String` variable. Therefore, its name is `str` & `MessageClass` or `strMessageClass`.

> Even though VBScript variables all use the `Variant` data type, giving them prefixes will help remind you when you are working with strings, when you expect a particular variable to contain numeric data, and so on.

Understanding Scope

The examples you have seen so far deal with variables only as they occur inside a particular procedure. Sometimes, though, you want variables to be in wider use.

For example, when you open an Outlook item, you might want to find out what folder the user is viewing and save that information to a variable another procedure might use later. Here is some VBScript that gets the current folder and saves it to a variable named `g_objMyFolder`.

```
Dim g_objMyFolder

Function Item_Open()
    Set objExplorer = Application.ActiveExplorer
    Set g_objMyFolder = objExplorer.CurrentFolder
End Function
```

By declaring the `g_objMyFolder` variable at the beginning of the script (before the first procedure), you make it a global variable, one that any other procedure in the script can use to obtain information about the folder or change it. I prefixed the variable name with `g_` to highlight that it's a global variable. This is another common naming convention.

The `ActiveExplorer` method is one of several techniques you will use in Hour 12, "Handling User Input and Feedback," to find out what Outlook folders and items the user is currently using.

In VBScript, all variables are either procedural or global. In VBA, an in-between option exists: You can also have module-level variables. Table 9.2 summarizes the scopes a variable can have.

TABLE 9.2 Variable Scope Definitions

Scope	VBA	VBScript	Description
Procedure	Yes	Yes	Available only within the current procedure. Declare with a `Dim` statement at the beginning of the procedure.
Module	Yes	No	Available only to procedures within the current module. Declare with a `Dim` or `Private` statement in the declarations section of the module.
Global	Yes	Yes	In VBA, available to procedures in any module in the Project Explorer. Declare with a `Public` statement in the declarations section of any module.
			In VBScript, available to any procedure in the script. Declare with a `Dim` statement at the beginning of the script.

You can use either `Dim` or `Private` to declare private scope variables in modules, but `Private` makes your intent perfectly clear.

Some VBA documentation uses the term *public module scope* instead of *global scope* or *private scope* instead of *module scope*. I think it's easier to think in terms of *global* versus *module*, than *public* versus *private*, especially if you are in the habit of using g_ and m_ as prefixes to denote the different scopes.

Scope also affects variable names. You cannot have a module-level variable named strMsg and also use a procedure variable with the same name. If you did, how would the program know which one you meant to use inside that procedure? However, you can repeat variable names, as long as the variables are local to the procedures in which they are used. For example, it's common to use variable names such as intAns and strAns across many procedures to hold the results from MsgBox() and InputBox() functions. This isn't a problem if you declare the variable as a local variable inside the procedure each time.

These two lines of code, placed in the declarations section of a module, declare a module-level Date variable, using a prefix of m_, and a global-level String variable:

```
Private m_dteLastVacationDay
Public g_strUserName
```

Why care about scope at all? For two main reasons: to make code run more efficiently and to keep two procedures from inadvertently changing the same variable.

The efficiency issue involves memory: The broader the scope, the longer the variable remains in memory. A variable is removed from memory when it goes out of scope, in other words, when all the code in the procedure or module has run and the variable is no longer needed.

The same scope concepts apply to procedures. In VBA, you can have Private procedures, available only in the current module (such as event handlers in form code modules) and Public procedures available to any other module. Use Private if you have an argumentless procedure that you do not want to appear in the macros list.

In general, you should use the tightest scope possible. Because you can use arguments to pass variables from one procedure to another (as you will see shortly), global and module variables should be the exception, not the rule.

Declaring Constants

Constants can have scope, too. You can have constants that are available only to a procedure's code, others that work in the current module, and still others that are global. You declare a constant with a Const, Private, or Public statement that also assigns its value.

Names for constants follow the same pattern as variable names, using con as a prefix for procedure constants, m_con for module constants, and g_con for global constants.

For procedure constants, place the Const statement after any Dim statements. For module constants in VBA, place the Const statement in the declarations section of the module, and use the optional `Private` or `Public` keyword to define the scope. For global constants in VBA, use a constant assignment statement with the Public keyword in the declarations section of the module. These are all examples of constant declaration statements:

```
Const conAttempts = 5
```

```
Private m_conCompanyName = "Slipstick Systems"
```

```
Public g_conVacationDays = 10
```

Notice that constants can hold any kind of data; they're not limited to just numbers.

Both VBA and VBScript support some intrinsic constants whose names begin with vb. The names of these built-in constants are easier to remember than their corresponding values. Table 9.3 lists many you're likely to use. You will see others in Hour 12, when I talk about message boxes.

TABLE 9.3   Key VBScript Intrinsic Constants

Constant	Value	Description
	Color Constants	
vbBlack	&h00	Black
vbRed	&hFF	Red
vbGreen	&hFF00	Green
vbYellow	&hFFFF	Yellow
vbBlue	&hFF0000	Blue
vbMagenta	&hFF00FF	Magenta
vbCyan	&hFFFF00	Cyan
vbWhite	&hFFFFFF	White
	Date Constants	
vbSunday	1	Sunday
vbMonday	2	Monday
vbTuesday	3	Tuesday
vbWednesday	4	Wednesday
vbThursday	5	Thursday
vbFriday	6	Friday
vbSaturday	7	Saturday

continues

TABLE 9.3 continued

Constant	Value	Description
Date Format Constants		
vbGeneralDate	0	Displays a date and/or time formatted according to your system settings
vbLongDate	1	Displays a date using your computer's long date format
vbShortDate	2	Displays a date using your computer's short date format
vbLongTime	3	Displays a time using your computer's long time format
vbShortTime	4	Displays a time using your computer's short time format
String Constants		
vbCr	Chr(13)	Carriage return
vbCrLf	Chr(13) & Chr(10)	Carriage return + linefeed
vbLf	Chr(10)	Line feed
vbNewLine or, on the Macintosh, Chr(13)	Chr(13) & Chr(10)	Platform-specific newline character
vbTab	Chr(9)	Horizontal tab

Color constant values listed in Table 9.3 with &h prefixes are long integers written in hexadecimal format.

In Outlook VBA code, you will often see constants that begin with ol. However, VBScript does not support these. In VBScript, you must either use the actual value of the constant or include constant declarations in your code. To make it easier to write and test code ported to VBScript from VBA, many Outlook programmers include key Outlook constants at the beginning of every script. You will look at this in more detail in a moment, under "Converting VBA Code to VBScript."

Coding Style

If you looked closely at some of the screen shots of the VBA code window in earlier lessons, you probably saw two style conventions that tend to make code easier to read:

- Keep statements together in blocks indented the same amount of space. (Press Tab at the beginning of a line to indent the default four characters.)

- Use an underscore (_) as a continuation character at the end of a line when the statement code would otherwise run off the screen. (For an example, see Listing 9.1 later in this lesson.)

> In the VBA code editor, to change the indent of a group of statements at one time, select the statements. Then, press Tab to increase the indent, or press Shift+Tab to decrease the indent.

The order in which procedures occur in a module doesn't really matter to VBA or VBScript, but it does matter to someone (you!) who's trying to understand the code. The drop-down list on the upper-right corner of the code window keeps track of procedures in alphabetical order. Within a module, you might want to keep them in order of importance: main procedure first and then subsidiary subroutines and functions.

In VBScript, you might want to put all event handlers for the Outlook form at the beginning, in alphabetical order, and then follow with user-named subroutines and functions.

At the beginning of this lesson, I promised that you could cut down on the amount of typing you do in the VBA code window if you declare all your variables. When you do this, as you use any object variable, VBA displays a list of members of that object class. Members include the events, methods, and properties—in other words, everything you might be able to do with or find out about an object.

You saw a small demonstration of this when you added Dim statements earlier; VBA helped you pick the right data or object type. It gets even better when you start using those object variables.

To see how this feature works, create a new VBA procedure, and add this code:

```
Dim objApp As Application
Dim objAppt As AppointmentItem
Set objApp = CreateObject("Outlook.Application")
```

On a new line, type **Set objAppt = objApp.** and then pause for a moment. After you type the period, you will see a list of all the methods, properties, and events for an Application object variable (see Figure 9.3).

FIGURE 9.3

The Auto List Members feature helps automatically complete your VBA code statements.

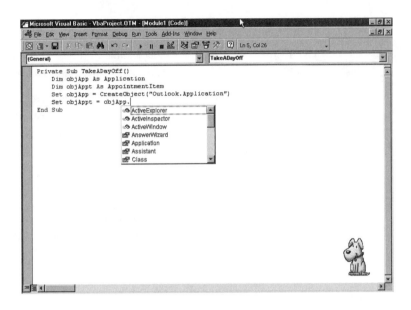

Type **cr**, and the members list jumps to CreateItem, which is the method you want for this example. Press Tab to paste **CreateItem** into the text of the statement. Then, type an open parenthesis. As soon as you type the parenthesis, VBA again pops up a list—this time one of appropriate intrinsic constants—as well as information on the CreateItem method and its parameters (see Figure 9.4).

FIGURE 9.4

The Auto Quick Info feature provides the syntax for functions, methods, and their parameters as you type in the code window.

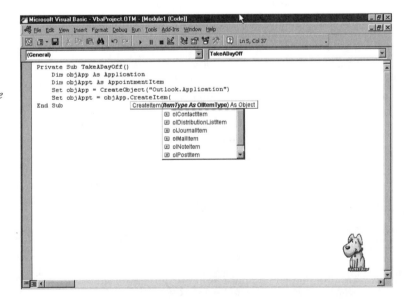

To finish the statement, press the down arrow key to select olAppointmentItem, press Tab to add it to the code window, and type a closing parenthesis. The code statement you entered looks like this:

```
Set objAppt = objApp.CreateItem(olAppointmentItem)
```

but all you typed was

```
Set objAppt = objApp.Cr[Tab]([Down Arrow])
```

That's 27 keystrokes using the Auto List Members feature (as it's called), versus 50 keystrokes to type the entire statement by hand. See, it really will save you lots of typing and prevent many mistakes!

Before leaving general style issues, I want to introduce one more concept that makes your code infinitely more readable when you work with object variables. You can use a With...End With code block to set properties and invoke methods on a single object. For example, if you have a ContactItem object variable named objContact (in other words, an Outlook Contact item), you can set the name and other properties and then save the item with a block of statements, like this:

```
With objContact
    .Name = "Sue Mosher"
    .Company = "Slipstick Systems"
    .BusinessAddressCity = "Moscow"
    .BusinessAddressCountry = "Russia"
    .Save
End With
```

You can even nest With ... End With blocks, as long as the inner block refers to an object that is a child of the object referred to with the outer block.

Calling Procedures

You've probably heard of programs that number thousands or millions of lines of code. All that code is not contained in just one procedure. Programs typically break down into many small chunks, each of which performs a certain role in the larger application.

To transfer control from one procedure to another, the program calls another procedure. A procedure that invokes another subroutine or function is the *calling procedure*, and the other procedure is the *called procedure*. Most functions and many subroutines have one or more arguments that pass a value, as either a variable or a literal, from one procedure to another.

User-defined functions are called the same as built-in functions, by giving the function name and then any arguments in parentheses.

Subroutines can be called with the subroutine name, followed by arguments separated by commas, or with the Call keyword and the arguments in parentheses. Both these statements call the same procedure:

```
MyProc arg1, arg2, arg3

Call MyProc(arg1, arg2, arg3)
```

Using the Call type of statement to call a subprocedure is less ambiguous and makes it easier to spot the points in your code where you branch to a different procedure.

When you call a subroutine, the code in the called procedure executes, and then control returns to the next line of the calling procedure. For example, in these two procedures,

```
Sub ProcOne()
    Dim intA as Integer
    intA = 10
    Call ProcTwo()
    intA = 10 * 10
End Sub

Sub ProcTwo()
    Dim intB as Integer
    intB = 20
    intB = 20 * 20
End Sub
```

the value of intA is set to 10. Then, ProcTwo executes and sets the value of intB. Finally, execution returns to ProcOne to change the value of intA once more.

Passing Arguments

One way in which VBA and VBScript differ is in how they handle a variable passed to another procedure through the called procedure's arguments. VBA's default is to pass the variable by reference. This means that the value of the original variable can be changed through the statements inside the called procedure. VBScript always passes variables by value, which means that the original variable remains unaltered, no matter what happens in the procedure to which it is passed.

This is a concept that's easier to see in action than read about. Listing 9.1 contains a demonstration you can add to a VBA module and run, to see for yourself what happens.

LISTING 9.1 ByVal Makes a Difference in How VBA Code Runs

```
Sub ByValDemo()
    Dim R As Integer, V As Integer
    R = 10
    V = 10
```

```
    Call ByRefSub(R, V)
    Debug.Print R, V
End Sub

Sub ByRefSub(X, ByVal Y)
    X = X + 20
    Y = Y + 20
End Sub
```

The code sets the value of both R and V to 10 and then calls the ByRefSub procedure, passing R by reference to the X argument and V by value to the Y argument. Because V is passed by value to the Y variable in the second procedure, the statement Y = Y + 20 has no effect on the value of V. However, the statement X = X + 20 not only changes X in the ByRefSub procedure, but also changes the value of R in the calling procedure to 30 because R was passed to the X variable by reference.

> Debug.Print is a convenient method for seeing the result of VBA code. It shows the data in columns in the Immediate window, which you can view by pressing Ctrl+G or choosing View, Immediate Window. Make sure, though, that you take Debug.Print statements out of your final code because they can slow down the program.

You could have used a ByRef keyword in the Sub ByRefSub() statement to make it perfectly clear that you're passing R by reference. However, because passing variables by reference is the default in VBA, you didn't have to.

Adding Data Types to Arguments and Functions

In VBA, you can improve the efficiency and consistency of your code by declaring the data type for the functions you create and for the arguments for both subroutines and functions. Use the same As data type syntax as you learned for Dim statements. For example, it's obvious from the data type declarations in this MailAddr() function that you have to supply an Outlook Contact and an integer as arguments.

```
Function MailAddr(obj As ContactItem, int As Integer) As String
    Select Case int
        Case 1
            strAddress = obj.Email1Address
        Case 2
            strAddress = obj.Email2Address
        Case 3
            strAddress = obj.Email3Address
    End Select
    MailAddr = strAddress
End Function
```

The function always returns a String value, corresponding to the first, second, or third e-mail address in the item (if there is one), or an empty string if you use a number other than 1, 2, or 3 for the int argument.

You don't declare data types for functions and arguments in VBScript because VBScript supports only the Variant data type. If you use data types in a Function statement in VBA, be sure to remove them if you copy the function to VBScript, as detailed in the next section.

Converting VBA Code to VBScript

If you have a procedure that works in VBA and you want to use it in an Outlook item's VBScript code, you should follow these basic steps:

1. Copy the VBA procedure code, and paste it into an Outlook form's script window.

2. Remove the As data type portion of any Dim declarations, function statements, and procedure arguments.

3. Remove any Dim variable As Application declaration.

4. Remove any statement that sets an Application object variable, such as

   ```
   Set objApp = CreateObject("Outlook.Application")
   ```

   This statement is not necessary because Application is an intrinsic object in Outlook form code.

> An alternative to steps 4–5 is to replace any Set objApp = CreateObject("Outlook.Application") statement with Set objApp = Application.

5. Change any reference to an Application object variable (such as objApp) to the Application intrinsic object.

6. If you used Outlook intrinsic constants, add Const statements at the beginning of the script to declare the constants you need. Use the same names as the VBA intrinsic constants to make your code more portable.

> To get the value of any intrinsic constant, in the VBA code editor, right-click the constant, and then choose Quick Info from the pop-up menu. You can also look up "Microsoft Outlook Constants" in Help or type ? followed by the name of the constant in the Immediate window and then press Enter.

7. Check all objects, methods, and properties to make sure that they are available in VBScript. The only way to know is to either read the help topics or try using the object, method or property and see what happens.

8. If the procedure was created as a VBA macro, attach it to an event handler in VBScript, such as the Click event for a command button.

Listing 9.2 is a VBA macro for creating a new Appointment item for a vacation day after the user answers a question. Listing 9.3 shows how the same procedure would look, running from a command button on an Outlook form.

LISTING 9.2   VBA Module Code Can Use Intrinsic Constants

```
Private Sub TakeADayOff
    Dim objApp As Application
    Dim objAppt As AppointmentItem
    Dim intAns As Integer
    Set objApp = CreateObject("Outlook.Application")
    intAns = MsgBox("Will you be gone all day?", _
                vbYesNo + vbQuestion, "Take a Day Off")
    Set objAppt = objApp.CreateItem(olAppointmentItem)
    If intAns = vbYes Then
        With objAppt
            .AllDayEvent = True
            .BusyStatus = olOutOfOffice
            .ReminderSet = False
        End With
    End If
    objAppt.Display
End Sub
```

LISTING 9.3   Declare Any Outlook Intrinsic Constants When You Port Code to VBScript

```
Const olAppointmentItem = 1
Const olOutOfOffice = 3

Sub cmdTakeADayOff_Click
    Dim objAppt
    Dim intAns
    intAns = MsgBox("Will you be gone all day?", _
                vbYesNo + vbQuestion, "Take a Day Off")
    Set objAppt = Application.CreateItem(olAppointmentItem)
    If intAns = vbYes Then
        With objAppt
```

continues

LISTING 9.3 continued

```
            .AllDayEvent = True
            .BusyStatus = olOutOfOffice
            .ReminderSet = False
        End With
    End If
    objAppt.Display
End Sub
```

You do not have to declare constants such as vbYes, vbYesNo, and vbQuestion, which are commonly used with the MsgBox() function, because VBScript supports these intrinsic Visual Basic constants. You will learn all about the MsgBox() function in Hour 12.

Summary

Knowledge of key code syntax elements such as variable and constant declarations, scope, and data types will enable you to write efficient and effective code. The VBA code window has several features that help automatically complete statements with a minimum of typing and a maximum of accuracy. When you've written all that beautiful code in VBA, you will be able to transfer it to the VBScript code window for an Outlook form in just a few simple steps.

In the next lesson, you turn to functions and expressions and, in the process, will build a nifty custom Outlook form to force users to pick at least one required category before they save an item.

Q&A

Q Will anything bad happen if I forget to declare a data type for a function or variable?

A The world won't end, but you will miss out on several important VBA features. You cannot take advantage of the Auto List Members feature to help you complete expressions by picking from a context-sensitive list. VBA cannot check for certain kinds of errors, such as passing a string to a function that requires a number. Finally, VBA cannot completely optimize your code when it compiles.

Q Are there other options in the VBA code editor that I need to know about?

A Choose Tools, Options to see all the available settings. The options on the Editor Format tab allow you to adjust the colors used for the code editor text.

Workshop

Work through the quiz questions and exercises so that you can understand Outlook programming better. See Appendix A for answers.

Quiz

1. If you write a function to return the number of days until (or since) the millennium, should that be a Public (global) or Private (module) procedure?

2. Does putting Option Explicit in the declarations section of one module make all your Outlook VBA modules require variable declarations?

Exercises

1. Devise variable names for the following:

   - A global variable storing information on whether an Outlook item is a newly created item

   - A procedure variable for the cost of your last meal

   - A module variable for the number of vacation days you have this year

2. Add the code in Listing 9.2 to a VBA module. Then, following the steps outlined in the section "Converting VBA Code to VBScript," create an Outlook form that performs the same operation from a command button.

Hour 10

Working with Expressions and Functions

Much of the work of programming involves performing calculations and updating variables with new values. The key tools for this work are expressions, built-in functions, and functions you create yourself. Outlook, like most programming environments, includes a variety of functions for manipulating dates and strings, as well as for doing math.

Highlights of this hour include

- How to tell variables and functions from literals
- Which functions extract and replace string parts
- How to add and subtract dates
- How to create a follow-up task for a certain number of days after a meeting
- How to replace one category with another

- How to use an array to fill a list box
- How to require the use of certain categories

I can't cover all of Outlook's functions in just one chapter—only those you're most likely to use. You can find out about others by reading the help topics.

Elements of an Expression

You have seen that many programming statements include a variable on the left side of an equals sign and terms on the right side that compose an expression. It may be a string value, a number, or a date, but the key concept is that an expression can be reduced to some finite value. A statement such as this

```
strPhoneNumber = "+1 (" & strAreaCode & ") " & strNumber
```

means "set the value of the `strPhoneNumber` variable equal to the expression on the right side of the equals sign." The expression itself consists of four terms joined by ampersand (&) string concatenation operators:

`"+1 ("`	String literal
`strAreaCode`	String variable
`") "`	String literal
`strNumber`	String variable

A phone number is a `String` because it contains characters as well as numbers.

Not all programming statements set a variable equal to an expression, of course. Some statements control program flow or set object variables.

A *literal value* is a specific value that doesn't change but is expressed in programming statements as the value itself, not as a programming constant. You must enclose string literals in quotation marks and date literals (which include time values) with number (#) signs. Here are more examples of literals:

```
"tomorrow"

#March 2, 2000#

#3/2/2000#

#10:00 a.m.#

3,298
```

The last item is a literal, too—a number literal. You do not have to enclose numbers with special characters when you use their literal values.

> The #3/2/2000# literal can actually mean two dates—March 2, 2000, or February 3, 2000—depending on the system settings found in the Control Panel, under Regional Settings.

10

The following are important uses for literals:

- As the arguments for a function, either built-in or user-defined
- In Outlook form VBScript code if you don't declare constants that are the equivalent of Outlook VBA intrinsic constants
- In code that validates the value of a field or control, comparing the field or control to a specific value

If you use the naming conventions introduced in Hour 9, "Code Grammar 101," you should have no problem distinguishing literals from variables and functions. Function names always end with parentheses, ( ), to hold arguments. Variable names and constants should follow the naming rules. String and date literals have their surrounding quotation marks and number signs, and number literals are, well, just numbers. You can combine functions, literals, variables, and constants in expressions.

Using Mathematical Expressions

You encountered the principle mathematical operators earlier in Hour 4, "Extending Form Design with a Custom Task Form." You do less math in Outlook programming than in some other applications because most of the time, you are manipulating Outlook items and working with text and dates.

When working with mathematical expressions, remember that mathematical expressions are evaluated from left to right. Also, if an expression contains more than one operator, the terms involving operators are evaluated in a particular sequence, according to the operator precedence order. However, you can control the order by adding parentheses to group terms.

Because VBScript allows only the Variant data type, you can't always be sure of what type of data a particular variable contains. Even if you give the variable a name that indicates it should contain numeric data, there could be something wrong with your code, or the variable could contain a value of Null. To avoid an error, you can perform a test first, using the built-in IsNumeric() function to find out whether the variable can be evaluated to a number:

```
If IsNumeric(intMyValue) Then
     code for math operations
Else
     MsgBox "intMyValue is not a number"
End If
```

> The presence of Null in any mathematical expression causes the entire expression to resolve to Null. For example, Null + 2 is not the same as 0 + 2. Null + 2 resolves to Null, not 2.

You might be puzzled by statements such as

```
D = D * 1.20
```

Why does the variable D appear on both sides of the equals sign? This statement updates the value of D by multiplying D by 1.20. If D equals 100, the new value of D after the statement runs is 120.

Working with Strings

A great deal of Outlook programming code is devoted to manipulating text, or more precisely, manipulating String variables—breaking them into parts and putting them back together. For example, if you have a variable named strPhoneNumber that contains a number using the standard pattern +xx (yyy) zzz-zzzz or (yyy) zzz-zzzz, this code extracts the area or city code from within the parentheses and assigns it to a new variable, strAreaCode:

```
intLeftPar = InStr(strPhoneNumber, "(")
intRightPar = InStr(intLeftPar, strPhoneNumber, ")")
strAreaCode = Mid(strPhoneNumber, intLeftPar + 1, _
  intRightPar - intLeftPar - 1)
```

Did you notice the string literals for the parenthesis characters?

Extracting String Parts

The preceding code uses two important string functions, `Instr()` and `Mid()`. `Instr()` finds the position of a single character or string within another string, and `Mid()` returns text from inside a string, starting at a particular position and continuing for a specific number of characters. Table 10.1 lists these and other essential string functions. The examples assume that `strPhoneNumber = "+1 (203) 456-7890"`.

TABLE 10.1 Functions to Extract String Parts

Function	Example	Evaluates To
`Left(string, length)`	`Left(strPhoneNumber,3)`	"+1 "
`Right(string, length)`	`Right(strPhoneNumber,8)`	"456-7890"
`Mid(string, start, length)`	`Mid(strPhoneNumber, 5, 3)`	"203"

Comparing Strings

Often you want to know whether one string is the same as another or is contained inside another. Table 10.2 lists three essential functions for comparing strings.

TABLE 10.2 Functions for Comparing Strings

Function	Example	Evaluates To
`InStr([start,] string1, string2[,compare])`	`InStr(3, "repeated","e")`	4
`InStrRev(string1, string2 [, start[,compare]])`	`InStrRev("repeated","e")`	7
`StrComp(string1, string2[, compare])`	`StrComp("ABCDE","AbCdE",1)`	0

`InStrRev()` works like `InStr()`, returning the position of the substring, only it starts looking from the end of `string1`, not the beginning. Its arguments are in a different order, too.

The `StrComp()` function returns these values:

If `string1` is less than `string2`	−1
If `string1` is equal to `string2`	0

If string1 is greater than string2   1

If string1 or string2 is Null   Null

Comparisons are case sensitive by default. To make string comparisons ignore uppercase and lowercase, set the optional compare argument to 1, as shown in the example for the StrComp() function.

> You can use the intrinsic constants vbTextCompare (= 1) and vbBinaryCompare (= 0) in functions that take a compare argument.

In VBA (but not VBScript), you can also set an entire module to use string comparison that is not case sensitive, by adding an Option Compare Text statement to the declarations section of the module. To use case-sensitive comparisons, add Option Compare Binary, which is the default if no Option Compare statement is present.

> Using text comparison, instead of binary comparison, can flatten the difference between letters in the standard English alphabet and letters from other languages that use diacritical marks. However, the result will depend on your Windows language settings, so you might have to experiment.

Replacing Parts of a String

You can replace part of a string with another in three basic ways:

- Break the string into substrings, change or substitute one or more substrings, and then join the substrings back together using the ampersand (&) concatenation operator.
- Use the Replace() function to create a new string that replaces part of the original string with another.
- In VBA but not VBScript, use the Mid statement to replace part of one string with another.

Let's go back to telephone numbers for some examples. Consider a situation in which your local area code, 717, is being split into 717 and 570. For a variable named strPhoneNumber containing the number in the standard format, using area and country code, these three lines return the updated number to a variable named strNewPhoneNumber by breaking out the country code and number and then concatenating them with the new area code—507—in the middle:

```
strCountryCode = Left(strPhoneNumber, 3)
strNumber = Right(strPhoneNumber, 8)
strNewPhoneNumber = strCountryCode & "(507) " & strNumber
```

The same operation performed with the Replace() function takes just one line of code:

```
strNewPhoneNumber = Replace(strPhoneNumber,"(717)","(507)")
```

> Replace() also supports optional start, count, and compare arguments to return only the portion of the string beginning at start, to make count replacements, and to set the comparison type, respectively, as with the InStr() function.

10

The final method is the Mid statement in VBA:

```
Mid(strPhoneNumber, 5) = "507"
```

> Don't confuse the Mid statement in VBA with the Mid() function, which works in both VBA and VBScript.

The basic syntax for Mid is Mid(*string*, *start*) = *substring*. It inserts the *substring* into the *string*, starting at the character in the *start* position. Although Mid works much like Replace(), it also differs significantly:

- You can't use the Mid statement in VBScript.
- Replace() allows you to replace a string that is x characters long with a string of a different length.
- Mid makes only one replacement, whereas Replace() can make multiple replacements within a string.
- Mid alters the original string variable, whereas Replace() leaves the original intact and returns a new value.

Other Useful String Functions

Not all string functions extract, compare, or combine text. Table 10.3 illustrates functions to fill a string with a particular character, return the length of a string, remove leading or trailing spaces, and change a string to uppercase or lowercase.

TABLE 10.3 Other Useful String Functions

Function	Example	Evaluates To
String(number, character)	String(4,"+")	"++++"
Space(number)	Space(10)	" "
Len(string)	Len("Microsoft Outlook")	17
Trim(string)	Trim(" sloppy text ")	"sloppy text"
LTrim(string)	LTrim(" sloppy text ")	"sloppy text "
RTrim(string)	RTrim(" sloppy text ")	" sloppy text"
UCase(string)	UCase("Microsoft Outlook")	"MICROSOFT OUTLOOK"
LCase(string)	LCase("Microsoft Outlook")	"microsoft outlook"

Working with Dates

Date manipulation skills are critical to Outlook programming because virtually every Outlook item has one or more important dates associated with it—the date an e-mail message was received, the due date for a task, a friend's birthday, the time of your appointment tomorrow, and so on. In this section, you will learn how to extract components from dates and perform date arithmetic. You will also briefly visit the issue of Year 2000 dates.

This section covers time issues, too, because the VBA Date data type and the Outlook Date/Time field type can contain both date and time data.

Extracting Date Components

Being able to extract components from dates means that you can find out whether Valentine's Day falls on a weekend or what journal entries you made on Monday. Table 10.4 lists functions you can use to obtain just the date or just the time portion of a date or extract any particular date component. Optional arguments are in brackets.

TABLE 10.4 Functions to Extract Date Parts

Function	Returns
Date	Current system date
DatePart(interval, date [, firstday [, firstweek])	Part specified by the interval string: "yyyy" Year "q" Quarter "m" Month "y" Day of the year "d" Day "w" Day of the week "ww" Week of the year "h" Hour "n" Minute "s" Second
DateValue(date)	Date component without any time value
Day(date)	Day of the year
Hour(time)	Hour of the day, from 0 to 23
Minute(time)	Minute of the hour, from 0 to 59
Month(date)	Month of the year, from 1 to 12
MonthName(month[, abbreviate])	Name of the month, given the number of the month
Now	Current system date and time
Second(time)	Second of the minute, from 0 to 59
Time	Current system time
Timer	Number of seconds since midnight
TimeValue(time)	Time component without any date value
Weekday(date[, firstdayofweek])	Number from 1 to 7 representing the day of the week, counting from firstdayofweek
WeekdayName(weekday[, abbreviate[, firstday]])	Name of the day, given its number

10

Unlike most other functions, the Date, Now, Time, and Timer functions do not use parentheses after the function name.

Here is an example of a function to check for weekend days. It evaluates to `True` if the `dteDate` argument falls on a Saturday or Sunday.

```
Function IsWeekend(dteDate)
    intWeekday = Weekday(dteDate, vbMonday)
    IsWeekend = (intWeekday >= 6)
End Function
```

The `IsWeekend` function uses the optional `firstday` parameter of the `DatePart()` function to set Monday as the first day of the week, using an intrinsic constant (`vbMonday`), so that Saturday is the sixth day of the week and Sunday the seventh. That makes it easy to test for Saturday or Sunday with the (`intWeekday >= 6`) expression, which evaluates to `True` or `False`.

A Custom Journal Form to Group by Date

Now for that question of what journal entries you made on Monday. You might have noticed that you can group items in Outlook views, but that there's no easy way to group everything you did on a particular date. You can sort by Start or any other date fields. However, because the date fields contain both date and time components, grouping by a date field usually produces just one item per group.

You can add grouping by date by creating a custom field to an Outlook Journal form and adding a few lines of code to the form. First, add a field named `DateNoTime` to a custom page, creating it as a Date/Time field. Then, use this code in the `Item_Write` event in the form's script:

```
Function Item_Write ()
Item.UserProperties.Find("DateNoTime") = DateValue(Item.Start)
End Function
```

Any new journal entries created with this form will have a `DateNoTime` field containing just the date portion of the `Start` date. You can then create a view grouping on these dates. I cover views in Hour 21, "Getting Started with Outlook Reports."

Performing Date Arithmetic

Date arithmetic involves calculating the time elapsed between two dates (or times) or adding time to a particular date to get a new date. Possible uses include

- Figuring the number of weeks since your last vacation day
- Calculating how long since you had any interaction with a contact
- Projecting the next date you should call a contact

Outlook stores dates in the same format as `Double` numbers: the integer portion representing the date and the decimal portion representing the time. This means that for the simplest sort of date arithmetic, you can just add the number of days. For example, `Now() + 3` is three days from the current date/time.

For more complicated calculations—such as the number of weeks between two dates or a date 13 months in the future—you use the `DateDiff()` and `DateAdd()` functions:

```
DateDiff(interval, date1, date2[, firstday, [,firstweek]])

DateAdd(interval, number, date)
```

The `interval` argument takes the same values as in the `DatePart()` function in Table 10.4. In the `DateAdd()` function, the `number` argument is the number of interval periods you want to add. It can be positive to get a date in the future or negative to get a date in the past.

`DateDiff()` returns a negative number if `date1` is later than `date2`. For example, `DateDiff("d", Date(), #1/1/2000#)` returns a positive number representing the number of days until the Year 2000 begins, or if you're already in the Year 2000, a negative number telling you the number of days since the year began.

The following function calculates the next business day that occurs `intAhead` days from `dteDate` by combining the `Weekday()` and `DateAdd()` functions and adding one or two days if the date falls on a weekend:

```
Function NextBusinessDay(dteDate, intAhead)
    dteNextDate = DateAdd("d", intAhead, dteDate)
    Select Case Weekday(dteNextDate)
        Case 1
            dteNextDate = dteNextDate + 1
        Case 7
            dteNextDate = dteNextDate + 2
    End Select
    NextBusinessDay = dteNextDate
End Function
```

> The `NextBusinessDay()` function is almost too easy! In Hour 15, "Working with Stores and Folders," you will enhance it by checking holidays and vacation days.

Year 2000 Issues

I can hardly overlook Year 2000 issues in this discussion of Outlook dates. Outlook 2000 is Y2K-compliant, so you really don't have much to worry about, as long as you use Date/Time fields and `Date` variables.

Whether the user sees two-digit or four-digit year numbers is another issue because it depends partially on the user's Windows settings, configured in the Control Panel's Regional Settings applet.

Using Functions

The NextBusinessDay() function is a good example of the kind of function you can create in Outlook and use over and over again. Let's finish this chapter on expressions and functions with a look at some of the finer points of using and creating functions.

User-defined functions help keep your code readable by breaking tasks down into manageable chunks. To help you see how this works, you will create a custom Outlook Appointment form with a button to create a follow-up task, based on an appointment's Start date and other information.

First, on a custom page, add a command button and name it cmdCreateFollowUpTask. Then, add the code in Listing 10.1 to the script for the form. This code calls the NextBusinessDay() function from inside the cmdCreateFollowUpTask_Click subroutine.

LISTING **10.1**   Incorporating a Function Makes It Easier to Follow the Code Logic

```
 1: Const olTaskItem = 3
 2:
 3: Sub cmdCreateFollowUpTask_Click()
 4:     Dim objTask
 5:     Set objTask = Application.CreateItem(olTaskItem)
 6:     With objTask
 7:         .StartDate = NextBusinessDay(Item.Start, 5)
 8:         .Subject = "Follow up"
 9:         .Body = "Follow up to appointment on " & _
10:                     FormatDateTime(Item.Start, vbLongDate) & _
11:                     vbCrLf & vbCrLf & "APPOINTMENT NOTES:" & _
12:                     vbCrLf & Item.Body
13:         .Display
14:     End With
15: End Sub
16:
17: Function NextBusinessDay(dteDate, intAhead)
18:     dteNextDate = DateAdd("d", intAhead, dteDate)
19:     Select Case Weekday(dteNextDate)
20:         Case 1
21:             dteNextDate = dteNextDate + 1
22:         Case 7
23:             dteNextDate = dteNextDate + 2
24:     End Select
```

```
25:      NextBusinessDay = dteNextDate
26: End Function
```

When the user clicks the cmdCreateFollowUpTask button, the code attached to the Click event for the button creates a new Task item five business days from the date of the appointment, copies information from the appointment to the task, and then displays the task for further modification.

Someone reading the code sees the With...End With block as a single set of logical steps, without any diversion into the details on how the NextBusinessDay() function works.

FormatDateTime() is a function that returns a string with the date or time in one of the user's system date and time formats.

Outlook items don't always use the same property for the same kind of information. Whereas the Appointment item has a Start property, the Task item has a StartDate property. However, the Body property always represents the large text box on the main page of any Outlook item.

To create other kinds of follow-up items from the same form, you could add more buttons and code for them. You could call the same NextBusinessDay() function from any button, passing it different arguments as needed. Writing frequently used routines like this as functions means you can reuse them whenever you need that particular calculation.

With more complex functions, you can use a feature called *named arguments* to make the calling code a little bit clearer. With named arguments, you can specify the arguments for a function in any order.

For example, you might have noticed that the InStr() and InStrRev() functions for searching inside one string for the presence of another use the same arguments, but in a different order. If you are accustomed to the order in InStr(), it's easy to make a mistake when using InStrRev(). You can avoid that kind of error if you specify the arguments by name. Get the names from the Auto Quick Info text that VBA pops up for each function. Then, use a colon followed by an equal sign (:=) to assign a value to each named argument—StringCheck, StringMatch, and Start in this example for InStrRev():

```
Sub NamedArgsDemo()
    Dim strLookIn As String
    Dim strLookFor As String
    Dim intFromRight As Integer
    strLookIn = "Able I was ere I saw Elba."
    strLookFor = "I"
    intFromRight = InStrRev(StringCheck:=strLookIn, _
                    StringMatch:=strLookFor, Start:=20)
    Debug.Print intFromRight
End Sub
```

Using `Split()`, `Join()`, and Arrays

I'd like to finish this chapter with two more string functions, `Split()` and `Join()`, to help introduce the topic of arrays. Use these functions to tinker with the Categories field on every Outlook item. Categories is a Keyword field; it consists of multiple string values separated by commas, which makes it a little more difficult to work with than a plain text string.

The comma that separates the individual categories is called a *delimiter*. The `Split()` and `Join()` functions are designed to make it easy to handle such a delimited list and its component substrings.

The full syntax for the `Split()` function is

```
Split(expression, delimiter, limit, compare)
```

where

`expression`	A delimited string expression
`delimiter`	(Optional) A single character; the default is the space character (" ")
`limit`	(Optional) The number of substrings to be returned; the default is −1, which means *return all*.
`compare`	(Optional) The comparison option, same as for `InStr()`

A statement such as

```
arr() = Split(objItem.Categories, ",")
```

returns an array. An *array* holds one or more values as separate elements. Refer to the elements of an array by subscript, starting with 0 for the first element. The first element in the array in Listing 10.2 would be `arr(0)`, the second `arr(1)`, and so forth.

> VBA allows you to create arrays that use 1 as the lowest subscript. However, because VBScript doesn't support this type of array, the examples in this book stick with 0 as the lowest subscript.

Join(), the opposite of Split(), uses this syntax:

```
Join(array, delimiter)
```

It returns a string consisting of the items in the array, separated by the delimiter character.

A Macro to Replace One Category with Another

Outlook does not include a feature to replace one category with another, but it's easy to build a macro to perform the replacement using these two functions. Take a look at the example in Listing 10.2.

LISTING 10.2   Use the Split() and Join() Functions to Work with Categories

```
 1: Sub ReplaceCat()
 2:     Dim objApp As Application
 3:     Dim objFolder As MAPIFolder
 4:     Dim objItem As Object
 5:     Dim arr() As String
 6:     Dim strOldCat As String
 7:     Dim strNewCat As String
 8:     Dim I As Integer
 9:     strOldCat = "Customer"
10:     strNewCat = "Client"
11:     Set objApp = CreateObject("Outlook.Application")
12:     Set objFolder = objApp.ActiveExplorer.CurrentFolder
13:     For Each objItem In objFolder.Items
14:         arr() = Split(objItem.Categories, ",")
15:         For I = 0 To UBound(arr)
16:             If arr(I) = strOldCat Then
17:                 arr(I) = strNewCat
18:                 Exit For
19:             End If
20:         Next
21:         objItem.Categories = Join(arr, ",")
22:         objItem.Save
23:     Next
24: End Sub
```

10

Lines 13–22 are the heart of the procedure. The `For Each...Next` loop gets each item in the current folder, uses the `Split()` function to convert the Categories field to an array, and then checks each element of the array to see whether it has to be updated. After the entire array has been checked, the `Join()` function reassembles the Categories for the item, which is then closed and saved.

> The `Exit For` statement inside the `If...End If` loop allows the program to go directly to refreshing the Categories field after it finds and updates the category value in the array. Because each category appears only once in the Categories field, after you find the category to be updated, it is not necessary to look at the other values in the array.

In this case, you don't even have to know how many categories each item has. The `For I = 0 To UBound(arr)...Next` loop cycles through all the elements of the array. `UBound()` is a function that returns the largest subscript for a particular array.

> In the next hour, you will look at `For...Next` loops, `If...End If` blocks, and other ways to control program flow.

The statement `If arr(I) = strOldCat Then` checks to see whether a given array element matches the old category (`strOldCat`). If it does, the routine changes that category to the new category with the statement `arr(I) = strNewCat`. Finally, the `objItem.Categories = Join(arr, ",")` statement puts the now updated elements of the array back into the Categories field. The default delimiter for `Join()` is the space character (`" "`); don't forget to specify the comma delimiter when working with the Categories field.

More on Arrays

An array requires a slightly different `Dim` statement. For a dynamic array such as the one in Listing 10.2—one that could be any size, depending on the number of Categories—use a `Dim` statement, following the variable name with empty parentheses, like this:

```
Dim arr() As String
```

The `As` data type keyword indicates the type of elements the array will contain. Later, use

```
ReDim arr(x)
```

to set or change the exact size of the array; x is not the number of elements but the upper bound of the array, the largest subscript. If you add the Preserve keyword, as in ReDim Preserve..., any existing data in the array is kept. Otherwise, a ReDim statement reinitializes the array, and any existing data is lost.

> You do not have to use a ReDim statement when you use the Join() function. The function redimensions the array automatically.

For fixed-dimension arrays, use

```
Dim arr(y)
```

You can also create multidimensional arrays. One convenient use of this type of array is to initialize List Box controls that contain data in more than one column. Here is the code used to initialize the cboCouples list box (Favorite Couples) that you saw in Figure 7.3 in Hour 7, "More on Controls."

```
Dim arrCouples(4, 2)
arrCouples(0, 0) = "Romeo"
arrCouples(0, 1) = "Juliet"
arrCouples(1, 0) = "Edward"
arrCouples(1, 1) = "Wallis"
arrCouples(2, 0) = "Robert"
arrCouples(2, 1) = "Sue"
arrCouples(3, 0) = "Dick"
arrCouples(3, 1) = "Linda"
cboCouples.List = arrCouples
```

It helps to think of two dimensional arrays, such as this one, as being similar to the tables that you might see in Access, Excel or Word. The first subscript corresponds to the number of the row, and the second subscript is analogous to the column number.

A Custom Contact Form with Required Categories

You know enough now about categories to create a really useful customized Contact form—one that makes you select one or more required categories before the item can be saved. To create the form, open a blank Contact form in design mode, and then follow these steps:

1. On the (P.2) page, add a List Box control named lstCategories.

2. On the Value tab of the list box's Properties dialog, set the bound field to Categories.

3. Rename the (P.2) page to Categories.

4. Place the code in Listing 10.3 in the code window for the form.

LISTING 10.3   VBScript Code for a Contact Form with Required Categories

```
 1: Dim g_strRequiredCats
 2:
 3: Function Item_Open()
 4:     g_strRequiredCats = "Prospect;Client;Former Client;Vendor"
 5:     Set objPage = _
 6:       Item.GetInspector.ModifiedFormPages("Categories")
 7:     Set objControl = objPage.Controls("lstCategories")
 8:     objControl.PossibleValues = g_strRequiredCats
 9: End Function
10:
11: Function Item_Write()
12:     If HasRequiredCategory() = False Then
13:         Item_Write = False
14:         Item.GetInspector.SetCurrentFormPage "Categories"
15:         Set objPage = _
16:           Item.GetInspector.ModifiedFormPages("Categories")
17:         Set objControl = objPage.Controls("lstCategories")
18:         objControl.SetFocus
19:     End If
20: End Function
21:
22: Function HasRequiredCategory()
23:     Set objPage = _
24:       Item.GetInspector.ModifiedFormPages("Categories")
25:     Set objControl = objPage.Controls("lstCategories")
26:     If g_strRequiredCats <> "" Then
27:         arrCats = Split(Item.Categories, ",")
28:         arrRequiredCats = Split(g_strRequiredCats, ";")
29:         For I = 0 To UBound(arrCats, 1)
30:             For J = 0 To UBound(arrRequiredCats, 1)
31:                 If arrCats(I) = arrRequiredCats(J) Then
32:                     blnMatch = True
33:                     Exit For
34:                 End If
35:             Next
36:             If blnMatch = True Then
37:                 Exit For
38:             End If
39:         Next
40:     Else
41:         blnMatch = True
42:     End If
43:     HasRequiredCategory = blnMatch
44: End Function
```

The Item_Open event (line 3) initializes the list box using a global String variable and the PossibleValues property of the control. If you want to use a different list of required categories, just change the String expression on the right side of line 4.

The Item_Write event (line 11) tests to see whether one of the required categories from the g_strRequiredCats variable was selected and, if not, moves the focus to the list box on the Categories page.

The test for a required category occurs in the HasRequiredCategory() function (line 22). It uses the Split() function twice to create two arrays—one of the user's existing category choices and one of the required categories—and then compares them.

The result is a form like that shown in Figure 10.1, which has been enhanced with a Label control to explain the list box.

FIGURE 10.1

To build a form that forces users to pick at least one required category, combine a list box with some array handling.

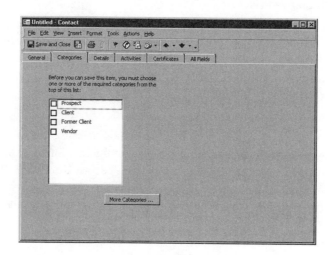

 The More Categories command button in Figure 10.1 was created by dragging the Categories... field from the All Contact Fields list in the Field Chooser and then changing its caption.

This form won't allow the user to save the item unless the Categories field contains at least one of the required categories.

Summary

With an arsenal of string and date functions, as well as functions to handle arrays, you are well equipped to start building routines to work with Outlook items. User-created functions enhance programs with reusable procedures that cut down the time necessary to build new applications.

In the next hour, you learn more about controlling the flow of a program and how to cycle through a group of items, such as all messages in your Inbox.

Q&A

Q Can you extract the area code from a phone number that doesn't follow a particular pattern?

A Not easily, if at all. That's why it's important to be consistent when you enter data. Outlook makes this easy with phone numbers by automatically formatting numbers in many counties into international format: +xx (yyy) zzz-zzzz where xx is the country code, yyy is the city or area code, and zzz-zzzz is the local number.

Q Why does 3/2/00 mean something different, depending on whether I'm working on a computer in London or Seattle?

A A "short" date such as 3/2/00 is ambiguous because not everyone interprets it the same way. North Americans use the first figure for the month, but to Europeans, that represents the day. Therefore, some people might see 3/2/00 as March 2, 2000, whereas to others, it's February 3, 2000. The Date/Time fields on Outlook forms interpret short dates according to the Regional Settings in the Control Panel. When a user enters a date in a text box on a VBA form, use the DateValue() function to convert it to a Date variable. You can then use the other date functions to break out any components you need.

Workshop

Work through the quiz questions and exercises so that you can better understand Outlook programming. See Appendix A for Answers.

Quiz

1. Can you extract the area code from a phone number that doesn't follow a particular pattern?

2. Did you really have to use the DateAdd() function to create the NextBusinessDay() function? If not, what would be the alternative?

3. If 0 is the lowest subscript for items in an array and the array contains 100 items, what is the value of the Ubound() for the array?

Exercises

1. Using the code in Listing 10.1 as a model, add another button to the customized Appointment form to create a follow-up meeting.

2. Create a VBA form with a text box for a category you want to replace, a text box for the replacement category, and a command button to perform the replacement. Adapt the code in Listing 10.2 to work with the form controls.

10

HOUR 11

Controlling Program Flow

It's hard to write code without running into issues of program flow. How do you get the program to perform a certain action under these conditions and a different action under other conditions? How do you work through all the items in a folder, examining each in turn? You've already looked at passing arguments from subroutine to subroutine as one way of controlling the flow of a program. You will learn several more methods in this lesson.

Highlights of this hour include

- How to use `If...Then...Else` statements to create branches in your program
- Why `Select Case` statements are essential to validating information in Outlook forms
- When to use `For Each...Next` versus `For...Next` loops
- How `GoTo` statements open the door to proper error handling

If...Then Statements

You have already seen several examples of `If...Then` statements in earlier lessons. The basic syntax is simple:

```
If expression Then
    code to perform actions
End If
```

The expression in the `If...Then` statement must evaluate to `True` or `False`. These are good examples of such expressions:

```
IsNumeric(txtDays.Value)

InStr(strSubject, "Birthday") > 0

strAddress <> ""

intDoIt = vbYes
```

> The intrinsic constant `vbYes` is used with message boxes, as you will see in the next hour.

Typically, the `If...Then` expression will be either a function that returns either `True` or `False` or an expression using one of the comparison operators you encountered in Hour 4, "Extending Form Design with a Custom Task Form."

You can also have a more complex expression involving more than one condition linked with the comparison operators `And`, `Or`, or `Not`, such as this one from the ReminderUpdate form in Hour 7, "More on Controls":

```
If InStr(strSubject, "Birthday") > 0 And _
  chkBirthdays.Value Then
```

Why didn't the above expression use `chkBirthdays.Value = True`? Because that would be redundant. Assuming that chkBirthdays represents a normal checkbox control, its `Value` property always evaluates to either `True` or `False`. You don't need to write chkBirthdays.Value = True; just chkBirthdays.Value is sufficient.

After the `If...Then` statement, you must supply one or more statements that you want the program to run if the expression is `True`. If you have only one statement to run, you can include it with the `If...Then` statement on a single line:

```
If D > 10 Then D = D * 1.20
```

Notice that you leave out the End If when you create an If...Then statement on a single line.

The single-line format works only for the simplest of If...Then statements. Most of the time, you have more than one code statement to execute and, therefore, must place each statement on a separate line after the If...Then statement and end the block with an End If statement. This example of an If...End If block tests whether a given Outlook item is a Contact and, if it is, assigns values to two String variables for the parent folder's StoreID and the item's EntryID.

```
If objItem.Class = olContact Then
    Set objFolder = objItem.Parent
    strStoreID = objFolder.StoreID
    strItemID = objItem.EntryID
End If
```

The StoreID of an Outlook folder and EntryID of an Outlook item can be used with the GetFolderFromID and GetItemFromID methods of the NameSpace object to retrieve a folder or item.

You can nest If...Then statement blocks inside each other, as in this example to manage the foreground and background colors for a Text Box control named txtOldCategory:

```
If txtOldCategory.ForeColor = vbRed Then
    If txtOldCategory.BackColor = vbRed Then
        txtOldCategory.BackColor = vbBlack
    End If
End If
```

VBA and VBScript provide constants, such as vbRed and vbBlack, for eight commonly used colors.

Too many levels of nesting make If...End If blocks very difficult to read and debug, especially when you start nesting them with other kinds of program control statements. All it takes is one extra or one missing End If to make your procedure stop dead in its tracks. When you find it necessary to use nested If...End If blocks, take extra care to indent all the statements within each block to make them look consistent.

A common variation on If...Then expressions adds an Else block so that you perform one set of actions if the expression is True and a second set if the expression is False.

Expanding on the earlier code to manage the foreground and background colors in a txtOldCategory control, you might have

```
If txtOldCategory.ForeColor = vbRed Then
    If txtOldCategory.BackColor = vbRed Then
        txtOldCategory.BackColor = vbBlack
    End If
Else
    txtOldCategory.BackColor = vbYellow
End If
```

A less common variation uses ElseIf to test for another condition. In fact, you can add several ElseIf statements, as shown in Listing 11.1.

LISTING 11.1 ElseIf Statements Provide More Complex Branching

```
1: If txtOldCategory.ForeColor = vbRed Then
2:      If txtOldCategory.BackColor = vbRed Then
3:          txtOldCategory.BackColor = vbBlack
4:      End If
5: ElseIf txtOldCategory.Forecolor = vbWhite Then
6:      txtOldCategory.BackColor = vbBlack
7: ElseIf txtOldCategory.Forecolor = vbBlue Then
8:      txtOldCategory.BackColor = vbWhite
9: End If
```

The logic in If...Then... ElseIf statements often is difficult to follow. A more readable way to accomplish the same result is to use a Select Case statement, which I cover in the next section.

If...End If blocks sometimes offer clues to where your code can be simplified. Take, for example, this code from Listing 7.1 in Hour 7:

```
If InStr(strSubject, "Birthday") > 0 And _
  chkBirthdays.Value Then
    objItem.ReminderSet = True
    objItem.ReminderMinutesBeforeStart = _
      24 * 60 * txtDays.Value
    objItem.Save
End If
If InStr(strSubject, "Anniversary") > 0 And _
  chkAnniversaries.Value Then
    objItem.ReminderSet = True
    objItem.ReminderMinutesBeforeStart = _
      24 * 60 * txtDays.Value
    objItem.Save
End If
```

Each If...End If block contains the same three objItem. statements. You can simplify the code by using the original If...End If blocks to set a Boolean variable, blnUpdate, that indicates whether to proceed with the update. Then, you add a third If...End If block to perform the actual update, only if blnUpdate is True:

```
If InStr(strSubject, "Birthday") > 0 And _
  chkBirthdays.Value = True Then
    blnUpdate = True
End If
If InStr(strSubject, "Anniversary") > 0 And _
  chkAnniversaries.Value = True Then
    blnUpdate = True
End If
If blnDoUpdate = True Then
    With objItem
        .ReminderSet = True
        .ReminderMinutesBeforeStart = _
            24 * 60 * txtDays.Value
        .Save
    End With
End If
```

This version is about the same length as the preceding code, but much easier to maintain. If you later decide to change the statements updating the item's reminder settings, you have to make the changes in only one location, in the If blnDoUpdate = True Then...End If block, not in two separate If...End If blocks.

> Did you notice that I also streamlined the new version by adding a With...End With block?

Select Case Statements

The next program flow control tool is the Select Case statement. Use this when you want to test a particular variable or property that could have several values, not just True or False. On Outlook forms, the Select Case statement is essential to event handlers for the PropertyChange and CustomPropertyChange events.

The syntax of Select Case looks like this:

```
Select Case expression
    Case value1
        code to perform actions
    Case value2
        code to perform actions
    Case value3
        code to perform actions
    ...
```

```
Case Else
        code to perform actions
End Select
```

The expression in a Select Case statement can be a variable, an object property, or a more complex expression. value1, value2, value3, and so on are possible values that expression might take. Because you can't always anticipate every possible value, the optional Case Else statement provides a way to handle exceptions to the known values. If you don't include Case Else and the expression does not match any of the given Case values, program control moves directly to the statement following End Select.

The code in Listing 11.1 uses too many ElseIf statements to be readable. However, if you transform it to a Select Case block, it is very easy to follow:

```
Select Case txtOldCategory.ForeColor
    Case vbRed
        If txtOldCategory.BackColor = vbRed Then
            txtOldCategory.BackColor = vbBlack
        End If
    Case vbWhite
        txtOldCategory.BackColor = vbBlack
    Case vbBlue
        txtOldCategory.BackColor = vbWhite
End Select
```

Notice that you can nest If...End If blocks inside Case blocks. The reverse is also true; you can nest a Select Case block inside an If...End If block. Be careful, though, to get the ending statements in the correct order. This example would trigger a compile error because the End Select statement appears before the End If of the nested If...End If block.

```
Select Case expression1
    Case value1
        your code here
    Case value2
        If expression2 Then
            your code here
End Select
End If
```

As noted earlier, Select Case is essential to event handlers for the PropertyChange and CustomPropertyChange events on Outlook forms, where you don't have BeforeUpdate and AfterUpdate events on controls. To see how this works, open a new Outlook Task item in design mode, display the code window, and insert an event handler for the PropertyChange event. Outlook pastes a

```
Sub Item_PropertyChange(ByVal Name)
```

statement into your code. Name is the expression you use in the Select Case statement. Add the following code, which reacts specifically to changes in the DueDate and Complete properties and also includes a generic property change handler under Case Else.

```
Sub Item_PropertyChange(ByVal Name)
    Select Case Name
        Case "DueDate"
            If DateDiff("w", Now, Item.DueDate) > 3 Then
                MsgBox "You shouldn't plan more than" _
                  & "3 weeks ahead."
            End If
        Case "Complete"
            If Item.Complete = True Then
                MsgBox "Congratulations! You finished this task!"
            End If
        Case Else
            MsgBox "You changed the " & Name & "property."
    End Select
End Sub
```

Run this form, and try changing values in different fields. You should find out several very interesting things about the PropertyChange event:

- The PropertyChange event fires not just for changes the user makes, but also when properties change because of actions that Outlook takes automatically.

- A change made to one property can cause a cascade of changes to several other properties. For example, changing the Status to Completed causes changes in the ReminderSet, PercentComplete, DateCompleted, Complete, and Status fields.

- Not all properties support the PropertyChange event. When you type in the large text box on the Task page, you are changing the Body property. However, you won't see a pop up You changed the Body property. message, not even when you press Tab to move the focus off that control.

Another important observation is that the Case statements for the PropertyChange event routine require you to supply the property names as string literals. However, if you want to access the property values themselves, you must use the familiar Item.property syntax.

> An event handler for the PropertyChange event provides one way to validate data entry on an Outlook form—immediately after the user makes a change to a property. Another validation method is to include code in the Item_Write event function to check values and use the statement Item_Write = False to cancel the write operation and allow the user to correct the error.

11

An event handler for the `CustomPropertyChange` event looks much the same. If you did exercise 2 in Hour 4, you have a custom Contact form with a formula field calculating the number of e-mail addresses for an item. If the name of that custom field is `NumAddresses`, you can add a `CustomPropertyChange` event handler to the form by using this code:

```
Sub Item_CustomPropertyChange(ByVal Name)
    Select Case Name
        Case "NumAddresses"
            Set objProperty = Item.UserProperties.Find(Name)
            MsgBox "This contact has " & objProperty.Value _
              " addresses."
        Case Else
            MsgBox "You changed the " & Name & "property."
    End Select
End Sub
```

With this event handler in place, you should see a message pop up each time you add a new e-mail address to this custom form. For changes to other custom fields, you see a message telling you that you changed a property.

 VBA supports a couple of refinements to `Case` statements, such as `Case expression1 To expression2` to specify a range of values and the `Case Is comparisonoperator` expression to allow the use of comparison operators in a `Case` statement. These are not available in VBScript.

Do Loops

The next program flow tool is the venerable `Do` loop. The basic principle of a `Do` loop is that it continues to run a series of statements until a certain condition is met. Here are several variations:

```
Do Until expression1
    code block 1
Loop

Do While expression2
    code block 2
Loop

Do
    code block 3
Loop While expression3
```

```
Do
    code block 4
Loop Until expression4
```

The first example repeats the statements in code block 1 until expression1 returns True. The second example repeats the statements in code block 2 as long as expression2 remains True. The third example runs once, but repeats only if expression3 is still True. Similarly, the fourth example runs once and keeps looping until expression4 returns True.

Use a Do loop when you don't know how many times a block of statements should run. If you want the loop to run at least once, consider using the syntax in the preceding third and fourth examples. If you can't be sure whether the loop will have to run at least once, the first or second version might be more appropriate.

Think through the logic of your Do loops carefully, and make sure that it includes a way for the procedure to exit the loop. Otherwise, the routine might find itself in an infinite loop.

If you run VBA code that you suspect is trapped in an infinite loop, press Esc or Ctrl+Break to break out of the routine.

Here is a practical example of a Do loop to remove all the controls from a custom "Project" page in the currently displayed Outlook form:

```
Sub CleanControls()
    Dim objApp As Application
    Dim objInspector As Inspector
    Dim objPage As Object
    Set objApp = CreateObject("Outlook.Application")
    Set objInspector = objApp.ActiveInspector
    Set objPage = objInspector.ModifiedFormPages("Project")
    If Not objPage Is Nothing Then
        Do While objPage.Controls.Count > 0
            objPage.Controls.Remove 0
        Loop
    End If
End Sub
```

This Do loop repeats as long as there are any controls on the page.

In addition to the Until expression or While expression keywords that control when looping stops, you might want to provide an additional test that causes the routine to exit the loop. For example, if you want to limit the operation to a particular amount of time, you can use the Timer function, which returns an Integer value representing the number of seconds elapsed since midnight. This code stops the loop after 60 seconds pass:

```
intStart = Timer
Do While X > Y
     your code that might take
       a long time to execute
       runs here
     If Timer - intStart > 60 Then
         Exit Do
     End If
Loop
```

Because the Timer function resets to 0 each day at midnight, if a procedure using Timer runs just before midnight, the results will not be what you expect.

For...Next Loops

You have already seen quite a few examples of For...Next loops. These loops cycle through either a known quantity of items or all the items within a set.

One type of For...Next loop continues until a particular number of iterations has occurred. Its syntax looks like this:

```
For I = intstart To intend
     your code runs here
Next
```

This type of For statement requires three elements:

- An Integer variable to hold the current value of the iteration; I is a customary choice.

- An Integer expression, intstart, that represents the starting value for I.

- An Integer expression, intend, that represents the ending value for I.

Both intstart and intend can be literal integers or any expression that evaluates to an integer. You saw an example in the last lesson, when you used a For...Next loop in Listing 10.2 to fill a list box from the values in an array. The For statement looked like this:

```
For I = 0 To UBound(arr)
```

because the subscripts for the `arr` array start with 0 and end with `Ubound(arr)`.

Handling Multi-Select List Boxes

The code inside a `For...Next` loop typically does something with the `I` counter value. For example, if you have a multi-select list box, you must check the `Selected` property of each item in the list to learn whether the user has chosen it. This code displays each selected item in a message box:

```
For I = 0 To (lstMyListBox.ListCount - 1)
    If lstMyListBox.Selected(I) = True Then
        MsgBox lstMyListBox.List(I)
    End If
Next
```

A loop for a list box named `lstBox` should begin with the statement

```
For I = 0 to (lstBox.ListCount - 1)
```

because the index number for items in the list box begins with 0. The syntax for getting a particular item from the list box is `lstBox.List(index)`.

A Custom Contact Form to Display All E-mail Addresses

Listing 11.2 is a practical example of a For...Next loop that puts the underlying e-mail addresses for an Outlook contact into a list box on a custom page. To make it work, create a list box named `lstAddresses` on the P.2 page of a Contact form in design mode. Then, add the code in Listing 11.2 to the form's code window.

LISTING 11.2   Obtain the Underlying E-mail Addresses in an Outlook Contact

```
1: Option Explicit
2:
3: Sub cmdShowAllAddresses_Click()
4:     Dim objPage
5:     Dim lstAddresses
6:     Dim strAddress
7:     Dim I
8:     Set objPage = Item.GetInspector.ModifiedFormPages("P.2")
9:     Set lstAddresses = objPage.Controls("lstAddresses")
10:    Call EmptyListBox(lstAddresses)
11:    For I = 1 To 3
12:        strAddress = OneAddress(Item, I)
13:        If strAddress <> "" Then
14:            lstAddresses.AddItem(strAddress)
```

continues

LISTING 11.2   continued

```
15:           End If
16:       Next
17: End Sub
18:
19: Sub EmptyListBox(objControl)
20:     Do Until objControl.ListCount = 0
21:         objControl.RemoveItem (0)
22:     Loop
23: End Sub
24:
25: Function OneAddress(objItem, intWhichAddress)
26:     Dim strAddress
27:     Select Case intWhichAddress
28:         Case 1
29:             strAddress = objItem.Email1Address
30:         Case 2
31:             strAddress = objItem.Email2Address
32:         Case 3
33:             strAddress = objItem.Email3Address
34:     End Select
35:     OneAddress = strAddress
36: End Function
```

The For...Next loop (lines 11–16) passes the value of I to a OneAddress function that returns one of the three e-mail addresses for the item. This routine lends itself well to a For...Next loop because you know that any Contact item contains, at most, three e-mail addresses—in the Email1Address, Email2Address, and Email3Address fields.

> Did you notice the Do loop in lines 19–23 of the generic EmptyListBox subroutine to remove all the items in a list box so that it can be refilled?

For Each...Next Loops for Collections

The other type of For...Next loop works with collection objects. A *collection* is an object that itself contains a set of other objects of a particular type. For example, each Outlook MAPIFolder object has an Items property that comprises the collection of all items in a folder. It also has a Folders property — a collection of all subfolders. Collection objects typically have a Count property, just as listboxes do, but you can work with them more efficiently by using this type of For...Next loop:

```
For Each object In collection
    your code runs here
Next
```

If, for example, you want to change one or more properties for all items in a folder, you use a For Each...Next loop to get each item in turn, alter the property, and then save the item. Listing 11.3 is a generic routine for working with the properties of items in the currently displayed Outlook folder.

LISTING 11.3   Use This Generic Code to Work with Item Properties in the Current Outlook Folder

```
 1: Private Sub WorkWithCurrentFolderItems()
 2:      Dim objApp As Application
 3:      Dim objItem As Object
 4:      Set objApp = CreateObject("Outlook.Application")
 5:      Set objFolder = objApp.ActiveExplorer.CurrentFolder
 6:      For Each objItem In objFolder.Items
 7:          With objItem
 8:              .property1 = newvalue1
 9:              .property2 = newvalue2
10:              more property changes
11:              .Save
12:          End With
13:      Next
14: End Sub
```

The WorkWithCurrentFolderItems procedure performs this sequence of operations:

1. Get the currently displayed folder (line 5).

2. Get the first item in the folder (lines 6–7).

3. Change some properties on the item (lines 8–10).

4. Save the item (line 11).

5. Repeat with the next item in the folder until all items have been used (line 13).

> If you have not already started building a library of generic VBA code modules, now is a good time to begin. Create a module named Generic, and then add the procedure in Listing 11.3. The next time you have to work with the properties of items in a folder, just make a copy of the WorkWithCurrentFolderItems procedure, change the name of the procedure, and update lines in the With objItem...End With block to set the item properties for your specific application.

11

At the end of a `For Each...Next` loop, you might want to report back to the user on the operations performed on the items in the collection. One way is to increment a variable each time an operation occurs.

For example, this code is based on the `For Each...Next` loop in the `ReplaceCat` subroutine in Listing 10.2 from Hour 10, "Working with Expressions and Functions." It has been updated to add an `intCount` variable to keep track of how many items were changed and to open a message box with the result at the end. (Note that this code also illustrates both types of `For...Next` loops!)

```
intCount = 0
For Each objItem In objFolder.Items
    arr() = Split(objItem.Categories, ",")
    For I = 0 To UBound(arr)
        If arr(I) = strOldCat Then
            arr(I) = strNewCat
            intCount = intCount + 1
            Exit For
        End If
    Next
    objItem.Categories = Join(arr, ",")
    objItem.Save
Next
MsgBox intCount & " items were changed."
```

The statement

```
intCount = intCount + 1
```

is a typical statement for keeping a running count. It takes the current value of `intCount`, adds one, and returns the incremented value to the `intCount` variable. Because it resides within the `If...End If` loop, the statement updates `intCount` only when a match is found for the category you want to replace.

The `Exit For` statement that follows works like the `Exit Do` statement you saw earlier for `Do` loops. It terminates the `For I = 0 To UBound(arr)...Next` loop after a matching value has been found in the array. Note that it terminates only the one `For I...Next` loop. The `For Each...Next` loop in which it is nested continues to operate until all items in the folder have been processed.

GoTo Statements

The last program flow technique in this lesson is the `GoTo` statement, which applies only to VBA and is used primarily for error handling. A `GoTo` statement works in conjunction with labels that set off subsections in your subroutines. Here's an example:

```
Sub GoToDemo()
    Dim intAns
    On Error GoTo Err_Handler
    intAns = MsgBox("Do you want to simulate an error?", vbYesNo)
    If intAns = vbYes Then Err.Raise 1
    MsgBox "No error occurred."
    Exit Sub
Err_Handler:
    MsgBox "Error Number " & Err & " occurred."
End Sub
```

The statement On Error GoTo Err_Handler tells the routine to branch to the section labeled Err_Handler: whenever it encounters an error. Program flow continues with the statements in the Err_Handler section, until the end of the subroutine.

An Exit Sub statement is placed before the Err_Handler: label so that, if no error has occurred, the program exits from the subroutine before running the statements in the Err_Handler: section.

Err.Raise is a method for simulating an error so that you can find out what your program will do when an error occurs.

You will look in detail at error handling and debugging in Hour 19, "Debugging Applications."

11

You could also use GoTo statements by themselves to branch from one portion of a procedure to another section. However, the other program flow methods you've studied in this lesson produce much clearer code. The GoTo statement, therefore, is pretty much relegated to use just in error handling in VBA.

Summary

In this hour, you have picked up a variety of ways to control the way your program flows within a particular subroutine or function. Along the way, you also learned how to deal with selected items in multi-select list boxes and how to work with collections, such as all Outlook items in a folder.

The next lesson concludes this section on general coding techniques, with methods for getting information from the user.

Q&A

Q **Will Outlook alert me if I leave out the required ending statement for a program control block?**

A In VBA, you can choose Debug, Compile at any time to check your code by compiling it. You will get an error message if any End If, End Select, Loop, or Next statement is missing.

Q **Why is a For Each...Next loop better than a For I = 1 to objFolder.Items.Count loop for working with all the items in a folder?**

A When you use a For Each...Next loop, you don't have to go through the extra steps of getting the count of items and using a Set objItem = ... statement to get the actual item.

Workshop

Work through the quiz questions and exercises so that you can better understand Outlook programming. See Appendix A for Answers.

Quiz

1. What are the advantages of using a For...Next loop in the cmdShowAllAddresses_Click subroutine in Listing 11.2 to get the three e-mail addresses for the Contact item?

2. Of the different program control methods you studied in this hour, which two have a built-in mechanism to handle exceptions?

Exercises

1. Use code for the PropertyChange event on a Contact form to find out what other properties change when you update a person's first name.

2. Write a subroutine to get all the items in the Tasks folder. For any items with due dates, set the date one day later. Can you reverse the process to make the due date one day earlier?

HOUR 12

Handling User Input and Feedback

This lesson deals with the practical matters of giving the user choices and receiving other input from the user. You will go beyond simple data entry to discover what Outlook items and folders the user is currently working with—an important first step to running macros that operate on such items.

Highlights of this hour include

- How to pop up a dialog from which the user can select any Outlook folder
- What are the mysterious `Inspector` and `Explorer` objects that operate within Outlook
- How to know what Outlook items and folders are currently displayed
- When to use message boxes, input boxes, and VBA dialogs to get information from the user

Accessing a Particular Folder

In the preceding lesson, you saw how a `For Each...Next` loop makes it easy to work with all the items in a particular folder. But first you need the folder object! That's your job in this section—finding out how to obtain a particular folder. You will look at methods to access the default folders (such as Inbox and Calendar), the folder the user is currently working with, and any particular Outlook folder the user might choose.

Getting a Default Folder

These nine default folders are always present:

- Calendar
- Contacts
- Deleted Items
- Drafts
- Inbox
- Journal
- Notes
- Outbox
- Sent Items
- Tasks

It's simple to get any of these default folders using the `GetDefaultFolder` method of the `NameSpace` object. Here's how to set an object variable named `objCalendar` to the Calendar folder:

```
Dim objApp As Application
Dim objNS As NameSpace
Dim objCalendar As MAPIFolder
Set objApp = CreateObject("Outlook.Application")
Set objNS = objApp.GetNamespace("MAPI")
Set objCalendar = objNS.GetDefaultFolder(olFolderCalendar)
```

Remember that folders are objects in Outlook. Declare folder object variables as the `MAPIFolder` type. Then, set the folder object variable to a particular folder, using the `GetDefaultFolder` method.

The `NameSpace` object itself represents the message store—either a Personal Folders file or an Exchange Server mailbox. But you don't have to worry about what it means. Just learn to use its methods and properties.

The single argument for GetDefaultFolder is an intrinsic constant; possible values are shown in Table 12.1. When you use GetDefaultFolder in VBScript, you must either include a Const declaration to initialize the appropriate constant or use the literal value.

TABLE 12.1 Intrinsic Constants for Default Folders

Folder	Constant	Value
Calendar	olFolderCalendar	9
Contacts	olFolderContacts	10
Deleted Items	olFolderDeletedItems	3
Drafts	olFolderDrafts	16
Inbox	olFolderInbox	6
Journal	olFolderJournal	11
Notes	olFolderNotes	12
Outbox	olFolderOutbox	4
Sent Items	olFolderSentMail	5
Tasks	olFolderTasks	13

Getting the Current Folder

Outlook includes Explorer objects that represent the Outlook windows the user has open. Because you can have more than one Outlook window open, more than one Explorer object may be available.

To access the folder window the user is currently using, use the ActiveExplorer method of the Application object. To get the folder displayed in the window, use the CurrentFolder property of the Explorer, as in this example:

```
Dim objApp As Application
Dim objCurrentFolder As MAPIFolder
Set objApp = CreateObject("Outlook.Application")
Set objCurrentFolder = objApp.ActiveExplorer.CurrentFolder
```

You don't necessarily have to use a separate object variable for the Explorer object. In this case, you can simply use objApp.ActiveExplorer.CurrentFolder to get the folder that the Explorer displays.

12

Don't assume that the `ActiveExplorer` method always returns an actual window displaying a folder. If the user has not yet started Outlook, but uses a mailto: link from a Web page to create a new message, a new message item is displayed, but no folder window is visible.

Also, remember that the user can switch folders unless a modal dialog box is active. This means that you should use the `ActiveExplorer` method carefully. For example, if you want to know the folder from which the user opened an item, use the `ActiveExplorer` method in the `Item_Open` event of the item. Don't wait and try to get it in a later procedure; the user might have switched folders by then.

For additional folder access techniques, such as locating a folder in someone else's mailbox, in one of several available folder windows, or within the Public Folder tree hierarchy on Exchange Server, see Hour 15, "Working with Stores and Folders."

Using the `PickFolder` Method

You've seen how to get any Outlook default folder or the currently displayed folder. You can also allow the user to choose from any folder in the Outlook hierarchy using the `PickFolder` method of the `NameSpace` object. A typical application looks like this:

```
Dim objApp As Application
Dim objNS As NameSpace
Dim objFolder As MAPIFolder
Set objApp = CreateObject("Outlook.Application")
Set objNS = objApp.GetNamespace("MAPI")
Set objFolder = objNS.PickFolder
If Not objFolder Is Nothing Then
    code to do something with the folder
End If
```

When this code runs, it pops up the Select Folder dialog, shown in Figure 12.1, where the user can create a new folder or select a folder. Select Folder is a *modal* dialog, which means that code execution stops until the user clicks OK or Cancel.

Because the user can click Cancel, code using the `PickFolder` method must handle the possibility of the user choosing no folder at all. The expression

```
Not objFolder Is Nothing
```

returns `True` if a folder was selected or `False` if the user clicked Cancel. `Nothing` is a keyword with a special meaning—the object variable is currently set to no particular object.

FIGURE 12.1

Use the PickFolder *method to pop up this dialog.*

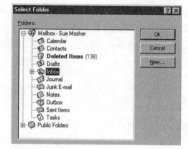

Accessing a Particular Item

When writing VBScript on an Outlook form, you can use an intrinsic Item object to refer to the current item. However, when coding in VBA, you must know how to get a particular item the user wants to work with. Looping through a folder and getting each item in turn, as you did in the preceding lesson, is one approach. Other methods for getting a single item are to work with the current item window and with the user's selection in a folder.

> I cover additional item access techniques, such as finding an item that meets certain conditions, in Hour 15, "Working with Stores and Folders."

Getting the Current Item

Where Explorer objects represent Outlook folder windows, Inspector objects correspond to Outlook item windows. Because you can have more than one Outlook window open, more than one Inspector object may be available.

To access the item window the user is currently using, use the ActiveInspector method of the Application object. To get the item displayed in the window, use the CurrentItem property of the Inspector, as in this example:

```
Dim objApp As Application
Dim objItem As Object
Set objApp = CreateObject("Outlook.Application")
Set objItem = objApp.ActiveInspector.CurrentItem
```

The current item could turn out to be any kind of Outlook item—a message, a contact, even a note. Because you can't predict the type of item, you must use the generic Dim objItem as Object statement to declare the object variable. If you have to know what kind of object it is before allowing the program to proceed, you can use either the TypeName() function or the Class property of the item.

TypeName() returns a String value providing information about the variable. For object variables, it returns the type of object. Table 12.2 lists the values for different types of Outlook items. The Class property returns an Integer value. Table 12.2 also lists the intrinsic constants for the Class property values and their literal values.

TABLE 12.2 TypeName() and Class Values for Outlook Object Variables

Object	TypeName(object)	object.Class
Message	"MailItem"	olMail (= 43)
Appointment	"AppointmentItem"	olAppointment (= 26)
Meeting Request	"AppointmentItem"	olMeetingRequest (= 53)
Contact	"ContactItem"	olContact (= 40)
Distribution List	"DistListItem"	olDistributionList (= 69)
Journal	"JournalItem"	olJournal (= 42)
Note	"NoteItem"	olNote (= 44)
Post	"PostItem"	olPost (= 45)
Task	"TaskItem"	olTask (= 48)
Task Request	"TaskItem"	olTaskRequest (= 49)
Folder	"MAPIFolder"	olFolder (= 2)
no object set	"Nothing"	error occurs

Table 12.2 lists just some of the TypeName() and Class values. For more information, look up "TypeName" in the Object Browser, as described in the next hour's lesson. To learn about other intrinsic constants for the Class property, look up "olObjectClass."

If you try to access the Class property for an object variable that has not been set to an object, Outlook generates an error. Therefore, if there is any chance that the object might not have been set, it might be better to use the TypeName() function to find out what kind of item you have, instead of the Class property. Note, however, that the Class property can help you distinguish between an appointment and a meeting request or between a task and a task request.

Working with Selected Items

Outlook 2000 offers a new method for working with particular items that previous versions lack: a `Selection` object containing the particular items selected by the user in a folder window. Use this code to set an `objSelection` variable to the items selected in the current folder (the `ActiveExplorer` window's folder):

```
Dim objApp As Application
Dim objItem As Object
Dim objSelection As Selection
Set objApp = CreateObject("Outlook.Application")
Set objSelection = objApp.ActiveExplorer.Selection
```

Because you have no way to know whether the user has selected one item or 100, you generally use a `For...Next` loop to work with each item in turn. Depending on the operation you plan to perform on the selection, you might want to check the count first with the `Count` property of the `Selection` object. This code alerts the user with a message box if no items are selected or if more than 30 are selected, but allows the code to proceed if there are between one and 30 items in the selection.

```
Select Case objSelection.Count
    Case 0
        MsgBox "No items were selected"
    Case 1 To 30
        your code goes here
    Case Is > 30
        MsgBox objSelection.Count & " items is too big " _
        & "a selection for this operation."
End Select
```

> The preceding `Select Case...End Select` block illustrates the additional `Case int1 to int2` and `Case Is` operator expression syntax for `Case` statements available only in VBA, not in VBScript.

After you decide that it's safe to proceed, given the number of items in the selection, use a `For Each...Next` loop to access each item in turn. This code pops up a series of message boxes showing the `Subject` property (in other words, the title) of each selected item.

```
For Each objItem In objSelection
    MsgBox objItem.Subject
Next
```

12

For Each statements involving Selection and MAPIFolder objects use different syntax. With a selection, use

For Each objItem In objSelection

When getting items from a folder, use

For Each objItem In objFolder.Items

Every item in an Outlook folder has a Subject property, so it's safe to use objItem.Subject without checking the type of object first.

You can use the Selection object from both VBA and VBScript. A common application is within VBA macros to perform batch operations that you can't do with Outlook's built-in menu and toolbar button commands. For example, the SetFlagOnSelection subroutine in Listing 12.1 sets an undated follow-up flag for all selected items. Notice that it checks the DefaultItemType property for the folder first (line 9) and also checks the Class property of each item (line 14) because only MailItem objects (in other words, Message items) support the FlagStatus property.

LISTING 12.1 Use the Selection Object to Perform Batch Operations on Items in a Folder

```
 1: Sub SetFlagOnSelection()
 2:     Dim objApp As Application
 3:     Dim objFolder As MAPIFolder
 4:     Dim lngType As Long
 5:     Dim objItem As Object
 6:     Dim objSelection As Selection
 7:     Set objApp = CreateObject("Outlook.Application")
 8:     Set objFolder = objApp.ActiveExplorer.CurrentFolder
 9:     lngType = objFolder.DefaultItemType
10:     If lngType = olMailItem Then
11:         Set objSelection = objApp.ActiveExplorer.Selection
12:         If objSelection.Count <> 0 Then
13:             For Each objItem In objSelection
14:                 If objItem.Class = olMail Then
15:                     With objItem
16:                         .FlagStatus = olFlagMarked
17:                         .FlagRequest = "Follow up"
18:                         .Save
19:                     End With
20:                 End If
21:             Next
```

```
22:          Else
23:              MsgBox "No items were selected"
24:          End If
25:      Else
26:          MsgBox "You can't flag items in this folder."
27:      End If
28: End Sub
```

 You can flag Contact items manually, but you cannot flag a ContactItem object with programming code.

Getting User Input

Having a particular Outlook folder or item to work with might not always be enough. Your program might have to get other input from the user on what to do with that item: whether to proceed if a certain condition is met, how many days ahead to set a reminder, or what the due date and flag should be for a message flag.

You've already seen examples of getting user input through fields on a custom page on an Outlook item or through a custom VBA form. New methods that you will learn in this lesson include message boxes, which can also be used for feedback to the user, and input boxes. You will also see how to integrate a VBA dialog form into a calling procedure.

Using Message Boxes

In several procedures, you have seen MsgBox statements displaying pop-up messages to the user. The syntax for this type of statement is

```
MsgBox(prompt, , title)
```

where prompt is the text you want the user to see and title is an optional title for the message box. If you omit the title argument, the title of the message box defaults to "Microsoft Outlook" for VBA routines and "VBScript" for procedures on Outlook forms.

Used in an expression, the MsgBox() function also provides a way to get a Yes or No answer from the user. A typical series of statements using a MsgBox() function looks like this:

```
intAns = MsgBox(prompt, buttons, title)
If intAns = vbYes Then
    your code runs here
Else
    alternative code runs here
End If
```

12

The arguments for the MsgBox() function include

prompt	String expression for the text that you want the user to see in the message box
buttons	Optional numeric expression that determines the number of command buttons, their labels, and the default button
title	Optional String expression for the title of the message box

If you omit the buttons argument, but want to include a title, you must leave the comma delimiter in place inside the parentheses. These are all valid MsgBox() expressions:

```
MsgBox("Will you be gone all day?")

MsgBox("Will you be gone all day?", , "Take a Day Off")

MsgBox("Will you be gone all day?", 36, "Take a Day Off")
```

However, MsgBox("Will you be gone all day?", "Take a Day Off") would not be a valid expression because it omits the comma that occurs after the optional buttons argument.

 The MsgBox() function also supports two optional arguments to supply the name of a Windows help file and the context number for the help topics you want to display. I don't cover the creation of help files in this book, however.

To get the value for the buttons argument, use the sum of three numbers:

```
buttontypes + icon + defaultbutton
```

where each of these values is a Visual Basic constant from one of the three groups listed in Table 12.3.

TABLE 12.3 Message Box Constants

Constant	Value	Description
Button Type Constants		
vbOKOnly	0	Display OK button only (default).
vbOKCancel	1	Display OK and Cancel buttons.
vbAbortRetryIgnore	2	Display Abort, Retry, and Ignore buttons.

Constant	Value	Description
vbYesNoCancel	3	Display Yes, No, and Cancel buttons.
vbYesNo	4	Display Yes and No buttons.
vbRetryCancel	5	Display Retry and Cancel buttons.
Icon Constants		
vbCritical	16	Display Critical Message icon (refer to Figure 12.2).
vbQuestion	32	Display Warning Query icon.
vbExclamation	48	Display Warning Message icon.
vbInformation	64	Display Information Message icon.
Default Button Constants		
vbDefaultButton1	0	First button is default.
vbDefaultButton2	256	Second button is default.
vbDefaultButton3	512	Third button is default.
vbDefaultButton4	768	Fourth button is default.

FIGURE 12.2

From left to right, the Critical Message, Warning Query, Warning Message, and Information Message icons.

You don't have to learn the numeric values for elements that make up the buttons argument because you can use the intrinsic constants in both VBA and VBScript.

Use only one constant from each group to build the buttons argument value. This message box asks the user whether they really want to proceed:

```
intAns = MsgBox("Do you really want to do this?", _
        vbYesNo + vbQuestion + vbDefaultButton2, _
        "Dangerous operation")
```

and sets the default button to the second button, No, so that the user must actively decide to proceed by clicking the Yes button. Figure 12.3 shows what the user sees.

FIGURE **12.3**

For risky operations, make No the default message box button.

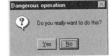

If the prompt for the message box is lengthy or is itself an expression, rather than use a string literal, use a separate String variable to build it. Here's an example using an objSelection variable to represent a Selection object:

```
strMsg = "This selection includes " & _
            objSelection.Count &" items. " & _
            "Do you want to continue?"
intAns = MsgBox(strMsg, _
            vbYesNo + vbQuestion, _
            "Process Selection")
```

The intAns variable in all the message box examples is the key to getting the user's response. The MsgBox() function returns one of the integers in Table 12.4, all of which have Visual Basic intrinsic constant equivalents.

TABLE 12.4   Return Values for the MsgBox() Function

When the User Presses	MsgBox() Returns	Constant
OK	1	vbOK
Cancel	2	vbCancel
Abort	3	vbAbort
Retry	4	vbRetry
Ignore	5	vbIgnore
Yes	6	vbYes
No	7	vbNo

Let's go back to the CleanAttachments subroutine created in the Hour 11, "Controlling Program Flow." Removing attachments is a slightly risky operation—because this routine deletes them completely from a message. Therefore, it's a good idea to ask the user to confirm the operation. The enhanced CleanAttachments subroutine in Listing 12.2 asks for user input in three places:

- Using the PickFolder method in line 11, it asks the user to select a folder.
- With the MsgBox() function in line 16, it asks whether the user wants to be prompted to remove attachments from each message in the folder. (The prompt was built in lines 13–15.)

- If the user chooses to be prompted, the MsgBox() function in line 26 provides a prompt for each message.

LISTING 12.2 Adding User Input to the CleanAttachments() Subroutine

```
 1: Sub CleanAttachments()
 2:     Dim objApp As Application
 3:     Dim objNS As NameSpace
 4:     Dim objFolder As MAPIFolder
 5:     Dim objItem As MailItem
 6:     Dim objAtts As Attachments
 7:     Dim strMsg As String
 8:     Dim intAns As Integer
 9:     Set objApp = CreateObject("Outlook.Application")
10:     Set objNS = objApp.GetNamespace("MAPI")
11:     Set objFolder = objNS.PickFolder
12:     If TypeName(objFolder) <> "Nothing" Then
13:         strMsg = "Do you want to be prompted to remove " & _
14:                     "attachments from each message in the " & _
15:                     objFolder.Name & " folder?"
16:         intRes = MsgBox(strMsg, vbQuestion + vbYesNoCancel, _
17:                     "Remove Attachments")
18:         If intRes <> vbCancel Then
19:             For Each objItem In objFolder.Items
20:                 Set objAtts = objItem.Attachments
21:                 If objAtts.Count > 0 Then
22:                     If intRes = vbYes Then
23:                         strMsg = "Remove attachments " & _
24:                             "from " & Quote(objItem.Subject) _
25:                             & "?"
26:                         intAns = MsgBox(strMsg, _
27:                                     vbYesNo + vbQuestion, _
28:                                     "Clean Attachments")
29:                     Else
30:                         intAns = vbYes
31:                     End If
32:                     If intAns = vbYes Then
33:                         For Each objAtt In objAtts
34:                             objAtt.Delete
35:                         Next
36:                     End If
37:                     objItem.Save
38:                 End If
39:             Next
40:         End If
41:     End If
42: End Sub
```

12

Line 24 uses the Quote() function you saw in Hour 8, "Code Basics," to put the name of the file in quotation marks so that it's easier to see in message boxes, such as the one in Figure 12.4.

FIGURE 12.4

Use message boxes to ask the user to confirm operations on a series of items.

Using Input Boxes

The MsgBox() function provides a limited number of possible responses—basically Yes, No, Cancel, and variations on those themes. If you want some other kind of input from the user, you need another method. The InputBox() function provides an easy way to get a single number, string, or date from the user.

Try not to beleaguer the user with a series of input and message boxes. If you need more input data or confirmations than a single InputBox() or MsgBox() function can provide, use either a VBA form, as described in the next section or, in VBScript, controls on the current Outlook item.

The basic InputBox() syntax looks like this:

```
InputBox(prompt, title, default, xpos, ypos)
```

All arguments except prompt are optional. prompt and title work as in the MsgBox() function. Default is an optional String expression for the text you want to display in the input box as the default response in case the user types nothing in.

The xpos and ypos arguments are optional numeric expressions that govern the screen location of the input box. They use the distance from the left and top of the screen, respectively, measured in twips; there are 1,440 twips to an inch. If you omit these arguments, Outlook centers the input box horizontally, about one-third of the way down the screen, as you can see in Figure 12.5.

Like the MsgBox() function, the InputBox() function also supports additional optional arguments that let you call a Windows Help file.

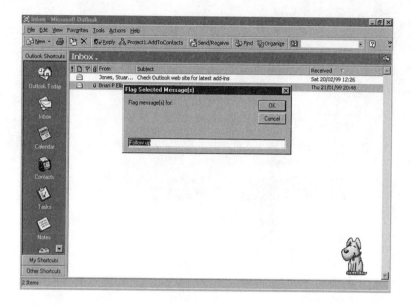

FIGURE 12.5

An input box asks the user for one piece of information.

An input box returns a String consisting of whatever the user types into the box. Here is the code that created the input box in Figure 12.5.

```
Dim strAns As String
strAns = InputBox("Flag message(s) for:", _
        "Flag Selected Message(s)", _
        "Follow up")
```

> A statement using InputBox() is often followed by one or more statements that test the value returned by the function to make sure that it's more than an empty string, that it's a number, and so on.

12

You could add this code to the SetFlagOnSelection subroutine in Listing 12.1 to get the user's flag preference as a strAns variable. Then, you could use strAns in the statement that sets the flag:

```
If objSelection.Count <> 0 Then
    strAns = InputBox("Flag message(s) for:", _
                "Flag Selected Message(s)", _
                "Follow up")
    For Each objItem In objSelection
        If objItem.Class = olMail Then
            With objItem
                .FlagStatus = olFlagMarked
```

```
                .FlagRequest = strAns
                .Save
            End With
        End If
    Next
End If
```

Using VBA Forms

What if you want the user to provide both a message flag and a due date to the
SetFlagOnSelection subroutine? Can you do that with an InputBox() function? No,
each input box returns only one piece of information, and popping up one input box after
another is not considered good design.

If you are working in VBScript on a form, your only alternative is to get the information
from controls on the current form. However, if you are programming in VBA, you can
call a VBA form for the extra information.

A VBA form for user input should be modal and have one or more controls where the
user enters data or makes selections, as well as an OK button to hide the form. The code
behind the form should set a global variable that the calling subroutine can use to determine whether the user clicked OK or cancelled the form dialog. To make use of the
form's data, the calling subroutine should follow these steps:

1. Use the Show method to display the form.
2. After the user interacts with the form, check the global variable to see whether the
   user clicked OK.
3. If the user did click OK, get data from the (now hidden) form's controls.
4. After obtaining all the necessary data from the form, unload it.

A Macro to Set a Flag on Selected Messages

In many cases, you can largely duplicate the look of Outlook's own dialog boxes with
VBA forms of your own. In this example, you will create a macro to set a message flag
on selected items, after prompting the user for the flag text and due date. Here's what
you have to do:

1. Create a new VBA form.
2. Add a text box named txtFlagTo and a matching label with the caption "Flag to".
3. Add a text box named txtDueBy and a matching label with the caption "Due by".
4. Add a command button named cmdOK with the caption "OK", and set its Default
   property to True.

5. Add a command button named cmdCancel with the caption "Cancel", and set its Cancel property to True.

6. In the form's code windows, add the code in Listing 12.3. When clicked, the command buttons set the value of a global variable (g_blnCancel) and then hide or unload the form. The UserForm_Terminate subroutine is necessary to make sure that the global variable is set even if the user clicks the form's Close button.

LISTING 12.4 Using a VBA Form for User Input

```
 1: Dim blnUserChose As Boolean
 2:
 3: Private Sub cmdCancel_Click()
 4:     g_blnCancel = True
 5:     blnUserChose = True
 6:     Unload Me
 7: End Sub
 8:
 9: Private Sub cmdOK_Click()
10:     g_blnCancel = False
11:     blnUserChose = True
12:     Me.Hide
13: End Sub
14:
15: Private Sub UserForm_Terminate()
16:     If blnUserChose = False Then
17:         g_blnCancel = True
18:     End If
19: End Sub
```

12

7. In the module containing the SetFlagOnSelection procedure, add the line

Public g_blnCancel As Boolean

in the declarations section to declare the global g_blnCancel variable.

8. Replace the If objSelection.Count <> 0 ... End If block (lines 12–24) for the SetFlagOnSelection procedure in Listing 12.1 with the code in Listing 12.5.

LISTING 12.5 A Procedure Calls a Modal VBA Form and Gets Its Data Before Unloading It

```
 1: If objSelection.Count <> 0 Then
 2:     frmFlagForFollowUp.Show
 3:     If g_blnCancel = False Then
 4:         strFlag = frmFlagForFollowUp.txtFlagTo.Value
 5:         If IsDate(frmFlagForFollowUp.txtDueBy.Value) Then
```

continues

LISTING 12.5 continued

```
 6:                dteDue = _
 7:                  DateValue(frmFlagForFollowUp.txtDueBy.Value)
 8:             Else
 9:                 dteDue = #1/1/4501#
10:             End If
11:             For Each objItem In objSelection
12:                 If objItem.Class = olMail Then
13:                     With objItem
14:                         .FlagStatus = olFlagMarked
15:                         .FlagRequest = strFlag
16:                         .FlagDueBy = dteDue
17:                         .Save
18:                     End With
19:                 End If
20:             Next
21:         End If
22:         Unload frmFlagForFollowUp
23: Else
24:      MsgBox "No items were selected"
25: End If
```

Here's how it works:

The `frmFlagForFollowUp.Show` statement (line 2) displays the Flag for Follow Up form shown in Figure 12.6. Because the form's `ShowModal` property is set to `True` (the default), execution of the `SetFlagOnSelection` procedure halts until the user interacts with the form by pressing one of the buttons or closing the form.

FIGURE 12.6

A VBA dialog can look very much like one of Outlook's built-in dialog boxes.

If the user clicks the OK button, the `g_blnCancel` variable is set to `False`. Otherwise, it's `False`. After the user finishes with the form, control returns to line 3 in Listing 12.4. If `g_blnCancel = False` (in other words, if the user clicked the OK button), the procedure gets the values from the list boxes on the form (which was just hidden, not unloaded) and uses those values to set a message flag on each selected item.

The `dteDue = #1/1/4501#` statement in line 9 looks very peculiar. It runs if the user enters something in the `txtDueBy` text box that is not a date. This date `#1/1/4501#` actually means "no date" to Outlook, not January 1, 4501. You can use this special date when you need a Date/Time field in an Outlook item to appear blank.

The other new line is line 22, `Unload frmFlagForFollowUp`, which terminates the form and releases its memory. In Listing 12.4, line 6, you see a variation, `Unload Me`, in which a form unloads itself.

Summary

Congratulations! You're halfway through your 24-hour introduction to Outlook 2000 programming. This lesson concluded the section on code essentials with techniques for getting an Outlook item or folder and handling user input through `MsgBox()` and `InputBox()` functions and VBA forms.

In the next hour, you will look in more detail at different object models at work in Outlook programming.

Q&A

Q Why doesn't the `MsgBox()` function use three separate arguments to get the information in the `buttons` argument?

A The `buttons` argument can do the work of three arguments in one because of the numbers chosen to represent each setting. The button type constants run from 0 to 5. The icon constants are multiples of 16, and the default button constants are multiples of 256. This ensures that each of the 120 types of message boxes can be represented by a unique number between 0 and 837. Where do you get 120 types of message boxes? Six button types times five icons (including none) times four default button options equals 120 message box variations.

Q How can I make sure that I'm getting the right kind of data from an `InputBox()` function?

A If `strAns` is the return variable for the function, use `If strAns <> ""` to check whether the user typed something in the input box. Use the `IsNumeric()` or `IsDate()` function to test whether the user typed a valid number or date.

Q Why does a VBA form used for user input have to be modal?

A When a procedure displays a modal form, program control passes to the form until the form is unloaded with an `Unload frm` statement or hidden with a `frm.Hide` statement. Data validation can occur in the code for the form. Then, if the code for the form's OK button hides the form, program control passes back to the program that originally called the form, which can now get the form's data and then unload the form.

12

Workshop

Work through the quiz questions and exercises so that you can better understand Outlook programming. See Appendix A for Answers.

Quiz

1. Which of Outlook's default folders can hold messages?

2. Name the methods you have used in this hour for the `Application` and `NameSpace` objects.

3. What function(s) could you use to add the current date to the message shown in a message box?

4. If you wanted to know whether a user prefers coffee or tea, would you be more likely to use a message box or an input box?

Exercises

1. Write a subroutine to assign each of the nine Outlook default folders to its own folder object variable. (You can save this boilerplate code in your Generic module and copy and paste it any time you have to get a default folder.)

2. Change the code in Listing 12.2 so that it cleans attachments from items the user has selected in a folder view.

3. Create message boxes with the title My Message Box Test, the prompt `This is a test of the MsgBox() function`, and these button and icon settings:

   • Question mark icon; Yes, No, and Cancel buttons; Cancel as the default button

   • Critical icon; Abort, Retry, and Ignore buttons; Abort as the default button

4. Modify the `ReplaceCat` subroutine in Listing 10.2 from Hour 10, "Working with Expressions and Functions," to use a VBA form to prompt the user for both the old category and the replacement category.

PART IV

Special Outlook Techniques

Hour

HOUR 13

Working with the Object Models

You've seen the term *object* many times in the course of the lessons so far. In this hour, you dive deeper into the subject of object models, not only for Outlook but also for other programming interfaces you might want to use to build Outlook applications.

Highlights of this hour include

- How to include additional object models in your Outlook project
- How to use the Object Browser to discover what you can accomplish with Outlook
- What you can do with the Collaboration Data Objects (CDO) model that you can't do with the Outlook Object model
- How to create a message with voting buttons through code
- How to work with collections of objects

Objects are special because they contain not only data, but also specific methods, events, and properties that determine how that data behaves and what you can do with it. Those shared characteristics define the object class. The methods, events, and properties are called *members* of the class.

Often, objects of different classes act much the same. For example, the different Outlook item objects support sets of properties that largely overlap, and all include many of the same events and methods.

Objects often exist in a parent-child relationship. An Outlook JournalItem object, for example, has a parent Folder object.

Trying to understand the concept of objects might seem like a lot of trouble when what you really want to do is write Outlook applications, but the effort pays off in the end. Grasping the core of the object model helps you know what you can do in Outlook—and how to accomplish it.

Using the VBA Object Browser

The main tool for exploring the object models is VBA's Object Browser. To display the Object Browser, choose View, Object Browser. You can also press F2 or click the Object Browser button on the toolbar. When the Object Browser appears, you might want to maximize it to be able to see more information on the screen.

When you start the Object Browser, it presents information on all the programming libraries available to you (more on that shortly, under "Understanding and Adding Libraries"). To get to a level of detail that should be familiar to you by now, just look at the Outlook objects. To do that, in the drop-down list at the top of the Object Browser (the one that defaults to <All Libraries>), select Outlook. Your screen should now look something like Figure 13.1, which shows the JournalItem class.

Pay close attention to the different icons that help distinguish the types of object classes and their members. For example, the JournalItem object class includes both a Close event and a Close action, but it's easy to tell them apart by the icon.

Understanding and Adding Libraries

The Object Browser displays information about not only Outlook objects, but also other objects you use in VBA, including the current Outlook project, listed as Project1 (unless you change the name). Information about each basic set of objects is contained in a library that loads when you start VBA. You can also add more libraries when you want to work with other object models, for example, with Word or Excel, to generate reports from Outlook data.

Search text   Library list

FIGURE 13.1

Use the Object Browser to explore Outlook's objects and their methods, properties, and events.

Object class

Constant class

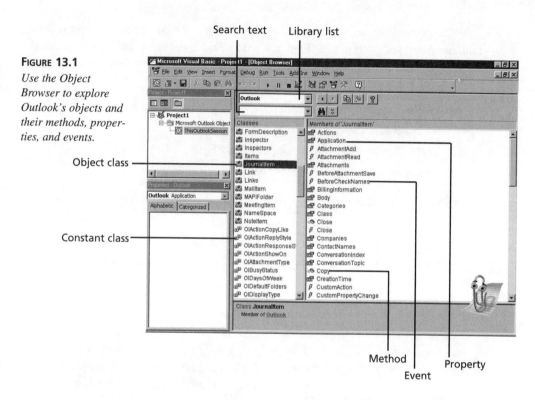

Method   Property
Event

To see the libraries currently installed and add more, choose Tools, References. In the References dialog box, shown in Figure 13.2, the items at the top marked with check marks are already installed and part of your VBA environment.

FIGURE 13.2

These libraries are installed in Outlook VBA by default.

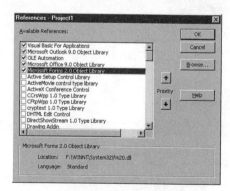

13

To add another reference, scroll down the alphabetical list of unchecked items until you find the library you want to use. Then, click the desired library's check box. You can also install new references by clicking the Browse button and finding the appropriate file on your system. Reference files can include the following:

Outlook VBA files	.otm files
Object Type libraries	.olb, .tlb, .dll files
Executable files	.exe, .dll files
ActiveX controls	.ocx files

To remove a reference if you're no longer using its objects in your project, clear its check box.

When two libraries contain objects with the same name, VBA uses the one listed higher in the Available References list. Use the Priority buttons in the References dialog box to change the order.

Searching for Objects and Getting Help

You can search the Object Browser for classes and members related to particular topics. Type a word in the second drop-down list box, and then press Enter or click the search text button. Figure 13.3 shows the results of a search of the Outlook library for the word *folder*. It turns up a long list of objects, methods, events, properties, and constants whose names contain Folder.

FIGURE 13.3

Search the Object Browser to find classes and members containing particular text.

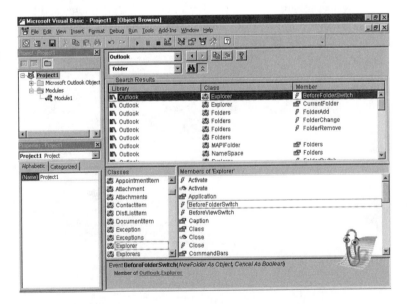

To hide the search results, click the Hide Search Results button next to the search text button. You can see the search results again by clicking the same button (now the Show Search Results button).

If you've been browsing an object model for a while and want to retrace your steps, use the right and left arrow buttons at the top of the Object Browser window, above the search text button.

One great use of the Object Browser is as an index to the help topics on the object models. Select any class or member, and then click the Help button or press F1 to get help on that item, including related properties, methods, and events.

Not all libraries shown in the Object Browser have help files associated with them. Sometimes, you will have to refer to a separate help file or other documentation.

Figure 13.4 shows a typical help topic for the DistListItem (distribution list) object. Notice the links for Properties, Methods, and Events at the top. The diagram showing the DistListItem object in context with its parent and child objects is also clickable, enabling you to explore the object hierarchy in the help system. If you keep moving up the hierarchy, eventually you will see the overall map of the Outlook Object Model, shown in Figure 13.5.

FIGURE 13.4

Help topics tell you how to create and use Outlook objects.

13

Microsoft Visual Basic Help

DistListItem Object

See Also   Example   Properties   Methods   Events

Multiple Objects
  DistListItem
    Multiple Objects

Represents a distribution list in a contacts folder. A distribution list can contain multiple recipients and is used to send messages to everyone in the list.

Using the DistListItem Object

Use the CreateItem method to create a DistListItem object that represents a new distribution list. The following Microsoft Visual Basic for Applications example creates and displays a new distribution list.

```
Set myOlApp = CreateObject("Outlook.Application")
Set myItem = myOlApp.CreateItem(olDistributionListItem)
myItem.Display
```

Use Items(*index*), where *index* is the index number of an item in a contacts folder or a value used to match the default property of an item in the folder, to return a single **DistListItem** object from a contacts folder (that is, a folder whose default item type is **olContactItem**, the value of which is 2). The following Visual Basic for Applications example sets the current folder as the contacts folder and displays an existing distribution list named Project Team in the folder.

FIGURE 13.5

Click on any branch in the help topic about the Outlook object to learn how to use the various objects.

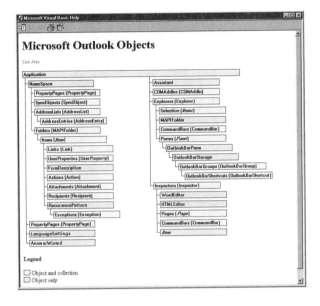

A more detailed map of the Outlook Object Model, suitable for printing in color and framing, can be found at the Outlook Exchange resource site for developers at http://www.microeye.com/outlook/ObjectModel.htm.

Using the Outlook Object Browser

The VBScript environment also includes a smaller version of the Object Browser. From the code window for a form, choose Script, Object Browser to display the Object Browser, shown in Figure 13.6. Click Object Help to see the help topic for the selected item. Click Insert to paste the name of the selected class or member or a selected constant value into your script.

FIGURE 13.6

This minibrowser helps you keep track of Outlook objects when you're working in VBScript.

Object Code Techniques

Programming with objects requires some special code techniques. You've already learned two:

- Using a Set statement to initialize an object variable
- Using a With...End With block to work with the properties and methods of a particular object

You are going to add two more skills: working with object collections and releasing objects.

Working with Collections

When you worked with items in a folder, you saw an example of an object *collection*, a set of objects of the same class that can be accessed through the properties and methods of the collection, not just via the individual item members. In Figure 13.5, all the objects that include a name in parentheses are collections. For example, the PropertyPages collection is a set of PropertyPage objects.

Using For Each...Next blocks to loop through all the objects in a collection is one important collection technique. You're going to look at others as you explore the properties, events, and methods you can expect to find in any collection.

A typical collection object includes the Application, Class, Count, Parent, and Session properties, listed in Table 13.1.

TABLE 13.1 Standard Collection Properties

Property	Returns
Application	Parent Application object (Microsoft Outlook)
Class	Constant representing the collection's class
Count	Number of objects in the collection
Parent	Parent object of the collection
Session	NameSpace object for the current Outlook session

13

The Count property is probably the most often used.

Most Outlook collections include these three methods:

- Add to add a new object to the collection
- Item to refer to a specific object in the collection
- Remove to delete an object from the collection

However, some collections do not support the Add or Remove methods, only the Item method.

To use the Item method to return a specific object, you must know either the index for the object or its default property. The index is the position of the object in the collection, starting with 1. For example, the following code uses the syntax objFolder.Items.Item(1) to open the first item in the Inbox:

```
Sub OpenFirstInboxItem()
    Dim objApp As Application
    Dim objNS As NameSpace
    Dim objFolder As MAPIFolder
    Dim objMessage As MailItem
    Set objApp = CreateObject("Outlook.Application")
    Set objNS = objApp.GetNamespace("MAPI")
    Set objFolder = objNS.GetDefaultFolder(olFolderInbox)
    Set objMessage = objFolder.Items.Item(1)
    objMessage.Display
End Sub
```

The collection of all items in a folder is folder.Items, not folder, so the Item method syntax is folder.Items.Item(index), even though that might seem redundant.

The problem with using an index is knowing exactly which object you're actually getting. In the preceding example, the oldest message in the Inbox is displayed because it has index position 1.

The other method is to use the default property for an item to look it up. This property varies from object to object. For Outlook items, it's the Subject property. This variation on the Item method prompts the user for the subject of a message and then displays that message.

```
Sub OpenAnyInboxItem()
    Dim strName As String
    Dim objApp As Application
    Dim objNS As NameSpace
    Dim objFolder As MAPIFolder
    Dim objMessage As MailItem
    strSubject = InputBox("Subject of message to open:", _
                "OpenFirstInboxItem")
    If strSubject <> "" Then
        Set objApp = CreateObject("Outlook.Application")
        Set objNS = objApp.GetNamespace("MAPI")
        Set objFolder = objNS.GetDefaultFolder(olFolderInbox)
```

```
            Set objMessage = objFolder.Items.Item(strSubject)
            If Not objMessage Is Nothing Then
                objMessage.Display
            End If
        End If
    End Sub
```

This version of the Item method has its limitations, too. It requires an exact match for
the text used as the argument for Item, and if there is more than one matching object,
only the first one is returned. You will learn some alternatives for finding particular
objects in Hour 15, "Working with Folders."

The Add method creates a new object in the collection and returns that new object to an
object variable. The syntax looks like this:

```
Set object = collection.Add(arguments)
```

Some objects support arguments in their Add method to set properties for the new object.
In other cases, you create the object with the Add method first and then set properties
separately.

This example of the Add method adds a new Explorer to open a new Outlook window
with the Calendar folder displayed. It requires two arguments—the MAPIFolder object to
be displayed and an Outlook constant specifying whether the view should include navigation tools such as the Outlook Bar:

```
Sub ShowCalendar()
    Dim objApp As Application
    Dim objNS As NameSpace
    Dim objExplorers As Explorers
    Dim objFolder As MAPIFolder
    Dim objExplorer As Explorer
    Set objApp = CreateObject("Outlook.Application")
    Set objNS = objApp.GetNamespace("MAPI")
    Set objExplorers = objApp.Explorers
    Set objFolder = objNS.GetDefaultFolder(olFolderCalendar)
    Set objExplorer = objExplorers.Add(objFolder, _
                        olFolderDisplayFolderOnly)
    objExplorer.Activate
End Sub
```

13

> Remember that, if you're writing VBScript code, you would omit the As por-
> tion of Dim statements, use the intrinsic Application object, and either
> declare the Outlook constants or provide the literal values.

> You can also use the Display method, as well as Activate, to show an Explorer or Inspector object.

Flip ahead to "Creating a Voting Button Message" for another example of the Add method.

The Remove method is the opposite of Add. It deletes an object from the collection, using this syntax:

```
collection.Remove index
```

Because you have to know the index first, you can't use Remove to specify that you want to remove a particular item. If you want to get rid of a particular object, it's usually easier to get the object with the Item method and then use the Delete method on the object to delete it from the collection.

Where Remove comes in handy is for bulk deletion operations, such as removing all controls from a form (as you saw in Hour 11). This code, rewritten from the Hour 11's CleanControls() subroutine to run in VBScript, removes all the controls from an Outlook form custom page named Project:

```
Sub cmdCleanControls_Click
    Set objInspector = Application.ActiveInspector
    Set objPage = objInspector.ModifiedFormPages("Project")
    Do While objPage.Controls.Count > 0
        objPage.Controls.Remove 0
    Loop
End Sub
```

How many collections are used in the preceding example? ModifiedFormPages is a Pages collection; you can return a single Page object without the Item method by using the ModifiedFormPages(name) syntax. (Some other collections use this syntax, without Item, as well.) Controls is another collection—the collection of all controls on the page.

> A VBA form has a Controls collection, too. It can be useful to cycle through the Controls collection with a For Each...Next block to find out which controls contain data, which are showing text in a particular color, and so on, or to change properties for several controls.

Creating a Voting Button Message

In most cases, the Add method requires one or more arguments, as you saw in the code for adding and displaying an Explorer object. In a few cases, though, you use the Add method with no argument and then work with the returned object's properties. Listing 13.1 illustrates the use of the Actions collection to create a message and add voting buttons after the user types in a comma-delimited list of voting button titles.

In the Hour 14, "Commanding with Custom Actions," you learn more about working with voting buttons and the Actions collection.

LISTING 13.1   Add Action Objects to Create a Voting Button Message

```
 1: Sub CreateVoteMessage()
 2:     Dim objApp As Application
 3:     Dim strMsg As String
 4:     Dim strActions As String
 5:     Dim arrActions() As String
 6:     Dim I As Integer
 7:     Dim objMessage As MailItem
 8:     Dim objAction As Action
 9:     strMsg = "Enter voting button titles, " _
10:             & "separated by commas."
11:     strActions = InputBox(strMsg, "CreateVoteMessage")
12:     If strActions <> "" Then
13:         arrActions = Split(strActions, ",")
14:         Set objApp = CreateObject("Outlook.Application")
15:         Set objMessage = objApp.CreateItem(olMailItem)
16:         For I = 0 To UBound(arrActions)
17:             Set objAction = objMessage.Actions.Add
18:             With objAction
19:                 .CopyLike = olRespond
20:                 .Enabled = True
21:                 .Name = arrActions(I)
22:                 .Prefix = ""
23:                 .ReplyStyle = olOmitOriginalText
24:                 .ResponseStyle = olPrompt
25:                 .ShowOn = olMenuAndToolbar
26:             End With
27:         Next I
28:         objMessage.Display
29:     End If
30: End Sub
```

13

Notice the syntax for the Add method in line 17:

```
Set objAction = objMessage.Actions.Add
```

This is equivalent to these two statements:

```
Set objActions = objMessage.Actions
Set objAction = objActions.Add
```

In other words, you do not have to declare an object variable to represent the collection. Instead, you can use its parent object with the syntax parent.collection.Add.

Releasing Objects

If you pay attention to scope when writing your procedures and declare variables with the narrowest scope possible, you shouldn't have any problem with procedure-level object variables staying in memory and using system resources after you need them. However, it doesn't hurt to release them anyway, as part of the end of each procedure, using a Set object = Nothing statement. Nothing is a special keyword that disassociates the variable from the object to which it refers.

> To save space, I will not show Set object = Nothing statements in every future procedure, but you should add them to your code.

> You can also use the statement If Not Object Is Nothing Then to test whether a previous Set object... statement was successful.

Always use a Set object = Nothing statement to release any module or global object variables.

Programming with Collaboration Data Objects

So far in this book, you've been working mainly with the Outlook Object Model, with a brief side trip to the MSForms Model when you were working with VBA forms and the events available for forms and controls. One other major object model deals with messages and contains some very useful methods that are not in the Outlook Model. Support for this model—called Collaboration Data Objects (CDO)—is not included in Outlook's default setup. If you don't find the Microsoft CDO 1.21 Library in the list of Available References (refer to Figure 13.2), rerun the Outlook setup, and select the Collaborative Data Objects component. Then, return to VBA, and use Tools, References to include CDO in your projects when you need it.

> You don't have to set any references to use CDO in VBScript code, but you do need to have the Cdo.dll file installed on your machine.

Among the useful things you can do with CDO are get the From address for an incoming message and open a Select Names dialog asking the user to choose recipients. You will look at the first task in this chapter and then work with the Select Names dialog in Chapter 16, "Working with Items," after you become familiar with the concept of recipients.

To browse the CDO object hierarchy, choose MAPI in the Library drop-down list. The CDO library does not include a help file integrated with the Object Browser. You can get the Cdo.hlp file from the Exchange Server CD or from the CDOLive Web site (http://www.cdolive.com), which provides independent support for CDO developers. An online version is available at the Microsoft Developers Network Web site at http://msdn.microsoft.com.

Before you can use CDO in a VBA or VBScript procedure, you must start a CDO session using this code:

```
Dim objSession As MAPI.Session
Set objSession = CreateObject("MAPI.Session")
objSession.Logon , , False, False
```

The Logon method initializes the CDO session using the currently active Outlook session. For VBScript, use just Dim objSession instead of Dim objSession As MAPI.Session.

Passing an Item from Outlook to CDO

CDO's main job is as a server component. It's a key element of Microsoft Exchange Server, which uses CDO to create the Outlook Web Access feature that provides Web-based e-mail from Exchange Server mailboxes. CDO is also the object model used with the Microsoft Exchange Event Service—scripts that run on the server to react to new and changed items in folders.

13

> You don't have to be connected to Exchange Server to use CDO, although
> Exchange Server users will be able to take advantage of some of CDO's more
> interesting features.

Because CDO is intended as a server component, it has no direct link to the user interface, as the Outlook Object Model does through its `Inspector` and `Explorer` objects.
Therefore, you must provide the code to pass a particular Outlook item or folder to CDO.
To do this, use the `EntryID` property of the item and its parent folder and the `StoreID` of
the Personal Folders file or Exchange Server mailbox containing the folder.

The code in Listing 13.2 gets the current Outlook item from the `ActiveInspector` object
and assigns it to a CDO `Message` object, while also assigning its parent folder to a CDO
`Folder` object:

LISTING 13.2   The CDO Procedure to Pass the Current Outlook Item to a CDO
Object

```
 1: Sub CDOPassItem()
 2:     Dim objApp As Application
 3:     Dim objItem As Object
 4:     Dim objFolder As MAPIFolder
 5:     Dim strEntryID As String
 6:     Dim strFolderID As String
 7:     Dim strStoreID As String
 8:     Dim objSession As MAPI.Session
 9:     Dim objCDOItem As Message
10:     Dim objCDOFolder As Folder
11:     Dim strAddress As String
12:     Set objApp = CreateObject("Outlook.Application")
13:     Set objItem = objApp.ActiveInspector.CurrentItem
14:     If TypeName(objItem) = "MailItem" Then
15:         strEntryID = objItem.EntryID
16:         Set objFolder = objItem.Parent
17:         strFolderID = objFolder.EntryID
18:         strStoreID = objFolder.StoreID
19:         Set objSession = CreateObject("MAPI.Session")
20:         objSession.Logon , , False, False
21:         Set objCDOFolder = _
22:            objSession.GetFolder(strFolderID, strStoreID)
23:         Debug.Print objFolder.Name, objCDOFolder.Name
24:         Set objCDOItem = _
25:            objSession.GetMessage(strEntryID, strStoreID)
26:         Debug.Print objItem.Subject, objCDOItem.Subject
```

```
27:      Else
28:          MsgBox "No Outlook message was open"
29:      End If
30: End Sub
```

The `GetFolder` and `GetMessage` methods on the `Session` object perform the actual work in this subroutine (lines 19–22). The two `Debug.Print` statements show, in the Immediate window, the display name of the Outlook object and the corresponding CDO object. You can see for yourself that they're identical.

Notice that, although you declare Outlook messages and folders as `MailItem` and `MAPIFolder` objects (lines 3–4), you declare CDO messages and folders as `Message` and `Folder` objects.

Getting a From Address

The Outlook Object Model does not include any direct way for you to get the e-mail address of the person who sent you a message. You can get the `SenderName` property, but that's not the same as an e-mail address. However, the CDO `Message` object includes a `Sender` property that returns an `AddressEntry` object containing the sender's name, the e-mail address, and the type of address.

If you use the code in Listing 13.2 to get a particular Outlook message, after you set the value of objCDOItem, you can add this statement to return the sender's e-mail address to a `String` variable:

```
strAddress = objCDOItem.Sender.Address
```

> In Hour 16, "Working with Items," you will discover another way to get the sender's address, one that involves generating a reply to a message.

Summary

With the aid of the Object Browser in VBA, I've explored new facets of the Outlook Object Model and introduced the Collaboration Data Objects Model. You also learned the standard methods and properties for the collection objects found throughout Outlook and saw how to create a message with voting buttons in code.

In the next hour, you will learn about custom form actions that make it easy for people to respond to your messages.

13

Q&A

Q How will I know when to use the Outlook Object Model and when to use CDO?

A Use the CDO Model when you want to take advantage of particular CDO features, such as the Sender property in this chapter's example and others you will see in upcoming chapters. Programming with CDO can become complicated when you go beyond the more common properties and methods.

Q What else can I do with CDO?

A Sample CDO applications available on the Internet (largely at http://www.cdo-live.com) demonstrate how to view the permissions and other configuration settings for folders, view the properties for forms libraries, and build server-based scripts to respond to incoming messages or send out messages at regular intervals.

Workshop

Work through the quiz questions and exercises so that you can better understand Outlook programming. See Appendix A for Answers.

Quiz

1. Can an object include an event and a method that use the same name? Give an example.

2. What's the difference between the Delete method and the Remove method?

Exercise

1. The Outlook Object Model and CDO both include a Recipient object. Explore its properties, actions, and methods. Are they the same object? If you use a Dim objRecip as Recipient statement in a procedure, which Recipient object are you referring to?

Hour 14

Commanding with Custom Actions

Custom actions are a unique Outlook technique for creating a new item from an existing item, with the option to include data from the original item. Voting buttons are one application of custom actions. Custom actions can also be used to run code that doesn't directly involve creating a new item.

You began looking at custom actions in the preceding hour. Listing 13.1 creates a voting button message by adding new custom actions to an item and setting their properties. In this hour, you will look at several other examples that illustrate ways to use custom actions.

Highlights of this hour include

- How to build a vacation approval form that sends back an Appointment item, ready to save to the Calendar folder

- How to add a button to run VBScript code without using a custom page

- How to add a Fax to Contact toolbar button to a Contact form

- What syntax to use when composing a fax as an e-mail message

A Vacation Approval Form

You will begin with a simple example that builds on the idea of voting buttons. Everyone likes to take vacations, right? However, unless you're the boss, someone must approve your time off. You will create a simple message form with Approve and Disapprove buttons that a supervisor can use to act on a vacation request.

First, customize a standard Message form in this fashion:

1. Set the Subject text box to read-only, and on the (All Fields) page, enter **Vacation request** as the text for the Subject field.

2. Select the large message body text box at the bottom of the form, and drag the top of it down to make some room between the Subject text box and the body of the message.

3. In the Field Chooser, create two new fields, **VacationStart** and **VacationEnd**, both as Date/Time fields. Drag them to the blank space above the message body to create two text boxes. Give these the names **txtVacationStart** and **txtVacationEnd**. Edit their labels so that the form looks like Figure 14.1.

FIGURE 14.1

This custom form makes it easy to request time off.

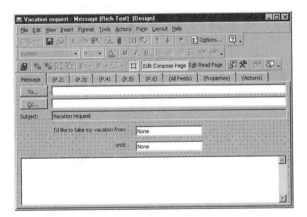

4. Adjust the tab order so that the txtVacationStart and txtVacationEnd text boxes are between Subject and Message.

5. Select the txtVacationStart and txtVacationEnd text boxes and their labels, and then copy them to the Clipboard.

6. Switch to the Read page, and adjust the height of the large text box as you did in step 2.

7. Paste the copied text boxes and labels from step 5 into the blank area.

8. Set the txtVacationStart and txtVacationEnd text boxes on the Read page to be read-only.

Now, you will make the custom actions that allow the supervisor to respond. The quickest method is to click Options and then type **Approve; Disapprove** in the Use Voting Buttons box. Switch to the (Actions) page of the form to see that two actions, Approve and Disapprove, were automatically added (see Figure 14.2). Select Approve, and then click Properties to see the details for the Approve action (see Figure 14.3).

> The Use Voting Buttons box is available only if you use Outlook in Corporate or Workgroup mode. In Internet Mail Only mode, you can still create voting buttons, but you must use the (Actions) page of the form and set Address Form Like A to Response, as described in the next section. You can also use the `CreateVoteMessage` procedure found in Hour 13, "Working with the Object Models."

FIGURE 14.2

Voting buttons create custom Response actions.

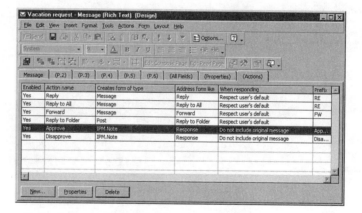

FIGURE 14.3

Action properties govern what kind of item the action will create and what it will look like.

14

Now, make one change on the properties so that the supervisor's action will look more like a normal reply. Under When Responding, select Include Original Message Text.

Run the form to test it, sending a vacation request to yourself if you don't have a friendly boss to test it with. The recipient should see a message such as that in Figure 14.4, with voting buttons. If you click Approve and choose Edit the Response Before Sending, you will see a standard Message form (see Figure 14.5) with these characteristics:

- *Approve* as the prefix for the Subject field
- The original sender's text in the body of the message

FIGURE 14.4

Click Approve or Disapprove to respond to the vacation request.

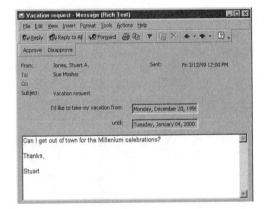

FIGURE 14.5

Clicking one of the custom action buttons produces a new item, using the form specified on the Form Action Properties dialog.

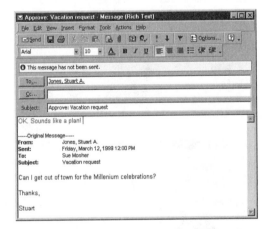

Try different ways of entering dates in the Date/Time text boxes. For example, to get the dates in Figure 14.4, I typed **third Monday in December** and **2 days after 1/1/2000**.

Users will see custom action buttons only on sent or saved items. You won't see them while you're composing a new item.

After looking at custom action properties, you will enhance this custom action so that it sends back not just a message, but an appointment ready to save to the Calendar folder.

Custom Action Properties

As you saw in Listing 13.1 in the preceding hour, you can create a new action for an Outlook item object named `objItem` by inserting an appropriate statement:

```
Set objAction = objItem.Actions.Add
```

and then setting the properties of the `Action` object. Table 14.1 relates the properties of an `Action` object to the settings in the Form Action Properties dialog box (refer to Figure 14.3), showing the corresponding Outlook constants, where appropriate.

TABLE 14.1 Outlook Form `Action` Properties

Form Action *Properties Setting*	*Object Property*	*Possible Values*	*Outlook Constant*
Address Form Like A	`CopyLike`	Reply	`olReply` (0)
		Reply to All	`olReplyAll` (1)
		Forward	`olForward` (2)
		Reply to Folder	`olReplyFolder` (3)
		Response	`olRespond` (4)
Enabled	`Enabled`	`True` or `False`	
Message Class	`MessageClass`	(Any published form)	
Action Name	`Name`	(Any name)	
Subject Prefix	`Prefix`	(Any prefix)	

14

continues

TABLE 14.1 continued

Form Action Properties Setting	Object Property	Possible Values	Outlook Constant
When Responding	ReplyStyle	Do Not Include Original Message Text	olOmitOriginalText (0)
		Attach Original Message	olEmbedOriginalItem (1)
		Include Original Message Text	olIncludeOriginalText (2)
		Include and Indent Original Message Text	olIndentOriginalText (3)
		Prefix Each Line of the Original Message	olReplyTickOriginalText (1000)
		Attach Link to Original Message	
		Respect User's Default	olUserPreference (5)
This Action Will	ResponseStyle	Open the Form	olOpen (0)
		Send the Form Immediately	olSend (1)
		Prompt the User to Open or Send	olPrompt (2)

Form Action Properties Setting	Object Property	Possible Values	Outlook Constan
Show Action on	ShowOn	Don't Show	olDontShow (0)
		Menu and Toolbar	olMenu (1)
		Menu Only	olMenuAndToolbar (2)

The Check button on the Form Action Properties dialog makes it easier for you to specify the form without going through the Choose Form dialog. You can type in the name of a form, such as **IPM.Appointment** for an Appointment form, and then click Check to make sure that the form is available in one of the form libraries. Alternatively, you can click the arrow in the Form Name box, choose Forms, and then pick from the Choose Form dialog.

The CopyLike property (labeled on the (Actions) tab as Address Form Like A) governs how properties are copied from the original item to the new item that the custom action creates. Table 14.2 offers suggestions on when to use which option.

TABLE 14.2 Address Form Usage

If You Want to...	Address Form like a...
Send a reply to the sender of the original item.	Reply
Send a reply to the sender of the original item and any Cc recipients.	Reply to All
Copy data from fields on one Post form to fields of the same name on a different Post form.	Reply to Folder (destination form must be published in the same folder)
Copy data from fields on one Task, Contact, or Appointment form to another form of the same type.	Forward
Have responses tracked on the Tracking tab.	Response

14

Adding Code to Custom Actions

So far, you've been working only with the settings available on the Actions tab. You can do quite a lot with just those, without writing any code. For example, using the Reply to Folder technique, you can create a Post form that inherits data from another Post form. This is very useful in folders for public discussions or for managing complex information, such as help desk requests.

To enhance custom actions with code, use the `CustomAction` event in VBScript code on an Outlook form. Typically, you use a `Select Case` statement to respond to the various actions that might be available. In the case of the Vacation Request form, the code would fit into a structure such as this:

```
Function Item_CustomAction(ByVal Action, ByVal NewItem)
    Select Case Action.Name
        Case "Approve"
            approval code goes here
        Case "Disapprove"
            disapproval code goes here
        Case Else
            'do nothing
    End Select
End Function
```

The two arguments for the `Item_CustomAction` function are

`Action`	The custom action executed by the user
`NewItem`	The new Outlook item that the custom action creates

The `Action` argument is an object representing the custom action created on the Actions tab. Use the `Name` property of the action in a `Select Case` block to specify different code for each action.

The `NewItem` argument gives you a way of working with the new item that the action creates, so you can change its data. You can also prevent the item from being created at all by setting the `Item.CustomAction()` function to `False`. This VBScript example sets the Importance to `High` on the new item created by the Approve action, but aborts the creation of a new item for the Disapprove action.

```
Function Item_CustomAction(ByVal Action, ByVal NewItem)
    Const olImportanceHigh = 2
    Select Case Action.Name
        Case "Approve"
            NewItem.Importance = olImportanceHigh
        Case "Disapprove"
            Item_CustomAction = False
        End Select
End Function
```

You can now do something very practical with the Vacation Request form: Have it automatically create an Appointment item and send it back with the approval. All the user has to do is open the appointment attached to the approval response and save it; it goes automatically into the Calendar folder.

First, on the (Custom Actions) page of the form, change the When Responding property to Do Not Include Original Message. Then, add code for the Approve action, as shown in Listing 14.1.

LISTING 14.1 Enhance a Custom Action with Code

```
 1: Const olOutOfOffice    = 3
 2: Const olAppointmentItem = 1
 3: Const olByValue         = 1
 4:
 5: Function Item_CustomAction(ByVal Action, ByVal NewItem)
 6:     Select Case Action.Name
 7:         Case "Approve"
 8:             dteStart = _
 9:               Item.UserProperties.Find("VacationStart")
10:             dteEnd = _
11:               Item.UserProperties.Find("VacationEnd")
12:             Set objAppt = _
13:               Application.CreateItem(olAppointmentItem)
14:             With objAppt
15:                 .Start = dteStart
16:                 .End = dteEnd
17:                 .ReminderSet = False
18:                 .Subject = "Vacation"
19:                 .AllDayEvent = True
20:                 .BusyStatus = olOutOfOffice
21:             End With
22:             objAppt.Save
23:             Set objAttachment = NewItem.Attachments.Add( _
24:                                 objAppt, olByValue, , _
25:                                 "Your Vacation")
26:             NewItem.Body = "Your vacation has been " & _
27:                            "approved. Open the attached " & _
28:                            "Appointment and save it to " & _
29:                            "your Calendar." & vbCrLf & vbCrLf
30:             objAppt.Delete
31:         Case Else
32:             'do nothing special for other actions
33:     End Select
34: End Function
```

14

Listing 14.1 enhances just the Approve action. It doesn't affect the operation of the Disapprove action. The code includes some interesting features:

- Declarations for global Outlook constants (lines 1–3) make the code more readable.
- A new appointment is created (lines 12–13), and data copied from the incoming message (lines 8–11 and 15–16). The appointment is saved (line 22) so that it can then be attached (lines 23–25). However, because the saved appointment is no longer needed, it's deleted (line 31).
- A `Case Else` statement indicates that any other actions do not have additional code associated with them. Line 32 is a comment, not a code statement; use an apostrophe to set off comments.

Figure 14.6 illustrates the message the user receives after the supervisor clicks the Approve button on a vacation request.

FIGURE 14.6

The user receives not just an approval but also an Appointment item all ready for the Calendar folder.

Because you chose Response under Address This Form Like A, the user can also look at the original item in the Sent Items folder and, on the Tracking tab, see the date that the request was approved.

Replacing Command Buttons with Custom Actions

Did you notice that this very functional Vacation Request form has no custom pages and no Command Button controls? That may be the most important reason to learn how to use custom actions in Outlook.

Say that you have a subroutine you want to run. Your first thought is probably to create a command button on a custom page, especially if you're working with the Task or Appointment form, whose first page cannot be customized. How does the user know that the custom page contains the button to run your procedure? Chances are, the user might never discover it, just because it's on a separate page.

Custom actions alleviate that problem. If you don't need a custom page for some other reason or if, in the case of a Message, Contact, or Post form, you don't want to clutter the main page, consider a custom action instead of a command button on a customized page.

A Contact Form with Fax Action

Take the Contact form, for example. If you use a fax component in Outlook—such as Microsoft Fax in Corporate or Workgroup mode or Symantec WinFax Special Edition in Internet Mail Only mode—you've probably found it odd that the Contact form has no Fax to Contact command on the Actions menu. A custom action designed to run a subroutine can put one there.

First, a little about faxes. Outlook supports many fax components, depending on whether you're working on a standalone system or in a corporation with big fax servers. Virtually every fax component allows you to compose a fax as an e-mail message and send it to an e-mail address that contains the fax number.

If you use Outlook in Corporate or Workgroup mode and have Microsoft Fax or the Fax Client from Microsoft Small Business Server installed, you use this e-mail address syntax: [FAX:name@+##(###)###-####]; name is the name of the recipient, and +##(###)###-#### is the complete number with country code, area code, and the local number. When you specify the full number in this fashion, these fax components can use Windows dialing properties to discover whether you need a 9 for an outside line, how to dial international calls, whether you have call waiting, and so on.

If you use Outlook in Internet Mail Only mode and have the Symantec WinFax Starter Edition installed, the syntax for the e-mail address is fax@9w###-####; ###-#### represents the local number to dial. Include the 9w if you must dial 9 for an outside line. If you're dialing long distance or international, you would have to include all the codes for the number, exactly as you want it dialed. To make this work in code on a form can become complicated because you also have to track your local country and area code to know when to provide that information as part of the e-mail address. Therefore, in this hour's example, you will do just the procedure for Corporate or Workgroup mode.

14

A custom action to create a fax from a Contact item must

- Obtain the contact's name.
- Obtain one fax number.
- Combine them into an address.
- Create a new message with that address in the To box.

Start by opening a new Contact form in design mode. Switch to the (Actions) page, and add a Fax to Contact action. You do not have to specify any form under Form Name because you will create the form in code. You can use the defaults for the other Form Action Properties settings.

Next, add the code in Listing 14.2 to the form. In this example, you will check the Business Fax first, then the Home Fax number, and finally the Other Fax number.

LISTING 14.2 A Custom Action Provides a Fax to Contact Button

```
 1: Const olMailItem = 0
 2:
 3: Function Item_CustomAction(ByVal Action, ByVal NewItem)
 4:     Select Case Action.Name
 5:         Case "Fax to Contact"
 6:             If Item.BusinessFaxNumber <> "" Then
 7:                 strTo = Item.BusinessFaxNumber
 8:             ElseIf Item.HomeFaxNumber <> "" Then
 9:                 strTo = Item.HomeFaxNumber
10:             ElseIf Item.OtherFaxNumber <> "" Then
11:                 strTo = Item.OtherFaxNumber
12:             Else
13:                 strTo = ""
14:             End If
15:             If strTo <> "" Then
16:                 strTo = "[FAX:" & _
17:                         Item.FullName & "@" & _
18:                         strTo & "]"
19:                 Set objFax = _
20:                     Application.CreateItem(olMailItem)
21:                 objFax.To = strTo
22:                 objFax.Recipients.ResolveAll
23:                 objFax.Display
24:             Else
25:                 MsgBox "This contact has no fax number."
26:             End If
27:             Item_CustomAction = False
28:         Case Else
29:             ' do nothing
30:     End Select
31: End Function
```

When users open a Contact item created with this form, they'll see a Fax to Contact button on the toolbar. Clicking it puts the code in Listing 14.2 to work:

- Lines 6–11 obtain the first fax number available among the Business Fax, Home Fax, and Other Fax fields.

- Lines 16–18 build the e-mail address using the syntax just discussed.

- Lines 19–23 create the new message, add the fax number to the To field, and then display the item.

Notice the Item_CustomAction = False statement to cancel the creation of any item from the custom action, just in case you forgot and specified a form on the Contact item's (Actions) tab.

By the way, if you later add a custom page to the Contact form and want to add a command button to generate a fax for the contact, you don't have to rewrite the code. You can run any custom action from code by using its Execute method. Here's how you would run the Fax to Contact action from a command button named cmdFaxToContact:

```
Sub cmdFaxToContact_Click()
    Item.CustomActions.Item("Fax to Contact").Execute
End Sub
```

Summary

Custom actions are a unique and powerful Outlook programming tool to help you generate new items that inherit properties. They also allow you to add toolbar buttons that run code in your forms without the need for command buttons on a custom page.

In the next hour, you will look more closely at Outlook folders—how to access any folder in the hierarchy and how to find particular items in a folder.

Q&A

Q Because I can customize the Outlook toolbar to add buttons that run VBA macros, why would I want to use custom action buttons instead?

A One reason is backwards compatibility. If you have to design for Outlook 97 or Outlook 98 users, you can't use VBA; everything must happen in form code.

Another reason is to keep things simple. If you use a particular procedure only in one certain form, there's no need to clutter your main Outlook toolbars with a button to run a macro. Instead, use a custom action to integrate the button and its code with the form itself. Also, as you will see in Hour 22, "Designing Reports with Microsoft Word," it's easier to distribute new forms than to distribute Outlook macros.

14

Q **Why do I have to choose Response under Address Form Like A if I want to create voting buttons?**

A It's the Response option that adds the tracking information so that the recipient sees your response on the Tracking tab of the original outgoing item in Sent Items.

Workshop

Work through the quiz questions and exercises so that you can better understand Outlook programming. See Appendix A for Answers.

Quiz

1. What event on an Outlook form lets you control custom actions?

2. In the event handler for the event in question 1, how do you refer to the new item that the custom action creates?

3. What statement do you use in the same event handler to avoid creating a new item by a custom action?

Exercises

1. For the Vacation Request form, add a validation formula and validation text to the txtVacationEnd text box on the Compose page to make sure that the user doesn't have a vacation that can end before it even begins.

2. Experiment with different combinations of the Message Class and Address Form Like A choices to get a feeling for what properties are transferred from the old item to the new item in different situations.

3. Assume that you have access to an Internet fax service that lets you send faxes by addressing them to number@myfaxservice.com, where number is the fax number with no punctuation. (In other words, to fax a document to +1 (202) 555-1234, you would e-mail it to 12025551234@myfaxservice.com.) Modify the Fax to Contact code in Listing 14.2 to send a fax through your Internet fax service.

HOUR 15

Working with Stores and Folders

This hour is devoted to techniques for working with Outlook information stores and folders—creating them, exploring their properties, accessing folders beyond the default set, and finding items within folders. Not every user sees the same set of folders, but the methods you learn in this lesson apply to all kinds of folders.

Highlights of this hour include

- Which types of information stores different kinds of users are likely to see
- How to access the default information store
- When you might want to use a new `Explorer` object to display a different folder
- How to access a folder that resides anywhere in the folder tree
- How to create, copy, move, and delete folders
- How to use the `Restrict` and `Sort` methods to build a better `NextBusinessDay()` function

Information Store Concepts

Messages and other Outlook items are stored in folders. Folders are kept in what is known as an *information store*. Every Outlook user has at least one information store. For a standalone user, the basic store is a Personal Folders .pst file. (*PST* stands for *Personal Store*.) For a user connected to Microsoft Exchange Server, the basic store is the Exchange Server mailbox.

Within the basic store, you can always find the default Outlook folders, such as Inbox and Calendar. These are the folders you can access with the `GetDefaultFolder` method on the `NameSpace` object.

Users connected to Microsoft Exchange Server also have access to *Public Folders*, a hierarchy of folders for shared access. Exchange Server users may have access to additional user mailboxes, each with its own Inbox and other default folders. For example, an executive assistant may have access to the boss's folders.

> When working with Exchange Server folders outside the basic mailbox store, you must allow for the possibility that the user might not have full access to a folder. A user might be able to see the folder in the hierarchy, but not be able to work with the items within the folder because of permission restrictions on the folder.

Standalone users connecting to an IMAP account will have an Inbox folder on the IMAP server, as well as the default Inbox in the Personal Folders file. They may also see a public folder hierarchy.

> For users running Outlook in Corporate or Workgroup mode, the available information stores are related to the services installed in Tools, Services. In Internet Mail Only mode, the stores depend on the accounts (in the case of IMAP folders) and what Personal Folders files are currently in use.

In addition to the preceding possibilities, any user may have more than one Personal Folders file. For instance, I have a Personal Folders file for this book, in addition to my basic Personal Folders file.

Information Store Techniques

You can access any Personal Folders file and create a new one through the Outlook object model. This code prompts the user to enter the path for a file and then uses the `AddStore` method on the `NameSpace` object to access an existing Personal Folders file or create a new one at the designated location.

```
Sub AddPST()
    Dim objApp As Application
    Dim objNS As NameSpace
    Dim strPath As String
    Set objApp = CreateObject("Outlook.Application")
    Set objNS = objApp.GetNamespace("MAPI")
    strPath = InputBox("Enter the full name and path for " & _
                       "a new or existing .pst file", _
                       "Add Personal Folders")
    If Right(strPath, 4) <> ".pst" Then
        strPath = strPath & ".pst"
    End If
    objNS.AddStore strPath
End Sub
```

Normally, you won't want the user to type in long pathnames and filenames. As you will see in Hour 20, "ActiveX and Other Controls," you can use a common dialog box control to make it easy for users to browse system files.

In the Outlook object model, all further work with stores takes place through `MAPIFolder` objects and `Folders` collections. To find out what kind of stores are currently available, you have to use CDO.

Remember that CDO is available only in Corporate or Workgroup mode and that you must add a reference to the Microsoft CDO 1.21 Library before you can use CDO objects in VBA code.

The following code uses CDO to get the display name of each available store from its `Name` property. The `ProviderName` property of the store indicates what kind of store it is, returning `"Microsoft Exchange Server"` and `"Personal Folders"` for the two most common sources of stores.

```
Sub EnumStoresCDO()
    Dim objSession As Session
    Dim objStore As InfoStore
    Dim strMsg As String
    Set objSession = CreateObject("MAPI.Session")
    objSession.Logon , , False, False
    strMsg = ""
    For Each objStore In objSession.InfoStores
        strMsg = strMsg & objStore.Name & " (" & _
                    objStore.ProviderName & ")" & vbCrLf
    Next
    strMsg = "These stores are available:" & vbCrLf & _
            vbCrLf & strMsg
    MsgBox strMsg, , "Available Stores"
End Sub
```

In the Outlook object model, you can get the names of the stores with the following code, but you don't get the additional information on the type of store:

```
Sub EnumStoresOOM()
    Dim objApp As Application
    Dim objNS As NameSpace
    Dim objFolders As Folders
    Dim objFolder As MAPIFolder
    Dim strMsg As String
    Set objApp = CreateObject("Outlook.Application")
    Set objNS = objApp.GetNamespace("MAPI")
    Set objFolders = objNS.Folders
    strMsg = ""
    For Each objFolder In objFolders
        strMsg = strMsg & objFolder.Name & vbCrLf
    Next
    strMsg = "These stores are available:" & vbCrLf & _
            vbCrLf & strMsg
    MsgBox strMsg, , "Available Stores"
End Sub
```

If you have multiple Personal Folders files or an Exchange Server mailbox, and at least one Personal Folders file, you might need to know which one is the default store. This DefaultStoreRoot() function uses the Inbox to get the root folder for the default store from the Parent property of the Inbox:

```
Function DefaultStoreRoot() As MAPIFolder
    Dim objApp As Application
    Dim objNS As NameSpace
    Dim objInbox As MAPIFolder
    Set objApp = CreateObject("Outlook.Application")
    Set objNS = objApp.GetNamespace("MAPI")
    Set objInbox = objNS.GetDefaultFolder(olFolderInbox)
    Set DefaultStoreRoot = objInbox.Parent
End Function
```

Working with Explorers

15

The Explorers collection is part of the Application object and represents all the viewer windows currently open in Outlook. For example, it's not unusual to have both the Inbox and Calendar open in separate windows so that you can switch back and forth between your e-mail and appointments. If your program needs to display the Calendar folder, it should first check whether an Explorer displaying the calendar is already available.

Listing 15.1 checks the CurrentFolder property of each Explorer object. It uses the DefaultStoreRoot() function just shown to make sure that any visible Calendar folder is the real default Calendar folder, not a folder named Calendar from somewhere else in the hierarchy.

LISTING 15.1 Check Whether the Folder Is Already Displayed Before Opening a New Explorer

```
 1: Sub ShowCalendar()
 2:     Dim objApp As Application
 3:     Dim objNS As NameSpace
 4:     Dim objExplorers As Explorers
 5:     Dim objExpl As Explorer
 6:     Dim objRoot As MAPIFolder
 7:     Dim objFolder As MAPIFolder
 8:     Dim blnIsCalOpen As Boolean
 9:     Set objApp = CreateObject("Outlook.Application")
10:     Set objNS = objApp.GetNamespace("MAPI")
11:     Set objExplorers = objApp.Explorers
12:     blnIsCalOpen = False
13:     Set objRoot = DefaultStoreRoot()
14:     For Each objExpl In objExplorers
15:         If objExpl.CurrentFolder.Name = "Calendar" And _
16:           objExpl.CurrentFolder.Parent = objRoot Then
17:             blnIsCalOpen = True
18:             objExpl.Activate
19:             Exit For
20:         End If
21:     Next
22:     If blnIsCalOpen = False Then
23:         Set objFolder = _
24:           objNS.GetDefaultFolder(olFolderCalendar)
25:         Set objExpl = objFolder.GetExplorer
26:         objExpl.Activate
27:     End If
28: End Sub
```

If an `Explorer` showing the desired folder is already available, use the `Activate` method (line 18) to switch to that `Explorer`.

If you want to display a folder in a new `Explorer`, first use the `GetExplorer` method on the folder to set an `Explorer` object variable. Then, use the `Activate` method on the `Explorer` object to show it.

To use the currently active `Explorer` to display a different folder, include a statement that sets the `CurrentFolder` on the `ActiveExplorer` object to a different `MAPIFolder` object:

```
Set objApp.ActiveExplorer.CurrentFolder = objFolder
```

Use the `Close` method to close any `Explorer`. The following code closes all `Explorer` windows and then activates a new one displaying the Inbox folder:

```
Sub CloseAllButInbox()
    Dim objApp As Application
    Dim objNS As NameSpace
    Dim objFolder As MAPIFolder
    Dim objFolderKeep As MAPIFolder
    Dim objExplorers As Explorers
    Dim objExpl As Explorer
    Set objApp = CreateObject("Outlook.Application")
    Set objNS = objApp.GetNamespace("MAPI")
    Set objExplorers = objApp.Explorers
    Do Until objExplorers.Count = 0
        objExplorers.Item(1).Close
    Loop
    Set objFolder = objNS.GetDefaultFolder(olFolderInbox)
    Set objExpl = objFolder.GetExplorer
    objExpl.Activate
End Sub
```

If you close all `Explorer` objects, including the `ActiveExplorer`, the user may no longer have any Outlook windows open. Therefore, it's a good idea to include code to make sure that at least one folder remains active in an `Explorer`.

Accessing Folders

In Hour 12, "Handling User Input and Feedback," you learned several techniques for accessing folders:

- The `Namespace.GetDefaultFolder` method to get one of the default Outlook folders
- The `Application.ActiveExplorer.CurrentFolder` object to get the folder currently displayed in the Outlook viewer
- The `Namespace.PickFolder` method to allow the user to choose a folder

The previous section on `Explorer` objects shows how to use an `Explorer`'s `CurrentFolder` property to get a folder displayed in windows other than the active folder viewer. In this section, you learn two more folder retrieval methods: getting a folder from another Exchange Server user's mailbox and getting a folder when you know the full path to the folder through the hierarchy.

Because you can have duplicate folder names and duplicate information store names, just knowing a folder's name isn't enough. In fact, if you look at Table 15.1, which summarizes methods that return a folder from the `Namespace` object, you will see that there is no direct way to retrieve a folder with only its name. You need to know either the mailbox where it resides—if you're getting another Exchange Server user's folder—or IDs for both the information store and the folder.

TABLE 15.1   Namespace Folder Methods

Method	Returns
`GetDefaultFolder` `(FolderType)`	Any of the default Outlook folders
`GetFolderFromID` `(EntryIdFolder,` `EntryIDStore)`	Any folder from any information store
`GetSharedDefaultFolder` `(Recipient,FolderType)`	Any default Outlook folder from another Exchange Server user's mailbox
`PickFolder()`	The folder chosen by the user from the folder hierarchy

The `GetFolderFromID` method is not commonly used because other available methods are more direct. Both the arguments for `GetFolderFromID`—the folder and store IDs—are `String` values. One situation in which `GetFolderFromID` can be useful is when you are working with a folder using CDO techniques and then want to pass it to the Outlook object model as an object variable.

Getting Default Folders from Another Mailbox

To get a default Outlook folder from another Exchange Server user's mailbox, you must have a resolved `Recipient` object before you can use the `GetSharedDefaultFolder` method. You will look in more detail at `Recipient` objects in the next hour. Listing 15.2 uses a dummy mail item to allow you to get a `Recipient` from a name entered in an input box. Lines 14–16 create the mail item, add the name to the `Recipients` collection, and then use the Resolve method on the Recipient. Resolving a recipient compares the display name to the names in the Address Book. If the Resolved property is True, you have a valid recipient and can continue with the GetSharedDefaultFolder method.

LISTING 15.2 Use a Dummy Mail Item to Resolve a Recipient

```
 1: Function GetOtherUserCalendar() As MAPIFolder
 2:     Dim objApp As Application
 3:     Dim objNS As NameSpace
 4:     Dim objFolder As MAPIFolder
 5:     Dim strName As String
 6:     Dim objDummy As MailItem
 7:     Dim objRecip As Recipient
 8:     Set objApp = CreateObject("Outlook.Application")
 9:     Set objNS = objApp.GetNamespace("MAPI")
10:     Set objFolder = Nothing
11:     strName = InputBox("Whose folder do you want to open?", _
12:                        "Get Other User Folder")
13:     If strName <> "" Then
14:         Set objDummy = objApp.CreateItem(olMailItem)
15:         Set objRecip = objDummy.Recipients.Add(strName)
16:         objRecip.Resolve
17:         If objRecip.Resolved = True Then
18:             On Error Resume Next
19:             Set objFolder = _
20:               objNS.GetSharedDefaultFolder(objRecip, _
21:                 olFolderCalendar)
22:             On Error GoTo 0
23:         Else
24:             MsgBox "Could not find " & Quote(strName), , _
25:                     "User not found"
26:         End If
27:     End If
28:     Set GetOtherUserCalendar = objFolder
29: End Function
```

It's important to notice that there is every possibility that you won't find the user. If that happens, the statement

```
Set GetOtherUserCalendar = objFolder
```

results in the GetOtherUserCalendar function returning Nothing. The calling subroutine has to test for that possible result, as in this example:

```
Set objFolder = GetOtherUserCalendar()
    If objFolder Is Nothing Then
        your code to handle this case here
    Else
        your code to work with folder here
    End If
```

The statements On Error Resume Next, in line 18, and On Error GoTo 0, in line 22, turn on error handling then back off. This allows the code to keep running without displaying an error to the user, even if it can't open the other user's folder. You learn more about error handling in Hour 19, "Debugging Applications."

Walking the Folder Tree

What if you know the full path and name of the folder? How can you open it? Your code has to start at the top of the folder tree, walk through each level to find a matching folder, and then move on to the subfolders at the next level.

The GetExchangeListFolder subroutine in Listing 15.3 looks for a folder whose full path is "Public Folders/All Public Folders/Mailing Lists/Msexchange list" and displays it in a new Explorer if found.

LISTING 15.3 Walk the Folder Tree by Parsing the Path

```
 1: Sub GetExchangeListFolder ()
 2:     Dim objApp As Application
 3:     Dim objNS As NameSpace
 4:     Dim objFolder As MAPIFolder
 5:     Dim objFolders As Folders
 6:     Dim strName As String
 7:     Dim arrName() As String
 8:     Dim objExpl As Explorer
 9:     Dim I as Integer
10:     Dim blnFound As Boolean
11:     Set objApp = CreateObject("Outlook.Application")
12:     Set objNS = objApp.GetNamespace("MAPI")
13:     strName = "Public Folders/All Public Folders/" & _
14:             "Mailing Lists/Msexchange list"
15:     arrName = Split(strName, "/")
16:     Set objFolders = objNS.Folders
17:     blnFound = False
18:     For I = 0 To UBound(arrName)
19:         For Each objFolder In objFolders
20:             If objFolder.Name = arrName(I) Then
21:                 Set objFolders = objFolder.Folders
22:                 blnFound = True
23:                 Exit For
24:             Else
25:                 blnFound = False
26:             End If
```

continues

LISTING 15.3   continued

```
27:            Next
28:            If blnFound = False Then
29:                Exit For
30:            End If
31:        Next
32:        If blnFound = True Then
33:            Set objExpl = objFolder.GetExplorer
34:            objExpl.Display
35:        End If
36: End Sub
```

The Split(strName, "/") function in line 14 turns the path into a String array. Each entry in the array represents a different level of the folder hierarchy. The two nested For...Next loops test the folder names at each level, comparing them with the name stored in the array. If there is a match, the blnFound flag is set to True. If blnFound is still True after processing the entire array, objFolder represents a folder that can be displayed in an Explorer window.

In Listing 15.3, because objFolders is a collection and the array contains the name you're looking for, why can't you just use

Set objFolder = objFolders.Item(arrName(I))

to get the folder from the name? This is certainly a more direct technique than using a For Each...Next loop to check each folder name. However, if there is no matching item in the objFolders collection, you will receive a runtime error, the user will get an indecipherable error message, and the rest of the subroutine will not run. To make use of the more direct technique, you have to know how to handle runtime errors, so you will return to this example in Hour 19, "Debugging Applications."

Folder Techniques

You already know many useful techniques for working with Outlook folders. Because an Outlook folder is a member of a Folders collection, you use the Add or Remove method on the parent Folders collection to create or delete a folder. Table 15.2 lists other methods for an individual Outlook folder, which is represented by a MAPIFolder object.

TABLE 15.2   MAPIFolder Object Methods

Method	Description	Returns
CopyTo	Copies the entire folder	The MAPIFolder object representing the newly copied folder.
Delete	Deletes the current folder	N/A
GetExplorer	Initializes an Explorer object for the folder	The Explorer object representing the folder; use the Activate method to show it.
MoveTo	Moves the entire folder	N/A

> The Outlook object model and the CDO model use two different types of objects for folders. In the Outlook object model, a folder uses the MAPIFolder object. With CDO, a folder uses the Folder object. They have different properties and methods. When declaring object folder variables, be sure to use the correct type—MAPIFolder or Folder—in your Dim statement.

You learned how to use the GetExplorer method earlier in this hour. The remaining sections introduce other useful folder techniques.

Creating and Deleting Folders

To create a folder, use the Add method on the parent folder where you want to create the new folder. The Add method takes two arguments: the name of the folder and an optional type constant that defines what kind of items the folder can hold. Table 15.3 lists the possible values for type.

TABLE 15.3   Add Folder Types

Folder Contains	Type Constant (Value)
Appointment items	olFolderCalendar (9)
Contact items	olFolderContacts (10)
Journal items	olFolderJournal (11)
Message items	olFolderInbox (6) or olFolderDrafts (16)
Note items	olFolderNotes (12)
Task items	olFolderTasks (13)

For example, this statement creates a new folder within an objFolders collection to hold Contact items in a folder named Old Contacts:

```
Set objFolder = objFolders.Add("Old Contacts", olFolderContacts)
```

If you omit the second argument, the folder type, the new folder inherits its type setting from the parent folder. This code creates a new folder named Subscriptions as a subfolder of the Inbox folder. Because the type argument is omitted, the new folder will also be a folder to hold Message items.

```
Sub CreateSubsFolder()
    Dim objApp As Application
    Dim objNS As NameSpace
    Dim objFolder As MAPIFolder
    Dim objNewFolder As MAPIFolder
    Set objApp = CreateObject("Outlook.Application")
    Set objNS = objApp.GetNamespace("MAPI")
    Set objFolder = objNS.GetDefaultFolder(olFolderInbox)
    Set objNewFolder = objFolder.Folders.Add("Subscriptions")
End Sub
```

You will get a runtime error if you try to add a new folder with the same name as an existing folder in the same Folders collection.

Notice the use of objFolder.Folders.Add to add a new folder to the Folders collection of the objFolder object. You don't add the folder to the objFolder itself, but to its Folders collection.

To remove a folder, use the statement objFolder.Delete. You can also use the Remove method on its parent Folders collection, as described in Hour 13, "Working with the Object Models."

Moving and Copying Folders

You can copy or move entire folders, with all their items, to a new location in the folder hierarchy. You need two object variables: one for the folder being moved or copied and the second for the destination parent folder. The syntax for these two methods is similar, but CopyTo operates as a function, returning the newly copied folder as a MAPIFolder object:

```
Set objNewFolder = objFolder.CopyTo(objDestFolder)
objFolder.MoveTo objDestFolder
```

Filtering and Sorting Folders

Find, FindNext, Restrict, and Sort are four methods that work with a folder's Items collection to provide some control over what items are available and in what order. Find returns the first item that meets your conditions; FindNext, subsequent items. Restrict is another type of filter, returning a subset of the Items collection. Sort returns the same collection, but sorted.

> Find, Restrict, and Sort do not change the way a folder is displayed in an Explorer.

Here is the basic syntax for Find and its associated method, FindNext:

```
Set objItem = objFolder.Items.Find(filter)
Set objItem = objFolder.Items.FindNext
```

The Restrict method uses a similar syntax, but returns an Items collection, instead of a single object representing an Outlook item:

```
Set objItems = objFolder.Items.Restrict(filter)
```

The filter argument is a String expression that evaluates to True or False. It includes at least one field, a comparison operator, and the value you want to find for that field. Field names are in brackets. The field can be either intrinsic or user-defined. String values must be surrounded by either one set of single quotation marks or two sets of double quotation marks. Date/Time values must be expressed as strings and also surrounded with quotes. Here are some examples of simple filters:

```
"[City] = 'Moscow'"
```

```
"[Unread] = True"
```

```
"[Start] >= ""March 3, 2000"" "
```

Filters can be difficult to build because of the need to surround the entire expression with quotation marks and enclose String and Date/Time literals in quotation marks. That's one reason you created the Quote() function in Hour 8, "Code Basics." Another trick to making filters easier to work with is to build the filter as a separate series of statements and then apply it with the Find or Restrict method. This code builds a filter to obtain all items during the months of June, July, and August 2000.

```
strFilter = "[Start] >= " & Quote("6/1/2000") & _
            " And [Start] <= " & Quote("8/31/2000")
Set objItems = objFolder.Items.Restrict(strFilter)
```

The complete `strFilter` expression is

```
"[Start] >= ""6/1/2000"" And [Start] <= ""8/31/2000"""
```

See the help topics on the `Find` and `Restrict` methods for important information on what fields cannot be used in filters.

You cannot use variables, constants, or functions in the `String` expression itself because they won't be evaluated. For example, in the filter `"[Start] >= Now"`, the expression `"Now"` is not equivalent to the `Now` function.

However, you can use variables, constants, and functions in the filter expression with the ampersand (&) concatenation operator. Use the `Quote()` function from Hour 8 to add the required surrounding quotation marks for dates and strings. This code builds a filter to return appointments that begin later than seven days from today.

```
strFilter = "[Start] >= " & _
            Quote(Format(Now + 7, "Short Date"))
```

If today's date is March 15, 2000, the expression `Now + 7` evaluates to the `Date/Time` value March 22, 2000. To use that value in a filter, you must convert it to a `String`. The VBA `Format()` function, which can convert any numeric or date value to a string, is particularly helpful because it includes several intrinsic date and time formats. `Format(Now + 7, "Short Date")` returns the `String` value `"3/22/2000"` or `"3/22/00"`, depending on the Regional Settings set in the Control Panel. In VBScript, the equivalent function would be `FormatDateTime(date, vbShortDate)`. You might see different formats outside the U.S. and Canada, but they should still work in your filters.

You can use a filter such as `"[Categories] = 'mycat'"` to look for a single category, even if the items in question fall into more than one category.

The `Sort` method comes into play when you not only want to retrieve certain items, but you also want to get them in a particular order. Use `Sort` like this:

```
objItems.Sort property, descending
```

The `property` argument is a `String` value—the name of the property you want to sort by. You can enclose a built-in property's name in brackets if you want to stay consistent with the `Find` and `Restrict` syntax. However, if you sort by a user-defined field, do not enclose the name in brackets. The `descending` argument is optional. The default is `False`. Set it to `True` if you want the returned `Items` collection to be sorted in descending order.

15

> Sort can help when you want to display Outlook data in a list box on a VBA form. Without it, you must either write your own sort routine for the list box items or live with the items appearing in what might look like a random order.

A Better `NextBusinessDay()` Function

Back in Hour 10, "Working with Expressions and Functions," I promised that you would revisit the `NextBusinessDay()` function to make it cognizant of holidays and vacations. Listing 15.4 combines `Restrict` and `Sort` to accomplish this and also introduces two new methods you can use on `Items` collections, `GetFirst` and `GetNext`.

This version of the `NextBusinessDay()` function makes several key assumptions:

- That both vacation and holiday days are marked with corresponding categories
- That your business does not operate on holiday days
- That holidays and vacations are listed as all-day events

In your own business world, some or all of these assumptions might not hold. The code would be more complex in that case. For example, if you don't have vacation days categorized as such, you might have to rely on the `Subject` or some other property to indicate that a particular Appointment item is a vacation day. However, you could build on the basic techniques in Listing 15.4.

LISTING 15.4   Accounting for Holidays and Vacations, as Well as Weekends

```
 1: Function NextBusinessDay2(ByVal dteDate, intAhead)
 2:     Dim objApp As Application
 3:     Dim objNS As NameSpace
 4:     Dim objFolder As MAPIFolder
 5:     Dim objItems As Items
 6:     Dim objAppt As AppointmentItem
 7:     Dim strFilter As String
 8:     Dim intDayCount As Integer
 9:     Dim blnSkip As Boolean
10:     strFilter = "[AllDayEvent] = True And " & _
11:       "[End] > " & Quote(Format(dteDate, "Short Date")) & _
12:       " And ([Categories] = " & Quote("Holiday") & _
13:       " Or [Categories] = " & Quote("Vacation") & ")"
14:     Set objApp = CreateObject("Outlook.Application")
15:     Set objNS = objApp.GetNamespace("MAPI")
16:     Set objFolder = objNS.GetDefaultFolder(olFolderCalendar)
17:     Set objItems = objFolder.Items.Restrict(strFilter)
```

continues

LISTING 15.4   continued

```
18:        objItems.Sort "[Start]"
19:        objItems.IncludeRecurrences = True
20:        intDayCount = 1
21:        Do
22:            dteDate = dteDate + 1
23:            blnSkip = False
24:            If Weekday(dteDate, vbMonday) >= 6 Then
25:                blnSkip = True
26:            ElseIf objItems.Count > 0 Then
27:                Set objAppt = objItems.GetFirst
28:                Do While objAppt.Start <= dteDate
29:                    If objAppt.End > dteDate Then
30:                        blnSkip = True
31:                    End If
32:                    Set objAppt = objItems.GetNext
33:                    If objAppt Is Nothing Then
34:                        Exit Do
35:                    End If
36:                Loop
37:            End If
38:            If blnSkip = False Then
39:                intDayCount = intDayCount + 1
40:            End If
41:        Loop Until intDayCount > intAhead
42:        NextBusinessDay2 = dteDate
43: End Function
```

If the dteDate argument is 3/15/2000, the filter constructed in lines 10–13 as strFilter looks like this: "[AllDayEvent] = True And [End] > '3/15/2000' And ([Categories] = 'Holiday' Or [Categories] = 'Vacation')".

The Restrict method using this filter returns all holiday and vacation events that don't occur before the date in question.

The outer Do loop (lines 20–40) uses a variable, intDayCount, to keep track of the number of valid business days encountered. It is incremented only for days that are not weekends and do not overlap any appointments in the objItems collection.

When testing a filter in VBA code, add a Debug.Print strFilter statement so that you can see the results in the Immediate window.

The objItems collection was filtered to eliminate events that were too early and was sorted on the Start property (line 18). It also uses the IncludeRecurrences property (line 19) to include individual instances of recurring events. (This property does not work if you sort by anything other than Start. It also can create an infinitely large Items collection.)

In the inner Do loop, lines 28–29 check whether the date currently under consideration overlaps with any holiday or vacation events. The GetFirst method returns the first item in the objItems collection, and the GetNext method returns subsequent items. Line 33 uses the expression objAppt Is Nothing to test whether the loop has exhausted the supply of events in objItems; if so, it exits the loop.

> You can also use the GetLast and GetPrevious methods on an Items collection. Always use GetFirst before GetNext, and GetLast before GetPrevious.

Filters can become complicated, but this example should help you see how the combination of the Restrict and Sort methods can bring order to what can seem at first like an impossibly complex task.

Summary

We've covered many new concepts and methods in this hour. You should have a good understanding of the various information stores you might encounter and the relationship between Explorer objects and the MAPIFolder objects they display. Your toolkit also now includes a host of methods for creating, deleting, moving, filtering, and sorting folders.

In the next hour, you get down to the same level of detail with Outlook items.

Q&A

Q Why can't I just refer to folders by name? Getting an object every time seems like a lot of trouble.

A Folder names can be duplicated. You can have a Calendar folder that's a subfolder of a Calendar folder that itself is a subfolder of the default Calendar folder. A name just isn't enough to uniquely identify a folder.

Q Is there any advantage to using Find versus Restrict (or vice versa)?

A Find tends to be better when you have to work with only a few items. Restrict lends itself well to situations in which performance is not an issue and you have to work with an Items collection.

Q Can I use wildcards in a `Find` or `Restrict` filter, for example, to find all the Contact items with zip codes that begin with *303*?

A Although the `Find` and `Restrict` methods require exact and complete matches, you can build your own wildcard filter by taking advantage of the fact that you can compare strings with operators such as > and <. For example, `"[BusinessAddressPostalCode] > '303' And [BusinessAddressPostalCode] < '304'"` is a filter that finds all Contact items with zip codes starting with *303*. It works because `"30329"` is greater than `"303"` in the world of comparing String values, but less than `"304"`.

Q Can I use the `Find` and `Restrict` methods on several folders at once, perhaps to get a list of all unread items?

A This is beyond the capability of these methods, which work on just one Items collection at a time. You would have to get a separate Items collection for each folder.

Workshop

Work through the quiz questions and exercises so that you can better understand Outlook Programming. See Appendix A for Answers.

Quiz

1. What kind of information store can be present more than once in an Outlook profile?

2. What do you think would happen if you tried to use the `GetSharedDefaultFolder` method with a recipient argument that had not been resolved?

Exercises

1. Using Tools, Services (assuming you use Outlook in Corporate or Workgroup mode), determine which information stores are in your default mail profile. Use the `EnumCDOStores` subroutine to list the stores. Do you get the same result?

2. Modify Listing 15.3 to add a message box to handle the case of a folder not being found. Try to use the information in the `arrName()` array to tell the user exactly what part of the folder hierarchy could not be found.

3. Adapt the code for the `GetExchangeListFolder` subroutine in Listing 15.3 to convert it into a function named `GetAnyFolder()` that returns the `MAPIFolder` object for a given folder path.

HOUR 16

Working with Items

In Hour 15, you explored the workings of folders and the Explorer windows that display them. In this hour, you will work with items and their Inspector windows. You will learn about the many methods available for Outlook items and get some tips for dealing with recipients and message bodies.

Highlights of this hour include

- How to work with the Inspector objects that display Outlook items
- How to create, move, copy, delete, and perform other common item tasks
- How to display the Select Names dialog box from code
- Where to find the e-mail address for the sender or recipient of a message
- Why you have to know the format of an item before finding and replacing text

Working with Inspectors

The Inspectors collection is part of the Application object and represents all Outlook items displayed in their own windows. You should already be familiar with the ActiveInspector object, which you used in Hour 12, "Handling User Input and Feedback," to create macros that operate on the currently displayed item.

If an Inspector showing the desired item is already available, you can use the Activate method to switch to that Inspector.

Use the Close method to close any Inspector, using this syntax:

objInspector.Close *savemode*

You must supply a value for the *savemode* argument. Table 16.1 lists possible values. The following code closes all Inspector windows. It then uses the GetInspector method on the item most recently displayed (ActiveInspector.CurrentItem) to get a new Inspector and applies the Activate method to show it.

```
Sub CloseAllInspectors()
    Dim objApp As Application
    Dim objInspectors As Inspectors
    Dim objInspector As Inspector
    Dim objItemKeep As Object
    Set objApp = CreateObject("Outlook.Application")
    Set objInspectors = objApp.Inspectors
    Set objItemKeep = objApp.ActiveInspector.CurrentItem
    Do Until objInspectors.Count = 0
        objInspectors.Item(1).Close olPromptForSave
    Loop
    Set objInspector = objItemKeep.GetInspector
    objInspector.Activate
End Sub
```

TABLE 16.1 The savemode Argument Values for the Close Method

Option	savemode *Value*
Close without saving changes.	olDiscard (1)
If the item was changed, prompt the user to save changes.	olPromptForSave (2)
Close and save changes.	olSave (0)

Table 16.2 lists useful methods for working with form pages in an Inspector window.

TABLE 16.2 The Inspector Methods for Form Pages

Method	Description
HideFormPage(pagename)	Hides the pagename page.
SetCurrentFormPage pagename	Switches to the pagename page.
ShowFormPage(pagename)	Shows the pagename page.

You might, for example, use the ShowFormPage method to display a page that is normally hidden.

Item Techniques

In this section, I will review the wide range of techniques for accessing items and creating new items. You will also see what methods Outlook items have in common and which are particular to specific item types.

Accessing Items

In Hour 12, you saw several methods for accessing specific items. You learned more during the preceding hour, when you worked with the Find and Restrict methods on a Folder.Items collection. There is one more access method, not commonly used—GetItemFromID, which takes as its arguments the String values for the item's EntryID and StoreID properties:

```
Set objApp = CreateObject("Outlook.Application")
Set objNS = objApp.GetNamespace("MAPI")
Set objItem = objNSGetFolderFromID(entryID, storeID)
```

You will see an example of the GetItemFromID method later in the chapter when you use CDO to populate the addresses on a message before displaying it in an Inspector.

> An item does not have an EntryID until it has been saved. The EntryID for an item changes if you move the item to a different folder.

Creating Items

Outlook has three main methods for creating new items. Which one should you use? It depends on whether you are creating a standard item or using a custom template or form. Table 16.3 summarizes the available methods.

TABLE 16.3 Item Creation Methods

Method	Use
Add(*form*) (on a Folder.Items collection)	Create a new item in the folder, with the option of specifying a published *form* as an argument.
CreateItem(*itemtype*)	Create a new default Outlook item, using one of these constants for the *itemtype* argument: olMailItem (0) olAppointmentItem (1) olContactItem (2) olTaskItem (3) olJournalItem (4) olNoteItem (5) olPostItem (6) olDistributionListItem (7)
CreateItemFromTemplate(*template*)	Create a new item from an Outlook .oft *template* file.

Here is an example of each method:

```
Function NewCustomContact() As ContactItem
    Dim objApp As Application
    Dim objNS As NameSpace
    Dim objFolder As MAPIFolder
    Dim objNewContact As ContactItem
    Set objApp = CreateObject("Outlook.Application")
    Set objNS = objApp.GetNamespace("MAPI")
    Set objFolder = objNS.GetDefaultFolder(olFolderContacts)
    Set objNewContact = _
      objFolder.Items.Add("IPM.Contact.MyContact")
    Set NewCustomContact = objNewContact
End Function

Function NewStandardTask() As TaskItem
    Dim objApp As Application
    Set objApp = CreateObject("Outlook.Application")
    Set NewStandardTask = objApp.CreateItem(olTaskItem)
End Function

Function NewCustomAppointment() As AppointmentItem
    Dim objApp As Application
    Dim objNS As NameSpace
    Dim strPath As String
    Set objApp = CreateObject("Outlook.Application")
    Set objNS = objApp.GetNamespace("MAPI")
```

```
    strPath = "C:\Program Files\Microsoft Office\Templates\" & _
            "MyAppt.oft"
    Set NewCustomAppointment = _
      objApp.CreateItemFromTemplate(strPath)
End Function
```

> If you create an Outlook item using code on a VBA form, make sure that either the VBA form is nonmodal or you unload it before you display the new Outlook item. Otherwise, you will get a `dialog box is open` error.

16

In addition to the three methods in Table 16.3, a number of other methods return new items, including `Reply`, `ReplyToAll`, `Forward`, `ForwardAsVcal`, and `ForwardAsVcard`. As you saw in Hour 13, "Working with the Object Models," custom actions on Outlook forms also create new items.

Common Item Methods

The different Outlook items have many methods in common. Table 16.4 provides a summary. Not all methods apply to every item. See the help topic for an individual method for details.

TABLE 16.4 Common Item Methods

Method	Description
Close	Closes the `Inspector` for the item, saving changes if desired
Copy	Returns a copy of the item
Delete	Deletes the item
Display	Displays the item in an `Inspector`
Forward	Executes the Forward action, returning a new `MailItem` object
Move	Moves the item to a different folder
PrintOut	Prints the item with default settings
Reply	Returns a `MailItem` addressed to the original sender
ReplyAll	Returns a `MailItem` addressed to the original sender and any Cc recipients
Save	Saves the item to the folder from which it was opened or to which it was added or, for a new item, to the default folder for the item type
SaveAs	Saves the item to a system file using the specified path and file format
Send	Sends the item (appointment, meeting item, message, or task request)

To copy an item to another folder, first use the Copy method to get a copy of the item, and then use the Move method to place the copy in the destination folder, as in this example:

```
Sub CopyToFolder(objItem as Object, objFolder as MAPIFolder)
    Dim objApp As Application
    Dim objNewItem As Object
    Set objApp = CreateObject("Outlook.Application")
    Set objNewItem = objItem.Copy
    objNewItem.Move objFolder
End Sub
```

Outlook can save items as files in system folders in the formats shown in Table 16.5.

TABLE 16.5   SaveAs Format Constants

Format	Constant
Text only (.txt)	olTXT (0)
Rich Text Format (.rtf)	olRTF (1)
Outlook template (.otf)	olTemplate (2)
Message format(.msg)	olMSG (3)
HTML format (.htm)	olHTML (5)
vCard file (.vcf)	olVCard (6)
VCal format (.vcs)	olVCal (7)

If you do not specify the format with the SaveAs method, the default Message (.msg) format is used.

The vCard and vCal formats are emerging standards for exchanging contact and schedule data and are used by many programs besides Outlook. You can use those formats only to save contact and appointment items, respectively.

Other Item Methods

The various Outlook items have their own specific methods, many of which apply to only one or two item types. Table 16.6 summarizes these methods. For more information and usage examples, see the help topic for each method.

TABLE 16.6   Item-Specific Methods

Item Type	Method	Description
AppointmentItem	ClearRecurrencePattern	Changes an appointment to a single occurrence
	ForwardAsVcal	Returns a MailItem object with an attached vCal file for the appointment
	GetOccurrence	Returns a specific instance of a recurring AppointmentItem for a certain date
	GetRecurrencePattern	Returns the RecurrencePattern object defining a recurring appointment
	Respond	Responds to an AppointmentItem contained in a meeting request
ContactItem	ForwardAsVcard	Returns a MailItem object with an attached vCard file for the contact
DistListItem	AddMembers	Adds a specified Recipients collection of members to a distribution list
	GetMember	Returns a Recipient object representing a distribution list member
	RemoveMembers	Removes a specified Recipients collection of members from a distribution list
JournalItem	StartTimer	Starts the timer on the Journal item
	StopTimer	Stops the timer on the Journal item
MailItem	ClearConversationIndex	Clears the ConversationIndex property
MeetingItem	GetAssociatedAppointment	Returns the AppointmentItem object associated with a meeting request
PostItem	ClearConversationIndex	Clears the ConversationIndex property
	Post	Saves the item to the target folder
TaskItem	Assign	Assigns a task and returns a TaskItem object that can be sent to the assignee

16

continues

TABLE 16.6 continued

Item Type	Method	Description
	CancelResponseState	Resets the ResponseState property to its original value before responding to a task request
	ClearRecurrencePattern	Changes a task to a single occurrence
	GetRecurrencePattern	Returns the RecurrencePattern object defining a recurring task
	MarkComplete	Updates PercentComplete to 100%, Complete to True, and DateCompleted to the current date
	Respond	Responds to a TaskItem contained in a task request
	StatusReport	Sends a status report to all recipients listed in the StatusUpdateRecipients property
TaskRequestItem	GetAssociatedTask	Returns the TaskItem object associated with a task request

Working with Recipients

Two key Outlook objects are Recipients collections and Recipient items. These represent the people and e-mail addresses with whom you communicate in Outlook. The principle use of a Recipients collection is to represent the addressees on a sent or received item—not just messages, but also appointments and assigned tasks as well.

Each Recipient in a Recipients collection includes the basic properties in Table 16.7.

TABLE 16.7 Key Recipient Properties

Property	Description
Address	E-mail address.
Index	Position in the Recipients collection.
Name	Display name.
Resolved	True, if the recipient has been successfully validated against the Address Book.
Type	Type of entry, such as To, Cc, or Bcc, using the constants in Table 16.8.

Adding Recipients

One way to add a recipient to an item is to use the Add method to supply the name or the Internet address in *name@domain* format. You can then set the Type, using one of the constants in Table 16.8. This example assumes that you already have an objItem variable representing a MailItem:

```
Set objRecip = objItem.Recipients.Add("mswish@microsoft.com")
Set objRecip = objItem.Recipients.Add("Henry J. Mudd")
objRecip.Type = olBCC
```

16

Generally, supply a name to the Add method when sending to someone in your Address Book. Use an Internet address instead of a name for a one-time message to a particular address, someone not listed in the Address Book.

TABLE 16.8 Recipient Type Constants

Item Type	Recipient *Type Constants*
JournalItem	olAssociatedContact (1)
MailItem	olTo (1)—default
	olCC (2)
	olBCC (3)
MeetingItem	olRequired (1)—default
	olOptional (2)
	olResource (3)
TaskItem	olUpdate (2)
	olFinalStatus (3)

Another method is to use the CDO AddressBook method to display a Select Names dialog, such as that shown in Figure 16.1. This is a powerful method that allows you to completely customize the look of the Select Names dialog: its title, the number of boxes for recipients, and the labels for those boxes. The AddressBook method returns a Recipients collection. Typically, you then set the Recipients collection on the current Outlook item to the Recipients collection returned by AddressBook.

FIGURE 16.1

Use the AddressBook *method to display the Select Names dialog.*

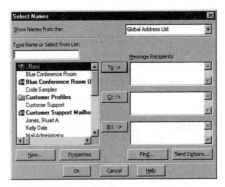

Don't forget that, to use CDO methods, you must use Tools, References to add the Microsoft CDO 1.21 Library to your project. Also, you must declare object variables with CDO data types, not data types for the Outlook object model equivalents.

In particular, note that both models use a Recipient object, but the two objects are not equivalent; you cannot set a CDO Recipients object equal to an Outlook Recipients object. The upcoming code example for the AddressBook method sets the Recipients collection on a CDO Message object, rather than try to copy the recipients to an Outlook MailItem object.

AddressBook is a relatively complex method with quite a few arguments, listed in Table 16.9. In Listing 16.1, you use the named arguments method of specifying parameters to make it easier to follow the code.

TABLE 16.9 AddressBook **Arguments**

Argument	Description
Recipients	Optional. Recipients collection holding initial values for the boxes in the Select Names dialog.
Title	Optional. Caption for the Select Names dialog box.
OneAddress	Optional. Boolean value for whether user can select only one address entry at a time. Default is False.
ForceResolution	Optional. Boolean value for whether the program should try to resolve all names before closing the Select Names dialog. Default is True.
RecipLists	Optional. How many recipient boxes to display. Default is 1. Possible values:

Argument	Description
	−1—Three boxes with default captions and ForceResolution:=False
	0—No boxes
	1—One box for To recipients
	2—Two boxes for To and Cc recipients
	3—Three boxes for To, Cc, and Bcc recipients
ToLabel	Optional. Label for To box. Default: "To:"
CcLabel	Optional. Label for Cc box. Default: "Cc:"
BccLabel	Optional. Label for Bcc box. Default: "Bcc:"

LISTING 16.1   Using the AddressBook Method to Populate a Recipients Collection

```
 1: Sub AddressBookDemo()
 2:     Dim objApp As Application
 3:     Dim objNS As NameSpace
 4:     Dim objItem As MailItem
 5:     Dim objMessage As Message
 6:     Dim objSession As Session
 7:     Dim objRecipients As Object
 8:     Dim strEntryID As String
 9:     Dim strStoreID As String
10:     Set objSession = CreateObject("MAPI.Session")
11:     objSession.Logon , , False, False
12:     Set objRecipients = objSession.AddressBook( _
13:       Title:="Select Students and Parents", _
14:       OneAddress:=False, _
15:       ForceResolution:=True, _
16:       RecipLists:=3, _
17:       ToLabel:="&Students", _
18:       CcLabel:="&Parents", _
19:       BccLabel:="&Teachers")
20:     Set objMessage = objSession.Inbox.Messages.Add
21:     Set objMessage.Recipients = objRecipients
22:     objMessage.Update
23:     strEntryID = objMessage.ID
24:     strStoreID = objMessage.StoreID
25:     Set objApp = CreateObject("Outlook.Application")
26:     Set objNS = objApp.GetNamespace("MAPI")
27:     Set objItem = objNS.GetItemFromID(strEntryID, strStoreID)
28:     objItem.Display
29: End Sub
```

16

After setting the `Recipients` collection for the CDO `Message` object, the code uses the `Update` method to save the CDO item so that you can get its `ID` and `StoreID` properties. You then use those properties in the `GetItemFromID` method on the `NameSpace` object to access an Outlook `MailItem` object (`objItem`) and display it.

Working with Addresses

You need to understand two key issues related to recipients: address resolution and working with e-mail addresses.

Before you can successfully send any Outlook item, all recipient addresses must be *resolved*, that is, they must be validated against the user's Address Book. Internet addresses in *name@domain* format are resolved automatically. For other addresses, Outlook looks for a match in the various address lists in the Address Book.

Resolution occurs in any of these situations:

- The user clicks the Send button.
- The user clicks the Check Names button.
- Background name resolution is turned on, and Outlook finds a match as a background process.
- Program code uses the `Resolve` method on a `Recipient` item or the `ResolveAll` method on a `Recipients` collection.

In the first two situations, if Outlook does not find a match, it displays a dialog where the user can either try to find the recipient or create a new address.

 In Listing 15.2 in Hour 15, "Working with Stores and Folders," you saw an example using the `Resolve` method on a `Recipient` in a dummy `MailItem` before trying to use the `GetSharedDefaultFolder` method with that `Recipient`.

In a displayed Outlook item, resolved recipients are shown underlined. You can check the `Resolved` property for any recipient to find out whether address resolution was successful. This VBScript `ConfirmNames` subroutine pops up a message with the names of unresolved recipients:

```
Sub ConfirmNames()
    Item.Recipients.ResolveAll
    For Each objRecip In Item.Recipients
        If objRecip.Resolved = False Then
            strDontKnow = strDontKnow & objRecip.Name & vbCrLf
        End If
```

```
        Next
        If strDontKnow <> "" Then
            MsgBox "I don't know who these people are:" & _
                    vbCrLf & vbCrLf & strDontKnow, , _
                    "Unknown Recipients"
        End If
End Sub
```

You could call the ConfirmNames subroutine from the Click event on a form button or from a custom action.

16

> Outlook addresses don't always act as you might expect. For instance, the Address property for a Recipient is read-only. To change the actual e-mail address, you must remove the Recipient from the collection and then add a new Recipient. Also, the e-mail addresses on a ContactItem look like resolved recipients, but you can't change the display name by changing the EmailDisplayName property because it's read-only.
>
> Another example of an address oddity is that the MailItem object includes a SenderName property, but no property that returns the e-mail address for the sender. You will deal with that in the next section.

Adding Contacts with a Macro

On an open message, you can right-click the name in the From field and choose Add to Contacts to create a new item in the Contacts folder using the sender's information. However, if you read most of your messages in the preview pane, opening the message just to be able to save the sender might seem like a lot of trouble.

Therefore, you will create a macro that works with a selected item in a folder and creates a new Contact item using the sender's display name and e-mail address.

You already saw how to get the From address by using CDO in Hour 13 in the section "Getting a From Address." This time, in Listing 16.2, you stick to the Outlook object model and get the sender's return address by creating a reply first.

LISTING 16.2   Adding a Sender to the Contacts Folder

```
1: Sub AddSenderToContacts()
2:     Dim objApp As Application
3:     Dim objItem As Object
4:     Dim objContact As ContactItem
```

continues

LISTING 16.2 continued

```
 5:      Dim objReply As MailItem
 6:      Dim objRecip As Recipient
 7:      Dim strAddress As String
 8:      Set objApp = CreateObject("Outlook.Application")
 9:      Set objItem = objApp.ActiveExplorer.Selection.Item(1)
10:      If objItem.Class = olMail Then
11:          Set objContact = objApp.CreateItem(olContactItem)
12:          objContact.FullName = objItem.SenderName
13:          Set objReply = objItem.Reply
14:          Set objRecip = objReply.Recipients.Item(1)
15:          strAddress = objRecip.Address
16:          If strAddress = "" Then
17:              strAddress = objRecip.Name
18:          End If
19:          objContact.Email1Address = strAddress
20:          objContact.Display
21:      End If
22: End Sub
```

Lines 15–17 allow for the possibility that the e-mail address will not be in the Address
property of the Recipient, but instead in the Name property. This is often the case with
Internet addresses.

Displaying Recipient Properties

Another feature of the Outlook user interface is the ability to right-click on a resolved
(that is, underlined) recipient and then choose Properties to display details about the
recipient. You can duplicate this feature in code with this DisplayAddress subroutine,
which uses a Recipient's child AddressEntry, an object that contains the e-mail
address and other information:

```
Sub DisplayAddress(objRecip As Recipient)
    If objRecip.Resolved = True Then
        objRecip.AddressEntry.Details
    End If
End Sub
```

The Properties dialog box that the Details method displays is modal. No other Outlook
code will run until you close it.

Working with the Item Body

For Outlook items other than the MailItem, when you want to modify the text in the large text box on the item, you work with the Body property. Body is a String property, so you can use all the normal String parsing and manipulation functions on it. For example, place the following VBScript code in a Contact form, and create a custom action named **Add Time Stamp** on the (Actions) page, as described in Hour 14, "Commanding with Custom Actions." When users open a Contact item saved with this form, they see an Add Time Stamp toolbar button. Clicking it adds the current date and user to the top of the form, as shown in Figure 16.2.

```
Function Item_CustomAction(ByVal Action, ByVal NewItem)
    Select Case Action.Name
        Case "Add Time Stamp"
            Item_CustomAction = False
            Set objSession = CreateObject("MAPI.Session")
            objSession.Logon , , False, False
            Item.Body = vbCrLf & vbCrLf & _
              "Last updated on " & _
              FormatDateTime(Date, vbLongDate) & " by " & _
              objSession.CurrentUser & vbCrLf & _
              String(72, "*") & vbCrLf
        Case Else
    End Select
End Function
```

FIGURE 16.2

The Add Time Stamp button executes a custom action.

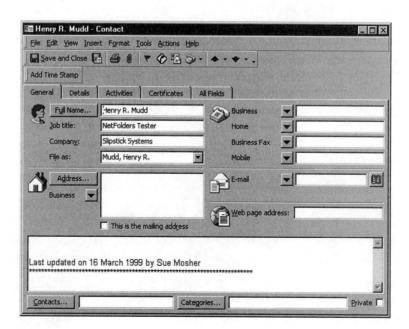

> All Outlook items other than the Message item use Rich Text Format for the item body. If you set the Body property, any formatting that the user may have applied is lost.
>
> Also, if you set the Body property on a Message item, the item switches to Rich Text format. While you can change it to HTML format by setting the HTMLBody property, there is no programming method to change a Rich Text message to a Plain Text message.

Although you can manipulate the Body property itself, you cannot do much with the Text Box control that displays it on an Outlook form. You cannot position the insertion point in the text box at a particular location, nor can you change the formatting of text.

Working with the Message Body

Working with the body of a message is much more complicated. Outlook supports three formats for messages (plain text, Rich Text, and HTML) and two editors (the built-in editor and WordMail—Microsoft Word as the editor). In addition to the Body property, MailItem items also have an HTMLBody property for storing text and formatting using HTML syntax. If you change the HTMLBody property, the Body property is updated automatically with matching text.

The EditorType is a read-only property of the item's Inspector and may have the values shown in Table 16.10.

TABLE 16.10 Values for Inspector.EditorType

Editor	EditorType *Value*
Plain text	olEditorText (1)
HTML	olEditorHTML (2)
Rich Text	olEditorRTF (3)
WordMail	olEditorWord(4)

A user sets the default format and editor by choosing Tools, Options and changing the options on the Mail Format tab.

If you are designing a custom Message form that uses RTF format, you can set it to always use WordMail by checking the Always Use Microsoft Word as the E-Mail Editor box on the (Properties) page. This has the effect of setting the Item.FormDescription.UseWordMail property to True.

Although EditorType itself is read-only, certain code statements can have the effect of changing the editor or format for a particular item.

If you set the HTMLBody property, the EditorType automatically changes to olEditorHTML.

If you set the Body property, the EditorType reverts to olEditorRTF. Furthermore, if you set the Body property, the HTMLBody property is cleared, losing any HTML formatting. All formatting is lost in Rich Text messages, also.

A Simple Search and Replace Form

Knowing that you have to always work with the HTMLBody property in HTML messages and the Body property in plain text and Rich Text messages, you can now construct a simple VBA form to search and replace text in any Outlook item. Follow these steps to construct the form:

1. Create a new VBA form named Ch16FindReplace. Set its ShowModal property to False.

2. Add two text boxes named txtFind and txtReplace.

3. Add a check box named chkMatchCase.

4. Add three command buttons named cmdReplace, cmdReplaceAll, and cmdCancel.

5. Add labels and arrange the controls, as shown in Figure 16.3, so that they look like the Find and Replace dialog box that you see in many Windows programs.

FIGURE 16.3

Try to make VBA forms resemble standard application dialogs.

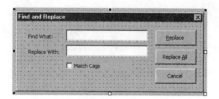

Next, add the following code to the form's code window to set module-level constants, and add code to the command buttons' Click events.

```
Private Const m_conReplaceOnce = 1
Private Const m_conReplaceAll = -1

Private Sub cmdCancel_Click()
    Unload Me
End Sub

Private Sub cmdReplaceAll_Click()
    Call DoReplace(m_conReplaceAll)
```

```
End Sub

Private Sub cmdReplace_Click()
    Call DoReplace(m_conReplaceOnce)
End Sub
```

Finally, add the code in Listing 16.3 to the form's code module. This is the `DoReplace()`
function called by the `cmdReplace` and `cmdReplaceAll` buttons.

LISTING 16.3 The Heart of the Find and Replace Form

```
 1: Private Sub DoReplace(intReplaceAll As Integer)
 2:     Dim objApp As Application
 3:     Dim objInspector As Inspector
 4:     Dim objItem As Object
 5:     Dim strBody As String
 6:     Dim blnIsHTML As Boolean
 7:     Dim intRes As Integer
 8:     Dim intMatchCase As Integer
 9:     Set objApp = CreateObject("Outlook.Application")
10:     Set objInspector = objApp.ActiveInspector
11:     Set objItem = objInspector.CurrentItem
12:     Select Case objInspector.EditorType
13:         Case olEditorText
14:             blnIsHTML = False
15:             strBody = objItem.Body
16:         Case olEditorHTML
17:             blnIsHTML = True
18:             strBody = objItem.HTMLBody
19:         Case olEditorRTF
20:             intRes = MsgBox( _
21:                "If you use this form to replace text in a " & _
22:                "Rich Text message, you will lose all " & _
23:                "formatting." & vbCrLf & vbCrLf & _
24:                "Do you want to continue?", _
25:                vbYesNo + vbDefaultButton2 + vbQuestion, _
26:                "Replace Text")
27:             If intRes = vbYes Then
28:                 blnIsHTML = False
29:                 strBody = objItem.Body
30:             Else
31:                 strBody = ""
32:             End If
33:     End Select
34:     If strBody <> "" Then
35:         If Me.chkMatchCase = False Then
36:             intMatchCase = vbTextCompare
37:         Else
38:             intMatchCase = vbBinaryCompare
39:         End If
```

```
40:          strBody = Replace( _
41:                  Expression:=strBody, _
42:                  Find:=Me.txtFind, Replace:=Me.txtReplace, _
43:                  Start:=1, Count:=intReplaceAll, _
44:                  Compare:=intMatchCase)
45:          If blnIsHTML = True Then
46:              objItem.HTMLBody = strBody
47:          Else
48:              objItem.Body = strBody
49:          End If
50:      End If
51: End Sub
```

Finally, in a separate VBA module, add this code so that you can call the form from a macro:

```
Sub SearchReplace()
    Ch16FindReplace.Show
End Sub
```

In the `DoReplace` subroutine, for Rich Text items, you warn the user that performing the replace operation will wipe out all formatting in the item. The user has the option to cancel the operation by responding No to the `MsgBox()` pop-up.

> You don't have to consider items that use the WordMail editor, because they have access to Word's more powerful Find and Replace operations. Also, a WordMail item does not produce an `ActiveInspector` object, even if it is the only Outlook item open.

> The code in Listing 16.3 does not distinguish between HTML tags and the text of the item. It is possible to mangle the HTML formatting by replacing text that could appear inside an HTML tag. Therefore, this technique should be used with care.

Summary

You have furthered your understanding of Outlook items in this hour by exploring the `Inspector` object, reviewing item methods, working with `Recipient` objects, and experimenting with the `Body` and `HTMLBody` properties. Keep in mind that not every item method works with each type of Outlook item.

16

In the next hour, you will learn how to write procedures that react to application-level events, such as the arrival of new mail or the user switching to a different folder.

Q&A

Q Can I work with an item without first displaying it in an `Inspector`?

A Certainly. You only have to activate an `Inspector` when you want the user to interact with the item.

Q Why don't Outlook items have an `RTFBody` property for handling Rich Text Format items?

A Microsoft seems to be of two minds about RTF. While custom forms and all Outlook items except messages use RTF by default, RTF is generally considered an outdated, hard-to-manage format. With a bit of work, however, you can read and write an RTF message body. The Microsoft Knowledgebase contains an article, "FILE: DLL to Read and Write RTF with Active Messaging," at `http://support.microsoft.com/support/kb/articles/q172/0/38.asp` that explains how to get started.

Q Can a message with unresolved addresses be sent?

A Normally not. If the user clicks the Send button on a message with unresolved addresses, Outlook pops up a dialog suggesting names from the Address Book and offering other options for resolving the name. Outlook doesn't send the message until you provide a valid address for each name. However, if in Corporate or Workgroup mode, you add a new recipient as part of an `Application.ItemSend` event handler, that recipient is not automatically resolved, even if it's a simple SMTP address in `name@domain` format. If you don't use the `Resolve` method to resolve the recipient, you will get a "no transport provider" error message in your Inbox for that recipient.

Workshop

Work through the quiz question and exercises so that you can better understand Outlook Programming. See Appendix A for answers.

Quiz

1. Does the `Copy` method copy an item to a folder?

2. What property of a received message represents the name of the person who sent the message?

Exercises

1. Compare the method of getting a sender address in Listing 16.2 with the CDO method in Hour 13 by running them with some actual messages. Do they always return the same address? Why or why not?

2. How would you enhance the DoReplace subroutine in Listing 16.3 to ignore text in HTML tags? Hint: Tags always take the format <tag>. Try to at least write the pseudocode.

16

Hour 17

Responding to Outlook Events in VBA

Before Outlook 2000, the only way to respond to events in Outlook was through VBScript code on a form. Programmers were limited to just the few item events. Outlook 2000 opens the door to programming event handlers at the application level with the more powerful VBA language. Although not every possible event is included in the object model, the range of available events is enough to keep any programmer busy for a long, long time. Here are just a few of the events for which you can write code:

- Outlook starting and stopping
- Sending an item
- Receiving new mail
- Items or folders being created or modified
- Switching to a different folder or to a different view

You will look first at the events on the Application object that can be easily programmed and then move on to items and other object events that require a little more effort. This lesson is strictly about VBA because the application-level events are available only to VBA, not to VBScript.

Highlights of this hour include

- What event code to place in the ThisOutlookSession module
- How to set up folders for monitoring new and changed items
- How to forward reminders to a pager
- Why you can't reliably react to the deletion of items and folders in code
- How to make Outlook automatically copy personal Journal entries to a Public Journal folder

Application Object Events

The Application object offers five events that are useful to any Outlook user and one (OptionsPagesAdd) of interest mainly to programmers building COM add-ins. Table 17.1 lists the five key events. Only ItemSend can be cancelled. The arguments for both ItemSend and Reminder include the associated item so that you work with it in your code.

TABLE 17.1 Key Application Object Events

Event	Description
ItemSend	Occurs when you send an item. Includes the item as an argument. Can be cancelled.
NewMail	Occurs when new mail arrives, even if a Rules Wizard rule moves it out of the Inbox.
Quit	Occurs when Outlook shuts down, after all Explorer and Inspector windows have closed.
Reminder	Occurs when a reminder is triggered by an Appointment or Task item or for a flagged Message or Contact item. If the option to display reminders is turned on, the event occurs just before the reminder is displayed. Includes the item that triggered the reminder as an argument.
Startup	Occurs when Microsoft Outlook starts, after all add-in programs have loaded.

Code for any of these events is placed in the `ThisOutlookSession` module found in the Project Explorer under Project1 and then Microsoft Outlook Objects, as shown in Figure 17.1. Double-click `ThisOutlookSession` to open it in a module window.

FIGURE 17.1

Place application-level event code in the `ThisOutlookSession` *class module.*

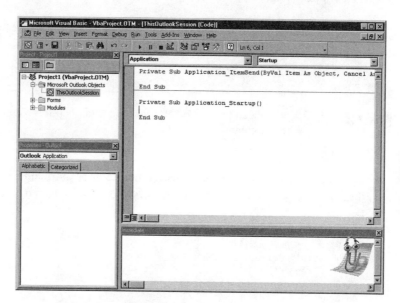

To add an `Application` event handler, select Application from the list at the top left of the module window. Then, from the list on the right, select the event for which you want to write code. VBA places a wrapper for the procedure in the module window, with the correct syntax. Figure 17.1 depicts wrappers for the `ItemSend` and `Startup` events.

As you will see later in the hour, one important use of the `Startup` event is to initialize event handlers for other Outlook object events. The `Quit` event is not quite as useful because the `Application` object is already destroyed when the `Quit` event fires. Therefore, you no longer have access to Outlook items and folders. However, you can use the `Quit` event to set any global object variables to `Nothing`. The next few sections offer some practical suggestions for using the `ItemSend`, `NewMail`, and `Reminder` events.

New Mail Pop-up

Outlook offers several built-in options for notifying the user that new mail has arrived, but maybe you want something more customized. Try creating a VBA form, such as that in Figure 17.2, which pops up when new mail arrives and displays the time of the latest mail delivery.

FIGURE **17.2**

This VBA form is dis-
played whenever the
NewMail *event fires.*

The form in Figure 17.2 has just three controls: an Image control to show the picture and two labels. The one to hold the date and time information is named lblReceived. I named the form frmCh17NewMail.

> Skip ahead to Hour 20, "ActiveX and Other Controls," to learn about the
> Image control.

To make the form display the most recent mail delivery time, add the following code to the Application_NewMail event in the ThisOutlookSession module:

```
Private Sub Application_NewMail()
    frmCh17NewMail.Show vbModeless
    With frmCh17NewMail
        .lblReceived.Caption = Now
        .Repaint
    End With
End Sub
```

> The new mail notification options that you can set through the Outlook user
> interface do not fire on every incoming message. Otherwise, your computer
> would be alerting you all day with new mail notification sounds. However,
> the NewMail event does fire on every incoming item. At the same time that
> this provides an opportunity to do more detailed tracking of incoming mail
> events, it also calls for caution in not putting so much into the
> Application_NewMail procedure that it slows down your machine as it
> responds to each new mail arrival.

Because you used vbModeless as a parameter with Show, you can leave the form on the screen while you do other work in Outlook. The form doesn't need a command button to close it, because you can use the close (×) button in the upper-right corner.

E-Mailing Reminders

Not everyone likes to be reminded of tasks and appointments with a pop-up message. Some people prefer to see reminders as items in their Inbox. Still others are out of the office and want reminders forwarded to another e-mail account or perhaps even to an e-mail address for a pager. Because the Reminder event gives you access to the item that triggered the reminder, you can place a message in your own Inbox or send the information to another address. The code in Listing 17.1 creates a Message item from the reminder item and then places the new item in the Inbox.

LISTING 17.1 Placing Reminders in the Inbox

```
 1: Private Sub Application_Reminder(ByVal Item As Object)
 2:     Dim objNS As NameSpace
 3:     Dim objItem As MailItem
 4:     Dim objFolder As MAPIFolder
 5:     Dim strDue As String
 6:     Dim objAttachments As Attachments
 7:     Set objNS = Application.GetNamespace("MAPI")
 8:     Set objItem = Application.CreateItem(olMailItem)
 9:     Set objFolder = objNS.GetDefaultFolder(olFolderInbox)
10:     Select Case Item.Class
11:         Case olMail
12:             strDue = " Due " & Item.FlagDueBy
13:         Case olAppointment
14:             If Item.Location <> "" Then
15:                 strDue = " (" & Item.Location & ")"
16:             End If
17:             strDue = strDue & " At " & Item.Start
18:         Case olContact
19:             Case olTask
20:                 strDue = " Due " & Item.DueDate
21:     End Select
22:     If Item.Importance = olImportanceHigh Then
23:         strDue = strDue & " (High)"
24:     End If
25:     With objItem
26:         .Subject = Replace(TypeName(Item), "Item", "") & _
27:                     ": " & Item.Subject & strDue
28:         .Body = Item.Body
29:         .Save
30:         .Move objFolder
31:     End With
32: End Sub
```

17

Because the `Application_Reminder` subroutine is in the `ThisOutlookSession` module, `Application` is an intrinsic object; you do not have to declare an object variable for it (see lines 7–8.)

> Outlook automatically saves unsent items in the Drafts folder. That's why you have to use the `Move` method to get the reminder notice into the Inbox. Moving an item to the Inbox does not trigger the `NewMail` event.

> Only items in your default Outlook folders will trigger the `Application.Reminder` event.
>
> You can't include the due date from a flag on a Contact item in the `Application_Reminder` procedure because that information is not exposed in the Outlook object model.

There are lots of variations on this technique for processing reminders. Substitute this code for the `With...End With` block to put a shortcut to the original item into the Inbox message.

```
objItem.Subject = "Reminder - " & Item.Subject & strDue
objItem.Body = Item.Body
Set objAttachments = objItem.Attachments
Set objAttachment = objAttachments.Add(Item, olEmbeddeditem)
objItem.Save
objItem.Move objFolder
```

To send information about the reminder to a pager address, instead of filing it as an Inbox message, provide the address in a `String` variable named `strPagerAddress`, and substitute this `With...End With` block.

```
With objItem
    .Subject = "Reminder - " & Item.Subject & strDue
    .To = strPagerAddress
    .Send
End With
```

Sending Items Immediately

In many Outlook configurations, messages are delivered from the Outbox folder to the mail server immediately. In others, they remain in the Outbox until either a scheduled delivery session takes place or the user clicks the Send/Receive button. With the `ItemSend` event and CDO's `DeliverNow` method, you can use this code to send important items — that is, items with Importance set to High — immediately:

```
Private Sub Application_ItemSend(ByVal Item As Object, _
   Cancel As Boolean)
     Dim objSession As MAPI.Session
     If Item.Importance = olImportanceHigh Then
         Set objSession = CreateObject("MAPI.Session")
         objSession.Logon , , False, False
         objSession.DeliverNow
     End If
End Sub
```

You wouldn't want to use the DeliverNow method on every item that you send, because it also retrieves all waiting mail and, therefore, may tie up Outlook for a few minutes.

Refiling Sent Items

The Outlook Rules Wizard offers an option to move or copy outgoing items to different folders, but can't handle complex conditions. For example, you might want to file messages marked with the Critical category in a subfolder of Sent Items named Important and also place other outgoing items marked with High importance there. In the Rules Wizard, this would take two rules. You can handle this case of two conditions with one Application_ItemSend procedure:

```
Private Sub Application_ItemSend(ByVal Item As Object, _
   Cancel As Boolean)
     Dim objItem As MailItem
     Dim objNS As NameSpace
     Dim objSentItems As MAPIFolder
     Dim objFolder As MAPIFolder
     Set objNS = Application.GetNamespace("MAPI")
     Set objSentItems = objNS.GetDefaultFolder(olFolderSentMail)
     Set objFolder = objSentItems.Folders.Item("Important")
     If InStr(1, Item.Categories, "Critical", vbTextCompare) > 0 _
       Or Item.Importance = olImportanceHigh Then
         Set objItem = Item.Copy
         objItem.Move objFolder
     End If
End Sub
```

Because the item has not yet been sent, if you try to use the Move method directly on the Item object provided by the ItemSend event, you get a run-time error notifying you that the item was copied, not moved. To avoid the error, your code should make a copy of Item first and then use Move on the copy. Also note that the item copied to the Important folder does not display a Sent time because the copy itself was never sent. However, you can add the Received field to the folder view to see when the item was created in the folder.

When the `ItemSend` event fires, the item has not yet been sent. This means that you can use the `ItemSend` event to change the item before it is sent. For example, you could use this code fragment to add a blind carbon copy (Bcc) recipient (`"anybody@anywhere.com"`) to the outgoing item—something the Rules Wizard can't do:

```
Dim objRecip as Recipient
Set objRecip = Item.Recipients.Add("anybody@anywhere.com")
objRecip.Type = olBcc
objRecip.Resolve
```

Another important use for the `ItemSend` event is to check for conditions under which you might want to cancel sending the item — such as an attachment that's too large or too many recipients. Add this statement to your code:

```
Cancel = True
```

when you want to cancel the sending of the item.

Item Object Events

VBA handling of Outlook events is not limited to events associated with the `Application` object. Look at Table 8.2 in Hour 8, "Code Basics," for a list of events associated with Outlook objects. You can write event handlers for these, too, not just in VBScript code on a form but at the application level so that they apply to all items, not just items using custom forms.

Setting this up is a little more involved because you must first declare object variables using a `Dim WithEvents` statement. `WithEvents` can be used only in *class modules*—special code modules that establish and work with object classes and their methods, events, and properties. The `ThisOutlookSession` module itself is a class module.

Here's the basic procedure to follow for any Outlook event other than `Application` events:

1. Declare an object variable `WithEvents` in the `ThisOutlookSession` module.

2. Initialize the declared object with a statement in either the `Application_Startup` procedure, if you always want it to run, or some other procedure, if you want to run it only on demand.

3. Write code in the `ThisOutlookSession` module to respond to the declared object's events.

If you want to deal with events that take place as users work with Outlook items, remember that most of that interaction takes place through `Inspector` objects. Therefore, you need event handlers not just for the Outlook item objects, but also for the `Inspector` objects that display them.

To set up a basic framework for trapping item events, add these statements to the declarations section of the ThisOutlookSession module:

```
Private WithEvents objInsp As Outlook.Inspector
Private WithEvents objInspectors As Outlook.Inspectors
Private WithEvents objMailItem As Outlook.MailItem
Private WithEvents objPostItem As Outlook.PostItem
Private WithEvents objContactItem As Outlook.ContactItem
Private WithEvents objDistListItem As Outlook.DistListItem
Private WithEvents objApptItem As Outlook.AppointmentItem
Private WithEvents objTaskItem As Outlook.TaskItem
Private WithEvents objJournalItem As Outlook.JournalItem
Private WithEvents objDocumentItem As Outlook.DocumentItem
```

After you declare these objects, you should see them in the list at the top left of the ThisOutlookSession module and be able to select item events from the list on the right. Next, add the following procedures to the ThisOutlookSession module. The Application_Startup procedure initializes the objInspectors object, and the objInspectors_NewInspector procedure gets the new Inspector that is added when a new window opens and assigns its CurrentItem to the objInsp object variable.

17

```
Private Sub Application_Startup()
    Set objInspectors = Application.Inspectors
End Sub

Private Sub objInspectors_NewInspector(ByVal Inspector _
  As Inspector)
    Set objInsp = Inspector
    Select Case objInsp.CurrentItem.Class
        Case olMail
            Set objMailItem = objInsp.CurrentItem
        Case olAppointment
            Set objApptItem = objInsp.CurrentItem
        Case olContact
            Set objContactItem = objInsp.CurrentItem
        Case olDistributionList
            Set objDistListItem = objInsp.CurrentItem
        Case olJournal
            Set objJournalItem = objInsp.CurrentItem
        Case olPost
            Set objPostItem = objInsp.CurrentItem
        Case olTask
            Set objTaskItem = objInsp.CurrentItem
    End Select
End Sub
```

You're now ready for step 3, writing code for the object variables assigned in the objInspectors_NewInspector procedure. You can use any of the techniques you've already learned for manipulating Outlook items. Start with something easy, such as this procedure, which reacts to the Open event on a MailItem object and displays a message:

```
Private Sub objMailItem_Open(Cancel As Boolean)
    MsgBox "You opened an message."
End Sub
```

Try adapting any of the item procedures that you developed for custom forms in earlier chapters.

The one major limitation of the item event approach is that you can gain access only to the item in the last Inspector to be opened. The events available to VBA do not provide a way to switch from one Inspector to another and determine the CurrentItem in the newly activated Inspector.

Explorer Events

Events related to the Explorer object can be triggered when the user changes views, selects items, or switches to a new folder. Table 17.2 summarizes the Explorer events.

TABLE 17.2 Explorer Events

Event	Description
Activate	Occurs when the user switches to the Explorer window.
BeforeFolderSwitch	Occurs just before the Explorer displays a new folder. Includes the new folder as an argument. Cancellable.
BeforeViewSwitch	Occurs just before the Explorer displays a new view. Includes the new view as an argument. Cancellable.
Close	Occurs when the Explorer closes.
Deactivate	Occurs just before the focus switches from the Explorer to another window.
FolderSwitch	Occurs just after the Explorer displays a new folder.
SelectionChange	Occurs when the user selects different items. Does not apply to Outlook Today or file system folders.
ViewSwitch	Occurs after the Explorer displays a new view.

The BeforeFolderSwitch, BeforeViewSwitch, FolderSwitch, and ViewSwitch events can be triggered either by the user changing the folder or view or by code that assigns a new value to the Explorer's CurrentFolder or CurrentView property.

To make use of these events, you must declare appropriate object variables and initialize them in the ThisOutlookSession module. Add these statements to the declarations section:

```
Private WithEvents objExpl As Outlook.Explorer
Private WithEvents objExplorers As Outlook.Explorers
```

Next, add the following code to initialize the objExplorers and objExpl variables. (If you already have an Application_Startup procedure, don't create a new one; just add these statements to the existing procedure.)

```
Private Sub Application_Startup()
    Set objExplorers = Application.Explorers
    If TypeName(Application.ActiveWindow) = "Explorer" Then
        Set objExpl = Application.ActiveWindow
    End If
End Sub

Private Sub objExplorers_NewExplorer(ByVal Explorer As Explorer)
    Set objExpl = Explorer
End Sub
```

It is possible to start Outlook without first displaying a folder—for example, by using a shortcut to display a new message window. Therefore, the preceding Application_Startup procedure uses the TypeName() function to check what kind of window is open when Outlook starts. TypeName(), which you first saw in Hour 12, "Handling User Input and Feedback," returns a string representing the data type for a variable or object. If TypeName() reveals that an Explorer window is active, the procedure can set the objExpl object.

> The implementation of Explorer events suffers from the same limitation as Inspector events: You can gain sure access only to the last Explorer window opened.

Practical applications for Explorer events include the following:

- Turning off the preview pane when you switch to a view with *AutoPreview* in its name
- Turning on a custom toolbar when you switch to a particular folder and turning it off again when you switch to a different folder
- Showing the number of items selected in the current Explorer window
- Automatically showing a certain view when you switch to a folder, rather than showing the last view used on that folder

17

You will do the last two as examples.

Setting a Default Folder View

If you're like me and have several thousand items in your Sent Items folder, viewing just the last few days' worth makes the folder seem to run faster. Outlook includes a Last Seven Days view that filters out all but the last week's worth of items.

> You may want to create an additional Sent in Last Seven Days view to replace the Received and From fields with the Sent and To fields. You will look at customizing views in Hour 20, "ActiveX and Other Controls."

To make Outlook automatically turn on the Last Seven Days view, you must add an event handler for the FolderSwitch event, using the code in Listing 17.2.

LISTING 17.2 Enforcing a Default Folder View

```
 1: Private Sub objExpl_FolderSwitch()
 2:     Dim objNS As NameSpace
 3:     Dim objSentItems As MAPIFolder
 4:     Set objNS = Application.GetNamespace("MAPI")
 5:     Set objSentItems = _
 6:       objNS.GetDefaultFolder(olFolderSentMail)
 7:     If objExpl.CurrentFolder = objSentItems Then
 8:         objExpl.CurrentView = "Last Seven Days"
 9:     End If
10: End Sub
```

This code depends on having an objExpl object declared WithEvents and initialized, as described in the previous section.

Showing the Number of Selected Items

Before you run a macro that operates on the Selection object that represents the number of items selected in a folder view, you might want to know how many items you have selected. This procedure pops up a small nonmodal VBA form that tells you how many items are currently selected. Every time you change the selection, the number shown on the form changes.

Follow these steps to create the form:

1. Insert a form, and name it **frmCh17Selection**.
2. Add a single large label control to the form, and name it **lblCaption**.
3. Set the following form property values:

Caption	"Selected Items"
ShowModal	False
StartUpPosition	0 - Manual

Next, add this procedure to the ThisOutlookSession module:

```
Private Sub objExpl_SelectionChange()
    If objExpl.Selection.Count > 1 Then
        frmCh17Selection.Show
        With frmCh17Selection
            .lblCaption = "You have selected " & _
                          objExpl.Selection.Count & _
                          " items in the " & _
                          objExpl.CurrentFolder.Name & _
                          "."

            .Repaint
        End With
    End If
End Sub
```

This code depends on having an objExpl object declared WithEvents and initialized, as described earlier.

When the user selects more than one item in the Explorer, the objExpl_SelectionChange procedure pops up the frmCh17Selection form (see Figure 17.3), which stays on the screen until the user closes it. The selection count does not update automatically when you switch to a new folder, until you select new items in that folder. In that situation, you could use the FolderSwitch event to update the information displayed in the form.

Because Outlook does not have a built-in technique to show the number of items in a filtered view, try adding this form and procedure and then choosing Edit, Select All to see how many items are in the view.

FIGURE 17.3

The Selected Items form is updated whenever the user selects more than one item in a view.

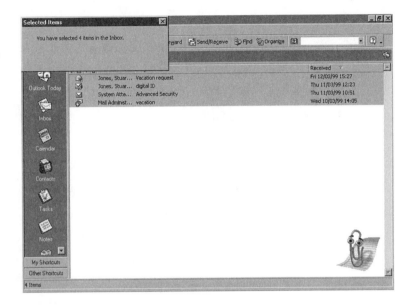

Folders and Items Events

Another major category of events is those that affect the Folders and Items collections—in other words, Outlook folders and the items they contain. This is where Outlook reacts to the creation of a new folder or item, a change to an existing folder or item, or the deletion of a folder or item. Table 17.3 summarizes these events.

TABLE 17.3 Folders and Items Events

Event	Description
Folders Events	
FolderAdd	Occurs when a new folder is created. Includes the new MAPIFolder as an argument.
FolderChange	Occurs when a folder is modified. Includes the modified MAPIFolder as an argument.
FolderRemove	Occurs after a folder has been deleted.
Items Events	
ItemAdd	Occurs when a new item is created. Includes the new Item as an argument.
ItemChange	Occurs when an item is modified. Includes the modified Item as an argument.
ItemRemove	Occurs after an item has been deleted.

The `FolderRemove` and `ItemRemove` events have a severe limitation in that they fire only after the folder or item has been deleted—in other words, when it's too late to do anything about it! One workaround is to set up event handlers on the Deleted Items folder itself to watch for the addition of new folders and items. You will do a folder deletion monitor in the next section.

Preventing Folder Deletion

If you work with the Folder List turned on, sooner or later you're bound to delete a folder accidentally. Outlook is good about asking you whether you really want to delete a folder, but it doesn't hurt to have extra protection. One application of `Folders` events is to monitor the Deleted Items folder for any new folders added to it and ask users whether they really want to delete that folder.

As with other events, you must declare a `Folders` or `Items` object variable `WithEvents`, initialize it, and write code for the event handler. First, add this statement to the declarations section of the `ThisOutlookSession` module:

```
Private WithEvents objDeletedItemsFolders As Outlook.Folders
```

Next, you must initialize the `objDeletedItemsFolders` at startup by adding these statements to the `Sub Application_StartUp` procedure:

```
Dim objNS As NameSpace
Set objNS = Application.GetNamespace("MAPI")
Set objDeletedItemsFolders = _
  objNS.GetDefaultFolder(olFolderDeletedItems).Folders
```

Finally, add the event handler in Listing 17.3 to the `ThisOutlookSession` module.

LISTING 17.3 Watching for Deleted Folders

```
 1: Private Sub objDeletedItemsFolders_FolderAdd(ByVal Folder _
 2:    As MAPIFolder)
 3:     Dim strMsg As String
 4:     Dim objNS As NameSpace
 5:     Dim objDestFolder As MAPIFolder
 6:     If Folder.Items.Count <> 0 Then
 7:         strMsg = "Did you really mean to delete the " & _
 8:                 Folder.Name & " Folder?" & vbCrLf & _
 9:                 vbCrLf & "If you click No, you " & _
10:                 "will need to choose the parent " & _
11:                 "folder where it belongs."
12:         intRes = MsgBox(strMsg, _
13:                 vbYesNo + vbDefaultButton2 + vbQuestion , _
14:                 "Delete Folder?")
```

continues

17

LISTING 17.3   continued

```
15:           If intRes = vbNo Then
16:               Set objNS = Application.GetNamespace("MAPI")
17:               Set objDestFolder = objNS.PickFolder
18:               If Not objDestFolder Is Nothing Then
19:                   Folder.MoveTo objDestFolder
20:               End If
21:           End If
22:       End If
23: End Sub
```

It's too bad that Outlook can't remember the original location of the folder before it was deleted. That's why Listing 17.3 must include a PickFolder method, so the user can indicate where the folder should be relocated.

Copying to a Public Journal

A common frustration in the Exchange Server world is that Outlook allows you to create a public Contacts folder and a public Journal folder, but automatically stores any Journal item to a user's mailbox Journal folder. Getting it into the public folder requires extra effort on the user's part. In this example, you copy all Journal items from the user's mailbox Journal folder to a public folder located at Public Folders/All Public Folders/Public Journal.

Add this code to the ThisOutlookSession module:

```
Private WithEvents objJournalItems as Outlook.Items

Private Sub Application_Startup()
    Dim objNS As NameSpace
    Set objNS = Application.GetNamespace("MAPI")
    Set objJournalItems = _
      objNS.GetDefaultFolder(olFolderJournal).Items
End Sub

Private Sub objJournalItems_ItemAdd(ByVal Item As Object)
    Dim objDestFolder As MAPIFolder
    Dim objItem as JournalItem
    Dim strFolder As String
    strFolder = "Public Folders/All Public Folders/Public Journal"
    Set objDestFolder = GetAnyFolder(strFolder)
    Set objItem = objItem.Copy
    objItem.Move objDestFolder
End Sub
```

GetAnyFolder() is the function you created in Exercise 14.3 to return any folder from its complete path.

The objJournalItems_ItemAdd procedure copies all new Journal items from the local Journal folder to the Public Journal folder.

Other Events

In the next hour, "Menus, Toolbars, and the Outlook Bar," you will examine events related to the Outlook Bar.

One final category of events is associated with synchronization of Outlook with an Exchange Server mailbox using a SyncObject object. The SyncObject object is a named set of synchronization settings. Table 17.4 lists its events.

TABLE 17.4 SyncObject Events

Event	Description
OnError	Occurs when an error occurs during synchronization. Includes the error Code and Description as arguments.
Progress	Occurs periodically during a synchronization session. Includes several arguments providing information on the process, including the number of items to be synchronized.
SyncEnd	Occurs after synchronization has completed.
SyncStart	Occurs when synchronization begins.

An event handler for a SyncObject event might be initialized in a procedure that uses the Start method to perform synchronization using a particular SyncObject object. You could also choose to initialize it in the Application_StartUp procedure by referencing a particular item in the Application.Session.SyncObjects collection. You cannot, however, create a new SyncObject in code, only through the Outlook user interface.

Summary

VBA event handling takes Outlook programming to a new level of utility not available in previous versions. Through events related to the application itself—folders, items, and the windows that display them—you gain much greater control over what happens in Outlook.

In the next hour, you will learn new events related to the Outlook Bar and find out how to control toolbars and menus.

Q&A

Q Why doesn't Outlook react to even more events, such as a `BeforePrint` event or a `SelectionChange` event within an Outlook item body?

A Compared with previous versions, the event handling capability of Outlook 2000 has taken a giant leap. In future versions, you can expect some of the limitations in current events to be eliminated and more events to be added.

Q What is the advantage of handling Outlook item events at the application level instead of the form level? Are there any disadvantages?

A With an application-level event, you can perform operations of all items of a certain class, whether they use a custom form or not. One disadvantage is that it is harder to distribute application-level event code than it is to publish custom form code. You will probably find that both methods have their place.

Workshop

Work through the quiz questions and exercises so that you can better understand Outlook programming. See Appendix A for answers.

Quiz

1. In Listing 17.2, why do you have to use the `GetDefaultFolder` method in lines 5–6?
2. What's the difference between the `BeforeFolderSwitch` and `FolderSwitch` events? In each case, how would you retrieve the folder being switched to?

Exercises

1. Using the code in Listing 17.1 as a model, write an `Application_Reminder` procedure to forward items that trigger reminders to an Internet address, with the item as an attachment.
2. What would you add to `ThisOutlookSession` in order to be able to write code to respond to events on Meeting Request items?
3. Adapt the code in Listing 17.3 to monitor the Deleted Items folder for items with attachments.

HOUR **18**

Menus, Toolbars, and the Outlook Bar

The preceding chapters in this section teach you a lot about working with Outlook folders and items and dealing with the events that happen as a user interacts with the application. In this hour, you explore some of the key elements of Outlook's user interface—the menus and toolbars and the optional Outlook Bar that displays shortcuts to folders and files. All of these are much more programmable in Outlook 2000 than in previous versions of Outlook.

Highlights of this hour include

- Why menus and toolbars are actually the same thing
- How to add a new custom toolbar through code and populate it with controls
- How to create a toolbar control that launches any message form
- How to change the toolbars displayed when a user switches folders
- How to write code to add and remove groups and shortcuts on the Outlook Bar

Programming Outlook Menus and Toolbars

Menus and toolbars are actually both examples of CommandBar objects. The Explorer and Inspector objects include child CommandBars collections consisting of all the menus and toolbars. Each CommandBar in the collection contains a CommandBarControls collection holding buttons, combo boxes, and submenus.

 If you use the Object Browser to locate information on the CommandBar object, don't look in the Outlook library. The CommandBar object is common to all Office programs, so you will find it in the Office library.

To see what CommandBars objects are intrinsic to the main Outlook window (the Explorer object), run this code and then look in the Immediate window in VBA (View, Immediate Window) for a list of menus and toolbars:

```
Sub EnumCommandBars()
    Dim objApp As Application
    Dim objExplorer As Explorer
    Dim objCB As CommandBar
    Dim objControl As CommandBarControl
    Set objApp = CreateObject("Outlook.Application")
    Set objExplorer = objApp.ActiveExplorer
    For Each objCB In objExplorer.CommandBars
        Debug.Print "CommandBar: " & objCB.Name
        For Each objControl In objCB.Controls
            Debug.Print objControl.Caption
        Next
        Debug.Print
    Next
End Sub
```

The Immediate window will list toolbars that are currently visible and those that are not currently activated. Visible is one of the key CommandBar properties listed in Table 18.1.

TABLE 18.1 Key CommandBar Properties

Property	Description
BuiltIn	True if the CommandBar is a built-in menu or toolbar (read-only).
Controls	Returns a CommandBarControls object that represents all the controls on the toolbar or menu.
Enabled	True if the CommandBar is enabled.
Left	The distance in pixels from the left edge of the screen to the left edge of the CommandBar.

Property	Description
Name	The display name.
NameLocal	The display name in the current language version of Outlook.
Parent	The parent object of the CommandBar.
Position	The screen location, using one of these msoBarPosition constants: msoBarLeft (0) msoBarTop (1) msoBarRight (2) msoBarBottom (3) msoBarFloating (4) msoBarPopup (5) msoBarMenuBar (6)
Protection	Whether the toolbar or menu is protected from customization, using one of these msoBarProtection constants: msoBarNoProtection (0) msoBarNoCustomize (1) msoBarNoResize (2) msoBarNoMove (4) msoBarNoChangeVisible (8) msoBarNoChangeDock (16) msoBarNoVerticalDock (32) msoBarNoHorizontalDock (64)
Top	The distance in pixels from the top of the screen or, for docked menus or toolbars, from the top of the docking area, to the top of the CommandBar.
Type	The type of toolbar or menu, using one of these MsoBarType constants: msoBarTypeNormal (0) msoBarTypeMenuBar (1) msoBarTypePopup (2)
Visible	True if the toolbar or menu is visible. The Enabled property must be True before Visible can be set to True.
Width	The width in pixels.

18

To work with a specific CommandBar object menu or toolbar, use its name or index number to retrieve it from the CommandBars collection, as you would with any other collection. This code, for example, toggles the Visible property of the Standard toolbar on the current Inspector object. Make sure that you have an Outlook item open before you run it; otherwise, there will be no ActiveInspector object.

For more information on `CommandBar` and `CommandBarControl` properties, events, and methods, consult the Object Browser and help file.

```
Sub ToggleInspectorStandard()
    Dim objApp As Application
    Dim objInspector As Inspector
    Dim objBars As CommandBars
    Set objApp = CreateObject("Outlook.Application")
    Set objInspector = objApp.ActiveInspector
    Set objBars = objInspector.CommandBars
    ObjBars.Item("Standard").Visible = _
      Not objBars.Item("Standard").Visible
End Sub
```

Working with Submenus

To access submenus, you have to work with the `CommandBarControls` collection. Each submenu on a menu `CommandBar` consists of a `CommandBarPopup` object, which in turn contains its own `CommandBarControls` collection of menu commands. The menu commands are normally implemented as `CommandBarButton` objects.

A `CommandBarControls` collection can contain objects of these four types:

`CommandBarButton`	A toolbar button or menu command
`CommandBarComboBox`	A toolbar or menu combo box
`CommandBarPopup`	A submenu
`CommandBarControl`	Built-in controls that don't fit one of the other three types of command bar control objects

Each `CommandBarPopup` object has a child `CommandBar` object with the same properties listed in Table 18.1, including a `Controls` collection. This can become confusing because the `CommandBarPopup` object itself has a `Controls` collection. Just keep in mind that the `CommandBarPopup.Controls` collection is the same as the `CommandBarPopup.CommandBar.Controls` collection.

Just as you were able earlier to list all `CommandBar` objects, you can also list menus and their submenus. The following code looks only at menu bars (`objCB.Type = msoBarTypeMenuBar`). For each `CommandBarPopup` control on the menu (`objControl.Type = msoControlPopup`), it prints to the Immediate window the `Caption` and `Index` of each control in the `CommandBarPopup`'s `Controls` collection:

```
Sub EnumMenus()
    Dim objApp As Application
    Dim objExplorer As Explorer
    Dim objCB As CommandBar
    Dim objControl As CommandBarControl
    Dim objSubCB As CommandBar
    Dim objSubCBCtrl As CommandBarControl
    Set objApp = CreateObject("Outlook.Application")
    Set objExplorer = objApp.ActiveExplorer
    For Each objCB In objExplorer.CommandBars
        If objCB.Type = msoBarTypeMenuBar Then
            For Each objControl In objCB.Controls
                Debug.Print "Menu: " & objControl.Caption, _
                        objControl.Index, objControl.Id
                If objControl.Type = msoControlPopup Then
                    For Each objSubCBCtrl In objControl.Controls
                        Debug.Print objSubCBCtrl.Caption, _
                                objSubCBCtrl.Index, _
                                objSubCBCtrl.Id
                    Next
                    Debug.Print
                End If
            Next
            Debug.Print
        End If
    Next
End Sub
```

Notice that the Debug.Print statements include the Id and Index properties of each control representing a menu command. You will see how to use the Id to access controls in the next section. Later, you will see how knowing the Index property enables you to position new controls on a menu or toolbar.

If the menus have been customized to delete commands, the EnumMenus procedure does not list those removed commands. To get a full listing, run EnumMenus again on a system where the Outlook menus have not been customized. You can reset the menus to their original state by choosing View, Toolbars, Customize. On the Toolbars tab, select Menu Bar, and then click Reset.

Accessing Controls

To access a particular control on a CommandBar with the standard collection syntax, use the Caption property of the control or its Index. For example, this code fragment sets objControl to the Reply button on the Standard toolbar:

```
Set objApp = CreateObject("Outlook.Application")
Set objExplorer = objApp.ActiveExplorer
Set objCB = objExplorer.CommandBars.Item("Standard")
Set objControl = objCB.Controls("Reply")
```

But what if the user has renamed a toolbar button or menu command? If the user renames the Reply command with a new `Caption` of **Send Reply**, the `Set objControl` statement in the preceding snippet fails.

In the preceding section, you saw that each control also has an `Index` property. This represents its position on the toolbar. For example, if the File menu has not been customized, the Save As command's control has an `Index` of 4. However, if the user adds a new command above Save As, the control representing Save As now has an `Index` of 5. This makes the `Index` property unreliable for accessing a particular control.

If you can't count on the `Caption` or `Index` property, what can you use to access a particular control? The secret is the `Id` property. The `EnumMenus` subroutine in the preceding section uses `Debug.Print` statements to display the `Id` property for all built-in menu commands in the `Immediate` window.

> After running `EnumMenus`, you can copy the list of commands from the Immediate window to a text file and save it to keep the `Id` values handy.

If you know the `Id`, you can use the `FindControl` method on the `CommandBar` object to return the corresponding control. For example, by running the `EnumMenus` procedure, you find out that the `Id` for the File menu is 30002 and the `Id` for the Share command is 31128. This code fragment, which assumes that you already have an `objMenuCB` `CommandBar` object, returns the `CommandBarControl` object representing the Share command:

```
Set objFileMenu = objMenuCB.FindControl(ID:=30002)
Set objShareCtrl = objFileMenu.CommandBar.FindControl(ID:=31128)
```

The following code disables the Share command so that the user cannot create new Net Folders shares:

```
Sub DisableNetFolderShare()
    Dim objApp As Application
    Dim objExplorer As Explorer
    Dim objMenuCB As CommandBar
    Dim objFileMenu As CommandBarControl
    Dim objFileCB As CommandBar
    Dim objShareCtrl As CommandBarControl
```

```
      Set objApp = CreateObject("Outlook.Application")
      Set objExplorer = objApp.ActiveExplorer
      Set objMenuCB = objExplorer.CommandBars("Menu Bar")
      Set objFileMenu = objMenuCB.FindControl(ID:=30002)
      Set objShareCtrl = _
        objFileMenu.CommandBar.FindControl(ID:=31128)
      objShareCtrl.Enabled = False
End Sub
```

The preceding code disables the Share command by setting the Enabled property for its menu bar control to False. That's not the only way to prevent a user from accessing a menu command. You can also set the Visible property to False or remove the control from the CommandBar completely using the Delete method, as in objShareCtrl.Delete.

> Removing a menu or toolbar control may not be as effective as you might think. Unless you disable the Customize command on the View menu or set all menus and toolbars so that they cannot be customized, the user can manually add any built-in command to any toolbar.

Adding a New Toolbar and Controls

You can create a new toolbar in code and populate it with controls for both built-in functions and VBA macros.

Because CommandBars is a collection, as with other collections, you use the Add method to create a new toolbar. The Add method takes the optional arguments listed in Table 18.2.

TABLE 18.2 Arguments for Adding a CommandBar

Argument	Description
Name	The display name for the command bar. If omitted, Outlook uses a default name such as Custom 1.
Position	The position or type of command bar, using one of these constants: msoBarLeft (0) msoBarTop (1) msoBarRight (2) msoBarBottom (3) msoBarFloating (4)
MenuBar	If True, replaces the current menu bar with the new command bar (Default = False).

18

If you compare the Position property in Table 18.2 with that in Table 18.1, you might notice that the msoBarPopup (5) constant is not supported. Unlike other Office applications, Outlook does not allow you to create custom pop-up menus that appear when you right-click in the application.

You also don't see msoBarMenuBar as an option for the Position property in Table 18.2. Instead, set the MenuBar property to True, and set the Position to msoBarTop to place your replacement menu above the toolbars. Only one CommandBar object at a time can have MenuBar set to True.

The Add method also takes an optional Temporary argument. However, this argument has no effect in Outlook. Even if you set a command bar's Temporary property to True, it is not automatically removed when Outlook closes.

This CreateSampleToolbar subroutine creates a new floating toolbar named Sample and displays it in the current Explorer window:

```
Sub CreateSampleToolbar()
    Dim objApp As Application
    Dim objExplorer As Explorer
    Dim objCBars As CommandBars
    Dim objCB As CommandBar
    Set objApp = CreateObject("Outlook.Application")
    Set objExplorer = objApp.ActiveExplorer
    Set objCBars = objExplorer.CommandBars
    Set objCB = objCBars.Add("Sample", msoBarFloating)
    objCB.Visible = True
End Sub
```

Outlook does not prevent you from creating multiple toolbars with the same name. As an exercise at the end of this chapter, you will write code to check the names of existing toolbars.

After you create a toolbar, you will want to add controls to it. To add a button that duplicates one of the built-in toolbar buttons, you need to obtain the Id, a property of CommandBarControl objects. For example, this syntax returns the Id of the Find button on the Standard toolbar in an Explorer window:

```
objCBars("Standard").Controls("Find").ID
```

Table 18.3 lists additional arguments, all optional, for adding controls.

TABLE 18.3 Arguments for Adding CommandBar Controls

Argument	Description
Type	The type of control, using one of these constants: msoControlButton (1) msoControlEdit (2) msoControlDropdown (3) msoControlComboBox (4) msoControlPopup (10)
Id	The integer specifying a built-in control.
Parameter	The argument used by Outlook to run built-in controls or by a custom control to store information for the control's VBA procedure.
Before	The number indicating the position of the control on the command bar. If omitted, the control is added at the end.
Temporary	If True, the control is temporary and will be deleted when Outlook closes (Default = False).

> Controls you create with the Type property equal to msoControlEdit (2), msoControlDropdown (3), and msoControlComboBox (4) are all CommandBarComboBox control objects. Use the Text property of a CommandBarComboBox control, as shown in the example in the next section, to retrieve either text typed by the user or a selection from a list.

This statement assumes that you have already initialized an objCBControls object representing the Controls collection of the current CommandBar; it adds a button for the built-in Find command:

```
Set objControl = objCBControls.Add(msoControlButton, _
                    objCBars("Standard").Controls("Find").ID)
```

When you add a custom control to run VBA code, you not only need to use the Add method to create the control on the CommandBar, but you also must specify what the control should do and how the control should look. Table 18.4 shows the key CommandBarControl properties you should consider setting.

18

TABLE **18.4** Key CommandBarControl Properties

Property	Description
Caption	The text shown on the control.
FaceID	The ID number for the picture shown on a control. You can use the CopyFace and PasteFace methods to copy and paste the face from one control to another.
HyperlinkType	Determines whether the control runs an Internet URL. Can be one of these constants: msoCommandBarButtonHyperlinkNone (0) msoCommandBarButtonHyperlinkOpen (1) msoCommandBarButtonHyperlinkInsertPicture (2)
OnAction	The name of the VBA macro to run when the control is clicked or its value is changed.
Parameter	Stores information for the control's VBA procedure.
Style	For a CommandBarButton object, sets whether the button is displayed with a caption, icon, or both. Can be any of the following constants: msoButtonAutomatic (0) msoButtonIcon (1) msoButtonCaption (2) msoButtonIconAndCaption (3) msoButtonIconAndCaptionBelow (11) msoButtonIconAndWrapCaption (7) msoButtonIconAndWrapCaptionBelow (15) msoButtonWrapCaption (14) For a CommandBarComboBox object, sets the appearance of the combo box. Can be either of these constants: msoComboNormal (0) msoComboLabel (1)
TooltipText	The text displayed when the user pauses the mouse over the control; uses the Caption value by default.

As you saw earlier in the discussion of submenus, a CommandBarPopup object also has child CommandBar and Controls objects that you use to build the menu for the CommandBarPopup object.

A Toolbar Control to Launch Any Message Form

The procedure listed in the OnAction property must be a VBA macro; in other words, it must be a subroutine with no arguments. However, the subroutine itself can use the properties of the control to obtain information for use in the procedure. The following AddFormLaunchCombo subroutine adds a CommandBarComboBox control and populates it with a list of favorite published IPM.Note forms by using the AddItem method, just as you would with a combo box control on a form:

```
Sub AddFormLaunchCombo()
    Dim objApp As Application
    Dim objCBars As CommandBars
    Dim objCB As CommandBar
    Dim objCBControls As CommandBarControls
    Dim objControl As CommandBarControl
    Set objApp = CreateObject("Outlook.Application")
    Set objCBars = objApp.ActiveExplorer.CommandBars
    Set objCB = objCBars("Sample")
    Set objCBControls = objCB.Controls
    Set objControl = objCBControls.Add(msoControlComboBox)
    With objControl
        .AddItem "IPM.Note.Info"
        .AddItem "IPM.Note.Notice"
        .AddItem "IPM.Note.Report"
        .OnAction = "RunForm"
        .Style = msoComboLabel
        .Caption = "Run Form"
    End With
End Sub
```

When the user selects a form from the toolbar control, the RunForm subroutine (from the OnAction property of the control) checks the Text property of the control and uses that information to display the form:

```
Sub RunForm()
    Dim objApp As Application
    Dim objNS As NameSpace
    Dim objFolder As MAPIFolder
    Dim objItems As Items
    Dim objCB As CommandBar
    Dim objControl As CommandBarComboBox
    Dim strMessageClass As String
    Set objApp = CreateObject("Outlook.Application")
    Set objNS = objApp.GetNamespace("MAPI")
    Set objCB = objApp.ActiveExplorer.CommandBars("Sample")
    Set objControl = objCB.Controls("Run Form")
    strMessageClass = objControl.Text
    If Left(strMessageClass, 8) = "IPM.Note" Then
        Set objFolder = objNS.GetDefaultFolder(olFolderDrafts)
        Set objItems = objFolder.Items
        Set objItem = objItems.Add(strMessageClass)
        objItem.Display
    Else
        MsgBox "Not a valid message form"
    End If
End Sub
```

18

In procedures such as this, you could also use the `Parameter` or `Tag` property of the control to return information to the subroutine that you had stored earlier with other code.

Folder-Specific Toolbars

One simple practical application of the `CommandBars` object is to display a particular custom toolbar when the user switches to a certain folder. For example, perhaps you have a Help Desk folder containing custom items. If you initialize an `objExpl` object variable at the `Application` level, as described in the preceding hour, you can use this code to display a corresponding Help Desk custom toolbar that you've already created either in code or manually:

```
Private Sub objExpl_FolderSwitch()
    If objExpl.CurrentFolder.Name = "Help Desk" Then
        objExpl.CommandBars("Help Desk").Visible = True
    End If
End Sub
```

You don't have to create a custom toolbar in code. Just choose the View, Toolbars, Customize, and click the New button on the Toolbars tab. You will have to close the VBA window first, though.

Do you recognize this as an application-level event handler for the `FolderSwitch` event? If you need to, look back at the section on "Explorer Events" in the preceding lesson for details on how to declare the `objExpl` variable `WithEvents` and initialize it.

Programming the Outlook Bar

Outlook 2000 adds programmability to the Outlook Bar—the collection of shortcuts optionally displayed on the left side of Explorer windows. Another innovation is that the Outlook Bar can now hold shortcuts not just to Outlook and system folders but also to individual files, including program executables.

You can add and remove both Outlook Bar groups and individual items. You can also program event handlers to react to switching between groups and adding and removing shortcuts and groups.

Access the Outlook Bar through the `Panes` collection of an `Explorer` object. Access the `Groups` collection of Outlook Bar groups through the `Contents` child object of the Outlook Bar `Pane`. This example displays a message box with the number of groups in the Outlook Bar:

```
Sub CountOBGroups()
    Dim objApp As Application
    Dim objOB As OutlookBarPane
    Set objApp = CreateObject("Outlook.Application")
    Set objOB = objApp.ActiveExplorer.Panes.Item("OutlookBar")
    MsgBox "My Outlook Bar contains " & _
            objOB.Contents.Groups.Count & " groups."
End Sub
```

Each OutlookBarGroup object contains a child Shortcuts collection. Each
OutlookBarShortcut object in this collection includes Name and Target properties. The
Target is set when the shortcut is created and cannot be changed later.

Adding Groups and Shortcuts

To add a new Outlook Bar group, use the Add method and provide a name for the group,
as in this example, which adds a Favorites group:

```
Sub AddFavoritesGroup()
    Dim objApp As Application
    Dim objOB As OutlookBarPane
    Dim objOBGroups As OutlookBarGroups
    Dim objNewOBGroup As OutlookBarGroup
    Set objApp = CreateObject("Outlook.Application")
    Set objOB = objApp.ActiveExplorer.Panes.Item("OutlookBar")
    Set objOBGroups = objOB.Contents.Groups
    Set objNewOBGroup = objOBGroups.Add("Favorites")
End Sub
```

The Add method also supports an optional position argument within the Outlook Bar. For
example, objOBGroups.Add("Favorites", 1) would add the Favorites group as the
first group in the Outlook Bar.

To add a shortcut, use the syntax Shortcuts.Add(target, name, index). The target
can be either a MAPIFolder object or a String representing a system file, folder path, or
an Internet URL. This code fragment adds a shortcut to Microsoft's Outlook Developers
Web page to the bottom of the Favorites group you just created:

```
Set objOBShortcuts = _
  objOB.Contents.Groups("Favorites").Shortcuts
Set objOBShortcut = objOBShortcuts.Add( _
  "http://www.microsoft.com/outlookdev/", _
  "Outlook Developers page")
```

The position index within the group is optional. Because the preceding code omitted it,
the Outlook Developers shortcut would be added to the bottom of the group.

Removing Groups and Shortcuts

To remove a group or shortcut, use the Remove index method on a Shortcuts or Groups collection. You must know the specific index number of the shortcut or group you want to remove. The procedure in the next section includes an example. The individual OutlookBarShortcut or OutlookBarGroup objects do not support the Delete method.

Maintaining a Favorites Group

The Advanced toolbar includes a Previous Folder button that keeps a history of most recently accessed Outlook folders. You can accomplish the same thing with the Favorites group created on the Outlook Bar earlier in the hour. This code gives you a good review of using collection techniques to examine, add, and remove items. The objExpl_FolderSwitch subroutine is, of course, an event handler for the FolderSwitch event. The objExpl variable representing the current Explorer object needs to be initialized as described in Hour 17, "Responding to Outlook Events in VBA." The event handler calls the AddFolderToFavorites procedure, passing the current folder as an argument.

```
Private Sub objExpl_FolderSwitch()
    Call AddFolderToFavorites(objExpl.CurrentFolder)
End Sub

Sub AddFolderToFavorites(objFolder As MAPIFolder)
    Dim objApp As Application
    Dim objOB As OutlookBarPane
    Dim objOBShortcuts As OutlookBarShortcuts
    Dim objOBShortcut As OutlookBarShortcut
    Dim intMaxShortcuts As Integer
    Dim I As Integer
    intMaxShortcuts = 10
    Set objApp = CreateObject("Outlook.Application")
    Set objOB = objApp.ActiveExplorer.Panes.Item("OutlookBar")
    Set objOBShortcuts = _
      objOB.Contents.Groups("Favorites").Shortcuts
    For I = 1 To objOBShortcuts.Count
        Set objOBShortcut = objOBShortcuts.Item(I)
        If objOBShortcut.Target = objFolder Then
            objOBShortcuts.Remove I
            Exit For
        End If
    Next
    If objOBShortcuts.Count = intMaxShortcuts Then
        objOBShortcuts.Remove 1
    End If
    Set objOBShortcut = objOBShortcuts.Add( _
                        objFolder, objFolder.Name, 1)
End Sub
```

A few notes on the `AddFolderToFavorites` procedure:

- `intMaxShortcuts` is a variable representing the maximum number of shortcuts that you want to keep in the Favorites group.
- If the target folder already has a shortcut in the group, the original shortcut is removed, and then a new shortcut to the folder is added at the top of the group.
- With the `Add` method, you can specify an optional position index. An index of 1 puts the new shortcut at the top of the group.

Outlook Bar Events

The objects associated with the Outlook Bar support a variety of useful events for which you can write event handlers, following the examples in Hour 17. Table 18.5 lists the available events for each object.

TABLE 18.5   Outlook Bar Events

Object	Event	Occurs
OutlookBarPane	BeforeGroupSwitch	Immediately before a different Outlook Bar group is opened. Can be canceled.
	BeforeNavigate	Before a different folder is displayed as a result of clicking on an Outlook Bar shortcut. Can be canceled.
OutlookBarGroups	BeforeGroupAdd	Before a new group is added. Can be canceled.
	BeforeGroupRemove	Before a group is removed. Can be canceled.
	GroupAdd	After a new group has been added.
OutlookBarShortcuts	BeforeShortcutAdd	Before a shortcut is added. Can be canceled.
	BeforeShortcutRemove	Before a shortcut is removed. Can be canceled.
	ShortcutAdd	After a new shortcut has been added.

18

Summary

Custom toolbars, menu bars, and Outlook Bar groups and shortcuts make it easy for users to run the VBA subroutines for your Outlook applications. You can also set them to jump to specific Web pages or even run other programs. Finally, you can tie toolbars, menus, and the Outlook Bar to other Outlook events, displaying only those commands that the user is likely to need in your application.

In the next hour, you get a respite from coding while you find out how to debug your Outlook applications.

Q&A

Q Can I modify the menus that pop up when I right-click in Outlook?

A No, whereas other Office programs allow you to customize these context-sensitive menus, Outlook doesn't.

Q How can I get a list of the `Id` property values for all Outlook toolbar buttons and for the menus and toolbars on Outlook items?

A The `EnumMenus` routine in this hour gives you a basic syntax for looping through menus and submenus, but it applies only to the `Explorer` object. You can make a copy and modify the copied procedure to work with an `ActiveInspector` object instead of `ActiveExplorer`. Additionally, you can change the

```
If objCB.Type = msoBarTypeMenuBar Then
```

statement to

```
If objCB.Type = msoBarTypeNormal Then
```

so that it looks for toolbars, rather than menu bars.

Workshop

Work through the quiz questions and exercises so that you can better understand Outlook programming. See Appendix A for answers.

Quiz

1. What is the relationship between a `CommandBar` object and a `CommandBarControls` object?

2. What type of control is used to produce a drop-down menu? A text box on a menu?

3. Can a shortcut on the Outlook Bar run a VBA procedure?

Exercises

1. Write an `objExpl_FolderSwitch` event handler for a folder named Help Desk that not only displays a Help Desk custom toolbar but also turns off any other toolbars (but not the menu bar). To simplify the task, assume that the Help Desk name is unique among all your folders. (If it weren't, you would have to add code to make sure that this particular Help Desk folder is the one you want to work with.)

2. Modify the `CreateSampleToolbar` subroutine to check first for the existence of a toolbar named Sample so that you can avoid creating two toolbars with the same name.

18

PART V
Finishing Touches

Hour

HOUR 19

Debugging Applications

This lesson gives you a break from writing procedures. It explores what might go wrong with your Outlook code and how to fix it. Outlook includes many tools to assist you in tracking down such problems, both in VBA and in VBScript.

In addition, you will get a few tips on how to make things go right.

Highlights of this hour include

- What types of errors you are likely to encounter
- What debugging techniques Outlook supports
- How to handle errors you can't avoid
- Why it's worth taking the time to add comments to your application

Understanding Errors

If you're going to learn how to debug Outlook applications, you need to understand that many types of errors can occur in the course of designing and running an Outlook form or VBA procedure. One classification scheme might divide them into five varieties:

- Simple syntax errors
- Errors that appear when you compile the routine
- Runtime errors
- Logic errors
- Outlook application bugs

Simple syntax errors occur as you type code statements in VBA. For example, you might type

```
Set objApp + CreateObject("Outlook.Application")
```

when what you mean to type is

```
Set objApp = CreateObject("Outlook.Application")
```

When you press the Enter key at the end of the statement, VBA pops up a message such as that in Figure 19.1, colors the problem statement in red, and highlights the portion of the statement that appears to be in error.

FIGURE 19.1

VBA tries to help you correct simple syntax errors as you type.

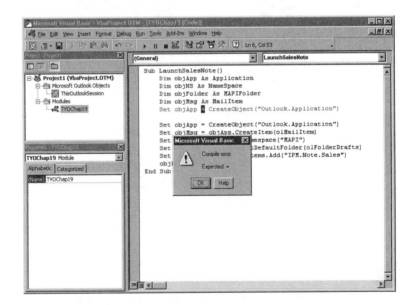

This kind of error checking is analogous to the spelling and grammar checker in Microsoft Word. Like Word's spell check, you can turn off VBA's syntax checker if you find it intrusive. Choose Tools, Options, and then clear the box for Auto Syntax Check.

The Auto Syntax Check feature detects errors only in single statements. It doesn't alert you to missing `End If` statements or undeclared variables in modules where `Option Explicit` is set. To find those kinds of errors, you can *compile* your VBA procedure. A procedure must be compiled before it can run. VBA automatically compiles procedures when you run them, but you can also compile manually by choosing Debug, Compile.

Errors detected when you compile may not be as easy to find as simple syntax errors. For example, take a look at Figure 19.2. The error message indicates that something is wrong with the `If...End If` block. However, you can see clearly that you have both an `If` statement and an `End If` statement. In a case like this, examine the statements above the highlighted statement to find the error. In the code in Figure 19.2, the problem is a missing `End Select` statement.

FIGURE 19.2

Some errors, such as a missing `End Select` *statement, are detected only when you compile.*

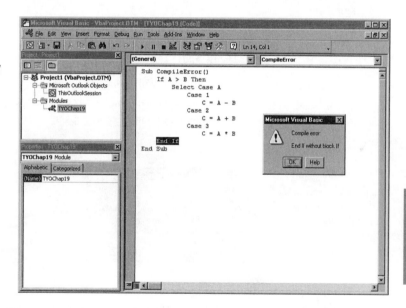

19

When you compile, only one error is highlighted at a time. After correcting the first error, compile again to see whether additional errors are present. Keep compiling until you receive no error messages.

In VBScript, no distinction exists between simple syntax errors and compile errors because VBScript does not include the Auto Syntax Check feature. Instead, code on a VBScript form is compiled when you run the form. If there is a compile error, you receive an error message. To fix it, you have to return to the form's design mode and edit the code.

The third type of error, a runtime error, comes to light only when a procedure runs and a statement with an error executes—making this type of error potentially difficult to find. The following procedure contains one of the most common runtime errors you are likely to encounter in Outlook programming. Can you find it?

```
Sub NoObjectError()
    Dim objApp As Application
    Dim objNS As NameSpace
    Dim objFolder As MAPIFolder
    Dim objMsg As MailItem
    Set objApp = CreateObject("Outlook.Application")
    Set objNS = objApp.GetNamespace("MAPI")
    Set objFolder = objNS.GetDefaultFolder(olFolderDrafts)
    objMsg = objFolder.Items.Add("IPM.Note.Sales")
    objMsg.Display
End Sub
```

The error is in the statement

```
objMsg = objFolder.Items.Add("IPM.Note.Sales")
```

Because `objMsg` is an object variable, you cannot assign it a value with a simple = statement. It requires a `Set` keyword. If you run the `NoObjectError` subroutine, when the program gets to that statement, it cannot continue and pops up the error message shown in Figure 19.3.

FIGURE 19.3

Runtime errors usually halt the execution of your procedure.

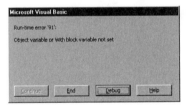

The runtime error dialog gives you several choices. The Continue button is usually unavailable because most runtime errors are so bad that the program cannot continue to run until you correct the problem.

If you choose End, program execution halts. After you correct the problem, you can run the procedure again from the beginning.

If you choose Debug, VBA pauses program execution, switching to what's called *break mode*. (Notice the word [break] in the title bar in Figure 19.4.) The next statement to be executed is highlighted in yellow and marked with an arrow to the left. This is the statement you must fix before the program can continue. After you correct it, click the Continue button on the toolbar, or choose Run, Continue to pick up execution with the highlighted statement.

FIGURE 19.4

In break mode, VBA highlights the next statement to be executed.

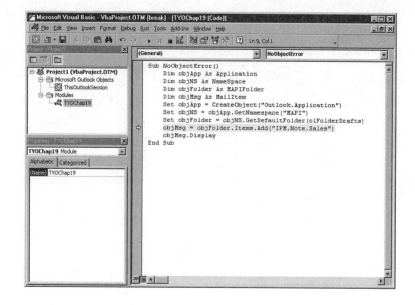

The next sections discuss break mode's debugging tools and techniques in more detail.

If you are unsure about the meaning of a runtime error, click the Help button on the dialog (refer to Figure 19.3). In most cases, a Help topic (see Figure 19.5) appears, explaining why the error may have occurred and how you might correct it.

19

FIGURE 19.5

Click Help on a runtime error message dialog to see more information on the problem.

Some runtime errors are unavoidable. You learn how to build error handling into your Outlook applications later in this hour.

In VBScript on Outlook forms, runtime errors also halt program execution, but do not automatically allow you to debug them unless you have installed the Microsoft Script Debugger, as described under "Debugging in VBScript."

The next type of error is the logic error or, as many programmers call them, dumb mistakes. You can't blame the program for these. They represent flaws in the logic of your procedures.

For example, an application includes a VBA form containing two Text Box controls, `txtStart` and `txtEnd`, where the user enters start and end dates. Before processing Outlook items in that date range, your code uses a `DatesOK()` function to make sure that both entries are dates and that the end date is later than the start date. At least, that's what you think your code does. However, when you run the form and enter what seem to be valid dates, `DatesOK()` often returns a value of `False`. Take a look at the code for `DatesOK()`, and see whether you can pick out the logic error:

```
Function DatesOK() As Boolean
    If IsDate(txtStart.Value) And IsDate(txtEnd.Value) Then
        If txtEnd.Value >= txtStart.Value Then
            DatesOK = True
        Else
            Exit Function
        End If
    Else
        Exit Function
    End If
End Function
```

Did you find it? The problem is with the expression `txtEnd.Value >= txtStart.Value`. The `Value` for each Text Box control is not `Date/Time` data; it's a `Variant`, like the values returned by all form controls. This means that when you apply a comparison operator such as `>=`, the two terms are compared as if they were `String` values, a fatal flaw when you're trying to compare dates. For example, 4/10/99 may be a later date than 4/4/99, but the expression `"4/10/99" >= "4/4/99"` is `False`.

To fix this logic error, you must make sure that you are actually comparing dates. The `CDate()` date conversion function does the trick. Change the errant expression to

```
CDate(txtEnd.Value) >= CDate(txtStart.Value)
```

As you can see, logic errors can be tough to track down. These defensive strategies can help prevent them:

- Plan your procedures well before coding.
- Use properly declared and typed variables.
- Test with lots of different data.

The final type of error can be the most frustrating—the bug built into Outlook. No matter how much testing takes place before the product is released, some known problems remain, and others come to light only after thousands of developers begin putting all the new features to use. When you encounter a suspected program bug, you don't have to suffer in silence and solitude. The resources listed in Appendix B, "Resources for Outlook 2000 Programming," will help you confirm whether you've run up against a program limitation and whether a patch or workaround is available.

Debugging in VBA

Debugging is the process of tracking down errors—mainly logic and runtime errors—by following the sequence in which code statements execute and monitoring the resulting changes in the values of your variables. VBA includes several tools that allow you to set the location where you want to start debugging and follow the variable values. These include

- Breakpoints
- The Immediate window
- The Watch window and Quick Watch feature
- The Locals window
- The Call Stack

These tools are found on the Debug and View menus in VBA.

Using Breakpoints

The idea of a breakpoint is to pause program execution so that you can take a look at the code and variable values and make any necessary changes before continuing with the next statements. You can set manual breakpoints or have VBA switch to break mode automatically under conditions that you set.

 As you saw in the previous section, you can switch to break mode by clicking Debug if a runtime error message appears. You can also get into break mode by pressing Ctrl+Break while the program is executing. However, this method provides no control over which procedure will be interrupted.

19

To set a breakpoint, click in the gray left margin of the module window next to the line of code where you want to place the breakpoint. You can also click in the code line and then press F9, or choose Debug, Toggle Breakpoint. Follow the same procedure to remove a breakpoint. To remove all breakpoints in your project, choose Debug, Clear All Breakpoints.

To have VBA switch to break mode automatically under a certain condition, you must set a *watch* for a particular variable. The easiest way is to right-click on the variable name that you want to watch and then choose Add Watch. The Add Watch dialog (see Figure 19.6) appears. Check to make sure that you picked the right variable and context and then set the Watch Type at the bottom. You can have VBA go into break mode either when the value in the Expression box is True or when it changes.

FIGURE 19.6

Watch expressions can switch VBA to break mode automatically while your code is executing.

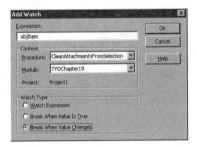

Watches are shown in the Watches window (see Figure 19.7). You can toggle this window on and off with the View, Watch Window command. To change or remove a watch, right-click it in the Watches window; then choose Edit Watch or Delete Watch. When VBA is in break mode, you can use the Watches window to examine the values of the watch expressions. For object variables, you will see a + sign to the left of the expression. Click it to expand the information about the object to show all its properties and their values.

FIGURE 19.7

The Watches window shows each expression for which you have set a watch, along with its current value if VBA is in break mode.

If you just want to add a watch without setting it to break, select a variable or expression and then choose Debug, Quick Watch.

Working in Break Mode

What can you do when you're in break mode? Here are some of the techniques that programmers use in break mode to work out the problems in their code:

- Check the sequence of procedures that have already run.
- Edit code to correct problems.
- Examine and change the values of variables.
- Restart the procedure from the breakpoint or another statement.
- Step through the code, statement by statement or procedure by procedure.

To check what procedures ran before the break occurred, choose View, Call Stack. The Call Stack window shows the sequence of procedures, with the most recent at the top of the list.

While in break mode, you can edit your program code. Some changes, such as adding a Dim statement for a new variable, will cause a message to appear that the project will be reset. This means that program execution will halt and VBA will return to design mode.

As you saw in Figure 19.7, the Watches window shows the current values of any variables or expressions for which you set a watch. Another way to see the value of any variable or object variable property is to pause the mouse pointer over the variable. After a second or two, a screen tip will appear, giving the current value (see Figure 19.8).

FIGURE 19.8

Screen tips pop up with the current variable values.

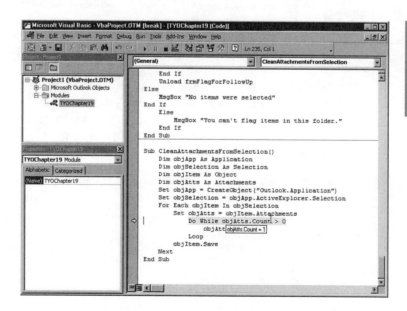

19

To see more values, choose View, Locals. The Locals window (see Figure 19.9) works much like the Watches window, only it shows all variables, not just those for which watches were set.

FIGURE 19.9

The Locals window tracks all variable values.

Locals		
Project1.TYOChapter19.NextBusinessDay		
Expression	Value	Type
TYOChapter19		TYOChapter19/TYOChapter19
IntAhead	10	Variant/Integer
NextBusinessDay	Empty	Variant/Empty
dteDate	#1/1/00#	Variant/Date
objApp		Application/ThisOutlookSession
objNS		NameSpace/NameSpace
objFolder		MAPIFolder/MAPIFolder

Using the Immediate Window

Another tool for examining variables is the Immediate window, which you can display by choosing View, Immediate Window. In the Immediate window, you can not only check the value of any variable, but also change values and even evaluate functions or run code statements.

To check the value of any variable, in the Immediate window, type ? or Print, followed by the variable name, and then press Enter. The variable's value appears on the next line in the Immediate window.

One advantage of the Immediate window over the Watches or Locals window is that it's easier to check the value of string variables containing long blocks of text—even multiple lines of text.

You can also add a Debug.Print statement to your program code and have it print information to the Immediate window as the code executes. Figure 19.10 shows the Immediate window in the process of evaluating the NextBusinessDay function. First, the Debug.Print statement in the function prints the value for the strFilter variable. Then, the value of the function, 1/14/00, is printed to the Immediate window.

While in break mode, you can change the value of any variable by typing the appropriate Set objVariable = new value or variable = new value statement in the Immediate window and then pressing Enter. When you continue with code execution, the code runs with the new value of the variable.

FIGURE 19.10

Use the Immediate window to evaluate functions, check the values of variables, and execute single code statements.

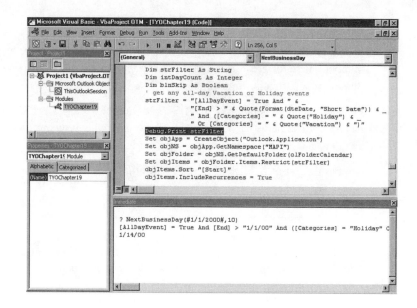

Continuing Program Execution

After making changes to your code, checking variable values, and executing statements in the Immediate window, you may want to continue running the procedure. To continue from the breakpoint, click the Continue button or choose Run, Continue.

To restart from the beginning, click the Reset button or choose Run, Reset. You can then restart the current procedure or any other procedure with the Run button.

To continue from a statement other than the breakpoint, select the statement you want to start from; choose Debug, Set Next Statement; and then click the Continue button, or choose Run, Continue.

These methods continue program execution until the end of the current procedure (or its calling procedure) or the next breakpoint. You can also step through the code, statement by statement, to get a feeling for exactly what happens when each statement executes. To continue program execution in this fashion, press F8 or choose Debug, Step Into.

19

You can also choose Debug, Step Into instead of Run to begin execution of a procedure in step mode. The Debug menu includes several other commands to help you step through your code in various ways: Step Over, Step Out, and Run to Cursor.

Debugging in VBScript

When an error occurs in VBScript code, Outlook pops up an error message with the line number where the error occurred. In the script editor, you can choose Edit, GoTo to go directly to a particular line number.

For more detailed debugging in VBScript, Outlook includes the Microsoft Script Debugger. The Script Debugger is available only when you are running an Outlook form and does not allow you to edit the script code.

To start the Script Debugger, run any form that includes VBScript code, and then choose Tools, Forms, Script Debugger.

> The Script Debugger is part of Web Scripting, one of the Office Tools components included with Outlook 2000. If Web Scripting is not already installed when you try to use the Script Debugger, you will be prompted to install it from your Outlook or Office CD-ROM or shared installation files on your network.

Another way to launch the Script Debugger is to place a Stop statement in your code. When the Stop statement executes, you receive a runtime error message and can choose to debug the application.

> You can use a Stop statement in VBA code as well to force VBA to switch to break mode.

As you can see in Figure 19.11, the Script Debugger is part of the Microsoft Development Environment, which can also be used to write scripts for Web pages. It includes many of the same tools as VBA, including Watch, Locals, and Immediate windows. The Debug menu contains the same Step Into and Set Next Statement commands, as well as other functions. You also see toolbar buttons for the most frequently used debugging commands.

The one thing you cannot do in the Script Debugger is edit the script code. If you find a program statement with an error and want to see whether fixing it solves a problem with your code, try this strategy to skip the problem statement and instead run an alternative version from the Immediate window:

FIGURE 19.11

Debug scripts on Outlook forms with the script debugging tools in the Microsoft Development Environment.

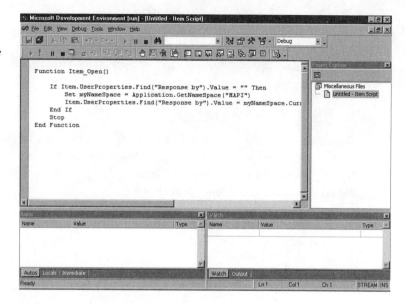

1. Step through the code until you reach the problem statement. Do not execute the problem statement.

2. Copy the problem statement to the Immediate window, edit it there, and then press Enter to execute it.

3. In the script code window, select the statement after the problem statement, and then choose Debug, Set Next Statement.

4. Click either the Continue or the Step Into button to continue script execution from the statement you set in step 3.

If the statement revised in step 2 solves the problem, copy it from the Immediate window to your form's code window.

Creating Clean Applications

This lesson on debugging concludes with some tips on avoiding problems with your Outlook applications: by writing error handlers, documenting the application, and writing reusable code.

Testing is another important issue. Remember that Outlook has two modes. Unless you know for certain that your application will be used only in Corporate or Workgroup mode or only in Internet Mail Only mode, you should test it in both modes.

19

Microsoft Office 2000 Developer—a special edition of Office for developers—includes several add-ins to help you create cleaner applications: Code Librarian, VBA Code Commenter, and VBA Error Handler.

Adding Error Handlers

The runtime error message that you saw in Figure 19.3 doesn't tell an end user what went wrong or how to fix it. To provide a friendlier message, you can add general error handling to any VBA procedure. The following procedure includes an error handler to display a message box whenever an error occurs:

```
Sub ErrorHandlerDemo()
    On Error GoTo MyError
    ' program code goes here
    Exit Sub
MyError:
    MsgBox "Error number " & Err.Number & _
           vbCrLf & vbCrLf & Err.Description, , _
           "Error in ErrorHandlerDemo"
End Sub
```

The On Error GoTo *linelabel* specifies that, if an error occurs, program execution continues with the section named *linelabel*. In general, named sections appear at the end of a procedure, with an Exit Sub statement before the named section, so that the statements in the named section do not execute except as the result of a GoTo statement. The line label itself must be followed by a colon.

The MsgBox statement uses two properties of the intrinsic Err object representing the error that occurs: Number and Description. Compare Figure 19.12 with Figure 19.3.

FIGURE 19.12

Your application can display its own message boxes in response to errors.

 Err.Number and Err by itself can be used interchangeably because Number is the default property of the Err object. If you have an error, the possible values for Err.Number are greater than zero. If Err = 0, you know that no error has occurred.

You are not limited to just displaying message boxes in response to errors, of course. If you want to trap particular known errors, you can expand the error-handling block with a Select...End Select block such as this one, in which err1 and err2 represent specific errors that you want to react to:

```
Select Case Err.Number
    Case err1
        ' error-handling code goes here
    Case err2
        ' error—handling code goes here
    ' additional Case statements
    Case Else
        ' error-handling code goes here
End Select
```

In such an error-handling block, a useful statement is Resume Next. This causes program execution to continue with the statement immediately following the one in which the error occurred.

> To test how your code responds to a particular error, add an Err.Raise errnum statement to your code, in which errnum is the specific number for the error. The statement Err.Clear clears the current error number.

Error handling in VBScript must take place in the body of the procedure because line labels are not allowed in VBScript. You can use On Error Resume Next to turn on inline error handling and On Error GoTo 0 to turn it off again.

A good example of a situation in which you must provide error handling in VBScript code is when you use the CDO AddressBook method to display the Address Book so that the user can choose one or more recipients. The CDO documentation warns that if the user cancels the dialog, the CdoE_USER_CANCEL error occurs. If you do not handle that error in your code, the resulting runtime error will halt execution of your script. Therefore, you must include code that specifically watches for the CdoE_USER_CANCEL error, such as this:

```
Sub CDOErrDemo()
    Const CdoE_USER_CANCEL = -2147221229
    Set objSession = CreateObject("MAPI.Session")
    objSession.Logon , , False, False
    On Error Resume Next
    Set oRecips = _
      objSession.AddressBook(, "Pick One Person", True, , 1)
    If Err <> CdoE_USER_CANCEL Then
        ' program code that runs if no error occurred
```

19

```
    Else
        ' program code that runs if the error occurred
    End If
    On Error GoTo 0
End Sub
```

> Remember to declare any CDO error codes as constants in your VBScript code. After you add the CDO library to your project, as described in Hour 13, "Working with the Object Models," you can use the VBA Immediate window to get the value of any CDO error code.

You can use an If...Else...End If block to handle both the error and non-error conditions.

Documenting Your Application

To document your application, add comments to your program code. A *comment* is any text preceded with an apostrophe character ('). VBA shows comment text in green.

Comments can introduce sections in your code and explain what each section does and also provide remarks on variables as you declare them. In complex modules, you may want to provide the author, purpose, history, arguments and other information on each procedure. The following code provides an example of each of these types of comments:

```
' ************************************************************
' Name:     CommentTextExample
' Author:   Sue Mosher
' History:  Version 1.0, 8 Apr 1999
' Purpose:  Demonstrate placement of different types of
'           comments
' Args:     None
' Returns:  Nothing
' ************************************************************
Sub CommentTextExample()
    Dim strStart           ' start date from form
    Dim strEnd             ' end date from form
    ' get dates from form
    frmReminderUpdate.Show
    strStart = frmReminderUpdate.txtStartDate
    strEnd = frmReminderUpdate.txtEndDate
    Unload frmReminderUpdate
End Sub
```

You don't have to comment everything in every procedure, but try to provide enough comments so that you (or another developer) will be able to follow the code logic at any time in the future.

Making Code Reusable

Typos are one of the biggest sources of code errors. Therefore, one way to avoid many errors is to avoid typing. For example, going back to the first example in the lesson, you really should never have to type

```
Set objApp = CreateObject("Outlook.Application")
```

because this commonly used statement should be in a boilerplate module of frequently used Outlook code that you can copy and paste whenever you need it. If you don't have such a module, start one, or at least start copying statements like this from another procedure, rather than retype them every time.

Using variables instead of literals also makes it more likely that you will be able to reuse code between forms and modules. Here is a simple example involving the Selection object:

```
Sub ReusableCodeExample()
    Dim objApp As Application
    Dim objItem As Object
    Dim objSelection As Selection
    Dim intMaxItems As Integer
    ' *** Use next line to set maximum number ***
    ' *** of items this routine is allowed to ***
    ' *** process.                            ***
    intMaxItems = 5
    Set objApp = CreateObject("Outlook.Application")
    Set objSelection = objApp.ActiveExplorer.Selection
    Select Case objSelection.Count
        Case 0
            MsgBox "No items were selected"
            Exit Sub
        Case Is > intMaxItems
            MsgBox "Too many items were selected"
            Exit Sub
    End Select
    ' program code continues here
End Sub
```

19

In the second Case statement, you could include the literal value for the maximum number of selected items you want to process, rather than use the intMaxItems variable. However, whenever you copy that code to another module, you would have to dig down to the Case statement to change the maximum number of items. Including the intMaxItems = value statement near the beginning of the procedure makes it much easier to reuse this code in a variety of modules that process the Selection. The comment lines call attention to the statement setting variable's value.

Finally, if you have a routine that you want to run from the toolbar on either the main Outlook window or an open item window, don't write two complete versions—one for the `ActiveExplorer.Selection` and another for `ActiveInspector.CurrentItem`. You will have nightmares trying to keep the code consistent in the two versions.

This is a case where three procedures are more efficient than two. One contains the code that you want to run against a particular item. The other two call that procedure, passing the item as an argument.

For example, in Listing 19.1, the `SetFlag` procedure sets a message flag to remind you to make a decision on an item one week from today. The `FlagOpenItem` procedure calls `SetFlag` for the item in the `ActiveInspector` window, and the `FlagSelectedItems` procedure calls `SetFlag` for all items selected in the `ActiveExplorer` window.

LISTING 19.1   Running a Procedure from an Open Item or Folder Selection

```
 1: Sub FlagOpenItem()
 2:     Dim objApp As Application
 3:     Dim objOpenItem As Object
 4:     Set objApp = CreateObject("Outlook.Application")
 5:     Set objOpenItem = objApp.ActiveInspector.CurrentItem
 6:     Call SetFlag(objOpenItem)
 7: End Sub
 8:
 9: Sub FlagSelectedItems()
10:     Dim objApp As Application
11:     Dim objSelItem As Object
12:     Dim objSelection As Selection
13:     Set objApp = CreateObject("Outlook.Application")
14:     Set objSelection = objApp.ActiveExplorer.Selection
15:     For Each objSelItem In objSelection
16:         Call SetFlag(objSelItem)
17:     Next
18: End Sub
19:
20: Sub SetFlag(objItem As Object)
21:     If objItem.Class = olMail Then
22:         objItem.FlagStatus = olFlagMarked
23:         objItem.FlagRequest = "Make Decision"
24:         objItem.FlagDueBy = Now + 7 ' one week from today
25:         objItem.Save
26:     End If
27: End Sub
```

You can put `FlagOpenItem` and `FlagSelectedItems` on separate toolbar buttons for the item window and main Outlook window, respectively. If you ever want to change the text of the message flag, you must change it in only one place—in the `SetFlag` procedure.

Remember that any kind of item can be open or selected. If you use this technique, object variables representing items should be declared as Object, not as MailItem or another specific type (lines 3, 11, and 20). If your procedure uses methods or properties that apply only to certain kinds of items—such as the message flag properties in this example—you should check the Class of the item first (line 21). Otherwise, you will get runtime errors.

Summary

Producing reliable applications means testing your code and fixing problems as you go along. Outlook provides many debugging tools, especially in the VBA environment. Error handlers and comments also help fill out your code and make it more professional.

In the next hour, you will learn more about adding controls to forms—in particular, special controls called ActiveX controls that can add new capabilities.

Q&A

Q Why are programs released if there are known bugs in them?

A Nothing is perfect, including software. As functional requirements change, applications must be rewritten. Every time you change something in one portion of an application, you affect other parts. Given the complexity of programs such as Outlook, you might think the wonder is that software runs at all, not that it has a few bugs in it.

Q Do I need to put an error handler in every procedure?

A Although it doesn't hurt, you don't really have to use error handlers everywhere. For example, this book's Quote() function to return an input value as a String surrounded by quotation marks is simple enough that nothing should go wrong. However, good error handling is a hallmark of complete application development. Ideally, a user should never get an error message from Outlook itself (especially because these are often cryptic). Instead, the user should get your program's own error message, explaining how to fix or avoid the problem.

Q Should I debug each procedure or wait until I have finished all the procedures for a particular module?

A There is no hard and fast rule on when debugging should occur. However, just as writing applications as small interrelated procedures is easier than writing one long procedure, debugging in small chunks is a good idea. When you know a procedure is working fine, you can move on with confidence to the next one.

19

Q Can VBA perform a spell check as well as syntax check?

A No, but you could always copy and paste your code into Word and perform a spell check there.

Workshop

Work through the quiz questions and exercises so that you can better understand Outlook programming. See Appendix A for answers.

Quiz

1. What command do you use to run a procedure if you want to follow the progress of your code step by step?

2. Can you edit code in break mode in VBScript as you can in VBA?

3. What statement can you use in VBScript or VBA to force Outlook into break mode for debugging?

4. Name at least three methods you can use in break mode to get the current value of a variable.

Exercise

Use File, Export File to export a copy of one of the VBA modules you created in earlier lessons, so that you have a backup copy. Next, in one of the procedures in the module, deliberately delete a character here and there or add an apostrophe to turn a line of code into a comment. Run the procedure, and practice using VBA's debugging tools to find the errors and correct them. Continue until you fix all the errors and the procedure runs perfectly again.

Hour **20**

ActiveX and Other Controls

This lesson gathers an additional group of tips and techniques for working with forms, both Outlook and VBA, and controls. In particular, you will learn how to enhance forms with ActiveX controls from Microsoft or other sources.

Highlights of this hour include

- What other controls are available in the Toolbox
- How to add your own customized controls to the Toolbox
- How to add even more controls from other sources
- Why you can't exactly duplicate the drop-down date selection control from Outlook Appointment forms
- How to add Windows-style Open and Save As dialogs to your VBA applications

Adding More Controls from the Toolbox

The VBA and Outlook form Toolbox contains several more controls that you might find useful in particular situations:

- The Tab Strip control adds a strip of tabs to the form. The Value property of the control corresponds to the current tab, beginning with 0 for the first tab. You can use the Change event in VBA to build code that responds to the user clicking a tab, perhaps making some controls visible and hiding others.
- The Multipage control simulates the look of Outlook's tabbed pages. The Value property of the control corresponds to the current page, beginning with 0 for the first page. You can add a different set of controls to each page. At runtime, the SelectedItem property of the Multipage control indicates which page is currently selected and is used to access properties of that particular page.
- The Scroll Bar control can be set to appear as either a vertical or horizontal scroll-bar. On a VBA form, when the user scrolls it, the Change event fires.
- The Spin Button control is commonly used to set values in small increments, such as the number of copies to be printed.
- The Image control can display many types of picture files. If you don't set its Picture property, you can use it to enhance a form with simple lines and boxes in different colors.

Because Outlook forms already have tabbed pages, the Tab Strip and Multipage controls might be considered overkill on Outlook forms. However, you may find them handy for VBA forms.

Also, remember that the only event to which unbound controls on Outlook forms can respond is the Click event. For controls bound to fields, you must use the PropertyChange or CustomPropertyChange events.

To learn about the events associated with any of these controls, add the control to a VBA form, and then double-click the control. This opens the forms code module to the control's default event, usually Change or Click. You can then use the drop-down list at the top right of the code module to see the list of other events for the control.

To learn more about the properties of these additional controls, use the Object Browser to investigate the objects in the Microsoft Forms 2.0 library.

A Contact Form with Pictures

A common question about the Outlook Contact form is, "Can I use it to display an employee or client's picture?" That's exactly what the Image control is designed to do. You can follow these steps to add an Image control to a Contact form that loads a user's photo:

1. Open a Contact form in design mode, and switch to the (P.2) page.

2. Choose Form, Rename Page to change the name of the page to **Photo**.

3. In the Toolbox, click on the Image control, and drag a rectangle on the form, representing the size of the picture you want to display. (If you don't see the Toolbox, click the Toolbox button to display it.)

4. Right-click the Image control, choose Properties, and on the Display tab, change the name of the control to **imgPhoto**.

5. Click OK to save the changes to the control.

6. Add this code for the form's Open event:

```
Function Item_Open()
    Set objPage = Item.GetInspector.ModifiedFormPages("Photo")
    Set objCtrl = objPage.Controls("imgPhoto")
    If Item.User1 <> "" Then
        objCtrl.Picture = LoadPicture(Item.User1)
    End If
End Function
```

7. Publish the form as IPM.Contact.Photo.

Here's how to make it work: Use Tools, Forms, Choose Form to open a new IPM.Contact.Photo form. On the All Fields tab, under Miscellaneous Fields, for User Field 1, type in the full path and filename of the picture you want to load for this contact. User1 is the property name of the User Field 1 field. Save the item, then open it again. When the item opens, Outlook will use the data in User Field 1 to set the control's Picture property. Figure 20.1 shows the resulting Photo page.

20

If you develop a consistent naming convention for your contact pictures that uses the Full Name or another field from the Contact record, you can have Outlook fill in the User Field 1 value automatically as part of the form's code. You will do this as an exercise at the end of the lesson.

FIGURE 20.1

Use an Image control to put a face with the name of a contact.

Adding Customized Controls to the Toolbox

If you like consistent forms, you probably use exactly the same size OK and Cancel buttons on every form you create. You can make that task easier by adding your own customized versions of the standard controls to the Toolbox. Follow these steps:

1. In design mode of a form that has the control looking the way you want, drag the control to the Toolbox.

2. Right-click the newly added Toolbox control, and then choose Customize New. (For example, if you drag an OK button to the Toolbox, you see the Customize New CommandButton).

3. In the Customize Control dialog box (see Figure 20.2), change the ToolTip text to something appropriate for your control (such as `OK Button`), and then click OK.

FIGURE 20.2

Give customized controls you drag to the Toolbox their own names.

Optionally, if you have a .bmp, .dib, or .ico graphic that you want to use for the control's picture, you can click Load Picture to change the button's icon in the Customize Control dialog.

After you add a control to the Toolbox in this fashion, you can add it to any form, just as you would a built-in control, but it will retain its properties.

To remove a customized control you added to the Toolbox, right-click its Toolbox button, and then choose Delete New *control*.

Adding ActiveX Controls

Beyond the Toolbox controls is a rich world of additional controls called ActiveX controls. Programmers use these to add new capabilities not just to programs, but also to Web pages. Many are built into Windows, Office, Outlook, or Internet Explorer, and third-party sources offer even more controls.

> The drawback of using ActiveX controls from third-party sources is that you must install and register them on each computer that will run a form that uses them. Because many ActiveX controls are included with Windows, Office, and Internet Explorer, sticking to those will avoid the need to register additional controls.
>
> If you do decide to use a third-party control, check its documentation to make sure that you are licensed to redistribute the control with your Outlook project.

To browse the ActiveX controls already available on your system, right-click anywhere on the Toolbox, and then choose Additional Controls from the pop-up menu. You will see many controls (see Figure 20.3) that should suggest interesting possibilities. For example, you can use the Microsoft Progress Bar control to show the progress of time-consuming operations, such as processing a large number of selected items in an Outlook folder.

To add a control to the Toolbox, check the box next to the control, and then click OK to close the Additional Controls dialog box.

20

> If you check the Selected Items Only box, you will see a list of Microsoft Forms 2.0 controls. These are the standard controls that the Toolbox normally contains.

Figure 20.3

You can add custom controls to the Toolbox from the list of additional controls.

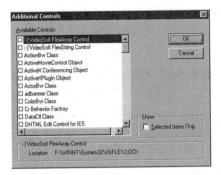

Third-party controls that you download from the Internet or buy separately may include a setup program that registers the controls. If not, you must install and register the control manually. Copy the control to your \Windows\System or \Winnt\System32 folder, and then run this command:

```
Regsvr32 mycontrol.dll
```

in which mycontrol.dll (or .ocx) is the filename of the control.

Microsoft will offer an Outlook View control via its Web site that will allow you to show the contents of Outlook folders on VBA forms, with all the view and other features you expect from folders.

Calendar Control

A common quandary for Outlook form designers is how to duplicate the drop-down calendar that appears on the Appointment and Task forms. This calendar control is private to Outlook and cannot be added to your own custom pages. However, if you have Microsoft Office 2000, you can use the Calendar control (Mscal.ocx) included with Microsoft Access. This isn't a pop-up control, but a full calendar you can put on a separate page.

To add the Calendar control to the Toolbox, follow these steps:

1. Open a Task form in design mode, and switch to the (P.2) page. (You could open any form, but this example will customize the Task form.)

2. Switch to the (P.2) page.

3. Click the Toolbox button to display the Toolbox.

4. Right-click anywhere on the Toolbox, and then choose Additional Controls.

5. In the Available Controls list, check the box next to Calendar Control 9.0.

6. Click OK to close the Additional Controls dialog box. You should now see the Calendar control on the Toolbox (see Figure 20.4).

FIGURE 20.4

Custom controls appear below the array of standard controls.

The next stage of the process is to add the Calendar control to the form and configure its properties. Follow these steps:

1. Select the Calendar control in the Toolbox, and then click on the (P.2) page of the Task form that you opened earlier. This places a calendar on the form with today's date selected.

2. Right-click the control and then choose Properties. On the Value page of the Properties dialog box, click New to create a new Date/Time field named NextBenchmark bound to the Calendar control. (You could also click Choose Field to bind the control to an existing field.)

3. Under Property to Use, choose Value.

4. Switch to the Display tab, and change the name of the control to `ctlCalendar`.

5. That's all there is to adding the Calendar control. Click OK to close the Properties dialog.

Because the `ctlCalendar` control is bound to the NextBenchmark field, the value of the NextBenchmark field will change when the user selects a different date in the control. Before you see this in action, rename the (P.2) page to `Next Benchmark Date`. Also, switch to the All Fields page, and choose Form, Display This Page so that you can easily track changes to the value of the NextBenchmark field.

20

 Because the `ctlCalendar` control is the only control on the page, you don't really need add a Label control to go with it. Instead, just rename the (P.2) page to something like Next Benchmark Date.

Try out your form with these steps:

1. Choose Form, Run This Form.

2. Switch to the Next Benchmark Date page (see Figure 20.5)—or the (P.2) page if you did not rename it—and click any date on the calendar.

3. Switch to the All Fields page, and select User-Defined Fields in Folder. The NextBenchmark field should show the same date as you picked in step 2.

FIGURE 20.5

The Calendar control on this form makes it easy for the user to select any date.

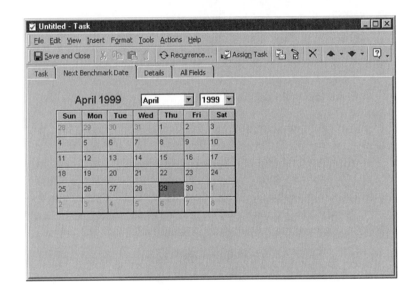

Custom controls sometimes have their quirks. For example, the Calendar control may not retain its size and shape when you switch from design mode to running the form. In that case, add code to the form's Item_Open event to set the Height and Width properties of the control; you may need to experiment a bit to find values that make the control look the way you want.

On Outlook forms, the only event available for a custom control is the Click event. If the control's Properties dialog does not allow you to bind an Outlook field to its Value property, use an unbound control instead. Then, you can write code for the form's Write event to transfer data from the control to an Outlook field.

Common Dialog Control

The preceding example adds an ActiveX control to an Outlook form. You can also add custom controls to VBA forms. For instance, you might want to write a procedure to save all attachments from an Outlook folder as system files. Instead of hard-coding the destination folder or making the user type in the path, you can pop up the same Save As dialog that you see in other Windows applications.

The Common Dialog control included with Microsoft Office 2000 Developer and Visual Basic 6 contains many useful dialogs, and you can add it to any form. In this example, you will add it to a VBA form and configure it to display the Save As dialog.

 Microsoft Office 2000 Developer also includes a pop-up Date/Time Picker control that's more like Outlook's built-in control than the Calendar control, plus several other ActiveX controls you can use in Outlook projects.

To get started, in VBA, add a new form to your project. Display the Toolbox, and then add the Microsoft Common Dialog control to the Toolbox as you added the Calendar control in the preceding section.

Next, drag the Common Dialog control from the Toolbox to your form. It doesn't matter where you put it because this control is invisible when you run the form. Change its Name property to **ctlCommonDialog**.

Add a Command Button control to the form, with the (Name) of cmdSaveAttachments and the Caption of Save Attachments. Add this code to the cmdSaveAttachments_Click event:

```
Private Sub cmdSaveAttachments_Click()
    Dim strPath As String
    Dim intPos As Integer
    Dim strFileName As String
    strFileName = GetFirstAttachment()
    ctlCommonDialog.FileName = strFileName
    ctlCommonDialog.ShowSave
    intPos = InStrRev(ctlCommonDialog.FileName, "\")
    If ctlCommonDialog.FileName <> "" Then
        strPath = Left(ctlCommonDialog.FileName, intPos)
        ' additional code to save attachments
    Else
        MsgBox "No file path chosen"
    End If
End Sub
```

20

Here's how it works: GetFirstAttachment() is a separate function (not shown in this example) designed to return the filename of the first attachment in the first message being processed. The value it returns to the strFileName variable is used to set the initial value of the Common Dialog control. After the user selects a path and clicks Save As, the code extracts the path from the FileName property of the control and then sets the strPath variable, which can be used in subsequent statements to process the attachments.

Like many custom controls, the Common Dialog control includes its own unique properties, such as FileName, that you can explore with the Object Browser. You can also set many of these properties in a special Property Pages dialog for the control, shown in Figure 20.6.

FIGURE 20.6

Set the caption for the Common Dialog control, along with other properties.

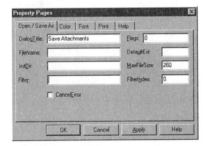

To display the Property Pages dialog, select the Common Dialog control on the form. Then, in the Properties window, click on the (Custom) property, and then click the button marked with an ellipsis (...).

Summary

Additional controls can enhance the functionality of Outlook and VBA forms. Sometimes they can even simplify what would be complex coding chores, such as duplicating a Save dialog. If you use ActiveX controls on your forms, make sure that they are properly registered and installed on all users' systems.

The next two lessons explore techniques to deal with "the feature that Microsoft forgot"—producing reports with Outlook.

Q&A

Q **Where can I find more ActiveX controls?**

A Both shareware and commercial ActiveX controls are available all over the Internet, from Microsoft's Web site at `http://www.microsoft.com`, to sites for companies that develop ActiveX controls, to shareware sites such as `http://www.winfiles.com` that list hundreds of add-ins. You can use Internet newsgroups to ask other developers what controls they found useful. Happy hunting!

Workshop

Work through the quiz questions and exercises so that you can better understand Outlook programming. See Appendix A for answers.

Quiz

1. What control would you use if you wanted to add a solid yellow line across your form?

2. What two things must be done before you can start using an ActiveX control in your Outlook applications?

3. What event is available for ActiveX controls that you add to an Outlook form?

Exercises

1. Create a new VBA form. Add an Image control, dragging the borders of the control so that it stretches the full width of the form and is one grid mark tall. Set control properties to turn it into a solid red horizontal line. What properties did you need to set?

2. On an Outlook Contact form, add an Image control named `imgPhoto` to the (P.2) page. Write code that sets the User Field 1 value for new items to a file for the user's picture. Hint: You will have to devise your own naming convention using perhaps the Full Name or File As field from the Contact.

3. For the Calendar control, add code to the form's `Item_Open` event to set the `Height` and `Width` properties of the control.

4. Customize the Cancel button and add it to the Toolbox, using the same techniques as you saw for the OK button.

20

Hour 21

Getting Started with Outlook Reports

If any single area of Outlook falls short, it's reporting. Outlook's built-in capabilities for regurgitating its data as printed reports and files in other formats are very, very limited. For example, when you use Outlook's File, Import and Export command, you cannot export user-defined fields. Items that use custom Outlook forms are not exported at all! Furthermore, there is no method for printing a custom form in a format that resembles the on-screen form. An individual form always prints in Outlook's memo style, which produces a simple list of fields. Because of these major limitations, being able to extract Outlook data into some other format—either a file or a printed report—is an essential skill for Outlook programmers.

This lesson discusses how you can export and print from Outlook without programming, using techniques such as Outlook views. You also see how to get Outlook data into Excel. In the following hour, you will learn how to use Word as a reporting tool—even combining data from different types of items.

Highlights of this hour include

- Why folder views are the key to simple tabular reports
- How to use Excel as a reporting tool
- How to extract details from a personal distribution list

Using Folder Views

Why are folder views important to Outlook reporting? Because anything you can show in a view can be printed out. Table-type views (such as the default view of your Inbox folder) are particularly useful for quick tabular reports on all kinds of Outlook data, including that contained in custom forms with custom fields.

You still have only limited control over how views look. For example, in a Calendar folder's Day/Week/Month view, you can't add any field you choose, only a few particular fields, nor can you use color-coding to highlight specific items. Still, for relatively simple reports, folder views are easy to create and can be saved for reuse.

> Can Outlook views be created in programming code? Unfortunately, no.
> That's a much requested enhancement for Outlook. Maybe it will appear in
> the next version of the program.

For printed reports, the most useful type of view is the Table view, which displays Outlook data in rows and columns. Other types of views include Timeline, Card, Icon, and for Calendar folders, Day/Week/Month.

> If you want to create a new view from scratch, choose View, Current View,
> Define Views. In the Define Views dialog box, click the New button.

Every folder has several built-in Table views, so you should never have to create a view from scratch. It's usually easier to make a copy of an existing Table view and then modify it to suit your needs. As an example, you can switch to the Sent Items folder and modify the Last Seven Days view to create a new view named Sent in Last 7 Days.

To make a copy of an existing view, follow these steps:

1. If the Advanced toolbar is not already displayed, turn it on by choosing View, Toolbars, Advanced.

2. In the Current View list on the Advanced toolbar, select the view you want to copy.

3. Type the name of the new view in the Current View box, and then press Enter.

4. In the Copy View dialog box that pops up (see Figure 21.1), under Can Be Used On, choose whether you want the new view to be available only in the current folder or in all similar folders. Click OK to finish copying the view.

FIGURE 21.1

The easiest way to create a new view is to copy an existing view.

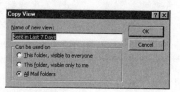

Customizing Views

After you create the view, you might want to modify it using any of the techniques listed in Table 21.1. These techniques can also be accessed by choosing View, Current View, Customize Current View and using the buttons on the View Summary dialog box, shown in Figure 21.2.

TABLE 21.1   View Customization Techniques

To Make This Change...	Do This...
Add columns showing other fields.	Right-click on any column heading in the view, choose Field Chooser, and then drag fields from the Field Chooser to the view.
Remove a field.	Drag the column heading for the field out of the view.
Display fields in a different order.	Drag a column heading to a new position.
Change the width of a column.	Drag the right border of a column heading to the left to make it narrower or to the right to make it wider.
Adjust the width of a column to the "best fit" for the data.	Double-click on the right border of the column heading.
Organize related items by values in a particular field.	Right-click the field's column heading, and then choose Group by This Field.
Sort by particular field(s).	Click the column heading for the field you want to sort by. To sort by up to three additional fields, hold down the Ctrl key as you click the column heading.
Show only items that meet particular criteria.	Choose View, Current View, Customize Current View; click Filter; and set criteria in the Filter dialog box.
Display data that meets particular criteria in a different font.	Choose View, Current View, Customize Current View; and click Automatic Formatting.

21

FIGURE 21.2

Modify a view with any of these commands.

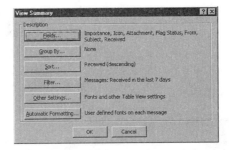

If you find yourself working a lot with the commands in the Customize Current View dialog, consider customizing the toolbars. You can either create a new custom toolbar or customize the Standard or Advanced toolbar. You may want to add the commands for Field Chooser, Format Columns, Filter, Group By, Automatic Formatting, and Other Settings.

To accurately adjust column widths so that they print the width you want, you might have to turn off automatic column sizing by following these steps:

1. Right-click on a column heading, and then choose Customize Current View.

2. In the View Summary dialog box (refer to Figure 21.2), click Other Settings.

3. On the Other Settings dialog box (see Figure 21.3), clear the box for Automatic Column Sizing, and then click OK twice to return to the view.

FIGURE 21.3

The choices in the Other Settings dialog box depend on the type of view you're modifying.

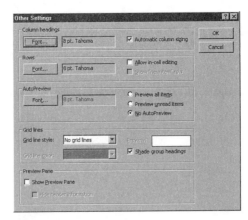

If you turn off automatic column sizing, be sure to use the Print Preview command to check whether all your columns fit on the page.

Notice the other choices in the Other Settings dialog box, shown in Figure 21.3. You can change the font for column headings and rows, turn AutoPreview on or off, and adjust grid line settings.

Printing from Outlook Views

Printing from an Outlook view is definitely a "what you see is what you get" operation. You should always check the way it will look by using the File, Print Preview command. Follow these steps:

1. Choose File, Print.

2. In the Print dialog box, under Print Style, choose Table Style.

3. Click the Preview button.

Click the close (×) button on the Print Preview window (see Figure 21.4) if you need to return to the view to make more modifications. You can also click Page Setup to change the margins and other page settings or Print if the view looks fine as it is.

FIGURE 21.4

It's always a good idea to use Print Preview to check your view-based report before printing it.

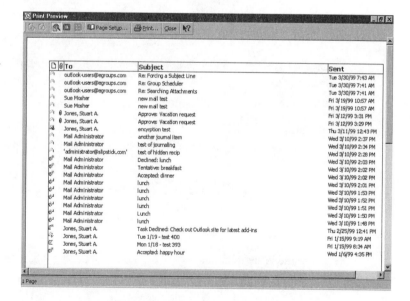

 If you want to experiment with variations on the table print style, perhaps using different margins and page sizes, choose File, Page Setup, Define Print Styles. In the Define Print Styles dialog box, choose Table Style, and then click Copy to create a new copy of the table style.

21

To change the print margins for a report printed from an Outlook view, follow these steps:

1. Choose File, Page Setup, Table Style.

2. In the Page Setup dialog box, switch to the Paper tab (see Figure 21.5).

FIGURE 21.5

The Paper tab controls settings that determine the layout of your view on the printed page.

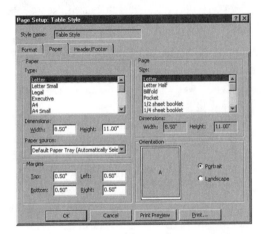

3. On the Paper tab, you can adjust the paper size, page size, page orientation, and margins.

4. When you finish your adjustments, click Print Preview to see the result.

You will return to views in Hour 23, "Exchange Server and Database Collaboration," which discusses how to restrict the views that users can see for a particular folder.

Other Built-in Report Techniques

Outlook includes a few other techniques that may be fine for simple reporting tasks. In this section, I will review these methods:

- Copy and paste to Excel
- Export to a delimited file

One side benefit of table-type folder views is that you can copy their data to Microsoft Excel with just a few keystrokes and then use Excel for additional formatting or data manipulation. Follow these steps in any Outlook Table view:

1. In an Outlook folder in a table-type view, choose Edit, Select All.

2. Choose Edit, Copy.

3. Switch to a blank Excel worksheet, and then choose Edit, Paste.

Another way to extract data from Outlook is to use the File, Import and Export command. This creates a file you can open in another program that may be able to produce better reports. You can export to a variety of database and text file formats. However, this method skips custom fields and data stored in Outlook custom forms.

Sending Output to Microsoft Excel

For reports that require more formatting than Outlook views can provide or in which you want to perform complex data manipulation, Microsoft Excel is a good tool. The row and column layout of an Excel worksheet is very similar to a Table view in Outlook and is easy to handle in code.

The feature that makes it possible for you to write code in Outlook to produce reports in Excel is called Office *automation*. You can start an instance of any other Microsoft Office program (or use an existing copy if it's already running), create a new document, and add data to it using the other program's object model.

First, you have to learn the basics of opening a worksheet in Excel and adding data to it. Then, you will look at a specific example, in which you extract the names and addresses from an Outlook distribution list.

Excel Report Basics

To work with another program, you must first add a reference to that program's library in VBA. Choose Tools, References, and then check the box for Microsoft Excel 9.0 Object Library. (If you have an earlier version of Excel, check the box for its library. Note, however, that you might have to modify the code in this section to work with the older version's object model.) Use the following code in an Outlook VBA project to start a copy of Excel and open a new, blank workbook:

```
Sub OpenExcelWB()
    Dim objExcel As Excel.Application
    Dim objWB As Excel.Workbook
    Dim objWS As Excel.Worksheet
    On Error Resume Next
    Set objExcel = GetObject(, "Excel.Application")
    If objExcel Is Nothing Then
        Set objExcel = CreateObject("Excel.Application")
    End If
    On Error GoTo 0
    objExcel.Visible = True
    Set objWB = objExcel.Workbooks.Add
    Set objWS = objWB.Worksheets(1)
End Sub
```

21

The Dim statements are a little different from those you've seen before. The
Excel.object syntax specifies that the object you're going to create is from the Excel
object model.

The Set objExcel = GetObject(, "Excel.Application") statement checks whether
Excel is already running. If Excel is not running, you create a new instance of Excel with
the Set objExcel = CreateObject("Excel.Application") statement. You must also
set the Visible property for the objExcel object to True, or the user will never see the
worksheet. Finally, you add a workbook using the Add method and then set the objWS
variable to the first worksheet in the workbook.

Within an Excel worksheet, use the Cells object to specify a particular cell and put data
into it. The Cells object takes row and column numbers as parameters, using the syntax
Cells(row, col). This code fragment puts the text "My First Excel Report" into cell
A1 (or row 1, column 1) and the text "End of Report" into cell E4 (or row 4, column 5)
of an objWS worksheet object:

```
objWS.Cells(1, 1) = "My First Excel Report"
objWS.Cells(4, 5) = "End of Report"
```

> Unlike Outlook, Excel includes a macro recorder that turns your keystrokes
> into VBA code. Choose Tools, Macro, Record New Macro to start the macro
> recorder. Perform various operations in Excel, and click the recorder's Stop
> button when you finish. Choose Tools, Macros; select your recorded macro;
> and then click Edit to open the macro in VBA. You can copy code from
> Excel's VBA window into your Outlook project, editing it as necessary to
> change the variable names.

Another useful Excel object is the Range object, which can cover an area that includes
more than one cell, even nonadjacent areas. For simple rectangular ranges, you can use
the Cells object to define a Range by its upper-left and lower-right corners. This code
fragment sets an objRange object to the cells in the rectangle defined by cells A1 and E4
as the upper-left and lower-right corners. It then turns on bold formatting in all the cells
in objRange.

```
Dim objRange As Excel.Range
Set objRange = objWS.Range(Cells(1, 1), Cells(4, 5))
objRange.Font.Bold = True
```

Use the Object Browser to find out more about Excel objects, properties, and methods.

A Distribution List Report

For a practical example of Excel as a report tool, consider the DistListItem object in Outlook—a personal distribution list contained in a Contacts folder. It holds a list of addresses that can either point to entries in your address books or be one-time addresses. The example in Listing 21.1 is designed to run from a toolbar button on an Inspector window and work with the currently displayed item (ActiveInspector.CurrentItem). It retrieves each member of the distribution list and puts its display name, e-mail address, and address type (such as SMTP for Internet mail) into an Excel worksheet.

LISTING 21.1   Extracting the Members of a Distribution List

```
 1: Sub DLToExcel()
 2:     Dim objApp As Application
 3:     Dim objDL As Object
 4:     Dim objRecip As Recipient
 5:     Dim objAddrEntry As AddressEntry
 6:     Dim objExcel As Excel.Application
 7:     Dim objWB As Excel.Workbook
 8:     Dim objWS As Excel.Worksheet
 9:     Dim objRange As Excel.Range
10:     Dim I As Integer
11:     Dim intRow As Integer
12:     Dim intStartRow As Integer
13:     Dim intCol As Integer
14:     Set objApp = CreateObject("Outlook.Application")
15:     If objApp.Inspectors.Count > 0 Then
16:         Set objDL = objApp.ActiveInspector.CurrentItem
17:         If objDL.Class <> olDistributionList Then
18:             MsgBox _
19:                 "The current item is not a distribution list."
20:             GoTo Exit_DLToExcel
21:         End If
22:     Else
23:         MsgBox "No open item"
24:         GoTo Exit_DLToExcel
25:     End If
26:     On Error Resume Next
27:     Set objExcel = GetObject(, "Excel.Application")
28:     On Error GoTo 0
29:     If objExcel Is Nothing Then
30:         Set objExcel = CreateObject("Excel.Application")
31:     End If
32:     objExcel.Visible = True
33:     Set objWB = objExcel.Workbooks.Add
34:     Set objWS = objWB.Worksheets(1)
```

21

continues

LISTING 21.1 continued

```
35:      objWS.Cells(1, 1) = objDL.Subject
36:      intStartRow = 3
37:      intRow = intStartRow
38:      For I = 1 To objDL.MemberCount
39:          Set objAddrEntry = objDL.GetMember(I).AddressEntry
40:          objWS.Cells(intRow, 1) = objAddrEntry.Name
41:          objWS.Cells(intRow, 2) = objAddrEntry.Address
42:          objWS.Cells(intRow, 3) = objAddrEntry.Type
43:          intRow = intRow + 1
44:      Next
45:      intRow = intRow - 1
46:      Set objRange = objWS.Range(Cells(3, 1), Cells(intRow, 3))
47:      For I = 1 To 3
48:          objRange.Columns(I).EntireColumn.AutoFit
49:      Next
50:      objWB.Names.Add _
51:          Name:=Replace(objDL.Subject, " ", ""), _
52:          RefersTo:="=" & "" & objWS.Name & _
53:          "!" & objRange.Address & ""
54:      objWS.Activate
55: Exit_DLToExcel:
56:      Set objApp = Nothing
57:      Set objDL = Nothing
58:      Set objRecip = Nothing
59:      Set objAddrEntry = Nothing
60:      Set objWB = Nothing
61:      Set objWS = Nothing
62:      Set objRange = Nothing
63:      Set objExcel = Nothing
64: End Sub
```

Here's how the code works:

- After the variables are declared (lines 2–13), an Outlook `Application` object is assigned. Lines 15–25 check whether any Outlook items are currently open and, in particular, whether the current item is a distribution list. If not, execution branches to the `Exit_DLToExcel:` label (line 55), where all object variables are set to `Nothing`.

- Lines 26–34 use the current instance of Excel (if there is one), start Excel if necessary, and then open a new workbook and assign variables for `Workbook` and `Worksheet` objects.

- Line 35 puts the name of the distribution list in the first cell of the worksheet.

- In lines 36–44, the procedure sets up a loop that gets each distribution list member (`objDL.GetMember(I)`) and copies data from three fields to cells in three columns, starting with row 3. `GetMember()` returns an Outlook `Recipient` object. The `AddressEntry` object property of the `Recipient` object is used so that you can get not just the `Name` and `Address` properties, but also the `Type` property, in case you have some non-Internet addresses and want to know what type of addresses they are.

- Line 46 sets a `Range` object (`objRange`) to the cells that contain the distribution list data.

- Lines 47–49 use the `Autofit` method on each column in `objRange` to make sure that the user can see the complete name and address.

- Lines 50–53 assign a name to `objRange`. Named ranges are an important Excel feature that make it easy to use a particular set of cells for mail merge and other functions.

- Line 54 displays the new worksheet to the user.

- The rest of the procedure, beginning with line 55, sets the object variables to `Nothing` to remove them from memory. Note the `GoTo Exit_DLToExcel` statements in lines 20 and 24, to cover the cases where a distribution list is not currently displayed.

Figures 21.6 and 21.7 show a distribution list created in a Contacts folder and the Excel worksheet that the code in Listing 21.1 produces.

FIGURE 21.6

An Outlook distribution list can mix and match different types of addresses.

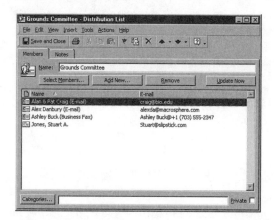

The icons in Figure 21.6 distinguish items from the Contacts folder (the first three) from other addresses, including both one-time addresses entered directly in the distribution list and addresses from a Microsoft Exchange Server Global Address List.

21

FIGURE 21.7

*The same list, ported
to Excel, adds the
address type to
column C.*

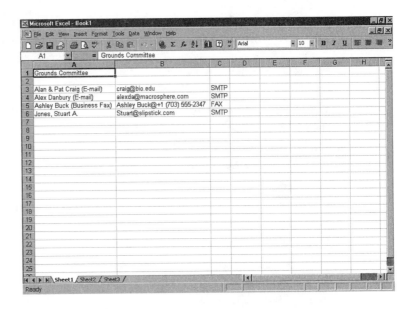

The For...Next block in lines 38–44 is the heart of the procedure, incrementing the row
number after each distribution list member's data has been added. You can use this type
of block to put any kind of Outlook data into Excel cells. For example, if you want to
copy data from all items in an Outlook MAPIFolder object named objFolder, you would
use a For Each...Next loop such as this one:

```
intRow = 1
For Each objItem in objFolder.Items
    objWS.Cells(intRow, 1) = objItem.property1
    objWS.Cells(intRow, 2) = objItem.property2
    ' more property statements
    objWS.Cells(intRow, n) = objItem.propertyn
    intRow = intRow + 1
Next
```

After the loop finishes with the last item, the worksheet will contain a block of
intRow - 1 rows and n columns containing data from n fields in intRow - 1 items from
the folder.

You could also use this technique to extract data from custom Outlook fields, using the
expression objItem.UserDefinedFields.Find(property) instead of
objItem.property. This is a valuable way to retrieve information from custom fields,
for use in Excel or in another program that can read either Excel data files or delimited
files (one of the Save As file formats available in Excel).

Summary

Making data available through reports is an important programming technique because chances are, not everyone who needs to see your data will have Outlook. Printing from Outlook views, exporting to files that can be read by other programs, and using code to send data to Excel are all methods that have a place in your reporting repertoire.

In the next hour, you will see how Microsoft Word is also a reporting tool, particularly if you need to print from a custom form or combine information from two types of folders.

Q&A

Q What if I have Outlook 2000, but Excel 97? Can I still use automation?

A Yes, the same techniques should work fine. If you run into any problems, your first troubleshooting effort should be to check the old Excel object model.

Q After I push Outlook data into an Excel worksheet, can I use Excel techniques such as pivot tables to analyze it further?

A. Sure! You can either perform the data manipulation manually, adding formulas as needed, or you can use the methods in the Excel object model to create pivot tables and charts and perform other analyses.

Workshop

Work through the quiz questions and exercises so that you can better understand Outlook programming. See Appendix A for answers.

Quiz

1. What technique(s) can you use to create a tabular (columnar) report of Outlook data from a single folder, including custom fields?

2. What if you need to include data from several folders, such as all the Appointment items in five users' Calendar folders—can you use the same techniques?

Exercise

Finish creating the Sent in Last 7 Days view, which you based on the built-in Last Seven Days view. What did you have to do to complete the view?

21

HOUR 22

Designing Reports with Microsoft Word

In the preceding hour, you learned two ways to use Microsoft Excel as a reporting tool—by copying data manually and by writing code to put Outlook data into Excel's rows and columns. Microsoft Word is an even more flexible reporting tool. Not only can it handle data in rows and columns, but it can also reproduce the look of a custom Outlook form.

Another important reporting technique that you will see in this hour is combining information from different types of Outlook items. For example, you might want your printed calendar to include the business and mobile phone numbers of the people you're meeting with, or perhaps you need an invoice that totals the time you have spent working on a particular contact's projects.

Highlights of this hour include

- How to use a Word mail merge as a reporting tool
- How to duplicate the look of an Outlook form with a Word template
- How to print invoices and other reports that combine data from two folders

Mail Merge to Word

Mail merge to Microsoft Word is a relatively easy reporting method, but it only works from folders that contain Contact items. In any Contacts folder, choose Tools, Mail Merge to display the Mail Merge Contacts dialog box, shown in Figure 22.1.

FIGURE 22.1

Perform a mail merge to Microsoft Word from within any Outlook Contacts folder.

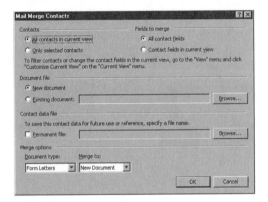

Mail merge is actually more flexible than it looks. You are not limited to producing just form letters, envelopes, and mailing labels. You can also choose Catalog from the Document Type list and lay out data fields in a table to create a columnar list of Contact data or, with comma delimiters, you can choose to create a comma-delimited list. Best of all, mail merge can handle custom Outlook forms and also allows you to include user-defined Outlook fields in the Word document.

Unlike previous versions, Microsoft Word 2000 allows you to use Outlook's Categories field in a mail merge query. However, this works effectively only in the limited case where each Contact item has no more than one entry in the Categories field.

Don't be discouraged by the fact that you can merge from Outlook directly to Word only from a Contacts folder. That's a limitation only when you start the merge from Outlook or if you choose Address Book as the data source in Word's Mail Merge Helper.

If you have custom fields that you want to use in a merge from other types of folders, try copying and pasting to Excel and then saving the resulting file as an Excel file or as a comma-delimited text file. Word can use either of those file formats as a data source for its mail merge feature.

Designing Custom Reports

22

Word is a particularly good vehicle for developing reports that duplicate the look of custom Outlook items. After an introduction to the basics of Word as an Outlook report tool, you will see an example of a custom report for a custom form. A second example shows how to combine information from items in more than one folder, as you might in an invoice.

Word Report Basics

Before writing code that uses Word, don't forget to add a reference to Word's library in VBA. Choose Tools, References, and then check the box for Microsoft Word 9.0 Object Library.

> If you have an earlier version of Word, check the box for its library. Note, however, that you might have to modify the code in this section to work with the older version's object model.

Use the following code in an Outlook VBA project to start Word, if it isn't already running, and open a new, blank document:

```
Sub OpenWordDoc()
    Dim objWord As Word.Application
    Dim objDoc As Word.Document
    On Error Resume Next
    Set objWord = GetObject(, "Word.Application")
    If objWord Is Nothing Then
        Set objWord = CreateObject("Word.Application")
    End If
    On Error GoTo 0
    objWord.Visible = True
    Set objDoc = objWord.Documents.Add
End Sub
```

It's very common to open Word with a document template (.dot file), instead of a blank document. The template can contain boilerplate text, as well as bookmarks, fields, or merge codes you can use to place Outlook data in the text. You can create a template from a new or existing Word document by choosing File, Save As and changing the Save as Type to Document Template. Templates that you create can be stored anywhere on your system, but usually are kept in one of these folders:

```
C:\Winnt\Profiles\profile name\Application Data\Microsoft\Templates
```

```
C:\Windows\Application Data\Microsoft\Templates
```

In Word, you can change the default location for templates by choosing Tools, Options, switching to the File Locations tab, and modifying the User Templates location.

Use this statement to open a new document based on a template named MyOutlookForm.dot, stored in your normal user templates folder:

```
Set objDoc = objWord.Documents.Add("MyOutlookForm.dot")
```

After you have a document open, you need to know how to add text to it. As with Excel, you can use the macro recorder to investigate Word's methods and properties and then adapt the resulting VBA code to your Outlook projects. For example, this code was generated by the Word macro recorder when I typed some text into a new document, pressed the Enter key twice to insert a line, and then typed in more text:

```
Sub Macro1()
'
' Macro1 Macro
' Macro recorded 4/16/99 by Sue Mosher
'
    Selection.TypeText Text:="This is the first paragraph. "
    Selection.TypeParagraph
    Selection.TypeParagraph
    Selection.TypeText Text:="This is the second paragraph."
End Sub
```

The Selection object refers to the currently selected text in Word. You can also use Range objects to refer to one or more ranges of text anywhere in the document. Both Range and Selection support somewhat similar methods for inserting text; the invoice example you will see later in this hour uses the InsertAfter method.

Duplicating a Custom Form

As you can imagine, it could be tedious to write code to type text into a Word document, then add data from an Outlook field, then add more text, then another field, and so on. In addition, it would be very difficult to revise such a report if you wanted to change a few words of text.

A better technique than inserting both standard text and Outlook fields in code is to lay out the report as a Word document, with Word fields acting as placeholders for the Outlook data. The code you write only has to place the data into the fields. It does not have to perform any layout chores; you take care of those simply by editing the Word template using Word's normal features.

This example creates a Word template to print the information shown on the Travel Request form in Figure 22.2 in a similar format. The Travel Request form is a custom Message form that displays a custom page instead of the default Message page. For this example, I modified a form downloaded from Microsoft's Web site to change a few of the field names to make them more intuitive and to add a command button that runs the code to produce the Word document. This latter is an important point: You can use automation in VBScript, not just VBA. The big difference is that VBScript doesn't require you to set a reference to Word first. (If fact, there is no place to set references.)

Figure 22.2

This Travel Request form has been modified to add a Print button with code that launches a Word document.

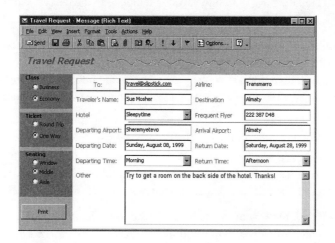

The Travel Request form is one of many free Outlook forms that you can download from `http://officeupdate.microsoft.com` and modify, rather than build a comparable Outlook form from scratch.

In a nutshell, here are the steps involved in creating a Word template that can be used to print the data from the Travel Request form:

1. In Word, choose File, New, and select Create New Template. Then click OK.

2. In the Template1 document, type in the title you want to appear on the printed form.

3. Choose Table, Insert Table to add a table with columns to match the number of apparent columns in the form's layout. The Travel Request form, for example, has labels and data controls arranged roughly in five columns, so you should use a five-column table in the Word template.

4. Turn off the borders for the Word table: Choose Table, Select, Table. Next, choose Format, Borders and Shading, and under Setting, choose None. Then click OK.

5. Choose View, Toolbars, Forms to display the Forms toolbar.

6. Type text into the table, and add form fields to duplicate the layout of the Outlook form. Use the Text Form Field and Check Box Form Field buttons on the Forms toolbar.

7. Set the properties for each form field, as described next.

8. Click the Save button to save the template to the default Word template location on your computer.

To add the form fields described in steps 5 and 6, use the buttons on the Forms toolbar. Click the Check Box Form Field button to duplicate both option buttons and check boxes from the Outlook form. Use the Text Form Field button to duplicate text boxes, combo boxes, and list boxes. Each button adds only the field. You also have to type text to label each field.

For example, start with the Class choices from the Travel Request form in Figure 22.2. In the cell at the upper-left of the table, type **Class** and then press Enter. Click the Check Box Form Field button and then type a space, followed by **Business**. Click the Check Box Form Field button again and then type a space, followed by **Economy**.

To finish the top row of the table, press Tab to move to the second cell. Type **Traveler's Name:**. Press Tab again to move to the third cell. Click the Text Form Field button. Press Tab to move to the second cell in the top row of the table. Type **Airline:**. Press Tab again to move to the last cell in the row. Click the Text Form Field button to add another field.

After formatting the text and form fields with the same formatting as on the Outlook form (8- and 9-point Tahoma), the template should now look like Figure 22.3.

Continue adding fields and text to the table. After you add all fields, use the commands on Word's Format toolbar to adjust the font settings and paragraph spacing. Adjust the column widths in the table, splitting and merging cells as needed. You might find it helpful to choose Table, Draw Table to display more table tools.

After the fields and text are in place, you have to set properties for each field. Right-click each shaded field, and then choose Properties to display the options for the selected field. Figure 22.4 shows the Options dialog box for the Business check box in Figure 22.3.

Under Bookmark, set the name that you want to use for this field in your code. Use a name that's as close as you can make it to the Outlook field name, given that Word bookmarks cannot use spaces or punctuation.

FIGURE 22.3

Use the Forms toolbar to insert form fields that your code can fill with Outlook data.

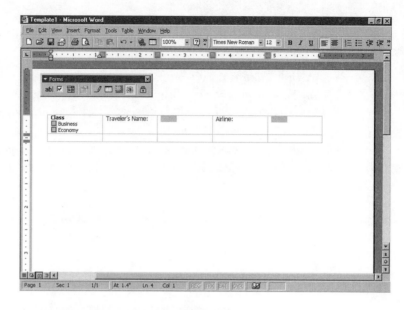

FIGURE 22.4

Set a bookmark and other options for each field in the template.

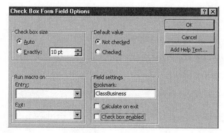

If you plan to allow users to view the form before printing, you might want to clear the Check Box Enabled option to prevent users from accidentally changing the value of a check box field. For text box fields, the equivalent option is Fill-In Enabled, as shown in Figure 22.5.

Here are a few more tips for working with form fields and templates:

- Before starting your template, compile a list of all the Outlook fields you want to include. Right-click each data control on the source Outlook form, and choose Properties to check the field name on the Value tab.

- Use just the Text Form Field and Check Box Form Field buttons on the Forms toolbar to insert fields. Because users won't be filling out this form in Word, you don't have to use the Drop-Down Form Field button at all.

- Choose Regular Text as the format for all text fields that you plan to fill with Outlook data. If special formatting is necessary, do it in your Outlook code, not in the field properties.

- Don't use a form field in Word to represent the large message box on an Outlook form. Form fields don't handle multiple paragraphs very well; they show boxes where you would expect to have carriage returns and line feeds. Instead, insert a bookmark without a form field.

- You can actually use bookmarks without the form fields to set the location for any of your Outlook data fields to be inserted. The advantage of form fields is that the field placeholders are easier to see and format.

FIGURE 22.5

Set Regular text as the Type for data that your code will copy from Outlook to text form fields.

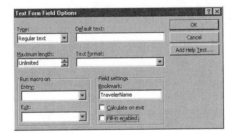

After laying out the fields and text, formatting the template, and setting up the properties for each field, you can choose File, Save to save the template.

Next, you have to set up the Travel Request form so that you can print it, by adding a Print button and some code. Open the form in design mode, and add a Command Button control to both the Compose and Read pages. Give it the name `cmdPrint` and use `Print` for its caption.

The `FormFields` collection on a Word `Document` object (for example, `objDoc`) contains all the fields you added. To copy data from an Outlook field to the corresponding field, you will use this syntax for check box form fields:

```
objDoc.FormFields(CheckBoxFieldName).CheckBox.Value = expr
```

`CheckBoxFieldName` is the bookmark you assigned to the field, and `expr` is either `True` or `False` or an expression that evaluates to `True` or `False`.

For Outlook form option buttons, you might want to use an `If...ElseIf...End If` block or a `Select Case...End Select` block to determine which check box field value needs to be set to `True`. See Listing 22.1 for examples.

Use this syntax for text form fields:

```
objDoc.FormFields(textboxfieldname1).Result = _
   Item.UserProperties(propertyname).Value
objDoc.FormFields(textboxfieldname2).Result = _
   Item.property
```

In this code, *textboxfieldnamex* is the bookmark assigned to the field, *propertyname* is the name of a custom Outlook item property, and *property* is the name of a built-in Outlook property.

Where you use a bookmark by itself, instead of with a form field, to mark the location of an Outlook field, use this syntax to insert text:

```
objDoc.Bookmarks(bookmarkname).Range.InsertAfter Item.property
```

The complete code for printing the Travel Request form is in Listing 22.1. The first procedure, cmdPrint_Click, is the event handler for the cmdPrint button's Click event. It starts Word, launches a new document based on the Travel Request.dot template, and then calls the AddTRData procedure (line 17). If you want users to review the document before printing, take out the objDoc.PrintOut statement (line 65).

LISTING 22.1 Using Word to Print a Custom Form

```
 1: Sub cmdPrint_Click()
 2:     Dim objWord
 3:     Dim objDoc
 4:     On Error Resume Next
 5:     Set objWord = GetObject(, "Word.Application")
 6:     If objWord Is Nothing Then
 7:         Set objWord = CreateObject("Word.Application")
 8:     End If
 9:     On Error GoTo 0
10:     objWord.Visible = True
11:     Set objDoc = objWord.Documents.Add("Travel Request.dot")
12:     Call AddTRData(objDoc)
13:     Set objDoc = Nothing
14:     Set objWord = Nothing
15: End Sub
16:
17: Sub AddTRData(objDoc)
18:     Dim strValue
19:     If Item.UserProperties("Flight Class").Value = _
20:        "Business Class" Then
22:          objDoc.FormFields("ClassBusiness"). _
22:             CheckBox.Value = True
23:     ElseIf Item.UserProperties("Flight Class") = _
24:        "Economy Class" Then
```

continues

LISTING 22.1 continued

```
25:          objDoc.FormFields("ClassEconomy").CheckBox.Value = True
26:      End If
27:      If Item.UserProperties("Ticket Type").Value = _
28:        "Round Trip" Then
29:          objDoc.FormFields("TicketRoundTrip"). _
30:             CheckBox.Value = True
31:      ElseIf Item.UserProperties("Ticket Type") = _
32:        "One Way" Then
33:          objDoc.FormFields("TicketOneWay").CheckBox.Value = True
34:      End If
35:      strValue = Item.UserProperties("Seating Type").Value
36:      If strValue <> "" Then
37:          objDoc.FormFields("Seating" & strValue) _
38:             .CheckBox.Value = True
39:      End If
40:      objDoc.FormFields("TravelerName").Result = _
41:        Item.UserProperties("Traveler's Name").Value
42:      objDoc.FormFields("Hotel").Result = _
43:        Item.UserProperties("Hotel").Value
44:      objDoc.FormFields("DepartingAirport").Result = _
45:        Item.UserProperties("Departing Airport").Value
46:      objDoc.FormFields("DepartingDate").Result = _
47:        ConvertOLDate(Item.UserProperties("Departing Date") _
48:        .Value)
49:      objDoc.FormFields("DepartingTime").Result = _
50:        Item.UserProperties("Departure Time").Value
51:      objDoc.FormFields("Airline").Result = _
52:        Item.UserProperties("Airlines").Value
53:      objDoc.FormFields("DestinationCity").Result = _
54:        Item.UserProperties("Destination City").Value
55:      objDoc.FormFields("FrequentFlyerNo").Result = _
56:        Item.UserProperties("Frequent Flyer No").Value
57:      objDoc.FormFields("DestinationAirport").Result = _
58:        Item.UserProperties("Destination  Airport").Value
59:      objDoc.FormFields("ReturnDate").Result = _
60:        ConvertOLDate(Item.UserProperties("Return Date").Value)
61:      objDoc.FormFields("ReturnTime").Result = _
62:        Item.UserProperties("Return Time").Value
63:      objDoc.Bookmarks("Other").Range.InsertAfter Item.Body
64:      objDoc.PrintOut
65: End Sub
66:
67: Function ConvertOLDate(dteDate)
68:      If dteDate = #1/1/4501# Then
69:          ConvertOLDate = "None"
70:      Else
71:          ConvertOLDate = FormatDateTime(dteDate, vbLongDate)
72:      End If
74: End Function
```

22

The AddTRData procedure does all the work of copying data from Outlook fields to the matching form fields in the Word document. This type of procedure requires a lot of testing to make sure that you get the exact names of the bookmarks and Outlook properties correct. However, after you perfect the code, printing a custom Outlook form is a snap.

> The property names for the Travel Request form in Listing 22.1 differ slightly from those in the Travel Request form you can download from Microsoft, because you made a few changes to make the property names more closely match their form labels. Be sure that you use the exact property name from the form in your own code.

The third procedure, the ConvertOLDate() function (line 68), controls the formatting for date fields and handles values that appear in Outlook Date/Time fields as None but are really the date 1/1/4501.

In line 63, note the special handling of the Item.Body property, labeled Other on the form. As noted earlier, a bookmark is better than a form field for working with the Body property, which represents the large message box on an Outlook form, because a bookmark handles multiple paragraphs better than a form field.

What does the finished document look like? Figure 22.6 shows the document that the code in Listing 22.1 creates when the user clicks the Print button on the form in Figure 22.2. The light gray shading on the form fields and the light gray table gridlines are just to make the document easier to view. They don't appear when you print it out.

> When you start designing Outlook reports in Word, you want to see the results each time. When you perfect the report, you will find that it prints much faster if you don't display the Word document to the user. That takes just a few changes to your code. First, at the beginning of the procedure, add this declaration:
>
> ```
> Dim blnPrintBackground
> ```
>
> To hold the user's current Word background printing setting Next, omit any
>
> ```
> objWord.Visible = True
> ```
>
> statement (line 10 in Listing 22.1). Finally, substitute these statements for the objDoc.PrintOut statement (line 64 in Listing 22.1):
>
> ```
> blnPrintBackground = objWord.Options.PrintBackground
> objWord.Options.PrintBackground = False
> ```

```
objDoc.PrintOut
objWord.Options.PrintBackground = blnPrintBackground
```

to set background printing to `False`, print the document, and then restore the user's background printing setting.

FIGURE 22.6

The Word version looks almost exactly like the Outlook form in Figure 22.2.

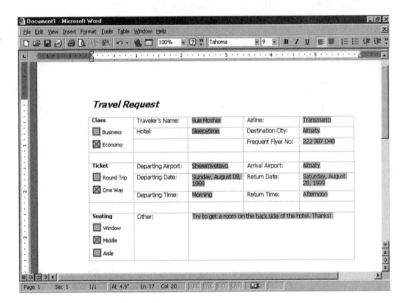

Reporting from Related Items

To complete your Outlook report skills, you must be able to combine related Outlook items from two folders. The example you will work with is an invoice listing the hours spent working for a particular contact, as recorded in the Journal folder. To produce this report, you will learn several additional coding skills:

- How to work with the `Links` collection in an Outlook item
- How to insert data into Word table rows and columns
- How to add a new row to a Word table

Every Outlook item includes as one of its properties a `Links` collection. (On Outlook forms, this field is labeled Contacts, not Links.) Each `Link` object in the collection points to an item in a Contacts folder. When you look at the Activities page of an Outlook Contact item, the list shows any items that contain a `Link` pointing to the current contact.

The `Links` collection and Activities page essentially enhance the original concept of the Journal folder with a much broader way of linking items to contacts. You can use the `Links` collection to loop through a folder and find items related to a contact by checking the `Link` object's `Name` property against the `FullName` property of the contact or, if the `FullName` property is empty, the `FileAs` property. In this `HasLinkToContact()` function, the `objItem` argument represents any type of Outlook item whose `Links` you want to examine. The `strName` argument represents either the `FullName` or `FileAs` property of the contact you're trying to match, depending on whether the contact's `FullName` property is empty.

```
Function HasLinkToContact(objItem As Object, _
        strName As String) As Boolean
    Dim objLinks As Links
    Dim objLink As Link
    Set objLinks = objItem.Links
    For Each objLink In objLinks
        If objLink.Name = strName Then
            HasLinkToContact = True
            GoTo Exit_HasLinkToContact
        End If
    Next
Exit_HasLinkToContact:
    Set objLink = Nothing
    Set objLinks = Nothing
End Function
```

Using a table in your Word template is simpler than it might look. Create a two-row table as you normally would, using either the Table, Insert, Table command or Table, Draw Table. In the first row, add the column heading text and formatting for the headings. Leave the cells in the second row blank; this will be the first data row. You can, however, add formatting to these cells.

In your code, assign an object variable to the table. If your template has only one table, the syntax looks like this because the first table has an index in the `Tables` collection of 1. (Assume that the current Word document is represented by the `objDoc` object variable.):

```
Set objTable = objDoc.Tables(1)
```

To add a new row to an `objTable` variable representing a `Table` object in VBA code, use this syntax:

```
objTable.Rows.Add
```

The syntax to fill a cell with data uses the `Cell` object and its `row` and `col` arguments:

```
objTable.Cell(row, col).Range.InsertAfter data
```

The data to be inserted should first be converted to a `String` and formatted appropriately by your code.

> Note that you refer to a single cell in a Word table with `Cell(row, col)`, whereas in Excel, you refer to a single cell with `Cells(row, col)`.

Listing 22.2 contains the entire code for the invoice application. It makes a few assumptions:

- You are running the code from an Explorer window using either a toolbar button or the Macros window.
- Only one Contact item is selected.
- The hourly billing rate for the Contact item is stored in the `BillingInformation` property.
- The Journal folder contains only all items that have not yet been invoiced.
- The `HasLinkToContact()` function is available either as a private function in the same module as the other procedures in Listing 22.2 or as a public function in another Outlook VBA module.

Put all the code for the invoice application in a separate Outlook module to make it easier to manage.

LISTING 22.2   Collating Data from Two Folders into One Word Document

```
 1: Option Explicit
 2: Private m_objDoc As Word.Document
 3: Private m_objItem As Object
 4: Private m_objJournal As MAPIFolder
 5:
 6: Sub WordInvoice()
 7:     Call OpenDoc("Invoice.dot")
 8:     Call GetContactAndJournal
 9:     Call FillFormFields
10:     Call FillTable
11:     Set m_objDoc = Nothing
12:     Set m_objItem = Nothing
13:     Set m_objJournal = Nothing
14: End Sub
```

22

```
15:
16: Private Sub OpenDoc(strTemplate as String)
17:     Dim objWord As Word.Application
18:     On Error Resume Next
19:     Set objWord = GetObject(, "Word.Application")
20:     If objWord Is Nothing Then
21:         Set objWord = CreateObject("Word.Application")
22:     End If
23:     On Error GoTo 0
24:     objWord.Visible = True
25:     Set m_objDoc = objWord.Documents.Add(strTemplate)
26: End Sub
27:
28: Private Sub GetContactAndJournal()
29:     Dim objApp As Application
30:     Dim objNS As NameSpace
31:     Dim objSelection As Selection
32:     Set objApp = CreateObject("Outlook.Application")
33:     Set objNS = objApp.GetNamespace("MAPI")
34:     Set objSelection = objApp.ActiveExplorer.Selection
35:     If objSelection.Count <> 1 Then
36:         MsgBox "Please select just one item."
37:         GoTo Exit_GetContactAndJournal
38:     Else
39:         Set m_objItem = objSelection.Item(1)
40:         If m_objItem.Class <> olContact Then
41:             MsgBox "Please choose a Contact."
42:             GoTo Exit_GetContactAndJournal
43:         End If
44:     End If
45:     Set m_objJournal = objNS.GetDefaultFolder(olFolderJournal)
46: Exit_GetContactAndJournal:
47:     Set objSelection = Nothing
48:     Set objNS = Nothing
49:     Set objApp = Nothing
50: End Sub
51:
52: Private Sub FillFormFields()
53:     m_objDoc.FormFields("FullName").Result = _
54:       m_objItem.FullName
55:     m_objDoc.FormFields("CompanyName").Result = _
56:       m_objItem.CompanyName
57:     m_objDoc.FormFields("BusinessAddressStree").Result = _
58:       m_objItem.BusinessAddressStreet
```

continues

LISTING 22.2   continued

```
59:        m_objDoc.FormFields("BusinessAddressCity").Result = _
60:         m_objItem.BusinessAddressCity
61:        m_objDoc.FormFields("BusinessAddressState").Result = _
62:         m_objItem.BusinessAddressState
63:        m_objDoc.FormFields("BusinessAddressZip").Result = _
64:         m_objItem.BusinessAddressPostalCode
65:        m_objDoc.FormFields("HourlyRate").Result = _
66:          Format(m_objItem.BillingInformation, "Currency")
67: End Sub
68:
69: Private Sub FillTable()
70:        Dim objTable As Word.Table
71:        Dim objJEntry As JournalItem
72:        Dim objItems As Items
73:        Dim intRow As Integer
74:        Dim curHourly As Currency
75:        Dim strContactName As String
76:        Dim curItem As Currency
77:        Dim curTotal As Currency
78:        Dim I As Integer
79:        Set objTable = m_objDoc.Tables(1)
80:        Set objItems = m_objJournal.Items
81:        objItems.Sort "[Start]"
82:        objItems.SetColumns "Start, Subject, Duration"
83:        curHourly = CCur(m_objItem.BillingInformation)
84:        strContactName = LinkName(m_objItem)
85:        intRow = 2
86:        For Each objJEntry In objItems
87:            If HasLinkToContact(objJEntry, strContactName) Then
88:                If intRow > 2 Then
89:                    objTable.Rows.Add
90:                End If
91:                objTable.Cell(intRow, 1).Range.InsertAfter _
92:                  FormatDateTime(objJEntry.Start, vbShortDate)
93:                objTable.Cell(intRow, 2).Range.InsertAfter _
94:                  objJEntry.Subject
95:                objTable.Cell(intRow, 3).Range.InsertAfter _
96:                  Format(objJEntry.Duration / 60, "Standard")
97:                curItem = objJEntry.Duration / 60 * curHourly
98:                objTable.Cell(intRow, 4).Range.InsertAfter _
99:                  Format(curItem, "Currency")
100:               curTotal = curTotal + curItem
101:               intRow = intRow + 1
102:           End If
```

```
103:     Next
104:     objTable.Rows.Add
105:     objTable.Cell(intRow, 3).Range.InsertAfter _
106:        "TOTAL"
107:     objTable.Cell(intRow, 4).Range.InsertAfter _
108:        Format(curTotal, "Currency")
109:     Set objTable = Nothing
110: End Sub
111:
112: Private Function LinkName(objContact As ContactItem) As String
113:     If objContact.FullName <> vbNullString Then
114:         LinkName = objContact.FullName
115:     Else
116:         LinkName = objContact.FileAs
117:     End If
118: End Function
```

Which procedure actually runs the invoice application? It's the WordInvoice subroutine—the only procedure not declared Private. The WordInvoice subroutine calls four other routines in turn:

- OpenDoc to create a new Word document and assign it to the m_objDoc module-level variable

- GetContactAndJournal to get the currently selected contact, assign it to the m_objItem module-level variable, and assign the user's Journal folder to the m_objJournal module-level variable

- FillFormFields to fill in the Word form fields in the template with corresponding data from Outlook fields, using the techniques described in the previous section

- FillTable to loop through the Journal folder, check each item using the HasLinkToContact() function, post entries linked to the contact to the Word table, calculate the charge for each entry, and keep a running total of the charges to post in the last row of the table

The LinkName() function makes it simpler to use the HasLinkToContact() function. It returns either the FileAs or FullName property of the contact.

Figure 22.7 shows the finished product: an invoice produced entirely from Outlook items, but laid out in Word.

FIGURE 22.7

This invoice demon-strates how well Word works as a reporting tool to combine items from different folders.

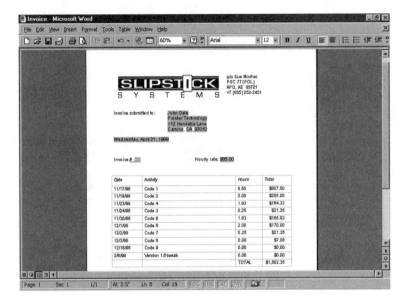

Summary

This second chapter on Outlook reports provides the skills you need to create printed or file output with either mail merge or code. Templates, form fields, and tables help you design Word reports to match a custom Outlook form or to produce reports in other formats. Using the Links property, you can locate items related to a particular Contact item and retrieve those items' data.

The next hour turns to the theme of collaboration, both with Microsoft Exchange Server as your mail server and with external databases.

Q&A

Q **In Listing 22.2, could the Restrict or Find method be used instead of looping through the Journal folder?**

A No, because Links is one Outlook item property that cannot be used in filters for the Restrict and Find methods. You will find others listed on the help topic for these methods.

Q In the invoice application, how do you know that the Journal item contains only entries that have not been invoiced?

A This is an example of a *business rule:* a standard operating procedure that embodies assumptions about your data and about the way your organization runs. These rules are not set in stone. Your organization might want to do things differently. For example, rather than keep only current Journal items in the Journal folder, you might want to keep all items there and select only Journal items that fall into a certain date range.

Workshop

Work through the quiz questions and exercises so that you can better understand Outlook programming. See Appendix A for answers.

Quiz

Imagine that you have been asked to write an application to print all appointments for any given day and include the business and mobile phone numbers of any contacts involved in a meeting or linked to an appointment. Answer the following questions:

1. What properties of the Appointment item would you examine for a link to Contacts?

2. What Contact properties would you want to include in your report?

3. Which built-in Outlook print styles might make good models for this kind of report?

4. What procedures from Listing 22.2 could you probably reuse in your application?

Exercise

Rewrite the `HasLinkToContact()` function to include the operations in the `LinkName()` function from Listing 22.2. Call it `HasLinkToContact2()`. The arguments for the `HasLinkToContact2()` function should be the item you want to test and the Contact item to which it might be linked. Which version of `HasLinkToContact()` is more efficient?

HOUR 23

Exchange Server and Database Collaboration

Outlook works great in a small workgroup with a POP3/SMTP mail server or the workgroup postoffice included with Windows. Using a feature called Net Folders, you can even share data with other people anywhere in the world, as long as they have an Internet mail address. However, to get the most out of Outlook, you need Microsoft Exchange Server as your mail server. Exchange Server supports shared folders with custom forms and views, scripts that react to new items even when you're not logged in, and Web access to mail and some other folders.

This lesson also takes a look at another high-end collaboration strategy: linking Outlook to an external database.

Highlights of this hour include

- How to create and configure Exchange Server public folders
- What folder events a server-based script can react to
- Which object model must be used in server-based scripts

- What Exchange Server tool converts Outlook forms to Web-based forms
- How Outlook can exchange data with an external database

Managing Public Folders

One of Exchange Server's key application-building components is the public folder. Public folders can hold any type of Outlook item and can be replicated between Exchange Server sites in different cities, offering truly global access to your applications.

Creating Public Folders

Before adding any public folders, check with the Exchange Server administrator to find out where in the All Public Folders hierarchy you have permission to create new folders. If you don't have permission to create new subfolders under a particular parent folder, you will get an error message.

To create a public folder, choose File, New, Folder. In the Create New Folder dialog box (see Figure 23.1), give the folder a name, indicate what type of items it contains, and specify its parent folder.

FIGURE 23.1

You can add your own folders to the Public Folders hierarchy if the Exchange Server administrator grants you permission.

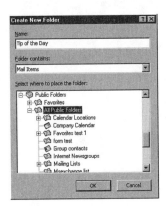

Setting Folder Properties

After creating the folder, right-click on it in the Outlook Folder List, and then choose Properties to see the dialog box shown in Figure 23.2.

On the General tab, you can rename the folder, provide an optional description, and check the folder size. The most important setting on the General tab is the selection under When Posting to This Folder, Use. This sets the default form for the folder—the form displayed when the user presses Ctrl+N or chooses Actions, New. You can use any published form as the folder default, as long as it matches the type of item selected for the folder in the Create New Folder dialog box in Figure 23.1. In other words, you can't use a modified Task form to post to a folder designed to hold Appointment items.

FIGURE 23.2

Set folder properties to control how your folder behaves.

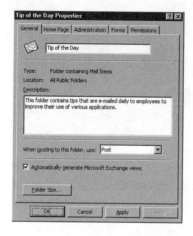

If people will access the folder with the Microsoft Exchange client software, as well as Outlook, check the box for Automatically Generate Microsoft Exchange Views. Also, note that Exchange client users cannot view Outlook forms, although Outlook users can work with folders created with the older Exchange Forms Designer tool.

On the second tab, Home Page, shown in Figure 23.3, you can associate a Web page with this folder and show it when the user switches to the folder. The user can use the View, Show Folder Home Page command to toggle between the home page and the items stored in the folder.

You can use any Web page as the folder home page, but Microsoft's intention for this feature is to have more pages like the Outlook Today page, which summarizes information in your own mailbox. To create a folder home page from scratch requires a knowledge of HTML and DHTML that goes beyond this book. However, Microsoft plans to offer a downloadable wizard that builds folder-based applications, including their home pages, after you answer a few simple questions.

23

FIGURE 23.3

You can provide a Web page that goes with a folder.

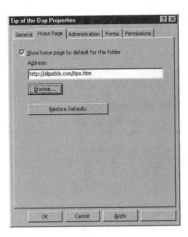

On the Administration tab (see Figure 23.4), set the initial view on the folder, the behavior of items dragged to the folder, and the current access to the folder. It's common to make the folder available only to owners until you finish modifying and testing its properties.

FIGURE 23.4

Set the default view on the Administration tab.

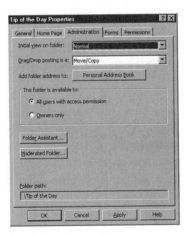

Folder views bring us back to a topic discussed in Hour 21, "Getting Started with Outlook Reports." In that chapter, you learned how to customize folder views to present Outlook data in a particular way. The focus of that chapter is on printed reports. However, Outlook uses the same views for printing and displaying data.

If you want to restrict the views available on a public folder to only those views you designate, follow these steps:

1. Switch to the folder whose views you want to restrict.

2. Right-click the folder name, and then choose Properties.

3. On the Administration tab of the properties dialog for the folder, set the Initial View on Folder to a custom view you have created.

4. Click OK to close the properties dialog.

5. Choose View, Current View, Define Views.

6. On the Define Views dialog box, check the box for Only Show Views Created for This Folder.

7. Click Close to return to the Outlook viewer.

Also on the Administration tab are the Folder Assistant and Moderated Folder buttons, which allow you to add automated responses to a folder without writing any programming code.

The fourth tab, Forms (see Figure 23.5), helps you manage forms that have been published to the folder's forms library.

Figure 23.5

Managing forms published in the folder.

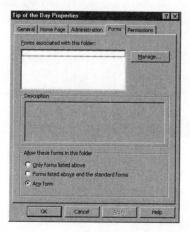

On the final tab (see Figure 23.6), you set permissions for everyone you want to have access to the folder. Click the Add button to add either individual names from the Exchange Server Global Address List or an Exchange Server distribution list holding the usernames. Then, choose a role from the Roles list, or select from among the individual check boxes and option buttons at the bottom of the Permissions section. Click Apply to set the permissions for each user or list, and then click OK to close the properties dialog box.

FIGURE 23.6

Setting permissions for a folder.

Copying Folder Design

Setting all those properties probably seems like a lot of trouble. You can copy all or selected settings from one folder to another by following these steps:

1. Switch to the folder that you want to copy the settings *to*.
2. Choose File, Folder, Copy Folder Design.
3. In the Copy Design From dialog box (see Figure 23.7), choose the folder you want to copy *from*.

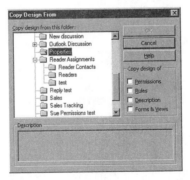

4. Check the boxes for the design elements you want to copy, and then click OK.

The tricky part about copying a folder design is to remember to start in the target folder and then select the source of the design from the Copy Design From dialog box.

Handling Exchange Server Folder Permissions

In Hour 15, "Working with Stores and Folders," you learned how to walk the folder tree to retrieve any folder. In a Microsoft Exchange Server environment, when you try to access folders in either Public Folders or another user's mailbox, you must consider these possibilities:

- The folder is not visible.
- The folder is visible, but the current user does not have permission to view its contents.
- The folder, along with its contents, is visible, but the user does not have permission to modify, create, or delete items in the folder.

If the folder is not visible, any code that walks the folder tree simply will not find the folder. Much of the time, the other two cases are handled with runtime error code.

It is possible to use CDO to test a folder to find out what a user can do with it. However, this requires the use of undocumented MAPI property tags. A good source for this type of application is the CDOLive Web site at http://www.cdolive.com.

Microsoft Exchange Event Service Scripts

Beginning with version 5.5, Microsoft Exchange Server includes an Event Service that allows you to install scripts on folders to react to certain events or to run at scheduled intervals. A script can be installed on any folder in an Exchange Server mailbox or Public Folders and always run from the server, regardless of whether any users are logged in. Table 23.1 lists scriptable events.

TABLE 23.1 Events Available in Exchange Server Scripts

Event	Description
OnMessageCreated	Runs when a new item is created in the folder
OnChange	Runs when an item in the folder is modified
OnMessageDeleted	Runs when an item in the folder is deleted
OnTimer	Runs when the timer (set through Outlook) on the folder expires

Typical uses for scripts include the following:

- Changing the message class to a custom form
- Accepting meeting requests for resources
- Responding to or routing incoming messages
- Copying items from user's mailboxes to Public Folders

> The Microsoft Exchange Routing engine, used for creating more complex workflow applications, also depends on the Event Service.

Scripts are written in VBScript using the CDO object model, not the Outlook object model, because they run unattended on the Exchange Server. However, if these scripts always run on the server, what do they have to do with Outlook programming? First, scripts generally are installed through Outlook. Also, you can cleverly integrate Outlook into scripts by writing a script that switches items to a custom Outlook form you have created. That way, when the user opens the form, your VBScript code behind the form runs.

Server configuration for scripting is handled by the Exchange Server administrator, who typically grants permission to a limited number people to add scripts. This is done in the Microsoft Exchange Administrator program by giving Author permission on the EventConfig object in the *organization*/Folders/System Folders/Events Root portion of the Exchange object hierarchy. You also need Owner permission on any folders where you will be adding scripts.

In Outlook itself, the Server Scripting add-in is not enabled by default. Follow these steps to enable scripting:

1. Choose Tools, Options, switch to the Other tab, click Advanced Options, and then click Add-In Manager.
2. In the Add-In Manager dialog box, check the box for Server Scripting.
3. Click OK three times to return to the Outlook viewer.

> A script runs in the security context of the user who set up the script. In general, this means that if you're setting up a script to work with a user's mailbox folders, you will want to log in to the Exchange Server as that user to set up the script.

After the Server Scripting add-in is enabled on the client and appropriate permissions are set on the server, you should be ready to install a script. (You will see a simple script analyzed in a moment.) Follow these steps:

1. Right-click on the folder where you want to install the script, choose Properties, and then switch to the Agents tab.

2. On the Agents tab, click New to display the New Agent dialog box in Figure 23.8.

23

FIGURE 23.8

Add new Exchange Server event scripts to a folder through Outlook.

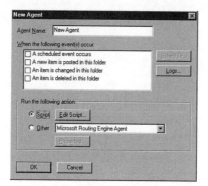

3. In the New Agent dialog box (see Figure 23.8), give the agent (that is, the script) a descriptive name, and select what event you want the script to react to. If you select A Scheduled Event Occurs, click the Schedule button, and set a time interval on the Scheduled Event dialog box. The minimum is every 15 minutes, and the maximum is once a week.

FIGURE 23.9

You must set the time interval for scheduled event scripts.

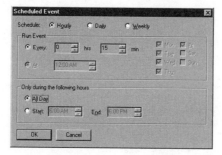

4. Under Run the Following Action, make sure that Script is selected, and then click Edit Script. The code in Listing 23.1 appears in Notepad. Notice that it includes event handlers for all four types of events listed in Table 23.1 and shown under When the Following Event(s) Occur in Figure 23.8.

5. You can create the script from scratch in Notepad, adding code for the appropriate event handler(s), or copy in code that you have written elsewhere. When you finish editing the script, close and save it.

6. Click OK on the New Agent dialog and on the folder properties dialog to complete installation of the script.

LISTING 23.1 The Shell for an Exchange Event Service Script

```
<SCRIPT RunAt=Server Language=VBScript>

'...........................................................
'FILE DESCRIPTION: Exchange Server Event Script
'...........................................................

Option Explicit

'...........................................................
' Global Variables
'...........................................................


'...........................................................
' Event Handlers
'...........................................................

' DESCRIPTION: This event is fired when a new message is _
' added to the folder
Public Sub Folder_OnMessageCreated
End Sub



' DESCRIPTION: This event is fired when a message in the _
' folder is changed
Public Sub Message_OnChange
End Sub

' DESCRIPTION: This event is fired when a message is deleted _
' from the folder
Public Sub Folder_OnMessageDeleted
End Sub

' DESCRIPTION: This event is fired when the timer on the _
' folder expires
Public Sub Folder_OnTimer
End Sub

</SCRIPT>
```

Your script code can use the four intrinsic objects listed in Table 23.2.

TABLE 23.2   Intrinsic Objects for Event Service Scripts

Object	Description
EventDetails.Session	Returns a CDO Session object representing the context in which the script is running.
EventDetails.FolderID	Returns a String value containing the unique FolderID for the folder in which the script is installed.
EventDetails.MessageID	Returns a String value containing the unique MessageID for the item whose addition, change, or deletion triggered the script to fire. This doesn't apply to the OnTimer event and isn't effective in the OnMessageDeleted event because the item has already been deleted.
Script.Response	Assigns a String value to this object using a normal assignment statement (no Set keyword) to add data to the script's log, which can hold up to 32KB of text entries. After the script is running, you can read the log through the Logs button on the New Agent dialog (refer to Figure 23.8).

The next example shows a simple script that you can use to change the form for Message items (default form IPM.Note) to IPM.Note.MyClass, a form you have published:

```
Public Sub Folder_OnMessageCreated()
    Dim objSession
    Dim strMessageClass
    Dim objItem
    strMessageClass = "IPM.Note.MyClass"
    Set objSession = EventDetails.Session
    Set objItem = _
      objSession.GetMessage(EventDetails.MessageID)
    If objItem.Type = "IPM.Note" Then
        objItem.Type = strMessageClass
        objItem.Update
    End If
    Script.Response = FormatDateTime(Now()) & _
                      objItem.Subject & " updated to " & _
                      strMessageClass
End Sub
```

Notice how you use the GetMessage method on the Session object to retrieve the message whose creation caused the script to fire, using the intrinsic MessageID object. The Script.Response statement writes a log entry.

Additional information on Exchange Server scripts and examples can be found at the resource sites listed in Appendix B, "Resources for Outlook Programming."

Outlook Web Access

Microsoft Exchange Server 5.5 supports access to mailboxes and public folders through the Internet HTTP protocol with a feature called Outlook Web Access (OWA). Users with compatible browsers log in to a Web page to get their mail and to post and send new items. This is an especially useful feature for organizations that have Macintosh and UNIX users. It is also attractive to companies that don't want to make the Exchange Server directly accessible from the Internet.

Message, Post, and Contact forms that you create in Outlook can be converted for OWA use with a tool on the Service Pack CD-ROMs for Exchange Server 5.5. Search the Service Pack CD-ROM for the setup file named Fcsetup.exe, and run that file to install the Forms Converter. The Forms Converter can also be downloaded from Microsoft's FTP site. Documentation is found in the Cdo.hlp file, also on the Service Pack CD-ROM, which is an essential reference for CDO, as well as the Forms Converter.

OWA forms are stored on the Exchange Server in the folder \Exchsrvr\Webdata*lang*\ Forms\Ipm, in which *lang* is the language used for the form. For example, forms created for U.S. English are stored in \Exchsrvr\Webdata\Usa\Forms\Ipm.

Using the Outlook HTML Forms Converter

Here is a step-by-step guide to converting a form:

1. Choose Start, Programs, Microsoft Outlook HTML Forms Converter to start the converter. The converter is a wizard with four screens where you enter information. Click Next to skip the first screen, which is for information only.

2. On screen 2 (see Figure 23.10), indicate whether you want to convert a published form or template file, and give the computer name of the server running Outlook Web Access. Click Next to continue.

3. If you chose Microsoft Exchange Forms Library form in step 2, the next screen of the wizard (see Figure 23.11) displays the forms and folder forms libraries from which you can select a form to convert.

   If you chose Outlook Template in step 2, you will see an Open Outlook Template dialog box, from which you can browse your system folders to select an .oft template file to convert.

   After you select a form or template, click Next to continue.

FIGURE 23.10

The Outlook HTML Form Converter can convert both published forms and forms saved as template files.

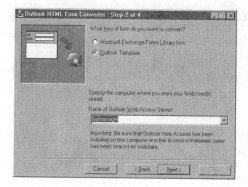

In step 3, you may be asked to choose a profile to log in to Outlook, even if Outlook is already running. Use a profile that will give you access to whatever forms you need to convert.

FIGURE 23.11

Choose a published form from any of the forms or folder forms libraries.

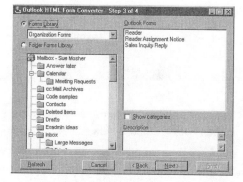

4. In step 4 of the wizard, you can choose to overwrite an existing OWA form with the same name. If you select Layout Debug Mode, the converter will show table borders in the converted form, making it easier to adjust controls to fit. However, you will want to edit the tables to remove the borders after you adjust the controls; the borders make the converted forms look too cluttered.

5. Click Finish to perform the conversion. The time required depends on the complexity of the form, but should not take more than a few minutes.

6. When the conversion completes, the Conversion Results dialog box (see Figure 23.12) appears, displaying a to-do list for cleaning up the form. This list is stored as ToDo.txt in the converted form's directory.

FIGURE 23.12

The wizard provides a to-do list of tasks necessary to finish converting the form.

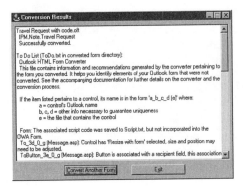

Look back in the preceding lesson at Figure 22.2, the Travel Request form. Figure 23.12 shows the conversion to-do list for this form, which was originally saved as an Outlook .oft template file. The converted form itself is stored on the OWA server as \Exchsrvr\Webdata\Usa\Forms\Ipm\Note\Travel_20Request as a series of .asp files. It's in the \Ipm\Note subfolder because it is a modified IPM.Note (Message) form.

To see how the form looks in OWA, follow these steps:

1. Point your browser to `http://owaserver/exchange/` where *owaserver* is the machine hosting OWA.

2. Log on with your Exchange mailbox alias, and provide your password if prompted to do so.

3. When the Inbox appears, from the Compose New list at the top right, choose Custom Form and then click Compose New.

4. A new browser window opens. In this Compose New Form window (see Figure 23.13), click on the underlined link for the Travel Request form.

5. The Compose New Form window switches to display the custom form. You might want to maximize the window, as shown in Figure 23.14, to see all the fields more easily.

Converting Form Code

As the to-do list for a converted form makes quite clear, code behind the Outlook form is not converted. Neither validation formulas in the form design nor VBScript code appears in the converted form. The VBScript code is saved in a file named Script.txt in the converted form's folder, but you must convert any such code yourself and add it to the Active Server Pages (ASP) code for the OWA form. This is a task requiring knowledge of HTML and ASP that goes beyond the scope of this book.

FIGURE 23.13
Outlook Web Access supports custom forms.

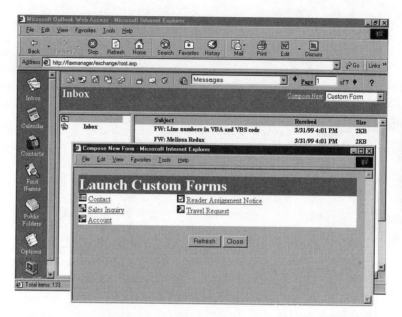

FIGURE 23.14
This converted form could use a little clean-up to reposition controls. Compare this with the original form in Figure 22.2.

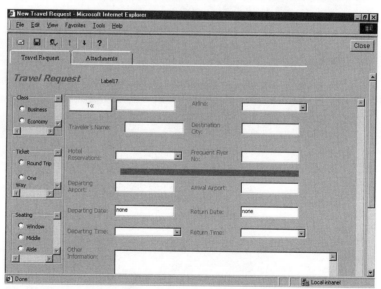

The good news is that custom actions that have no associated code—that is, actions created on the (Actions) tab of the Outlook form—are converted and run just fine under OWA.

Linking to Outside Data Sources

One much sought after collaboration element is linkage between Outlook (either with or without Exchange Server) and a separate database. The possible applications of this technique are countless. For example, you could display data on past products ordered by people listed in your Contacts folder in Outlook.

The latest Microsoft technique for linking to databases is called ActiveX Data Objects (ADO). It allows you to create connections to all kinds of databases, including those that use Open Database Connectivity (ODBC) drivers. Office 2000 ships with ADO version 2.1. To use ADO in an Outlook VBA project, you must use Tools, References to add a reference to the Microsoft ActiveX Data Objects 2.1 library.

If you want to use the Object Browser to examine the ADO object model, switch to ADODB in the libraries list. To get help on ADO objects, run \Program Files\Common Files\System\Ado\Ado210.chm.

Using ADO is another big topic that deserves a book in itself, but it's worth showing you just a bit of what it can do. This example uses a sample database for Microsoft Access, the Northwind Traders database, which you can install as part of the Microsoft Office 2000 setup. I used the ODBC Data Sources applet in Control Panel to add a User DSN (data source name) named Northwind to point to the sample database, which was installed as \Program Files\Microsoft Office\Office\Samples\Northwind.mdb. Having a DSN makes it just a little easier to use the Open method of an ADO Connection object to make a connection to a database.

You can also make a direct connection to an Access .mdb database. The ADO documentation explains the variations supported by the Open method for different types of databases.

I also modified a Contact form to

- Add a custom Northwind Order page.
- On the custom page, add two unbound text boxes (txtOrderDate and txtOrderAmount) to hold information on the contact's most recent order.

- On the custom page, add a text box named txtCustomerID bound to a custom CustomerID text field that matches the CustomerID field in the database's Customers table.
- Add code to the form's `Item_Open` event (discussed next) to pull information for the particular customer (based on the CustomerID field's value) from the Northwind database into the two unbound text boxes.
- Publish the form as IPM.Contact.Northwind.

In practice, every time a new customer is added to the Northwind database, you might use automation code to create a new, matching Outlook item using the IPM.Contact.Northwind form and fill in the CustomerID field, as well as matching Outlook Contact fields, from information in the database record. The focus of this example, however, is what happens in the Outlook form—in other words, how it pulls information from the Access database.

The basic technique for pulling data from ADO is to connect to a database, open a recordset, and retrieve data from fields in one or more records. A *recordset* is a collection of database records. It can be a full table from a database or a filtered set of records with only some of the fields from the original table. Some recordsets join data from two or more tables.

Listing 23.2 makes the connection to the database in lines 14 and 15 and then opens two different `RecordSet` objects, one with the `Open` method on the `RecordSet` and one with the `Execute` method on the `Connection` object. In both cases, the code uses Structured Query Language (SQL) statements (lines 17–21 and 28–31) to define the recordsets to be retrieved.

> This book doesn't have room to cover SQL syntax, but the basics are not hard to learn. Try creating a query in Microsoft Access and then using View, SQL View to see the SQL statement for the query.
>
> You might also find it useful, especially when you're just beginning to work with ADO and SQL, to add a `Debug.Print strSQL` statement to your code after each block of statements in which you build a SQL string. That will let you check the SQL statement's syntax in the Immediate window.

LISTING 23.2   Updating an Outlook Form from an Access Database

```
 1: Function Item_Open()
 2:     Call UpdateNorthwindData
 3: End Function
 4:
 5: Sub UpdateNorthwindData()
 6:     ' set Outlook object variables
 7:     Set objInsp = Item.GetInspector
 8:     Set objPage = objInsp.ModifiedFormPages("Northwind Order")
 9:     Set ctlOrderDate = objPage.Controls("txtOrderDate")
10:     Set ctlOrderAmount = objPage.Controls("txtOrderAmount")
11:     ' get customer ID from Contact item
12:     strCustID = Item.UserProperties.Find("CustomerID")
13:     ' make ADO connection to database
14:     Set objADOConn = CreateObject("ADODB.Connection")
15:     objADOConn.Open "DSN=Northwind"
16:     ' get order ID & date from Orders table
17:     strSQL = "SELECT OrderID, OrderDate " & _
18:             "FROM Orders " & _
19:             "WHERE (((CustomerID) = " & _
20:             SQLQuote(strCustID) & _
21:             ")) ORDER BY OrderDate DESC;"
22:     Set objRSOrders = CreateObject("ADODB.Recordset")
23:     objRSOrders.Open strSQL, objADOConn
24:     If Not objRSOrders.EOF Then
25:         ctlOrderDate.Value = objRSOrders.Fields("OrderDate")
26:         lngOrderID = objRSOrders.Fields("OrderID")
27:         ' get order amount from Order Subtotals query
28:         strSQL = "SELECT Subtotal " & _
29:                 "FROM [Order Subtotals] " & _
30:                 "WHERE ((OrderID)=" & _
31:                 CStr(lngOrderID) & ");"
32:         Set objRSTotal = objADOConn.Execute(strSQL)
33:         If Not objRSTotal.EOF Then
34:             ctlOrderAmount.Value = _
35:                 FormatCurrency(objRSTotal.Fields("Subtotal"))
36:         End If
37:     End If
38: End Sub
39:
40: Function SQLQuote(varInput)
41:     SQLQuote = Chr(39) & varInput & Chr(39)
42: End Function
```

Here are several notes on the code:

- To save space, this code is missing a few of the niceties. You should add an Option Explicit statement and use Dim statements to declare all variables. You should also use Set object = Nothing statements to release all the object variables at the end of the UpdateNorthwindData procedure. You would probably also want to add error handling to deal with such possibilities as either RecordSet object containing no records.

- The short SQLQuote() function (line 40) is used to surround the value of the CustomerID field in the Outlook form with single quotation marks (' '), which are required for String literals in SQL statements.

- The UpdateNorthwindData procedure was designed to retrieve just one value from the Orders table and only a single value from the Order Subtotals query. To get records for the objRSOrders, the SQL statement uses sorting (the ORDER BY clause) to ensure that the first record is the most recent order.

- Use the EOF (end of file) property of a RecordSet object to indicate whether you have reached the end of the record set. If EOF = True, there are no more records.

This example gives you just a taste of the kind of linkage you can create between Outlook and other data sources. In some cases, you might want to retrieve an entire table or query as a RecordSet object and loop through it, displaying the data in a List Box control on an Outlook form or in an HTML table on a folder home page.

Summary

Collaboration through Microsoft Exchange Server or an external database extends Outlook from a useful macro-writing tool to a means of creating enterprisewide applications. Public folders, folder scripts, and Outlook Web Access should become key elements of your Exchange Server development strategy.

The final chapter considers the issues you are likely to encounter as you start deploying your Outlook applications to other users.

Q&A

Q Can I restrict access to certain items or fields in a public folder?

A No. Neither Outlook nor Exchange Server provides for item-level or field-level permissions, as you might find in a relational database. There is at least one third-party product that adds security, though, through links to a SQL Server database.

Q **Why does the ADO example depend on retrieving information from the form when the user opens the custom Outlook contact? Why couldn't the order date and amount be updated whenever the data in the database changes?**

A You're absolutely right! Pushing the data to Outlook whenever records in the database change would be an excellent alternative to pulling the data into the Contact form when it's opened. This is one of those design decisions that you, as a programmer, get to make. Consider how often the data will be updated in the database versus how often the user is going to want to view it. If you want the user to be able to see that information through a folder view, you definitely will want to push it from the database. If it is only viewed through the Contact form, it may be more efficient to pull the data into the form only when the user is likely to want to see it, in other words, when the form is opened.

Workshop

Work through the quiz questions and exercises so that you can understand Outlook programming better. See Appendix A for answers.

Quiz

1. What object model is used in writing code for Exchange Event Service scripts? For connecting to a database?

2. Can Exchange Event Service scripts display user interface elements such as message boxes?

Exercise

Using the Tip of the Day public folder created as an example in this chapter, write a script that retrieves an item from the folder, forwards it to a distribution list named Tipsters, and then deletes the tip from the folder so that it is not repeated. Don't forget that you can use the Object Browser to scan the MAPI library for the CDO methods you will need. For example, try searching for Forward.

Hour 24

Deploying Forms and Applications

Congratulations! You've made it to the last hour! By now, you should have quite a few Outlook forms and VBA applications that you're eager to share with other people in your organization. In this hour, you learn how to make them available to your colleagues.

Highlights of this hour include

- How to use the Forms Manager to move and delete forms
- What code to use to import to a custom form
- How to convert existing data to a custom form
- How to distribute an Outlook VBA application to other users
- What tools you need for creating Outlook applications as COM add-ins

Deploying Forms

You have already digested many techniques for deploying forms. In Hour 2, "Six Forms in Search of a Designer," you saw how to publish a form to a forms library or save it as an Outlook template .oft file. In Hour 23, "Exchange Server and Database Collaboration," you learned how to set the default form for a folder, a particularly useful technique in Exchange Server public folders.

Outlook includes a Forms Manager tool for moving and deleting forms. Other key form techniques covered in this section include

- Creating self-installing forms to send to remote users
- Converting existing items to a custom form
- Replacing the default forms used by Outlook
- Converting existing data to a custom form
- Importing external data to a custom form

Managing Outlook Forms

To move published forms between locations and remove forms you no longer need, use the Forms Manager. This tool is available only if you installed Outlook in Corporate or Workgroup mode. To start the Forms Manager, choose Tools, Options from Outlook's main menu, and then switch to the Other tab. Click Advanced Options, then Custom Forms, and then Manage Forms.

In the Forms Manager dialog box (see Figure 24.1), use the Set buttons to select a folder or library. You can then use the Copy, Update, and Delete buttons to manage forms or the Properties button to find out more about a form.

FIGURE 24.1

The Forms Manager, Outlook's tool for maintaining forms, appears only in Corporate or Workgroup mode.

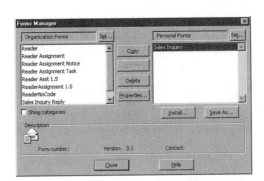

The Save As button on the Forms Manager allows you to save a form as an .fdm file. The Install button imports an .fdm file into a forms library. However, because the Forms Manager is so difficult to reach through the Outlook user interface, this method of installing forms is less convenient than the others discussed.

For example, if you have successfully tested a form in your Personal Forms library, you might want to copy it to the Organization Forms library. Remember that you must have appropriate permissions from the Exchange Administrator to put a form in the Organization Forms library and must be a folder owner to add to a folder forms library.

Self-Installing Forms for Remote Users

You have probably already realized that one way to distribute a form to remote users is to save it as an .oft template file and e-mail it to the users, along with instructions on how to publish it to the Personal Forms library.

In a Microsoft Exchange Server environment, the synchronization process ensures that remote users have the latest version of forms stored in folders set for offline use. However, there is no offline copy of the complete Organization Forms library. Offline users will have only the forms from that library that were used in messages they received. You have to provide a mechanism to distribute other forms—such as the monthly report for a traveling sales representative—to those off-site users.

Why not skip the instructions and make the form install itself automatically when the user opens the .oft file? Each Outlook item includes a `FormDescription` object that defines the properties of the form. After you retrieve this object from the item, you can set its `Name` property and then publish it with the `PublishForm` method to the user's Personal Forms library or any other forms library.

Here is the VBScript code to publish an item's own form to the user's Personal Forms library:

```
Option Explicit
Const olPersonalRegistry = 2
```

24

```
Sub PublishAsForm()
    Dim strName
    Dim strDisplayName
    Dim objForm
    ' *** Set name used in the message class here ***
    strName = "My Form"
    ' *** To set a different name for the display ***
    '      name, remove the apostrophe from the next
    '      line and specify a display name string
    ' strDisplayName = ""
    Set objForm = Item.FormDescription
    If Not IsCustomForm(objForm) Then
        objForm.Name = strName
        If strDisplayName <> "" Then
            objForm.DisplayName = strDisplayName
        End If
        objForm.PublishForm (olPersonalRegistry)
        MsgBox "Published the " & strName & " form to " _
               "Your Personal Forms library."
    End If
End Sub

Function IsCustomForm(objForm)
    IsCustomForm = False
    If objForm.Name <> "" Then
        IsCustomForm = True
    End If
End Function
```

The IsCustomForm() function tests whether the item uses a published form by checking the Name property of the FormDescription object.

The Name property is used to set the MessageClass property of the form when it is published. You can also have a separate DisplayName, which the user sees in the Choose Form dialog box.

> Notice how the PublishAsForm procedure uses comments to alert the creator of the form about the need to specify a Name and optional DisplayName property.

If you want the form to install automatically when the user opens the .oft file attachment, add this code for the item's Open event:

```
Function Item_Open()
    Call PublishAsForm
End Function
```

Another approach would be to call the `PublishAsForm` subroutine from the `Click` event on a custom Command Button control or via a custom action button.

You still have to instruct the user to click Enable Macros after opening the .oft file, so that the code in the form can run.

Converting Existing Data to a New Form

A key concern when publishing a new form or updating it is to make sure that existing data is converted. If there were few changes to the form, the best practice is to increment the form's version number on the (Properties) tab and republish it under the same name. Updating the version number ensures that users will load the latest version of the form when they open items that use it.

Sometimes, though, you have to convert data from one form to another. For example, you might have a Contacts folder with hundreds of items that you want to display in a new customized Contacts form. Converting data from one form to another is a matter of changing the `MessageClass` property of the individual items. You can run this VBA macro to update items in a folder to use a different form, whose name is supplied by the user through an input box:

```
Sub UpdateClass()
    Dim objApp As Application
    Dim objNS As NameSpace
    Dim objItem As Object
    Dim objFolder As MAPIFolder
    Dim strClass As String
    Dim strFolderClass As String
    Set objApp = CreateObject("Outlook.Application")
    Set objNS = objApp.GetNamespace("MAPI")
    Set objItem = objApp.ActiveInspector.CurrentItem
    Set objFolder = objNS.PickFolder
    If Not objFolder Is Nothing Then
        strClass = _
          InputBox("Change all items in folder to what class?")
        strFolderClass = objFolder.DefaultMessageClass
        If InStr(1, strClass, strFolderClass, vbTextCompare) Then
            For Each objItem In objFolder.Items
                If objItem.MessageClass = strFolderClass Then
                    objItem.MessageClass = strClass
                    objItem.Save
                End If
```

24

```
        Next
        MsgBox "Updated items in " & objFolder.Name & " Folder"
    Else
        MsgBox "The class you specified is not the normal " & _
               "type for this folder. " & _
               "No items will be updated."
    End If
End If
End Sub
```

> The DefaultMessageClass property of the folder does not indicate whether
> a custom form is the default form for that folder. It always returns the name
> of one of the built-in classes. This means that it's fine for testing whether
> the new class is appropriate for the folder, as in the If InStr(1, strClass,
> strFolderClass, vbTextCompare) Then statement. However, you cannot use
> it to discover the class of the default form for the folder.

The preceding code does some checking—first, to make sure that a folder has been
selected and then, that the new item class matches the default class for the folder. You
might want your routine to do additional validation, perhaps to change only items that
are already using a particular custom form.

Replacing the Default Forms

Users have often wanted to replace the default Message form (IPM.Note) with a custom
form to add functionality that the standard form does not include. In previous versions of
Outlook, it was not possible to replace the default forms with custom forms. However,
Outlook 2000 does support forms substitution; you can even specify separate forms for
read and compose operations.

> Replacing any default form is not a trivial matter. You must take care to
> ensure that your replacement form includes all the functionality of the
> default form, in addition to any special operations you have designed into
> the form.

Forms substitution is done in the Windows Registry. As with all work in the Registry, be sure to make a backup first. You can then follow these steps to specify the form used to read any type of Outlook item:

1. Choose Start, Run, and type **Regedit**. Then press Enter to start the Registry Editor.

2. Under the key HKEY_CURRENT_USER\Software\Microsoft\Office\9.0\Outlook\, choose Edit, New, Key to create a new key named Custom Forms. Under the Custom Forms key, create a subkey named **Read**.

3. Under the Read keys, choose Edit, New, String Value, and give the new value the name of the basic message class whose default form you want to change. For example, if you want to change the default Message form, give the string value the name **IPM.Note**.

4. Choose Edit, Modify to display the Edit String dialog. Under Value Data, enter the message class of the form that you want to use instead of the present form. It must be published to one of your forms libraries. For example, if you want to use a customized Message form named IPM.Note.CustomReply (maybe it has special custom actions for replies), you should enter **IPM.Note.CustomReply** as the value of the IPM.Note string. After you press Enter to save the new value, the Registry Editor should display it, as in Figure 24.2.

24

FIGURE 24.2

Outlook 2000 allows you to change the default form.

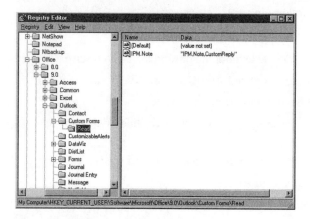

It is not so easy to substitute one form for another for composing and sending items because the required Registry string is complicated and includes null characters. Microsoft plans to release a tool to its http://officeupdate.Microsoft.com site to make the task easy.

After you add the substitution information to the Registry, Outlook will use the substitute form instead of the original form whenever you open an item of this type.

To remove a substitution, just delete the string value you just created.

Importing to a Custom Form

As you learned in Hour 21, "Getting Started with Outlook Reports," Outlook does not allow you to export directly to custom forms or custom fields using its File, Import and Export command. The same limitations apply to importing data. You must write custom code to copy the data field-by-field.

The exact code, of course, will depend on the source file. You must use its syntax to get the source records and fields. If the data is in a file that can be opened in a Microsoft Office program or in a database you can access with ADO, you can use VBA to write the code that follows this basic sequence:

1. Open the source file or database.
2. Create a new Outlook item using the custom form.
3. Get the first record from the source file or database.
4. Get the first field from the source.
5. Copy the data from the first source field to the corresponding field in the Outlook item.
6. Repeat steps 4–5 for all the fields you need to import.
7. Save the Outlook item.
8. Repeat steps 1–7 until you run out of source data.

To copy data to a field in Outlook, use either the property itself, for a built-in property, or the UserProperties property, for custom fields. This sample code gets a new custom Contact item using the NewCustomContact() function you saw in Hour 16, "Working with Items," and then updates two of its properties, one built-in (prop1) and one user-defined (prop2). The sourceprop1 and sourceprop2 expressions evaluate to properties from the source data.

```
Set objItem = NewCustomContact()
objItem.prop1 = sourceprop1
objItem.UserProperties("prop2") = sourceprop2
```

Writing an import routine is hard work, especially if you have dozens of fields to copy. Be sure to test it carefully.

Importing from a Comma-Delimited File to a Custom Form

Many programs can export to comma-delimited files. In a comma-delimited file, each line is a record. The fields in the record are separated by commas. Because this is such a common format, it's useful to know how to open a comma-delimited file and read its data. VBA has built-in file-handling methods. Create a new VBA module named ImportCSV and add this statement to the declarations section of the module:

```
Dim m_intFileNum As Integer
```

Then, add this function, which gets the next free file number, opens the file whose full path is indicated by strFileName with the file number (the m_intFileNum variable), and if successful, returns True. The GetFile() function returns False if it cannot open the file.

```
Function GetFile(strFileName) As Boolean
    On Error Resume Next
    m_intFile = FreeFile()
    Open strFileName For Input As #m_intFile
    If Err <> 0 Then
        MsgBox "Could not open " & strFileName & _
               vbCrLf & vbCrLf & Err.Description
        Exit Function
    Else
        GetFile = True
    End If
End Function
```

Where does strFileName get its value? It could come from an InputBox() function, from a Common Dialog control on a VBA form, or from a value hard-coded into the procedure that calls the function.

Next, you must know how to read data from a comma-delimited file. To create a simple example, open Notepad and type in these three lines:

```
John Doe, Lake Cleanup
Alice Channing, Air Quality
Marsha Kuong, Water Quality
```

24

Save the file as Project.csv. This gives you a comma-delimited file of people and the projects they're working on that you can import.

The default Contact form doesn't have a Project field, does it? Create a custom form with a Project field: Open the default Contact form in design mode, create a new Text field named Project, and drag the Project field to the P.2 page. Publish the form to your Personal Forms library or Contacts folder with the message class IPM.Contact.Project. Modify the NewCustomContact() function from Hour 16 to use that message class.

Now, you're ready to see the import code. The following ImportCSVToOutlook subroutine does this:

- Sets String variables for each field in the source file
- Prompts the user for a filename and then gets that file
- Reads each line from the file into the field String variables
- Gets a new custom Outlook item
- Copies the field data into the corresponding Outlook properties
- Saves the Outlook item
- Repeats the preceding process until it runs out of data

```
Sub ImportCSVToOutlook()
    Dim strFileName As String
    ' *** Declare variable for each field ***
    '     in the source CSV file
    Dim strFullName As String
    Dim strProject As String
    Dim objItem As ContactItem
    strFileName = _
      InputBox("File to import:", "Import to Outlook")
    If strFileName <> "" Then
        If GetFile(strFileName) Then
            Do While Not EOF(m_intFile)
                Input #m_intFile, strFullName, strProject
                Set objItem = NewCustomContact()
                With objItem
                    .FullName = strFullName
                    .UserProperties("Project") = strProject
                    .Save
                End With
            Loop
        End If
    End If
    Close #m_intFile
    Set objItem = Nothing
End Sub
```

Don't forget to modify the NewCustomContact() function so that it produces an item using your custom form.

If you find yourself using the NewCustomContact() function often, but with a different form each time, you might want to modify it to use a strMessageClass argument. That would enable you to pass the class to the function from other procedures.

For comma-delimited files, the Input # method separates each line into fields, based on the position of the commas. If another character other than a comma is used as a delimiter, you can use the Input method to read each entire line from the file into a String variable and then write your own parsing routine.

24

Did you remember that EOF means *end of file?* Using the EOF() function—as in the statement Do While Not EOF(m_intFile)—is a convenient way to set up a loop to read all the data in a file. You will have to close the file with the Close # method at the end of the procedure.

Distributing VBA Applications

So far in this hour on deployment, the focus has been on Outlook forms. What about your VBA applications? Can they be distributed as easily?

It is not as easy to distribute Outlook VBA applications as it is with Office programs such as Word and Excel, where you can embed VBA inside documents (more on that shortly). These are the methods available to you:

- Import and export.
- Automate Outlook from another program.
- Write a COM add-in.

COM add-ins are the recommended method for distributing Outlook VBA applications on any significant scale. If you just need to share your code with a few other people, try one of the other methods.

Using Import and Export

It's simple, but it works. VBA includes both Export File and Import File commands on its File menu. With these, you can export from VBA and then give the exported file to someone else to import. The exported files use these file extensions:

Modules	.bas files
Forms	.frm files
Class modules (including ThisOutlookSession)	.cls files

One catch with importing files is that you will get an error if the imported file duplicates any form name or public procedure name in the currently open projects.

Automation from Another Office Application

Remember how in Hour 21, "Getting Started with Outlook Reports," and Hour 22, "Designing Reports with Microsoft Word," you used automation code in Outlook to create printed output in Excel and Word? You can also reverse the process and put code to automate Outlook into macros attached to a Word and Excel document or template. Then, you can distribute that file to other users. Both Word and Excel documents include events that fire when a document opens, so it's easy to have a document display a VBA form or run code. You can also add a command button to an Excel worksheet or a double-clickable field to a Word document to run a macro on demand.

Take the ImportCSV module from the preceding section as an example. Here are the steps to follow to make it run from a Word document:

1. Make sure that all the procedures you need are included in the ImportCSV module. In particular, copy the NewCustomContact() function, which you should have created in Hour 16. Make sure that all procedures, except the main ImportCSVToOutlook subroutine, are set as Private procedures.

2. Choose File, Export File to save the module as ImportCSV.bas.

3. Open a new document in Word, and then press Alt+F11 to switch to Word's VBA environment. You should be in a project named Project (Document1)—or another document number if you have more than one unsaved document open in Word.

4. Choose Tools, References to set a reference to the Microsoft Outlook 9.0 Object library.

5. Choose File, Import File to import the ImportCSV.bas file into the Project (Document1) project.

6. Edit the type declaration for each of the Outlook object variables in the module to add Outlook as part of the type declaration. For example, in the NewCustomContact() function, you should have

```
Dim objApp As Outlook.Application
```

That's all there is to it! Switch back to the Word document, and press Alt+F8 to bring up the Macros dialog box. You should see ImportCSVToOutlook as an available macro. Try running the macro to make sure that it works.

> One of the benefits of using a Word document to distribute VBA code to perform Outlook tasks is that you can include an explanation of the application in the same document.

24

If you want to have the macro run when the user opens Word, switch back to the Word VBA window. Look in the Project Explorer under Project(Document1) and then under Microsoft Word Objects for ThisDocument. Double-click ThisDocument to display the code module for the document itself. From the drop-down list at the top left of the module window, select Document. From the list at the top right, select Open. This places a shell for the Document_Open procedure in the document. Add one line of code to the procedure to call ImportCSVToOutlook. The finished procedure should look like this:

```
Private Sub Document_Open()
    Call ImportCSVToOutlook
End Sub
```

Now, close and save the Word document, perhaps naming it ImportCSVToOutlook.doc. When you open it, the ImportCSVToOutlook procedure should run, just as it did when you ran it from Outlook's VBA window.

If you prefer to have the user read some instructions and then double-click a Word field to run the procedure, follow these steps:

1. In the VBA project for the Word document to which you added the Outlook code, remove the Document_Open subroutine that calls ImportCSVToOutlook.

2. Switch from VBA back to the document itself, and type in whatever explanatory text you'd like the user to read.

3. Choose Insert, Field to display the Field dialog box.

4. From the Field Names list on the right side of the Field dialog box, choose Macro Button.

5. In the box where you see MACROBUTTON, type a space, then the name of the macro (`ImportCSVToOutlook`), then another space, and then `To Import, Double-Click Here`.

6. Click OK to save the MACROBUTTON field.

You should now see the text `To Import, Double-Click Here` in the document and can test it by double-clicking it. You may want to use shading, highlighting, or a border to set it off from the rest of the text. All the user has to do to run the code is double-click on the field.

Creating COM Add-Ins

COM add-ins are separately compiled .dll (dynamic link library) files that hook into Outlook or other Office programs. Typically, a COM add-in project includes a combination of class modules, modules, and forms. It very likely has its own entries in the Windows Registry to track user preferences. In other words, COM add-ins are complex. There isn't enough room to provide step-by-step instructions for creating them in the few minutes remaining in this final hour.

The good news is that you can create and compile COM add-ins with either Visual Basic or Microsoft Office 2000 Developer (MOD), the programmer's edition of Office. MOD includes an add-ins template that makes the process a little easier.

> Microsoft Office 2000 Developer also includes a Packaging and Deployment Wizard for creating setup packages for COM add-ins and even Office documents.

An Outlook COM add-in typically loads either when Outlook starts or when a user invokes it through the COM Add-Ins dialog box. To enable and disable COM add-ins already installed on your system, choose Tools, Options and switch to the Other tab. Then click Advanced Options and then COM Add-Ins.

Summary

Whether you want to concentrate on Outlook forms, build programs in VBA, or do a bit of both, your job as a programmer is not finished until you make those applications available to the people who need to use them. Publishing to the forms libraries is the primary way to deploy Outlook forms, whereas COM add-ins are the way to go if you are distributing high-end applications written in VBA. For the small tasks that you run as macros from toolbar buttons, export and import may be good enough.

I hope that these 24 hours have given you a solid introduction to Outlook programming. I encourage you to explore the additional resources listed in Appendix B to see other techniques and discover source code that you can incorporate into your own projects.

Q&A

Q When creating a self-installing form, why did you have to send it as an e-mail message attachment? Couldn't you just make the `Form_Open` event on the e-mail message install the attached .oft template?

A That's certainly another valid approach. Its main disadvantage is that you would have to save the .oft file to the user's hard drive, but would not have a way to delete that file because VBScript normally runs without access to such file system commands. (Of course, leaving a copy of the .oft file on the user's system might not be a bad backup strategy.) The advantage is that the code on the e-mail message—not the template file—does the installation. This means that you don't have to include the `PublishAsForm` subroutine or `IsCustomForm()` in the code in the template.

24

Workshop

Work through the quiz questions and exercises so that you can better understand Outlook programming. See Appendix A for answers.

Quiz

1. If you can distribute a Word VBA macro in a Word document, why can't you distribute VBA code as part of an Outlook form?

2. Imagine that you have a public folder containing standard Contact items. You plan to import several hundred more items that contain information not covered in custom fields. Because you have to create a custom form for the extra fields anyway, you're going to add some additional functions that users want for the existing items. What tasks do you need to perform, and in what order, to get all the items into the folder, using the same form?

Exercises

1. Write a subroutine to update items in a folder to a message class of IPM.Post.MyNewForm only if they are not already using a custom form. (HINT: You can use a function listed in this chapter.)

2. Modify the `ImportCSVToOutlook` comma-delimited file import subroutine to keep a running total of the number of items imported and report the total to the user when the import is complete.

PART VI
Appendixes

APPENDIX A

Answers

Hour 1, "What You Can Do with Outlook 2000"

Quiz

1. Why does Outlook support both VBA and VBScript as programming languages?

   VBScript is a compact, portable language that allows Outlook developers to build intelligent forms that are not much larger than regular Outlook forms. VBA is a more powerful language, suitable for developing more complex routines that deal with Outlook at the application level, as well as at the item level.

2. Why are object models important to programming in Outlook?

   Object models provide the building blocks that determine what you can do with Outlook. The ability to include object models from Office programs and other applications that support VBA means that you can extend Outlook in many ways.

3. What are the two versions of Outlook?

   Internet Mail Only mode, for Internet mail and limited faxing, and Corporate or Workgroup mode, for Internet mail as well, but also for connecting to enterprise e-mail systems such as Microsoft Exchange Server.

Exercise

Write the pseudocode for a routine that forces the File As field on an Outlook Contact item to display the name in first name/last name order with the company name in parentheses. Do you want Outlook to update the File As field whenever any of the related name fields change or only when you save the contact? (Hint: It's your decision!)

```
When Item is saved
    DisplayName = FirstName & " " & LastName & "(" & Company & ")" (d)Quiz
```

Hour 2, "Six Forms in Search of a Designer"

Quiz

1. How many pages can you customize on a Message form? on a Task form?

   On a Message form, six (the five custom pages, plus the Message page)

   On a Task form, five (only the five custom pages)

2. What fields do the Appointment, Journal Entry, and Task forms use to measure time?

   Appointment: Duration, End, Recurrence Range End, Recurrence Range Start, Remind Beforehand, Start

   Journal: Duration, End, Start

   Task: Actual Work, Date Completed, Due Date, Reminder Time, Start Date, Total Work

3. What field(s) do all six basic forms show on their main page?

   Actually, there is no field that all six forms show on their main page. The Subject field is present on all but the Contact form, and the Categories field is present on all but the Message form.

4. What is different about the button in the upper-left corner of the Control Toolbox?

   This button, the Select Objects button, is the only button that does not represent a control you can place on a form.

Exercises

1. Search help until you find information on publishing forms.

   (No answer required)

2. In a Contact form, examine the list of frequently used fields. Which of these do not appear on the General or Details page of the built-in Contacts form?

   Business Home Page, Flag Status, Follow Up Flag, Journal, Personal Home Page (Any Phone, Address, or E-mail field can be displayed on the General page.)

3. Use voting buttons to create a document transmittal form that looks like Figure 2.17, and publish it to your Personal Folders with an appropriate display name and form name. (Hint: Click the Options button, and enter the names of the buttons in the Use Voting Buttons field, separated by semicolons.)

   (No answer required)

Hour 3, "Create Your First Custom Contact Form"

Quiz

1. What would be a good name for a Text Box control displaying the Due By field?

   `txtDueBy`

2. What is the difference between the Combo Box and List Box controls?

   The user can type new values into a combo box, but not into a list box.

3. The default icon for custom forms is the same as the icon for which basic built-in form?

   Post

Exercises

1. Change the name and add text in the `ControlTipText` property for each control on the custom Home Pages & Flag page of the customized Contact form.

   (No answer required)

2. Add a Frame control to the page, give it the caption `Follow Up`, and move the three fields related to flags so that they appear inside the frame.

   (No answer required)

3. After you save or publish the form, open it using the Tools, Forms, Choose Form command. Does it appear as you expected it to?

(No answer required)

Hour 4, "Extend Form Design with a Custom Task Form"

Quiz

1. What is the difference between a bound and an unbound control?

   A bound control gets its data from a particular Outlook field (or in wider applications, database field). When you change the data in a bound control, the data in the underlying field is updated. An unbound control gets its data either from what the user types in or from code that places data in the control. When you close a form, the data in any unbound controls is lost, unless you include code to save it.

2. What is the difference between a Duration field and a Date/Time field?

   A Duration field holds a number representing the number of minutes. A Date/Time field can hold any value representing a date or time.

3. Why is a Check Box control better for displaying a Yes/No field than a Text Box control? Can you use a Check Box control to display fields other than Yes/No fields?

   If you use a Text Box control to display a Yes/No field, the value for the field appears as the word *Yes* or *No*, making it harder for the user to accurately enter the correct value. If you use a Check Box control for a field other than Yes/No fields, the data for the field can only be -1 or 0, the numeric literal values that correspond to *Yes* and *No*.

4. What section of the Field Chooser lists fields that you yourself create?

   User-Defined Fields in Folder

5. Can you create separate Compose and Read layouts for any form or just the Message form?

   You can create separate Compose and Read layouts for any page that you can customize.

Exercises

1. On the Task form you modified in this lesson, drag the Completed or Due field to the form. Choose Form, Run This Form to create four Task items with the custom form: one with no Due Date, one with both a Due Date and a Status of Completed, one with a Due Date and a Status of Not Started, and one with no Due Date and a Status of Completed. For each of these items, check the value of the Completed or Due field. What is odd about some of the values? Can you think of a way to fix the problem by using a Formula field instead of a Combination field?

   If you follow the exercise instructions, you will see a value of "1/1/4501" in the instances where there is no due date or date of completion. This is a value that Outlook uses as the equivalent of "None" in Date/Time fields.

   Instead of a Combination field using

   `[Date Completed] [Due Date]`

   try this formula field:

   `IIf([Complete] = True, [Date Completed],[Due Date])`

   Outlook seems to be much better about handling Date/Time values with "None" in Formula fields than in Combination fields.

2. On the custom Task form, create a field named Next Status Check as a Date/Time field, and add it to the form's P.2 page. Use the basic Properties dialog for the control to change the format, trying out each of the 16 formats for Date/Time fields. Which do you think works best for this field?

   (No answer required)

3. Modify the built-in Contact form to use separate Read and Compose layouts for the General page. On the Read layout of the General page, add a Formula field to indicate the number of e-mail addresses for the contact, using the formula you saw in this lesson. Publish the form. Now run the form to try it out: Enter one, two, or three e-mail addresses, and then save the item. Open the item you just saved. Do you see the number of addresses?

   (No answer required)

4. Open the modified Contact form from exercise 3 again in design mode. Switch to the Compose page, and choose Form, Separate Read Layout to use just one layout for both composing and reading. Publish this form using a different name from that in exercise 3. Then run it, enter e-mail addresses, and save it. Open the saved item. Do you still see the number of addresses?

   You should not see the field with the number of e-mail addresses this time because only the Compose layout has a control for that field, not the Read layout.

A

Hour 5, "The VBA Design Environment"

Quiz

1. How do you start and end an Outlook VBA session?

   To start a session, press Alt+F11, or choose Tools, Macro, Visual Basic Editor. To end a session, either click the close button (×) in the upper-right corner of the VBA window, or choose File, Close and return to Microsoft Outlook.

2. Name six VBA windows that you studied in this lesson.

   UserForm, UserForm code, and Module windows, Project Explorer, Properties window, Object Browser.

3. Describe two ways you can back up your Outlook VBA project.

   Method 1: Exit Outlook and then make a backup copy of the VbaProject.OTM file.

   Method 2: Use File, Export File to export individual modules and forms.

4. If you switch from a VBA session back to Outlook, how can you return to the VBA session?

   If the VBA session is still active, click its button on the Windows task bar, or press Alt+Tab. If it is not still active, press Alt+F11 again.

Exercises

1. Examine the properties of a VBA project, form, and module. What property do they all have in common?

   The (Name) property

2. Locate the Outlook VBA project file on your computer.

   (No answer required)

3. Type **InputBox** into a module window, and then press F1 to view the help topic on the InputBox function.

   (No answer required)

4. Using the Office Assistant, type **Outlook fields and equivalent properties**, and retrieve and read the help topic by that name. (This is one topic you will come back to again and again.)

   (No answer required)

Hour 6, "A VBA Birthday/Anniversary Reminder Tool"

Quiz

1. What is the difference between a Label control and a Text Box control?

   A user can type into a Text Box control, but not into a Label control.

2. How do you run a VBA form to test it? How do you close it when you finish testing?

   To run a VBA form, select its window, and then click the Run Sub/User Form button. To close it, click the close button (×) in the upper-right corner.

3. What command removes a form from the display and from memory?

   `Unload`

4. If you added a Command Button control to a form and named it `cmdDoThis`, what would be the name of the code procedure that runs when you click that button?

   `cmdDoThis_Click`

5. Why does pressing Esc close the ReminderUpdate form after you add code to the `cmdClose` control, but not before?

   On the ReminderUpdate form, you set the `Cancel` property for the `cmdClose` control to `True`. All this does is make pressing the Esc key the equivalent of clicking the cmdClose button. After you add code to the `cmdClose_Click` event, pressing Esc causes that code to run.

Exercises

1. Write pseudocode to validate the entry in the `txtDays` control to make sure that a number greater than zero is present. What should happen if the control does not contain a valid number?

   It's up to you to decide what happens if the control does not contain a valid number. This pseudocode example pops up a message to the user:

   ```
   If txtDays is a number and that number is 0 or less
       Tell the user how to correct the mistake
   ```

2. Replace the `txtDays` control on the form with a Spin Button control. Give it an appropriate name, and update the `cmdUpdate_Click()` procedure to use your new control.

   (No answer required)

A

3. Can you think of other ways to enhance the ReminderUpdate form?

    (No answer required)

Hour 7, "More on Controls"

Quiz

1. When a user clicks on a check box or makes a selection in a combo box, what property of the control changes?

    The `Value` property.

2. What methods can you use to fill a list box on an Outlook form? Do they all work on a VBA form list box?

    For bound list boxes, enter the values on the Properties dialog, or set the `PossibleValues` property of the list box. For any list box, use the `AddItem` method or the `List` method. Only the latter two work on a VBA form list box.

3. If you have to present two choices to a user, which is better: check boxes, option buttons, a list box, or a combo box? What if you have three choices to present? Four?

    Two choices: Check box.

    Three choices: Option buttons if you have room; otherwise, list or combo box.

    Four or more choices: List or combo box, unless you have a lot of extra room on your form for option buttons.

Exercises

1. What do you think should happen if, in the form in Figure 7.1, both check boxes are unchecked when the user clicks the Update button?

    If both the Birthdays and Anniversaries boxes are unchecked, clicking the Update button should make no changes in the Calendar folder and probably should also tell the user that no actions were taken. Of course, you have to write code to make that happen.

2. You omitted keyboard accelerators for the option buttons in Figure 7.2. What would be good choices for the `Accelerator` property?

    Birthdays—B, Anniversaries—A, Both—o or t.

3. In the option button example in Figure 7.2, do you agree that the optBoth button should be the default (optBoth.Value = True)? Why or why not?

    (No answer required)

4. Using the code in Listing 7.1 for the check box form as a model, write a series of If...Then statements to handle the three option buttons. Don't worry about the exact syntax. Just see whether you can get the logic and sequence right.

```
If InStr(strSubject, "Anniversary") > 0 And _
  (chkAnniversaries.Value Or chkBoth.Value) Then
    objItem.ReminderSet = True
    objItem.ReminderMinutesBeforeStart = _
    24 * 60 * txtDays.Value
    objItem.Save
ElseIf Instr(strSubject, "Birthday") > 0 And _
  (chkBirthdays.Value Or chkBoth.Value) Then
    objItem.ReminderSet = True
    objItem.ReminderMinutesBeforeStart = _
    24 * 60 * txtDays.Value
    objItem.Save
End If
```

Hour 8, "Code Basics"

Quiz

1. What's the difference between a variable and a constant? Between a method and an event?

   After your code sets a constant, its value stays the same throughout the program. A variable, on the other hand, can have its value changed in code. A method is an action performed by code on an object; it may trigger an event. An event is something that happens to an object. You write code to *respond* to events and to *invoke* methods.

2. What steps must occur to create a new Outlook item using a custom form? (Hint: In your own words, summarize the macro you created.)

   Get the `Application` object. Get the `Namespace` object from the `Application` object. Use the `GetDefaultFolder` method on the `Namespace` object to get a folder. Use the `Add` method on the folder to create a new item. Change the `MessageClass` property of the new item to change it to a custom form.

Exercises

1. Open any Outlook form, add one or more custom fields, and write VBScript code to pop up a message box whenever any form event fires. Use the same `MsgBox` syntax as in Listing 8.1. Run the form, and experiment with changing data, saving, closing without saving, and so on.

   (No answer required)

2. For the custom Contact form you created in Hour 3, create a macro to launch the form, and customize the Standard toolbar with a button to run the macro.

In this procedure, change the strMessageClass = "IPM.Contact.Custom" statement to set the MessageClass to the name of your custom form:

```
Sub LaunchContactForm()
    Dim objApp As Application
    Dim objNS As NameSpace
    Dim objFolder As Folder
    Dim objItems As Items
    Dim objItem As ContactItem
    Dim strMessageClass As String
    strMessageClass = "IPM.Contact"
    Set objApp = CreateObject("Outlook.Application")
    Set objNS = objApp.GetNamespace("MAPI")
    Set objFolder = objNS.GetDefaultFolder(olFolderContacts)
    Set objItems = objFolder.Items
    Set objItem = objItems.Add(strMessageClass)
    objItem.Display
End Sub
```

Hour 9, "Code Grammar 101"

Quiz

1. If you write a function to return the number of days until (or since) the millennium, should that be a Public (global) or Private (module) procedure?

   You might want to make this a Public (global) function so that you can use it in any module.

2. Does putting Option Explicit in the declarations section of one module make all your Outlook VBA modules require variable declarations?

   No, an Option Explicit declaration affects only the current module.

Exercises

1. Devise variable names for the following:
   - A global variable storing information on whether an Outlook item is a newly created item
   - A procedure variable for the cost of your last meal
   - A module variable for the number of vacation days you have this year

   ```
   g_blnIsNew, curLastMealCost, m_intVacDays
   ```

2. Add the code in Listing 9.2 to a VBA module. Then, following the steps outlined in the section "Converting VBA Code to VBScript," create an Outlook form that performs the same operation from a command button.

```
Sub cmdTakeADayOff_Click
    Const olAppointmentItem = 1
    Const olOutOfOffice      = 3
    Dim objAppt
    Dim intAns
    intAns = MsgBox("Will you be gone all day?", _
                vbYesNo + vbQuestion, "Take a Day Off")
    Set objAppt = Application.CreateItem(olAppointmentItem)
    If intAns = vbYes Then
        With objAppt
            .AllDayEvent = True
            .BusyStatus = olOutOfOffice
            .ReminderSet = False
        End With
    End If
    objAppt.Display
End Sub
```

Hour 10, "Working with Expressions and Functions"

Quiz

1. Can you extract the area code from a phone number that doesn't follow a particular pattern?

   If you don't know the pattern for a phone number, all you can do is guess at which numbers compose the area code.

2. Did you really have to use the DateAdd() function to create the NextBusinessDay() function? If not, what would be the alternative?

   No, because intAhead is an integer representing the number of days, you could have instead used dteNextDate = dteDate + intAhead.

3. If 0 is the lowest subscript for items in array and the array contains 100 items, what is the value of the Ubound() for the array?

   99 is the upper bound of the array.

Exercises

1. Using the code in Listing 10.1 as a model, add another button to the customized Appointment form to create a follow-up meeting.

You call the same NextBusinessDay() function from this procedure to create a
new meeting.

```
Const olAppointmentItem = 1

Sub cmdCreateFollowUpMeeting_Click()
    Dim objAppt
    Set objAppt = Application.CreateItem(olAppointmentItem)
    With objAppt
        .StartDate = NextBusinessDay(Item.Start, 5)
        .Subject = "Follow up"
        .Body = "Follow up to appointment on " & _
                FormatDateTime(Item.Start, vbLongDate) & _
                vbCrLf & vbCrLf & "APPOINTMENT NOTES:" & _
                vbCrLf & Item.Body
        .Display
    End With
End Sub
```

2. Create a VBA form with a text box for a category you want to replace, a text box
    for the replacement category, and a command button to perform the replacement.
    Adapt the code in Listing 10.2 to work with the form controls.

    If the text boxes are named txtOldCat and txtNewCat and the command button is
    named cmdReplace, you can use this code. It just changes the name of the subrou-
    tine and the assignment statements for the strOldCat and strNewCat variables.

```
Sub cmdReplace_Click
    Dim objApp As Application
    Dim objFolder As MAPIFolder
    Dim objItem As Object
    Dim arr() As String
    Dim strOldCat As String
    Dim strNewCat As String
    Dim I As Integer
    strOldCat = Me.txtOldCat
    strNewCat = Me.txtNewCat
    Set objApp = CreateObject("Outlook.Application")
    Set objFolder = objApp.ActiveExplorer.CurrentFolder
    For Each objItem In objFolder.Items
        arr() = Split(objItem.Categories, ",")
        For I = 0 To UBound(arr)
            If arr(I) = strOldCat Then
                arr(I) = strNewCat
                Exit For
            End If
        Next
        objItem.Categories = Join(arr, ",")
        objItem.Save
    Next
End Sub
```

Hour 11, "Controlling Program Flow"

Quiz

1. What are the advantages of using a `For...Next` loop in the `cmdShowAllAddresses_Click` subroutine in Listing 11.2 to get the three e-mail addresses for the Contact item?

   The `For ... Next` loop makes the code more compact and easier to read and update because the details of the process of getting the e-mail addresses are contained in their own subroutine.

2. Of the different program control methods you studied in this hour, which have a built-in mechanism to handle exceptions?

   `If...Then...Else` blocks, `Select Case` blocks and `Do` loops.

Exercises

1. Use code for the `PropertyChange` event on a Contact form to find out what other properties change when you update a person's first name.

   If you use this code for the `PropertyChange` event on a Contact form, when you change the value in the Full Name box, you should be notified of changes to 21 properties, starting with `LastNameAndFirstName` and ending with `FullName`.

```
Sub Item_PropertyChange(ByVal Name)
    MsgBox "The " & Name & " property changed."
End Sub
```

2. Write a subroutine to get all the items in the Tasks folder. For any items with due dates, set the date one day later. Can you reverse the process to make the due date one day earlier?

   This code sets the due date one day later:

```
Sub Exercise2()
    Dim objApp As Application
    Dim objNS As NameSpace
    Dim objTasks As MAPIFolder
    Dim objTask As TaskItem
    Set objApp = CreateObject("Outlook.Application")
    Set objNS = objApp.GetNamespace("MAPI")
    Set objTasks = objNS.GetDefaultFolder(olFolderTasks)
    For Each objTask In objTasks
        If objTask.DueDate < #1/1/4501# Then
            objTask.DueDate = objTask.DueDate + 1
        End If
    Next
End Sub
```

To move the due dates up one day, use this assignment statement:

```
objTask.DueDate = objTask.DueDate - 1.
```

Hour 12, "Handling User Input and Feedback"

Quiz

1. Which of Outlook's default folders can hold messages?

   Deleted Items, Drafts, Inbox, Outbox, Sent Items

2. Name the methods you have used in this hour for the `Application` and `NameSpace` objects.

   Application: `GetNameSpace` and `ActiveExplorer`

   NameSpace: `GetDefaultFolder`, `PickFolder`

3. What function(s) could you use to add the current date to the message shown in a message box?

   `Now` and `Date`

4. If you wanted to know whether a user prefers coffee or tea, would you be more likely to use a message box or an input box?

   A message box with Yes and No buttons

Exercises

1. Write a subroutine to assign each of the nine Outlook default folders to its own folder object variable. (You can save this boilerplate code in your Generic module and copy and paste it any time you have to get a default folder.)

   The following code declares object variables for all the default folders and then sets each variable to its corresponding folder. Place these `Dim` and `Set` statements in a `GetDefaultFolders` subroutine in a boilerplate code module. You will then be ready to copy and paste the necessary code into another procedure and get any default folder.

   ```
   Dim objApp As Application
   Dim objNS As NameSpace
   Dim objCalendar As MAPIFolder
   Dim objContacts As MAPIFolder
   Dim objDeletedItems As MAPIFolder
   Dim objDrafts As MAPIFolder
   Dim objInbox As MAPIFolder
   Dim objJournal As MAPIFolder
   ```

```
Dim objNotes As MAPIFolder
Dim objOutbox As MAPIFolder
Dim objSentItems As MAPIFolder
Dim objTasks As MAPIFolder
Set objApp = CreateObject("Outlook.Application")
Set objNS = objApp.GetNamespace("MAPI")
Set objCalendar = objNS.GetDefaultFolder(olFolderCalendar)
Set objContacts = objNS.GetDefaultFolder(olFolderContacts)
Set objDeletedItems = objNS.GetDefaultFolder(olFolderDeletedItems)
Set objDrafts = objNS.GetDefaultFolder(olFolderDrafts)
Set objInbox = objNS.GetDefaultFolder(olFolderInbox)
Set objJournal = objNS.GetDefaultFolder(olFolderJournal)
Set objNotes = objNS.GetDefaultFolder(olFolderNotes)
Set objOutbox = objNS.GetDefaultFolder(olFolderOutbox)
Set objSentItems = objNS.GetDefaultFolder(olFolderSentMail)
Set objTasks = objNS.GetDefaultFolder(olFolderTasks)
```

2. Change the code in Listing 12.2 so that it cleans attachments from items the user has selected in a folder view.

```
Sub CleanAttachmentsFromSelection()
    Dim objApp As Application
    Dim objSelection as Selection
    Dim objItem As Object
    Dim objAtts As Attachments
    Set objApp = CreateObject("Outlook.Application")
    Set objSelection = objApp.ActiveExplorer.Selection
    For Each objItem In objSelection
        Set objAtts = objItem.Attachments
            Do While objAtts.Count > 0
                objAtts.Remove 1
            Loop
        objItem.Save
    Next
End Sub
```

3. Create message boxes with the title My Message Box Test, the prompt This is a test of the MsgBox() function, and these button and icon settings:

   • Question mark icon; Yes, No, and Cancel buttons; Cancel as the default button

   • Critical icon; Abort, Retry, and Ignore buttons; Abort as the default button

```
Sub MsgBoxExercise()
    Dim strMsg As String
    Dim strTitle As String
    strMsg = "This is a test of the MsgBox() function"
    strTitle = "My message box test"
    MsgBox strMsg, _
            vbQuestion + vbYesNoCancel + vbDefaultButton3, _
            strTitle
```

A

```
        MsgBox strMsg, _
                vbCritical + vbAbortRetryIgnore + vbDefaultButton1, _
                strTitle
    End Sub
```

4. Modify the `ReplaceCat` subroutine in Listing 10.2 from Hour 10 to use a VBA
   form to prompt the user for both the old category and the replacement category.

   Name the form `frmReplaceCat`, and place on it text boxes named `txtOldCat` and
   `txtNewCat` and command buttons named `cmdOK` and `cmdCancel`. Add the code in
   Listing 12.4 to the form's module. In another code module, add this code, adapted
   from Listing 10.2 to show and unload the form and assign the `strOldCat` and
   `strNewCat` variables to the data in the VBA form text boxes.

```
Sub ReplaceCat
    Dim objApp As Application
    Dim objFolder As MAPIFolder
    Dim objItem As Object
    Dim arr() As String
    Dim strOldCat As String
    Dim strNewCat As String
    Dim I As Integer
    frmReplaceCat.Show
    strOldCat = frmReplaceCat.txtOldCat
    strNewCat = frmReplaceCat.txtNewCat
    Unload frmReplaceCat
    Set objApp = CreateObject("Outlook.Application")
    Set objFolder = objApp.ActiveExplorer.CurrentFolder
    For Each objItem In objFolder.Items
        arr() = Split(objItem.Categories, ",")
        For I = 0 To UBound(arr)
            If arr(I) = strOldCat Then
                arr(I) = strNewCat
                Exit For
            End If
        Next
        objItem.Categories = Join(arr, ",")
        objItem.Save
    Next
End Sub
```

Hour 13, "Working with the Object Models"

Quiz

1. Can an object include an event and a method that use the same name? Give an
   example.

   Yes, `Close` is one example common to Outlook items.

2. What's the difference between the `Delete` method and the `Remove` method?

The `Delete` method applies to an individual object. The `Remove` method applies to a collection.

Exercise

The Outlook Object Model and CDO both include a `Recipient` object. Explore its properties, actions, and methods. Are they the same object? If you use a `Dim objRecip as Recipient` statement in a procedure, which `Recipient` object are you referring to?

The Outlook Object Model and CDO `Recipient` objects have different properties, methods, and events, which makes them different objects. A `Dim objRecip as Recipient` statement in a procedure will refer to whichever model is listed first in the Tools, References list, usually Outlook if you are writing VBA code in Outlook. If you must use two `Recipient` objects from different models in the same procedure, use `Dim objRecip as Recipient` for the Outlook Object Model recipient and `Dim objRecip as` MAPI.Recipient for the CDO Model recipient.

Hour 14, "Commanding with Custom Actions"

A

Quiz

1. What event on an Outlook form lets you control custom actions?

The `CustomAction` event

2. In the event handler for the event in question 1, how do you refer to the new item that the custom action creates?

With the `NewItem` object passed as an argument to the `CustomAction` event

3. What statement do you use in the same event handler to avoid creating a new item by a custom action?

`Item_CustomAction = False`

Exercises

1. For the Vacation Request form, add a validation formula and validation text to the txtVacationEnd text box on the Compose page to make sure that the user doesn't have a vacation that can end before it even begins.

For the validation formula, use

`[VacationEnd] > [VacationStart]`

Your validation text might read

```
Check the vacation dates to make that sure the start date is before
the end date.
```

2. Experiment with different combinations of the Message Class and Address Form like A choices to get a feeling for what properties are transferred from the old item to the new item in different situations.

   (No answer required)

3. Assume that you have access to an Internet fax service that lets you send faxes by addressing them to number@myfaxservice.com, where number is the fax number with no punctuation. (In other words, to fax a document to +1 (202) 555-1234, you would e-mail it to 12025551234@myfaxservice.com.) Modify the Fax to Contact code in Listing 14.2 to send a fax through your Internet fax service.

   Assuming that strTo contains a phone number from the Contact item, use this code to generate the e-mail address:

```
strCompactNum = ""
For I = 1 To Len(strTo)
    strChar = Mid(strTo, I, 1)
    If IsNumeric(strChar) Then
        strCompactNum = strCompactNum & strChar
    End If
Next
strTo = strCompactNum & "@myfaxservice.com"
```

Hour 15, "Working with Stores and Folders"

Quiz

1. What kind of information store can be present more than once in an Outlook profile?

   Personal Folders

2. What do you think would happen if you tried to use the GetSharedDefaultFolder method with a recipient argument that had not been resolved?

   You'd get a runtime error.

Exercises

1. Using Tools, Services (assuming you use Outlook in Corporate or Workgroup mode), determine which information stores are in your default mail profile. Use the EnumCDOStores subroutine to list the stores. Do you get the same result?

Tools, Services shows all services, not just information stores. The `EnumCDOStores` subroutine shows only information store components.

2. Modify Listing 15.3 to add a message box to handle the case of a folder not being found. Try to use the information in the `arrName()` array to tell the user exactly what part of the folder hierarchy could not be found.

You can use another `For...Next` loop to go back through the array, but only up to the point where a matching folder was not found. The `arrName(I)` element represents the level at which no match was found.

```
If blnFound = True Then
    Set objExpl = objFolder.GetExplorer
    objExpl.Display
Else
    strMsg = ""
    For J = 0 To I
        strMsg = strMsg & arrName(J) & "/"
    Next
    MsgBox "Could not find " & Quote(strMsg)
End If
```

3. Adapt the code for the `GetExchangeListFolder` subroutine in Listing 15.3 to convert it into a function named `GetAnyFolder()` that returns the `MAPIFolder` object for a given folder path.

You have to make only a couple of alterations: Change the first statement from `Sub GetExchangeListFolder()` to `Function GetAnyFolder(strName)`. (The `End Sub` statement at the end of the procedure should change automatically to `End Function`.) Then, delete lines 13–14. That's all!

Hour 16, "Working with Items"

Quiz

1. Does the `Copy` method copy an item to a folder?

No, the `Copy` method creates a new item that's a duplicate of the original.

2. What property of a received message represents the name of the person who sent the message?

The `SenderName` property.

Exercises

1. Compare the method of getting a sender address in Listing 16.2 with the CDO method in Hour 13 by running them with some actual messages. Do they always return the same address? Why or why not?

You probably will not see the same result with these two methods. The CDO method from Hour 13 gets the address that you see in the From field of the message. The method from this chapter gets the Reply To address—the address that the sender specified should be used for replies—or, if there is no Reply To address, it gets the From address.

2. How would you enhance the `DoReplace` subroutine in Listing 16.3 to ignore text in HTML tags? (Hint: Tags always take the format *<tag>*.) Try to at least write the pseudocode.

The pseudocode for this enhancement looks something like this:

```
Find the position of the first match for the string
Continue until there are no more matches in the message body
    Look to the left of the matching string to see if there
        is a "<" character (HTML tag open)
    If there is a "<" character Then
        Check the text between the "<" character and the
            string match to see if there is a ">" character
        If there is an intervening ">" character Then
            Replace the string
        End If
    Else
        Replace the string
    End If
    Find the position of the next match for the string
Next
Loop
```

Try your hand at writing the real code, using the `Mid()`, `Instr()`, and `InstrRev()` functions to handle the string testing.

Hour 17, "Responding to Outlook Events in VBA"

Quiz

1. In Listing 17.2, why do you have to use the `GetDefaultFolder` method in lines 5–6?

`GetDefaultFolder` is the easiest way to set a `MAPIFolder` object variable to one of Outlook's built-in folders, such as Sent Items.

2. What's the difference between the `BeforeFolderSwitch` and `FolderSwitch` events? In each case, how would you retrieve the folder being switched to?

The BeforeFolderSwitch event occurs just before the new folder is displayed; it passes the NewFolder object as an argument. The FolderSwitch event occurs after the new folder has been displayed. At that point, you can use the CurrentFolder property of the ActiveExplorer to get the current folder as a MAPIFolder object.

Exercises

1. Using the code in Listing 17.1 as a model, write an Application_Reminder procedure to forward items that trigger reminders to an Internet address, with the item as an attachment.

   If strAddress is a variable containing the target Internet address, you can replace the With...End With block in Listing 17.1 with these statements:

```
objItem.Subject  = Replace(TypeName(Item), "Item", "") & _
                   ": " & Item.Subject & strDue
objItem.Body = Item.Body
objItem.To = strAddress
Set objAttachments = objItem.Attachments
Set objAttachment = objAttachments.Add(Item, olEmbeddeditem)
objItem.Send
```

2. What would you add to ThisOutlookSession in order to write code to respond to events on Meeting Request items?

   You must add three things to ThisOutlookSession: an object variable declaration

```
Dim WithEvents objMeetingItem as MeetingItem
```

   these lines to the objInspectors_NewInspector event's Select Case block:

```
Case olMeetingRequest
    Set objMeetingItem = objInsp.CurrentItem
```

   and event handler procedures for the events that you want to respond to.

3. Adapt the code in Listing 17.3 to monitor the Deleted Items folder for items with attachments.

   Add your own code to this procedure, perhaps to suggest that the user might want to save the attachments first. You will also have to provide a Dim WithEvents statement and initialize the objDeletedItemsItems object variable in the Application_Start procedure.

```
Private Sub objDeletedItemsItems_ItemAdd(ByVal Item _
    As Object)
    If Item.Attachments.Count > 0 Then
        your code goes here
    End If
End Sub
```

A

Hour 18, "Menus, Toolbars, and the Outlook Bar"

Quiz

1. What is the relationship between a `CommandBar` object and a `CommandBarControls` object?

   Each `CommandBar` object has a child `CommandBarControls` object containing the controls that appear on the toolbar or menu bar.

2. What type of control is used to produce a drop-down menu? A text box on a menu?

   A `CommandBarComboBox` is used in both cases.

3. Can a shortcut on the Outlook Bar run a VBA procedure?

   No, Outlook Bar buttons can display Outlook folders, system folders, or Web pages or run a program, but they can't run a VBA procedure. If you want one-click access to a VBA procedure, use an Outlook toolbar button instead.

Exercises

1. Write an `objExpl_FolderSwitch` event handler for a folder named Help Desk that not only displays a Help Desk custom toolbar but also turns off any other toolbars (but not the menu bar). To simplify the task, assume that the Help Desk name is unique among all your folders. (If it weren't, you would have to add code to make sure that this particular Help Desk folder is the one you want to work with.)

```
Private Sub objExpl_FolderSwitch()
    Dim objCBars As CommandBars
    Dim objCB As CommandBar
    Set objApp = CreateObject("Outlook.Application")
    Set objExpl = objApp.ActiveExplorer
    Set objCBars = objExpl.CommandBars
    If objExpl.CurrentFolder.Name = "Help Desk" Then
        For Each objCB In objCBars
            If objCB.Type <> msoBarTypeMenuBar Then
                objCB.Visible = False
            End If
        Next
        objCBars("Help Desk").Visible = True
    End If
End Sub
```

2. Modify the `CreateSampleToolbar` subroutine to check first for the existence of a toolbar named Sample so that you can avoid creating two toolbars with the same name.

The revised version might look like this, adding a `blnIsSampleToolbar` variable, a `For Each...Next` loop to check the name of each toolbar, and an `If...End If` block to add the Sample toolbar only if `blnIsSampleToolbar` is False:

```
Sub CreateSampleToolbar2()
    Dim objApp As Application
    Dim objExplorer As Explorer
    Dim objCBars As CommandBars
    Dim objCB As CommandBar
    Dim blnIsSampleToolbar as Boolean
    Set objApp = CreateObject("Outlook.Application")
    Set objExplorer = objApp.ActiveExplorer
    Set objCBars = objExplorer.CommandBars
    For Each objCB In objCBars
        If objCB.Name = "Sample" Then
            blnIsSampleToolbar = True
            Exit For
        End If
    Next
    If Not blnIsSampleToolbar Then
        Set objCB = objCBars.Add("Sample", msoBarFloating)
        objCB.Visible = True
    End If
End Sub
```

A

Hour 19, "Debugging Applications"

Quiz

1. What command do you use to run a procedure if you want to follow the progress of your code step by step?

   Debug, Step Into

2. Can you edit code in break mode in VBScript as you can in VBA?

   No, the script can be edited only in the code window of the form in design mode, not in the Windows Script Debugger.

3. What statement can you use in VBScript or VBA to force Outlook into break mode for debugging?

   `Stop`

4. Name at least three methods you can use in break mode to get the current value of a variable.

   Check the Locals window, use ? or Print in the Immediate Window, or hover the mouse over the variable to see a screen tip with the value.

Exercise

Use File, Export File to export a copy of one of the VBA modules you created in earlier chapters. Next, deliberately delete a character here and there, or add an apostrophe to turn a line of code into a comment. Run the procedure, and practice using VBA's debugging tools to find the errors and correct them. Continue until you fix all the errors and the procedure runs perfectly again.

(No answer required)

Hour 20, "ActiveX and Other Controls"

Quiz

1. What control would you use if you wanted to add a solid yellow line across your form?

   An Image control.

2. What two things must be done before you can start using an ActiveX control in your Outlook applications?

   You must register the control using Regsvr32.exe, if it was not previously registered, and add it to the Toolbox.

3. What event is available for ActiveX controls that you add to an Outlook form?

   Only the Click event, and only for unbound controls.

Exercises

1. Create a new VBA form. Add an Image control, dragging the borders of the control so that it stretches the full width of the form and is one grid mark tall. Set control properties to turn it into a solid red horizontal line. What properties did you need to set?

   The BackColor and BorderStyle properties

2. On an Outlook Contact form, add an Image control named imgPhoto to the (P.2) page. Write code that sets the User Field 1 value for new items to a file for the user's picture. Hint: You will have to devise your own naming convention using perhaps the Full Name or File As field from the Contact.

   A simple naming convention for files might use the FullName property of the contact, minus any spaces. For example, the photo for Alan Dale might be stored as \\mainserver\photos\AlanDale.pcx if \\mainserver\photos is the path to the shared network folder where the photos reside. You could use code such as this:

```
Function Item_Write()
    If Item.User1 = "" Then
        Item.User1 = "\\mainserver\photos\" & _
          Replace(Item.FullName," ","") & _
          ".pcx"
    End If
```

3. For the Calendar control, add code to the form's `Item_Open` event to set the `Height` and `Width` properties of the control.

   After you determine the ideal dimensions for the control on the Photos page (x and y in the following code), your code might look like this:

```
Function Item_Open()
    Set objPage = Item.GetInspector.ModfiedFormPages("Photo")
    Set objCtrl = objPage.Controls("imgPhoto")
    objCtrl.Width = x
    objCtrl.Height = y
End Function
```

4. Customize the Cancel button and add it to the Toolbox, using the same techniques as you saw for the OK button.

   (No answer required)

Hour 21, "Getting Started with Outlook Reports"

Quiz

1. What technique(s) can you use to create a tabular (columnar) report of Outlook data from a single folder, including custom fields?

   Print from an Outlook folder view, copy and paste to Excel, and use code to export to Excel.

2. What if you need to include data from several folders, such as all the Appointment items in five users' Calendar folders—can you use the same techniques?

   You can use the two Excel techniques, but when you print from a folder view, you can print data from only one folder at a time.

Exercise

Finish creating the Sent in Last 7 Days view, which you based on the built-in Last Seven Days view. What did you have to do to complete the view?

You would want to add the To field to the view so that you can see the recipient of each item in the Sent Items folder.

Hour 22, "Designing Reports with Microsoft Word"

Quiz

Imagine that you have been asked to write an application to print all appointments for any given day and include the business and mobile phone numbers of any contacts involved in a meeting or linked to an appointment. Answer the following questions:

1. What properties of the Appointment item would you examine for a link to Contacts?

   `Links` and `Recipients`

2. What Contact properties would you want to include in your report?

   `FullName, Company, BusinessTelephoneNumber, MobileTelephoneNumber`

3. Which built-in Outlook print styles might make good models for this kind of report?

   Calendar Details Style and Memo Style, which is available only when one or more appointments are selected

4. What procedures from Listing 22.2 could you probably reuse in your application?

   `OpenDoc` to open the Word document, `FillFormFields` (with the fields changed, of course), `FillTable` (if you choose to design the report with a table)

Exercise

Rewrite the `HasLinkToContact()` function to include the operations in the `LinkName()` function from Listing 22.2. Call it `HasLinkToContact2()`. The arguments for the `HasLinkToContact2()` function should be the item you want to test and the Contact item to which it might be linked. Which version of `HasLinkToContact()` is more efficient?

The code for `HasLinkToContact2()` should look like this:

```
Function HasLinkToContact2(objItem As Object, _
          objContact As ContactItem) As Boolean
    Dim objLinks As Links
    Dim objLink As Link
    Dim strName As String
    Set objLinks = objItem.Links
    If objContact.FullName <> vbNullString Then
        strName = objContact.FullName
    Else
```

```
        strName = objContact.FileAs
    End If
    For Each objLink In objLinks
        If objLink.Name = strName Then
            HasLinkToContact = True
            GoTo Exit_HasLinkToContact
        End If
    Next
Exit_HasLinkToContact:
    Set objLink = Nothing
    Set objLinks = Nothing
End Function
```

This is less efficient than the original HasLinkToContact() function because this new version gets the name from the contact every time you make a comparison. If you are comparing one contact to many other Outlook items, you will save processing time by getting the contact's name once and then passing it repeatedly to comparison function.

Hour 23, "Exchange Server and Database Collaboration"

Quiz

1. What object model is used in writing code for Exchange Event Service scripts? For connecting to a database?

   CDO (Collaboration Data Objects)

   ADO (ActiveX Data Objects)

2. Can Exchange Event Service scripts display user interface elements such as message boxes?

   No, remember that scripts run unattended on the Exchange Server. If your script displays a message box or some other element that requires user interaction, execution of the script will halt because no user is present to interact.

Exercise

Using the Tip of the Day public folder created as an example in this chapter, write a script that retrieves on item from the folder, forwards it to a distribution list named Tipsters, and then deletes the tip from the folder so that it is not repeated. Don't forget that you can use the Object Browser to scan the MAPI library for the CDO methods you will need. For example, try searching for Forward.

You can use this code to write a script for the folder's `OnTimer` event:

```
Public Sub Folder_OnTimer()
    Dim objFolder As MAPI.Folder
    Dim objTip As MAPI.Message
    Dim objItem As MAPI.Message
    Dim objRecips As MAPI.Recipients
    Dim objRecip As MAPI.Recipient
    ' get the first item in the current folder
    Set objFolder = Session.GetFolderFromID(EventDetails.FolderID)
    Set objTip = objFolder.Messages.GetFirst
    If Not objTip Is Nothing Then
        Set objItem = objTip.Forward
        Set objRecips = objItem.Recipients
        Set objRecip = objRecips.Add("Tipsters")
        objRecip.Resolve
        ' if the address is successfully resolved,
        ' it's safe to send it
        If objRecips.Resolved Then
            objItem.Send
        Else
            ' otherwise, write a log entry
            Script.Response = FormatDateTime(Now()) & _
              " - Could not resolve Tipsters address"
        End If
    Else
        ' otherwise, write a log entry
        Script.Response = FormatDateTime(Now()) & _
            " - No items left in folder"
    End If
    ' delete the tip
    objTip.Delete
End Sub
```

Hour 24, "Deploying Forms and Applications"

Quiz

1. If you can distribute a Word VBA macro in a Word document, why can't you distribute VBA code as part of an Outlook form?

   Outlook forms use only VBScript code, not VBA.

2. Imagine that you have a public folder containing standard Contact items. You plan to import several hundred more items that contain information not covered in custom fields. Because you have to create a custom form for the extra fields anyway, you're going to add some additional functions that users want for the existing

items. What tasks do you need to perform, and in what order, to get all the items into the folder, using the same form?

First, design and publish the custom form. Then, perform these additional tasks in any order: Set the new form as the default for the folder. Convert the existing data to the new form. Import the new data to the new form.

Exercises

1. Write a subroutine to update items in a folder to a message class of IPM.Post.MyNewForm only if they are not already using a custom form. (Hint: You can use a function listed in this chapter.)

   Incorporate the IsCustomForm() function into your routine in this fashion:

   ```
   If Not IsCustomForm() Then
       objItem.MessageClass = strNewClass
   End If
   ```

2. Modify the ImportCSVToOutlook comma-delimited file import subroutine to keep a running total of the number of items imported and report the total to the user when the import is complete.

   Declare an intCount variable as an Integer. Include this statement within your Do While Not EOF loop:

   ```
   intCount = intCount+1
   ```

   Before the End Sub statement, display the result with a message box, like this:

   ```
   MsgBox "Imported " & intCount & " tems."
   ```

A

APPENDIX B

Resources for Outlook Programming

When you are ready to expand your knowledge of Outlook 2000, try some of these resources.

Web Sites

Most of these Web sites include both articles and links to other sources of Outlook programming information on the Internet:

Microsoft Outlook Developers Forum

`http://www.microsoft.com/outlookdev/`

Microsoft Exchange Developers' Resources

`http://www.microsoft.com/exchange/developers.htm`

Outlook & Exchange Developer Solutions

`http://www.slipstick.com/dev.htm`

Outlook and Exchange Developer Resource Center

http://www.outlookexchange.com/

Microsoft Scripting Technologies home page

http://msdn.microsoft.com/scripting/default.htm

VBScript documentation, including language reference and tutorial

http://msdn.microsoft.com/scripting/vbscript/techinfo/vbsdocs.htm

Visual Basic for Applications home page

http://msdn.microsoft.com/vba/

CDOLive

http://www.cdolive.com

The Exchange Code Exchange

http://www.exchangecode.com/

Mailing Lists

Mailing lists provide a way to exchange ideas with other developers or just "lurk" to see what everyone else thinks are the latest hot topics.

OUTLOOK-DEV

To subscribe to the OUTLOOK-DEV mailing list for Outlook programming issues, either visit http://www.egroups.com/group/outlook-dev/ or send a message to outlook-dev-subscribe@egroups.com.

MAPI-L

To subscribe to the MAPI-L mailing list for MAPI programming issues, send a message to LISTSERV@PEACH.EASE.LSOFT.COM with the text SUBSCRIBE MAPI-L *firstname lastname* (filling in your own name).

EXCHANGE SERVER

To subscribe to the EXCHANGE SERVER mailing list for Microsoft Exchange Server administrators, send a message to lyris@ls.swynk.com with subscribe exchange in the body, or visit http://ls.swynk.com.

Internet Newsgroups

Microsoft hosts several public newsgroups for the discussion of development issues related to Outlook and Exchange Server. If you don't find them on your ISP's news server, you can get them directly from Microsoft's news server at `msnews.microsoft.com`.

Outlook forms issues

`microsoft.public.outlook.program_forms`

Outlook VBA issues

`microsoft.public.outlook.program_vba`

Other Outlook programming issues

`microsoft.public.outlook.program_addins`

Exchange Server applications issues

`microsoft.public.exchange.applications`

The CDOLive Web site maintains links to additional mailing lists and newsgroups for particular topics, such as ADO, at `http://www.cdolive.com/ngml.htm` and hosts a discussion forum at `http://www.cdolive.com/ask.htm`.

Publications

These magazines and books take you deeper into Outlook development techniques and related topics.

B

Magazines

Microsoft Office & Visual Basic for Applications Developer magazine

`http://www.informant.com/mod/index.asp`

Access/Office/VB Advisor magazine

`http://www.advisor.com/wHome.nsf/wPages/Avmain`

Books

Gordon Padwick and Ken Slovak. *Programming Outlook 2000*. Indianapolis, Ind.: Sams, 1999. ISBN 0-672-31549-1.

Randy Byrne. *Building Applications with Microsoft Outlook 2000*. Redmond, Wash.: Microsoft Press, 1999. ISBN 0-7356-0581-5.

Thomas Rizzo. *Programming Microsoft Outlook and Microsoft Exchange*. Redmond, Wash.: Microsoft Press, 1999. ISBN 0-7356-0509-2.

Dwayne Gifford. *Outlook 2000 VBA Programmer's Reference*. Chicago: Wrox Press, 1999. ISBN 1-8610-0253-X.

Mikael Freidlitz and Todd Mondor. *Professional ADSI CDO Programming with ASP*. Chicago: Wrox Press, 1999. ISBN 1-8610-0190-8.

Raffaele Piemonte and Scott Jamison. *Developing Collaboration Applications with Outlook 2000, CDO, Exchange, and Visual Basic*. Reading, Mass.: Addison-Wesley, 1999. ISBN 0-201-61575-4.

Conferences

Attending a conference gives you the opportunity not just to preview new technologies, but also to brainstorm with other Outlook developers.

Microsoft Exchange Conference

`http://www.microsoft.com/exchange/`

Microsoft Office and VBA Solutions Conference

`http://www.informant.com`

Access/Office/VB Advisor Devcon

`http://www.advisor.com`

INDEX

Other Related Titles

Visual Basic for Applications for Office 2000 Unleashed
Paul McFedries
ISBN: 0-723-1567-x
$39.99 USA /
$59.95 CAN

Sams Teach Yourself Microsoft Outlook 2000 in 24 Hours
Herb Tyson
ISBN: 0-672-31449-5
$19.99 USA /
$29.95 CAN

Sams Teach Yourself Microsoft Office 2000 in 21 Days
Laurie Ulrich
ISBN: 0-672-31448-7
$29.99 USA /
$44.95 CAN

F. Scott Barker's Microsoft Access 2000 Power Programming
Scott Barker
ISBN: 0-672-31506-8
$49.99 USA /
$74.95 CAN

Sams Teach Yourself Microsoft FrontPage 2000 in 24 Hours
Rogers Cadenhead
ISBN: 0-672-31500-9
$19.99 USA /
$29.95 CAN

Sams Teach Yourself Microsoft Publisher 2000 in 24 Hours
Ned Snell
ISBN: 0-672-31572-6
$19.99 USA /
$29.95 CAN

Sams Teach Yourself Microsoft Excel 2000 Programming in 21 Days
Matthew Harris
ISBN: 0-672-31543-2
$29.99 USA /
$44.95 CAN

Microsoft Access 2000 Development Unleashed
Stephen Forte, Thomas Howe, and James Ralston
ISBN: 0-672-31291-3
$49.99 USA /
$59.95 CAN

SAMS

www.samspublishing.com

All prices are subject to change.

Get **FREE** books and more...when you register this book online for our Personal Bookshelf Program

http://register.samspublishing.com/

SAMS

Register online and you can sign up for our *FREE Personal Bookshelf Program*...unlimited access to the electronic version of more than 200 complete computer books—immediately! That means you'll have 100,000 pages of valuable information onscreen, at your fingertips!

Plus, you can access product support, including complimentary downloads, technical support files, book-focused links, companion Web sites, author sites, and more!

And you'll be automatically registered to receive a *FREE subscription to a weekly email newsletter* to help you stay current with news, announcements, sample book chapters, and special events, including sweepstakes, contests, and various product giveaways!

We value your comments! Best of all, the entire registration process takes only a few minutes to complete, so go online and get the greatest value going—absolutely FREE!

Don't Miss Out On This Great Opportunity!

Sams is a brand of Macmillan Computer Publishing USA.

For more information, please visit *www.mcp.com*